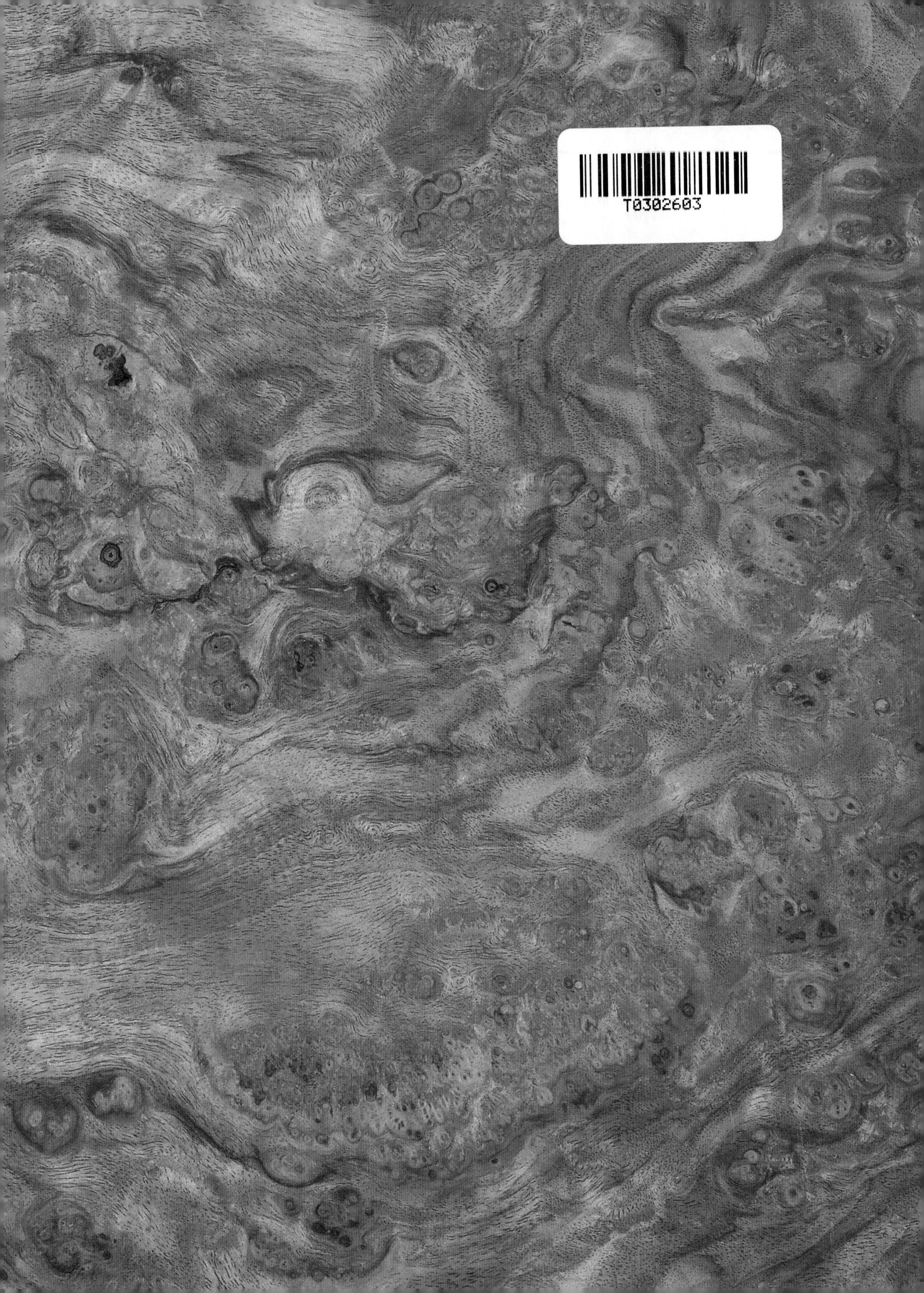

THE PRACTICAL ILLUSTRATED GUIDE TO FURNITURE REPAIR & RESTORATION

WILLIAM COOK · W.J. COOK & SONS

LORENZ BOOKS

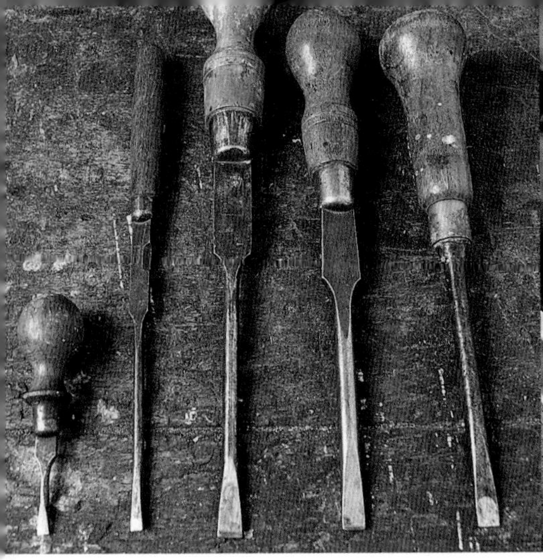

This edition is published by Lorenz Books, an imprint of Anness Publishing Ltd
info@anness.com
www.lorenzbooks.com; www.annesspublishing.com

A CIP catalogue record for this book is available from the British Library.

Publisher: Joanna Lorenz
Project editors: Charlotte Berman and Claire Folkard
Designer: Lisa Tai
Photographer: John Freeman
Technical director: Paul Lyon, W.J. Cook & Sons
Production controller: Ben Worley

PUBLISHER'S NOTE

The author and publisher have made every effort to ensure that all instructions contained in this book are accurate and that the safest methods are recommended. The publisher and the author cannot accept liability for any resulting injury, damage or loss to persons or property as a result of using any tools in this book or carrying out any of the techniques or projects. Before you begin any restoration task, you should know how to use all your tools and equipment safely and be sure and confident about what you are doing.

AUTHOR'S ACKNOWLEDGEMENTS

When approached to write this book we were delighted to accept. For a number of years we have been acutely aware of the absence of any book that was written and extensively photographed in a commercial restoration workshop and which showed and explained clearly how various techniques are carried out on a day to day basis. Drawing from almost 60 years of experience and a lifetime's collection of materials and tools, we hope to have given the reader an authoritative insight into the subject.

While the overwhelming majority of work was undertaken "in house", there are grateful thanks due to others who have been invaluable in their help both with advice and in the use of their facilities: Barry Ansell of R.D. Robins Ltd, London, on upholstery; Geoff Collier of Colliers Castings, Hooe, on casting methods; Les Crispin of Capital Crispin Veneer, London, on veneers; Alan Dallison on leathers, Bob Dunn of A. Dunn & Son, Chelmsford, on marquetry; and Optimum Brasses, Tiverton, on brassware.

Special thanks go to the staff in our workshops for making sure that the work needed for this book was always ready on time. A big thank you goes to Paul Lyon for his sterling work, without which this book would have been impossible.

On a personal note, like all family businesses, an unsung hero is our mother Catherine who has always been there keeping the wheels turning. Thanks also to my brothers Richard and Stephen with whom it is very much a team effort, and not to forget Justin, who has chosen to follow his own path.

Thanks to all those who have been encouraging and supportive throughout the whole process of writing this book, including Richard, my life-long friend, for his humour, often dispensed from across the world; Nathalie, whose words of wisdom, while not always fully appreciated are always carefully considered; and my four sons William, Henry, James and Felix, for just being themselves.

Finally this book is for my father from his sons, and for our sons and daughters from their fathers in the hope that they may one day take the business onwards for another generation. BILLY COOK

CONTENTS

Introduction

This book, which was written and photographed in a second-generation family workshop, demonstrates many of the techniques and methods used in the repair and restoration of antique furniture and aims to give readers the confidence to start restoring furniture themselves.

History of furniture restoration

By its very nature, all furniture will need attention of one form or another during its life. The approach toward restoration work has varied over the years as the type and nature of the problems facing the restorer have evolved. The numerous years of constant use, the action of the environment and various later alterations have all contributed to the need for a different approach to the general restoration of furniture.

Ever since furniture was first constructed there has been the need for a capable person to undertake necessary repairs and restoration work to combat daily wear and tear. From the medieval period, the original cabinet-maker or perhaps the local estate joiner could well have done this. Often one will see repairs carried out that are obviously not by the same hand as the rest of the piece; on occasion they are not even in the same wood. It is not unusual to find loose chairs being strengthened by elaborate, blacksmith-made brackets, which, ironically, would have taken more time to make than knocking apart the chair and undertaking the repair correctly. But as this would have involved removing the upholstery – thus requiring another tradesman, namely the upholsterer, to become involved – an "on-site" repair was usually facilitated.

It is worth remembering that often in the past and before the burgeoning interest in antiques (not to mention their rapidly increasing value), these items were considered as little more than second-hand pieces of furniture. Stories abound of large quantities of period pieces being either burnt or consigned to the dump when they required attention. Also, with the changing fashions, pieces were adapted or changed to make them more suitable for a particular task. This could range from legs being added or handles being changed to keep up with the latest styles, to pieces being reduced in size. A classic example is that of early bun feet, fashionable during the late 17th century, being replaced with the new style of

Above: *A selection of smith-made brackets, which were used to act as temporary strengtheners on loose furniture.*

Right: *This is a classic example of how furniture can be altered over the years as fashions change. The original bun feet on this late 17th-century chest were replaced with bracket versions some time during the 18th century. Note also the addition of later 18th-century swan-necked handles.*

Above: *An example of a late 17th-century drawer front which has been fitted with a Regency ring handle. Evidence can be seen of numerous previous handles.*

Above: *Having examined the evidence of a previous handle indicated by a darker shadow, an engraved plate handle suitable for the period has been selected and fitted. This has the advantage of overcoming the previous handle hole problems.*

bracket foot during the 18th century. Usually the change was due to necessity as well as aesthetics: standing on stone floors that were laid directly on earth foundations, the original bun feet would have absorbed moisture through the stone and eventually rotted away.

The term "antique restorer" is a comparatively new one: in earlier times it would have been the job of a trained cabinet-maker to attend to any necessary work. This cabinet-maker, however, would have been better qualified than most self-titled "cabinet-makers" today, as he would have served a lengthy apprenticeship, starting at the bottom and working his way through the ranks. Nowadays, however, with the lure of easier, better-paid and less manual jobs, combined with fewer workshops of a suitable calibre willing or perhaps financially able to take on apprentices, it is easy to see why those with the necessary skills, training and ability have moved from cabinet-maker to antique restorer.

There are a number of college courses designed to train the student restorer. These can range from short courses lasting a number of months to vocational courses that may take from one to three years. It should be remembered, however, that after the completion of any course, the gulf between classroom and workshop practice is wide. Nothing can replace the hours spent at the bench, honing and developing one's skills and benefiting from working with restorers who have spent a lifetime learning their craft.

In the past, a workshop would have been divided between the cabinet-maker, whose role was to undertake any necessary restoration work, and the polisher, who would attend to any necessary colouring, polishing or waxing. Today, however, restorers are increasingly undertaking both roles, and it is not uncommon to find a restorer who is both a cabinet-maker and a polisher. Again, with the lack of apprenticeships and the difficulty of finding suitable staff, today's restorer must be able to turn his or her hand to any role. This, of course, comes with its own problems, as it limits the time that can be spent on both polishing and cabinet making. Larger and more established workshops can and will employ both cabinet-maker and polisher, but the newly established or under-funded workshop can afford only one or the other. It is ironic that antique furniture has never been more highly valued or appreciated than it is today, and yet the restorer – whose work can play such a major part in increasing (or, as a result of bad restoration, decreasing) a piece's value – is frequently underrated.

One of the greatest changes in recent years is the ability of the restorer to charge a fee commensurate to his or her skills. This can, however, be a double-edged sword, since it provides a temptation for those who do not possess the necessary skills to make the jump from simple joiner or poorly trained cabinet-maker to self-styled "antique restorer". He or she may be able to use the tools to a proficient standard, but will not have learnt about the construction techniques of the 18th century and how the action of light, grease, waxes and wear will have altered the appearance and character of a piece. Lack of this knowledge could have dire consequences, since the character, colour and patination of an antique develop over

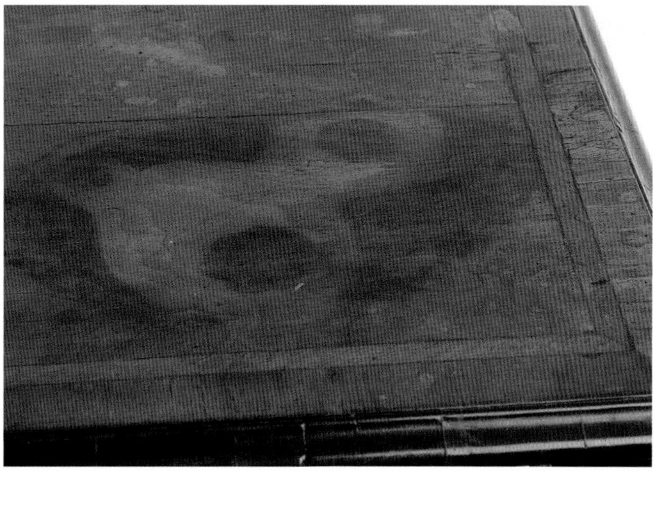

Left: *Often the role of the restorer is to attend to minor problems such as the water damage on this table top.*

Left: *During the 18th century even such esteemed cabinet-makers as Thomas Chippendale, to whom this fine breakfront bookcase is attributed, had to plead to his clients to settle their accounts.*

many years, not to say centuries, and once destroyed by bad restoration they can never be regained.

To try and combat this bad practice, various trade organizations have been founded. Perhaps the best known worldwide is the British Antique Furniture Restorers' Association (BAFRA), which was started during the early 1980s by a group of leading, established restorers to try to maintain a tradition and standard of work within the profession. Membership is limited by a strictly vetted application procedure, and a structured system is in place to deal with any disputes. The organization also works closely with colleges and students to try to make sure that the calibre of those entering the trade is suitably high and that theory never overtakes practice.

Until now, only the role and history of the polisher and cabinet-maker have been discussed. It should be remembered that there are other important disciplines that are vital to the restoration business. The upholsterer, leather-liner, lacquer-restorer and gilder, to name but a few, all make significant contributions to the upkeep and maintenance of antique furniture. It is a worrying trend that in some of the less-fashionable areas of antique restoration, there is a declining number of new recruits. Those who are prepared to spend years learning their trade, however, can be assured that they will never be short of work, and, as with all things, the greater their ability, the greater will be the demand for their time and skills.

In the past, the restorer's skills, while appreciated, were not always rewarded, and indeed the great furniture-makers of the 18th century, such as Thomas Chippendale, would often have to plead for monies owed. However, with the ever-increasing scarcity of fresh pieces to the market, and the rapidly increasing value of antiques, the position of the trained and knowledgeable restorer has never been better. Both trade and public are having to buy an increasing amount of furniture that requires attention in one form or another before it can be resold or used. Younger generations who inherit pieces are realizing the value of their legacies and appreciating the skill and workmanship involved in their original making. They know that their furniture must be well maintained and cared for if it is to survive and be treasured by succeeding generations.

The number of first-class pieces being offered on the open market is shrinking, while the demand for them is growing, causing prices to reach ever-higher levels at auction. As a result, collectors, dealers and private individuals are increasingly turning to the knowledgeable restorer to seek an opinion on the construction, condition and originality of a piece.

In short, the future of antique restoration and the role of the restorer have never looked healthier.

Right: *The aim of every restorer is to be able to restore a piece to its former glory.*

RESTORATION AND CONSERVATION

There are two main schools of thought with regard to furniture restoration: restoration and conservation. Restoring a piece of furniture is to fully renovate it to its original form, whereas conserving a piece is to simply return it to a serviceable condition. There are valid arguments for both approaches but essentially each has the same purpose – to bring a piece of antique furniture back to life.

The term "conservation", while known to everyone, is a relatively new school of thought in the area of furniture restoration. Ever since furniture was first manufactured, there has been a need to repair it to counter the damage caused by accidents, negligence and everyday wear and tear.

In the beginning the solution to these problems was simple: any damaged components were restored or replaced using a similar wood to the original. As little comparative time had passed since the piece's original manufacture, any concerns about colour matching and disguising repairs were unnecessary, and the aim of the restorer, or cabinet-maker as was more likely the case, was to bring the piece back into use again. However, with the passing of time and the ever-increasing value of a piece of furniture – in some cases to that of more than the cost of the average family car, or occasionally the family house – the parameters have vastly changed, and there now exist two schools of thought. The first is that a piece should be restored with the use of old or breaker pieces of wood to produce, as far as possible, unnoticeable repairs. The second is that any repairs should be carried out in as sympathetic a manner as possible, but that the line between old and new should be left unblurred.

Some restoration techniques are straightforward and involve simply regluing loose joints, broken legs and backs or attending to worn runners or lost stops. The debate begins, however, when a leg has been broken and misplaced or a piece of veneer lost. As the chapter on Tools, Equipment and Materials explains, a prerequisite of any serious workshop, and of membership of BAFRA (the British Antique Furniture Restorers' Association), is an adequate breaker store of various pieces of wood dating from the 17th, 18th and 19th centuries. These breakers will be invaluable for matching the colour, grain and texture of a piece under repair. The conservator will argue that any new pieces should be manufactured from new wood and simply matched in as best as possible. However, whichever argument you favour, it is important always to take advice from a valuer before repairing an important piece of furniture.

There is also an increasing debate concerning de-restoration, which involves reversing past bad repairs or alterations and redoing them to a higher standard. While to some this may seem unnecessary, for the majority of furniture lovers there is no eyesore quite so awful as a repair done badly or made using the wrong materials. Although the materials and skills available to the restorer of the original repair may have been adequate at the time, if the work can now be undertaken using the correct materials or better skill levels, then it should be done.

Some restorers will use modern adhesives that are reversible to enable their work to be undone at a later stage. While their intention is admirable, since most adhesives used in restoration are animal based and thus reversible anyway, this should be unnecessary. Of course, if the work is correctly undertaken and suitable materials and woods are used, there should be no need to undo the work.

No restorer should ever forget that a patinated surface has taken numerous generations to develop. Bad restoration or over-zealous cleaning by inexperienced, unqualified or unsupervised restorers is nothing short of criminal. As for surfaces, colour and patination should be retained wherever possible. The actual mechanics of polishing are dealt with in full detail in the chapter on Surfaces and Finishes, but it is worth noting here that again there are two schools of thought. The conservator will prefer that nothing other than wax should be applied to revive a surface. While in theory this would seem logical, and on occasion is the best way forward, it should be remembered that often a piece will lose its lustre because the top layers of polish have perished. In such cases, the restorer will gently remove and replace these layers in order to allow the various hues and tones of the wood below to be revealed in their full glory. It is this area that requires the greatest of skill, because, once generations of built-up surface have been stripped away, no amount of subsequent waxing will replace it. As with most things, a balance should be reached to get the best possible result.

Above: *Major structural damage, such as a broken upright, needs restoration rather than conservation.*

Purchasing

There are two main sources for buying antique furniture: a dealer (either trade or retail) and an auction room. Antique fairs are another good source, providing a range of competing stalls from which to buy. Lastly, there is online buying, which continues to grow in importance. All these sources have their advantages and disadvantages, and it is for individual buyers, after careful consideration, to choose their preferred method.

Auction rooms

Most towns and cities will have their own auction room holding regular sales of antiques. A catalogue describing each lot is provided, and, depending on the auction house and the sale being held, photographs will also often be included as well as pre-sale estimates. Always make sure you read the conditions of sale and the terms of business very carefully. Almost all auction rooms will charge a buyer's premium, with purchase tax being added on to this premium. Be sure to calculate this properly, since it can make a considerable difference between the bid price and the actual invoice figure.

View each lot carefully, making a note of any damage. If you want to make a bid, decide on a figure that you will be comfortable with paying, taking into account any buyer's premium and tax. Most auction rooms will require you to register before you can bid. Having decided on a price, stick to it, as the most common mistake when buying at auction is to enter into a battle with another bidder, secure the lot and then realize that, in your determination to have it, you have paid far more than you had intended. One of the biggest disadvantages of buying at auction is that once you have bid and secured your purchase, you cannot change your mind about buying the piece. Once the auctioneer's hammer has come down, the goods are yours.

Finally, most private individuals feel that by buying at auction they are getting the piece at a cheaper price than buying from a dealer. You may, on occasion, secure a bargain, but since most sales are well subscribed and viewed by dealers, you should remember that, more often than not, there may be a good reason why a dealer has decided not to bid.

Above: *Auction rooms, where both traders and private individuals can buy, are located in most towns and cities.*

Below: *A typical retail antique shop will usually display the furniture it has for sale in a sympathetic manner.*

Antique shops

Most large towns will have at least one antique dealer, dealing in antique furniture of varying quality. Antique dealers generally fall into two categories – the trade dealer and the retailer – although some dealers may operate in both trade and retail areas.

The trade dealer, as the name suggests, deals mainly with other dealers. The stock will turn over fairly quickly and, as a result, will not be fully on display. The prices will often be a little lower than the retail dealer, but, should you decide to buy and seek "trade prices", then restoration, delivery costs and the facility to return goods are often excluded. While these can be arranged, you should expect to pay extra.

The other type of dealer is the retailer. Here the stock will be clearly labelled, suitably lit and well laid out. You will find that retailers are happy to spend as much time as you require answering all your questions and will often give you the option of trying the piece on approval. Delivery costs are normally included in the price, and the piece will already have been restored if necessary, with the dealer happy to explain what, if any, restoration work has been carried out. The retailer's goods may cost a little more than the trade dealer's, but it is worth remembering that in life one generally gets what one pays for.

Whoever you decide to deal with, it is best to find someone with whom you feel comfortable, who knows the field well and with whom you wish to do business. With regards to pricing, most dealers are open to negotiation within a limit, and you will soon learn what sort of price movement a dealer is happy to make. Good dealers often belong to a recognized trade association, which will have a strict code of practice and which can act as an arbiter in the case of any dispute.

Antique fairs

Antique fairs are becoming an increasingly popular way to purchase antiques, as they offer buyers the opportunity to view the stock belonging to many different dealers in just one day. They range from one-day fairs held in a local venue to large exhibitions held over several days in hotels or purpose-built exhibition centres, with the participating dealers building elaborate stands on which to display their pieces.

When visiting a fair, make sure you view everything before deciding upon your purchase, and take time to talk to the dealers, who will be happy to answer any questions you may have. If necessary, take details and measurements to check that a selected item is suitable. Some dealers may be happy for you to try the piece on approval. Often some of the best working relationships between a dealer and patron have begun at an antique fair.

Above: *Antique fairs are an ideal way to view a large selection of furniture in a single day.*

Online

This method of purchasing antiques, continues to grow in importance and has had varying degrees of success. Some major auction rooms have set up elaborate online auctions, but while such auctions seem to do well in some fields, with furniture it seems that people still like to see the piece "in the flesh", to try sitting in or at it and to examine it in all its aspects. The same is true of dealers' websites, which are proving to be more of a marketing tool than a retail point of sale.

Tools, equipment and materials

The right tools, equipment and materials are the lifeblood of any restorer. Often passed from generation to generation, they must be cared for and used with the skill they deserve, for without them even the most gifted of restorers will be unable to undertake the most basic of restoration jobs.

CREATING A WORKSPACE

More often than not, financial limitations and space will dictate the location of a workshop. The most important piece of equipment in the workshop will be the bench, so it is important that any area under consideration should, as a basic requirement, be able to house both you and the bench, as well as allowing space for the furniture being restored. You will also need to surround yourself with tools and machinery, so plan your work area carefully.

YOUR WORKBENCH

Once you have decided where to site your workbench, you will need to assess the various factors that are vital for good work.

The most important factor is the quality of light available. Natural light is ideal, so, if possible, position the bench directly under a window or skylight. Hang fluorescent strip lights above the workbench and, if you are intending to undertake any polishing work, make sure that normal lights are also available (fluorescent light gives a false colour). Also paint the walls white to reflect, and so maximize, whatever light there is.

Rack your tools in an organized manner so that they are readily available. Keep groups of tools, such as hammers, saws or chisels, together for easy access. Keep tools that are not used daily, such as carving tools, carefully wrapped to protect their sharp edges, and stored neatly ready for use. Above all, keep the work area and bench clean and tidy.

Remember that most of your time will be spent standing at the workbench, so put blocks under it, if necessary, to set it at a height that is comfortable for you to work at. Also, if possible, opt for a wooden rather than a concrete floor, as concrete is very tiring on the feet and legs.

If space and funds permit, have two separate areas within the workshop: one for cabinet making and the other, in a dust-free area, for polishing. This dual use maximizes the available space.

An ideal workbench

YOUR TOOLKIT

When restoring antique furniture, the best tools are, without doubt, those that were originally used in the 18th and 19th centuries. For a hobby restorer, modern tools are a suitable, and realistic, substitute, but anyone wishing to pursue a career in the field of furniture restoration should endeavour to build up as wide a collection of antique tools as possible. Such tools were made by craftsmen for craftsmen. The steel used then is still the best for holding a suitable cutting edge now, and the handles, made from box or rosewood, feel more comfortable to the hand than modern materials such as plastic. Often you will see numerous names stamped into the handle of an antique tool, indicating how it has passed through the hands of generations of craftsmen.

Old tools can be found in a number of places, ranging from specialized tool auctions or car boot sales, to local fêtes and classified advertisements in the local paper. If you are really lucky, you may have the opportunity to buy the tools and contents of the workshop of a retiring cabinet-maker. If this happens, beg or borrow the funds to buy the tools, since such events are rare indeed.

In the absence of antique tools, or while you are building up your collection, start your toolkit by buying modern equivalents, but be sure to buy the best quality that is available within your budget. Clamps are an exception to this rule, and modern sash, snap and G-clamps are fine. These are expensive pieces of equipment, so it is a good idea to buy a few whenever you can afford them.

Modern screwdrivers, saws and chisels can be purchased to begin with, and you can gradually replace them with older examples if you want. Some tools and equipment, such as spring clips, can be made in the workshop (see p.215).

Most cabinet-makers take a lifetime to build up their collection of tools, and almost all craftsmen will prefer to work with only their own tools, which, once purchased, should last a lifetime.

If you become interested in restoring then you may become an avid collector of tools yourself. Certainly, if you decide to take up restoring as a job, then building up your stock of tools and materials can be seen as an investment in your own future. Remember always to respect your tools, keeping them clean and sharp, and wrapping them safely whenever they are not in use.

Safety

The safety rules of a workshop are esentially those of common sense. Always remember that the workshop is potentially a dangerous area, so make sure that children cannot get in. Always handle sharp tools with care and replace them in their rack after use. Keep a regularly tested fire extinguisher close to hand and lock any flammable materials away in a fireproof cabinet. Keep the work area clean and tidy and sweep up all shavings at the end of the day. Good ventilation is important, especially when using stripper or any other chemicals. Make sure any stains or other liquids are kept in jars and clearly labelled. Wear suitable safety clothing as the job dictates. Tie back long hair, remove any dangling jewellery and always wear a long apron to protect your clothes.

Above: *A fire extinguisher is essential. Install a powder-filled fire extinguisher at every exit door.*

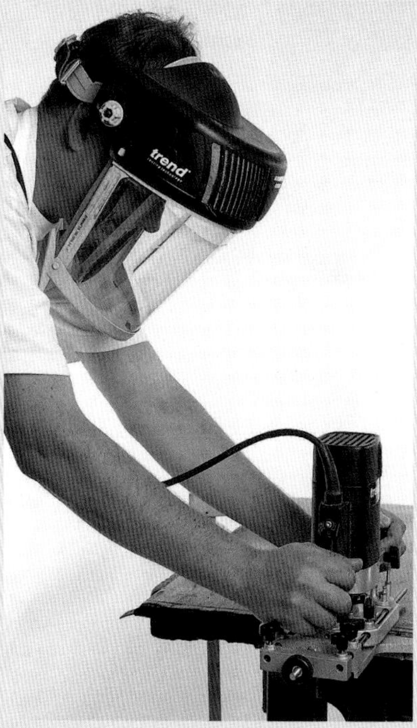

Above: *When using power tools likely to create a lot of dust or sparks, it is a good idea to wear a protective helmet.*

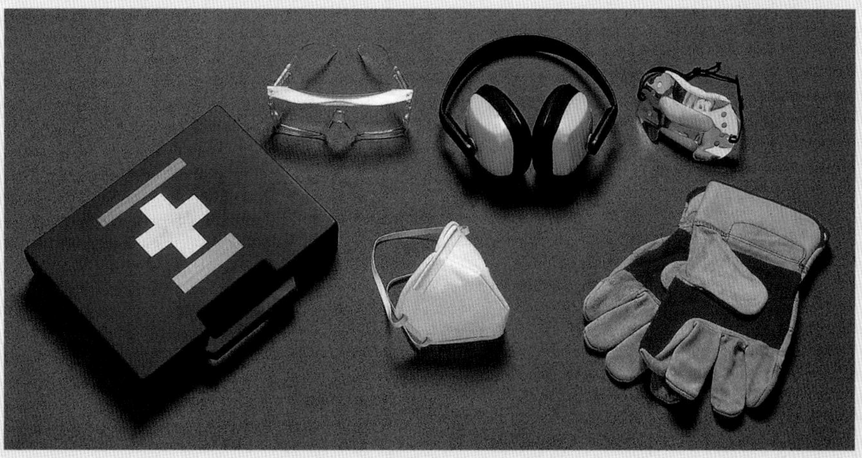

Left: *Basic safety equipment should include a first-aid kit, goggles, ear defenders, a filter mask, gloves and a disposable mask.*

SAWS AND MEASURING DEVICES

It is important that saws are kept in good condition because a sharp edge is essential, particularly when doing detailed work. Although modern power saws can take much of the effort out of sawing, and certainly have their place in a workshop, hand-held saws, such as the tenon saw, are invaluable for small-scale work. Measuring devices, including dividers, callipers and gauges, are the key to successful cabinet work, so look after them carefully.

SAWS

The three most commonly used saws in day-to-day restoration are the full tenon saw, the half-tenon saw and the dovetail saw, all of which have varying numbers of teeth per centimetre (inch). The more teeth per centimetre (inch), the finer the cut will be. Some of the finest cutting teeth are those of the fret and coping saws, designed for detailed shape work.

The large panel saw, used for cutting larger boards, comes with two teeth settings: the cross cut, designed to cut across the grain, and the ripsaw, designed to cut along the length of the grain. With the introduction of modern band saws and circular saws, large panel saws are used less frequently, but all workshops should have at least one of each type.

Saws will almost certainly be used on a daily basis and should be used only for the specific task for which they were designed. Using a fine dovetail saw for general work, for example, will damage the teeth and make it unsuitable for the finer work of cutting dovetails.

Above: *An extensive range of reliable measuring tools is essential for the furniture restorer to carry out accurate work.*

The saw is a precision cutting tool and should always be kept sharp and in good condition. While it is possible to sharpen the saw yourself, it is far better to send it to a professional saw doctor to have the teeth set and sharpened.

Left: *Three saws from a typical workshop, each with a different number of teeth per centimetre (inch). The more teeth a saw has, the finer the cut will be.*

When using a saw on a particularly difficult piece of wood, rub a little candle wax on the blade to help ease the cutting.

MEASURING DEVICES

"Measure twice, cut once" is an old cabinet-makers' saying, and it is as true today as it has always been. Accurate measuring is vital, since if the measuring is inaccurate then all the work that follows is wasted, at worst possibly leading to a ruined piece of valuable furniture, at best meaning you have to start all over again. Measuring tools include dividers, marking gauges, callipers, set (carpenter's) squares, sliding bevels and box rules, all of which are indispensable. Double-check every measurement and work from a face edge (the first edge cut and planed level, which is then used to take other measurements).

HAMMERS AND SCREWDRIVERS

Hammers, ranging from pin hammers for light work to heavier hammers for knocking apart furniture, are an essential part of any restoration work, as are the various types of mallet, particularly the carver's dummy, which is a very useful tool. A wide range of screwdrivers should also be kept to hand. Look out for examples with long and short shanks, which are useful in different situations. Be sure to keep the leading edge of a screwdriver sharp.

HAMMERS

The restorer will have two or three different types in the workshop, including the light pin hammer, the general cabinet hammer, which will be used on a daily basis, and a heavier hammer used to knock apart carcasses and drive in large nails. Hammers should never be used to hit another tool, such as a chisel – that is exclusively the role of the mallet.

When the face of a hammer becomes dirty and worn, file it flat then rub it lightly with fine-grade sandpaper to remove the dirt and score the surface. This enables the hammer to grip the head of the nail. This process, which is known as "dressing", will probably need to be done at least two or three times a month.

MALLETS

These were designed to be used against the handle of a tool such as a chisel or gouge. They come in different weights and shapes, and the greater the weight of the head, the more force it will exert. A good example of this is the carver's dummy, whose heavy lignum vitae head ensures that a simple wrist action gives a very strong blow. It also means that the carver need not look at the mallet as it swings down, since its rounded head will always strike the tool being used, thus allowing the carver to concentrate fully on the work in hand.

Above: *Two traditional mallets – it is useful to have a selection in your workshop.*

Larger mallets are for roughing off, while lighter ones are for delicate work. The square-headed mallet is for general cabinet work and knocking apart, where a large hammer might bruise the wood.

SCREWDRIVERS

It is best to equip yourself with as wide a range of screwdrivers as possible. It is well worth spending a little time at car boot sales or trawling through second-hand shops in order to build a collection of traditional tools at a lower price than new ones. Old screwdrivers tend to have a longer shank, which gives better leverage. They also have handles made from box-wood or beech, which are kinder to the hand than plastic. Small screwdrivers with short shanks can be very useful for removing screws in awkward locations.

When buying an old screwdriver, check that the leading edge is straight and even. If it is worn or uneven, you will have to grind it flush, because a screwdriver that does not fit snugly into a screw-head slot can break the screw. Remember that a screwdriver is designed for removing and putting in screws and should never be used as a lever, which could damage the edge and bend the shank.

Below: *A selection of old screwdrivers with shanks of varying lengths.*

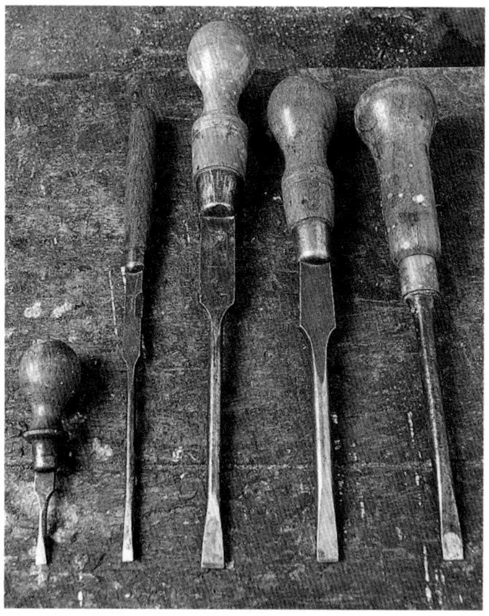

Holding a hammer

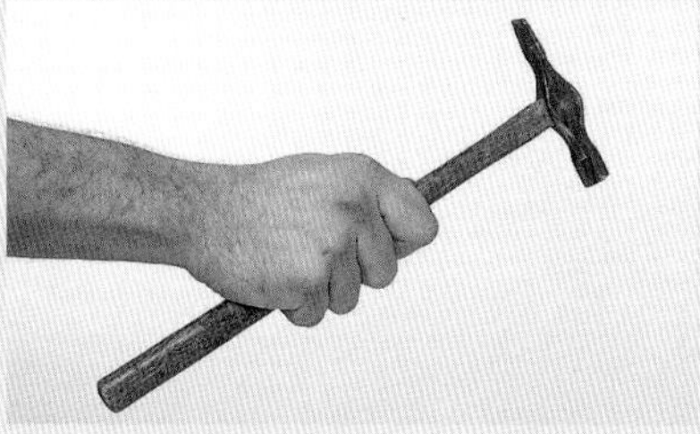

1 *When using a hammer, the most common mistake is to hold it half way down the handle in the belief that this allows more control and accuracy. In fact, it has the opposite effect.*

2 *The correct way to hold the hammer is at the end of its handle, which gives much better balance and control. When using a hammer, make several medium blows rather than trying to drive the nail home first time.*

SMOOTHING TOOLS AND CLAMPS

There are many different types of planes and clamps used in restoration work, and modern tools are very similar to their traditional counterparts. Some planes are fitted with their own guide fences and others with changeable blades, while moulding planes have specially shaped bases and blades for detailed shaping work. Different clamps, like planes, are designed for particular tasks and it is advisable to build up as wide a selection as possible.

PLANES

The earliest planes were made with wood bodies, but during the 18th and 19th centuries the metal-bodied plane took over, although the moulding planes remained wooden.

There are various examples of planes, each suited to a particular role, including the utilitarian jack plane, the smoothing plane, and the smaller block-and-shoulder plane for more intricate work. There are also specialized planes, such as moulding planes, with their specially shaped bases and blades, which are designed to cut the waist, base and other mouldings found on carcass furniture. However, the modern router, with its wide range of shaped cutters, has largely taken over this role. Although the spokeshave does not look like a plane, it is classed as one because it works along the same principle.

The blade of any plane is designed to cut the wood cleanly without tearing the grain, and so it is important that it is always kept sharp. When the blade is sharp and the plane is used correctly, it should made a wonderful slicing sound as it cuts through the wood.

SCRAPERS

The cabinet scraper, which is basically a piece of metal with a burred edge, is designed to clean up surfaces and remove any plane marks prior to sanding.

The most frequently used scraper will be a rectangular one for shaped mouldings, but tailor-made scrapers are also useful. The most common example is the French curve, which is shaped like a kidney and should be able to scrape any concave area.

Scrapers should always be used sharp and should produce shavings, not dust. To sharpen a scraper, you should draw a hard piece of rounded metal, such as the shank of a screwdriver, across the edge. This produces a burr, which is needed to cut the wood.

SANDING EQUIPMENT

The earliest types of sandpaper were, in fact, made from sharkskin, known as shagreen. It was dried and used very much in the same way as sandpaper is today. This was followed by the use of ground glass or sand, which was stuck to paper, and it is from this that the terms "glasspaper" and "sandpaper" are derived.

Nowadays there are many abrasive papers available, including silicon carbide, aluminium oxide and garnet paper, but the term "sandpaper" is still commonly used to describe them all. These papers are available in a number of different grits, or grades, with the most commonly used grits in the workshop ranging from 80 (the coarsest) to 320 (the finest).

Sandpaper is rarely used on its own but is wrapped around sanding blocks of cork or wood. If a specific moulding has to be sanded, you will need to make a shaped piece of wood (overloe) that matches the profile of the moulding, so that it can be sanded without having its shape altered. Over the years, the restorer will build up a wide selection of tailor-made overloes.

When you start sandpapering a piece of work, begin with the coarsest grade and work up through the grades to the finest. Wetting the wood between each grade, and allowing it to dry before you start with the next grade, will give a smoother finish. Also, if you intend to apply a water stain, this inter-grade wetting process will make sure that the grain does not rise at the staining stage.

Above: *A selection of planes showing some of the variety of shapes and materials used in their construction.*

Above: *The spokeshave is a cross between a plane and a scraper, and is a very versatile tool for shaping wood.*

Above: *Overloes are specially shaped wooden blocks that are used with sandpaper to smooth the profile of a moulding.*

Clamps

These tools come in a wide variety of styles, each suited to a particular role. The most common types are the long sash clamp, the G-clamp, which comes in different sizes, the band clamp, the snap clamp and the spring clip (see p.215). Modern clamps are similar to traditional ones, and although they are fairly expensive to buy, it is best to have as wide a range as possible.

When working with clamps, always use clamping blocks to prevent bruising and the appearance of "hoof" marks on the wood. Also, never over-tighten a clamp: the pressure it exerts can cause structural damage to delicate pieces.

When gluing up a complex job, it is a good idea to have a "dry" run beforehand, working out which clamps will be used and in which order. Spending a little time doing this may prevent problems later on when the glue has been applied and is setting. It also means that you will have everything you need to hand and will feel confident about starting the work.

Above: *A wide selection of modern and traditional clamps, including G-clamps and sash clamps, are essential for many types of restoration work.*

Making a band clamp

While most clamps can be bought, the steel band clamp is unique in that it is workshop made and tailored to a particular job in hand. Its role is to clamp an oval or round, creating an equal pressure around the circumference.

You will need a small block of hardwood, a steel band (as used for binding building materials), small screws and a clamp.

1 *Cut two lengths of the steel band to a length slightly shorter than the frame's circumference and punch two pilot holes into each end of them.*

2 *Using a metal bit, drill two small holes through the pilot holes. Be sure to place a scrap block of wood on the bench or worktop to protect it.*

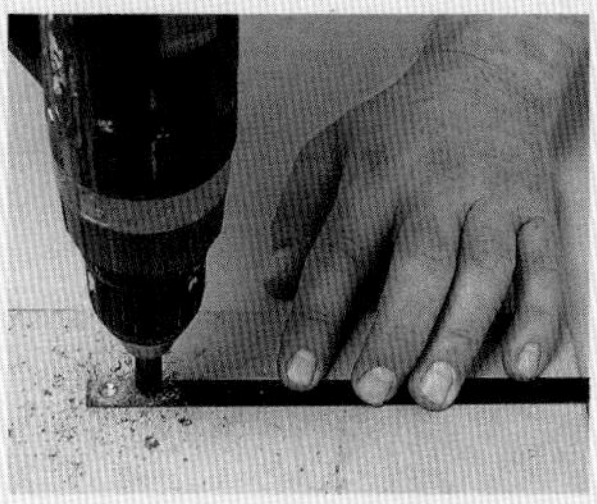

3 *Use a countersink drill bit to countersink the two holes previously drilled. This will make sure that the screw heads are level with the band.*

4 *After marking the shape of the frame on the hardwood, use a band saw to cut the concave profile. Cut the block in half.*

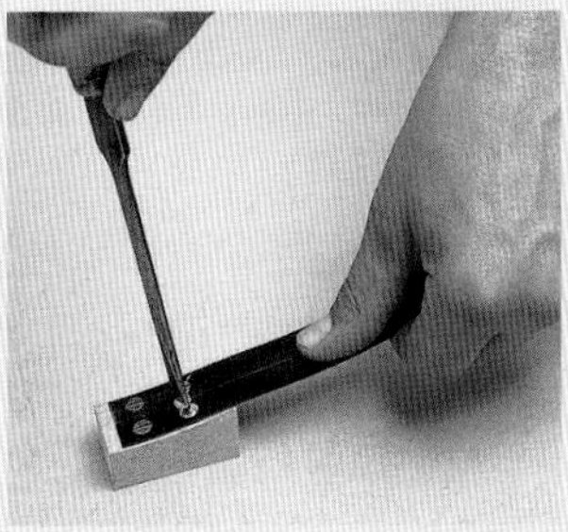

5 *Screw the two lengths of steel band to the shaped side of the hardwood, making sure that the countersunk hole side of the band is used.*

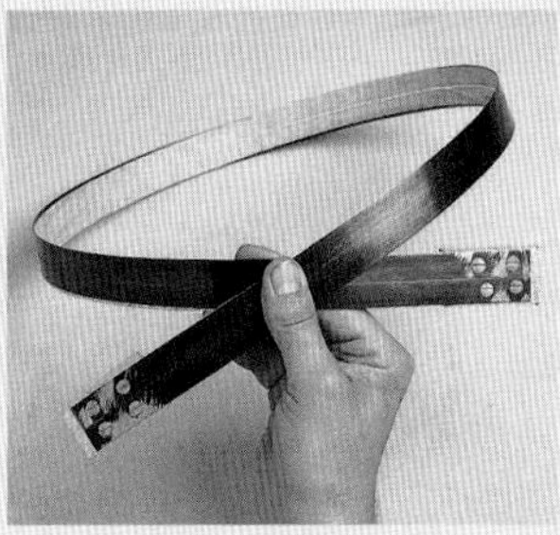

6 *Finish by filing the screw heads flush with the metal band, this will make sure that no unnecessary scratching or marking occurs.*

7 *The band clamp in use. The hardwood blocks are clamped together to create the tension.*

CHISELS AND CARVING TOOLS

All these implements have their own jobs, which involve paring away wood in one form or another, but one rule applicable to all is to keep their edges sharp so that they can cut through wood and not tear the grain. If you are interested in carving, you will start to amass a large collection of tools, since each has its own specific function. In general, old examples tend to keep their edge longer than modern versions, due to the better-quality steel.

CHISELS

The cabinet-maker or restorer will have three main types of chisel to hand on the workbench. These are the paring chisel, the mortise chisel and the firmer chisel. Within these groupings there should be a range of widths suitable for any task.

The paring chisel, with its bevelled edges and long blade, is primarily used for paring, levelling and chamfering. It is designed for hand-use only and should never be struck with a mallet.

The mortise chisel, as its name suggests, is used to cut out mortises, and for this reason its blade is noticeably thicker than that of both the paring and firmer chisels. The thickness of the blade means that it can withstand a heavy blow from a mallet and a certain amount of leverage when removing the waste wood from a mortise.

The firmer chisel, with its shorter, thicker blade without a bevelled side, is designed for heavier work and can be used in conjunction with a suitable mallet.

CARVING TOOLS

The carver is one of the most skilled craftspeople in the field of antique restoration. The skill of carving is similar to that of a painter, except that the carver's medium is wood and the end results are three-dimensional.

The required tools, which can number into the thousands, are known individually for their suitabilities and strengths, and before undertaking a carving project the carver will select the required implements and sharpen them. Indeed, depending on the hardness of the wood, it is not unknown for a carver to resharpen a blade every few minutes during carving work.

Small carving tools are essential for detailed and intricate work. They provide much greater control of the task in hand, allowing the carver to remove small slivers of wood with the minimum of effort.

There are numerous types of carving tools, including scrolls, which set out the shape of the carving; V- or parting tools, which produce long sweeps; grounders, which remove the background waste; veiners, which carve the fine details, such as flowers, leaves, etc; and fish tails, which, like the grounders, help to remove unwanted wood.

While this procedure may seem very complicated, it is worth noting that the complexity and intricacy of much of the work means that it takes several years for a carver to reach full potential.

Each carving project can often take hundreds of hours of painstaking work, and, aside from patience, the main skill a potential carver needs to learn is the ability to be able to study an existing carving closely and to mimic exactly the hand in which it was originally carved. The real test of the master carver is to restore carving to the extent that the new work blends in seamlessly with the original detail.

Above: *While gradually building up a collection of antique tools, which you can find in second-hand shops, it is a good idea to purchase modern equivalents too.*

Left: *A selection of chisels, gouges and bradawls (for making fine pilot holes) will be used on a daily basis.*

Left: *A small selection of the many hundreds of carving tools required by the master carver.*

Above: *A carver's vice allows free and easy access to any carved piece held in it.*

Sharpening a chisel

Some of the tools most used by the cabinet-maker or furniture restorer are the various chisels. These are used to pare, level and shape the wood. It is vital that the chisels are kept sharp at all times, as failure to do so will result in them tearing the grain rather than slicing through the wood. When a chisel loses its edge, the process of re-honing takes only a few minutes, and the procedure is very simple.

1 *Using a grinding wheel and selecting the finest grade of the two stones, offer the chisel at an angle of approximately 25–30 degrees. Remove the bevel as soon as it is flat, otherwise the chisel's length will be shortened too much and its working life substantially reduced.*

2 *Lightly lubricate an oil stone with a fine oil, then draw the chisel repeatedly along the stone at an angle of 30–35 degrees. This will produce the cutting edge.*

3 *Turn the chisel over and lay it flat down on the stone. Rub it back and forth two or three times. This process, known as "backing off", will weaken the burr that has built up. Strop the chisel on a piece of leather, which should remove the burr.*

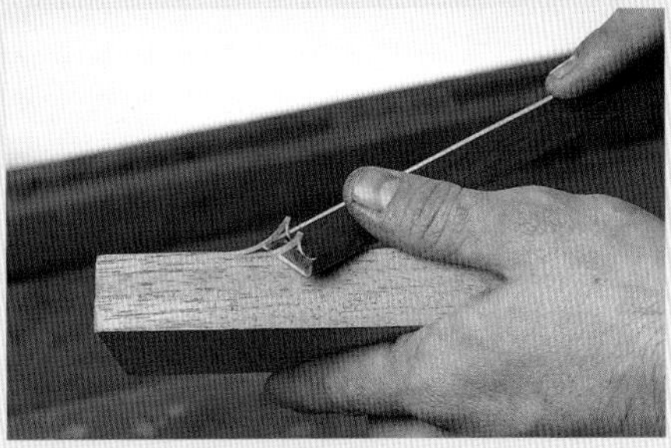

4 *Finally, use your newly sharpened chisel to cut a slither off a piece of wood. This will check for sharpness as well as removing the burr, should it not have come off on the leather strop.*

5 *The illustration shows how the finished edge should look if the chisel has been sharpened correctly.*

Turning tools

Since medieval times, turning has been used in the construction of furniture. While lathes have changed with the times – the earliest examples were human-powered – the basic techniques and principles used by the early bodgers (travelling lathe craftsmen) have remained much the same as they are today. Likewise, the tools used in modern workshops would still be recognizable to the turner of centuries past.

The tools of the turner are divided into measuring and turning tools. It is vital that accuracy is maintained, and this is done with the aid of the measuring tools: dividers to measure length and width and callipers to measure external or internal dimensions. Both take measurements from a template (pattern) and can be used easily when the lathe is in operation.

The turning tools, which have long blades and long handles to counteract the force of the lathe, are divided into four groups. First there are the gouges, which are used to rough off the wood to an approximate cylinder. Next are the skew chisels, used to refine the shape of the cylinder to its final form. The scrapers are used to make the grooves and turnings, and finally the parting tools are used to form long trenches and part the turnings from the waste wood.

Due to the stresses imposed on the tools they should be kept sharp and constantly checked for any possible stress fractures. This is one of the occasions when it is preferable for the restorer to use modern tools rather than their antique equivalents. This is because the latter may have developed stress factors in their blades or faults in their handles, which, if fractured during application, could cause serious injury to the turner. It is also important, therefore, to make sure that the tools are always used correctly. Due to the potential risks involved when using a lathe, it is essential to take an approved instructional course in turning before beginning lathe work (see Further Information, p.251).

Above: *A wide selection of measuring and turning tools is necessary to ensure that all turned work is accurate.*

Left: *The tap and die is a turning tool that is at the opposite end of the spectrum to high-speed lathes.*

Right: *Turning tools are distinctively different from woodworking chisels.*

Cutting a male screw thread

When turning and cutting a new thread, it is important to make sure that both male and female parts are of a corresponding size. As dies (internally threaded tools for cutting male threads) and screw taps (threaded steel cylinders for cutting female threads) exist in corresponding pairs, a match should be found. Remember that once you have started cutting, you must continue working until the thread is finished; stopping and starting will mean that you will not get a perfect match.

1 *Select and cut a piece of wood that is slightly larger in width than the diameter of the thread that is being replaced.*

2 *Turn the wood with a large gouge. Measure the size of the die housing using callipers, then compare the measurement to the size of the turned wood.*

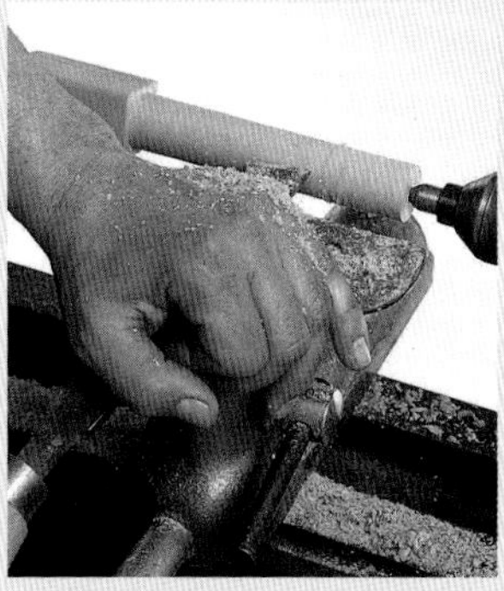

3 *Turn the column to the final diameter required, checking the measurements with the callipers as you work.*

4 *Place the turned column in the vice and, using a sharp chisel, cut a leading edge in the column. This will aid the beginning of the thread cutting.*

5 *Place the die, which has an inset cutting blade, on top of the turned column. Start turning it in a clockwise direction to cut the thread.*

6 *Keeping the die level, follow the technique of one full rotation clockwise followed by one half rotation counterclockwise. This clears the blade of shavings.*

7 *Continue all the way to the base and then remove the die. Remove the wood column and cut it to the required length.*

Cutting a female screw thread

A corresponding female thread now needs to be cut to match the male thread. Should the female and male threads be of different sizes, a solution is to plug the female thread with a suitable piece of wood and then recut the female wood to a size to correspond with the male thread.

1 *Place a piece of wood in a vice. Drill a corresponding hole into it of compatible size to the turned male thread, then pare a leading edge on the hole with a sharp chisel.*

2 *Grip the screw tap in the vice and place the leading edge on top of it. Turn the piece of wood one complete turn clockwise followed by a half turn counterclockwise.*

3 *When completed, the male and female parts should fit snuggly together and the thread should work with ease.*

MACHINERY

While antique restoration is traditionally a craft that relies on hand-held tools, the use of machinery can, in certain cases, make life much easier. It was the mass introduction of mechanized tools during the 19th century that radically altered furniture production. Although they can never replace the trained craftsman, the new generation of hand-held power tools available today will certainly save you many valuable hours in the workshop.

The use of heavy machinery in the restoration workshop is fairly limited. In fact, not many restoration workshops will have the space for a fully fitted machine shop, especially as the heavier types often require three-phase electricity supplies. (This involves installing a unit to boost the power from single to three phase, and is usually needed only in commercial workshops.) However, the inclusion of certain heavy machines can make life much easier, and two invaluable machines are the band saw and the lathe.

Hand-held machine tools, such as an electric or cordless drill, jigsaw and router, are a great help, and you should stock as wide a range of router cutters as possible. You could also buy a router bench, which extends the possibilities of the router. As finances and space allow, you can buy extra machinery, such as circular saws, thickness planers and pillar drills. While these will not be used on a daily basis, they can save hours of effort when they are required. As with all machinery, it is vital that you obtain the correct training before using it (see Further Information, p.251) and that you always carefully follow the safety instructions.

BAND SAW

The band saw's blade is a flexible length of steel that runs in a continuous loop. It is ideal for cutting curves and angles or for trimming strips from wider pieces. Its limitations are governed by the depth of the sawbed and the thickness of the blade. Never apply undue pressure to the blade, as this will damage it or the guiding rollers and cause it to snap.

As a general rule, allow the saw to cut at its own speed. Any excessive force will be indicated by the driving motors straining and starting to slow down.

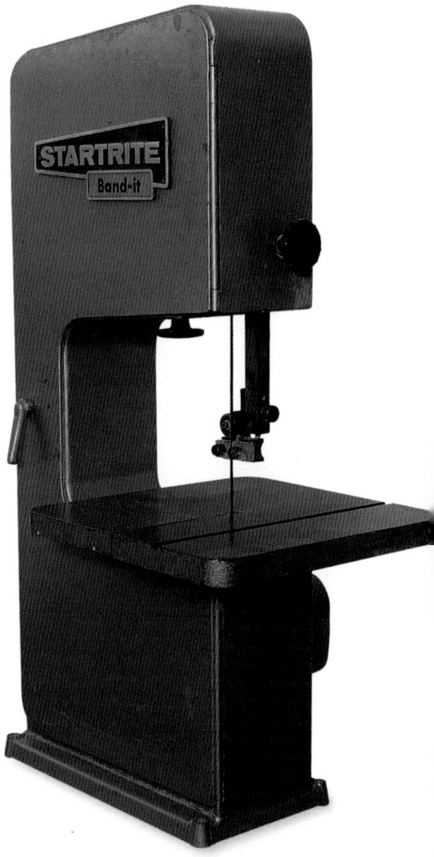

band saw

lathe

LATHE

The lathe allows you to accomplish a wide variety of tasks, ranging from the turning of legs, bobbins, bead mouldings and spindles to the copying of handles and decorative roundels or paterae.

Due to the speed and torque at which lathes operate, a lathe with a heavy cast body is ideal for restoration work, as this will counter any vibration. It is essential to take an approved instructional course in lathe work before you start using one as misuse can result in serious injury.

router bench

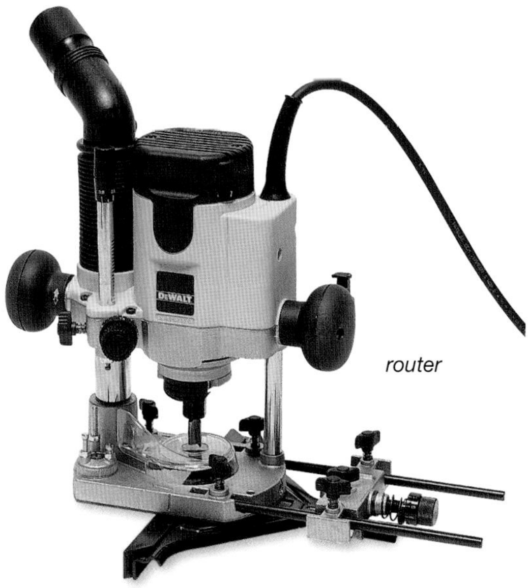

router

jigsaw

electric drill

cordless drill

ROUTER

The router is an extremely versatile hand tool. Its shaped cutter rotates at high speeds and will, if used correctly, give a clean, even cut. It can also be used with a guide fence or depth stop, and the range of cutters available is immense. Care should be taken in its use: no loose clothing should be worn, hair should be tied back and eye protection should be worn.

ROUTER BENCH

The router bench allows the router to be mounted upside down and so converted into a spindle moulder. The bench should always be used with guide fences and safety guards. The bench can often be dismantled, allowing for convenient storage when not in use.

POWER DRILLS

Cordless and electric drills are both ideal machines for workshop use. While you may sometimes require the use of a more traditional hand drill, such as when undertaking delicate work that may need to be executed one turn of the drill bit at a time, a power drill is one of the few modern tools that is preferred over the old version. Always buy the best model possible and, in the case of a cordless drill, always have the spare battery on charge ready to be changed over. These drills can also be used with screwdriver heads, although this would, of course, be for more general use and not for fine antique work, since the brass and steel antique screw heads would break if a power drill were used on them. Both types of drill can be used with a variety of bits and will accomplish a multitude of tasks. A drill stand can also be purchased to allow the drill to be used as a pillar drill.

JIGSAW

The jigsaw has a blade with a rise and fall action that cuts through sheet wood with ease. While it is not suitable for fine work, it is ideal for roughing out or cutting shaped templates (patterns) when the pieces are too large to fit into a band saw. Remember that the blade passes through the wood and continues to cut below, so care should be taken when using this tool.

COLLECTING AND STORING WOOD

A supply of suitable wood is an essential aspect of a restorer's workshop, and different kinds must be sourced, collected and properly stored. To the casual observer, such a collection of pieces of wood, salvaged from previous centuries of furniture making, may seem little more than firewood, but to the antique furniture restorer they are a priceless commodity, as without them his or her task would be impossible to undertake.

The aim of every restorer is, wherever possible, to restore a piece of furniture without trace. To do this requires the use of old surface woods and veneers that match the original as closely as possible in colour and grain. Also, when missing mouldings have to be remade, the material used must be of the same type as the original in order to make a good repair.

Two woods in constant demand by restorers are Cuban and Honduras mahogany, which, during the 18th century, were the woods of choice for furniture making. Both are now nearly impossible to buy from any wood merchant, and so any old examples found must be bought and put away until needed. This shows the vital importance of the restorer's "breaker store".

The breaker store, as the name so graphically describes, is a collection of pieces of antique furniture that have been bought not to be restored but to be carefully knocked apart, sorted into the various woods and stacked away for future reuse in the restoration of better pieces. Such an example might be a collection of quarter-sawn oak drawer sides, waiting to be used in the repair or replacement of a missing drawer, or perhaps an old Cuban mahogany table leaf, long ago separated from its table, waiting to be used in the making of a missing bracket foot or to be reshaped with a moulding plane to replace a missing section of top moulding.

The source of breakers is endless, and no opportunity should be missed to scour junk shops, local auctions or even skips. An old Victorian chest bought for very little indeed could provide enough oak linings, Cuban mahogany and even old locks to pay for itself many times over. Building a comprehensive breaker store can be a lifetime's work, and a useful tip to keep a store expanding is that every time some wood is used from the store, it should be replaced with more wood than was taken out. Indeed, it is a prerequisite for application to the antique restorers' most senior trade organization, The British Antique Furniture Restorers' Association (BAFRA), that the applicant is able to demonstrate the active building-up of a collection of breakers.

Right: *A well-stocked and logically arranged breaker store will supply a restorer with wood to match virtually any restoration project.*

The breaker store should be racked and labelled and the woods stored in the various marked sections. This saves both time and effort when searching for a particular piece and enables the restorer to see which, if any, types of veneer are running low or are not represented at all.

Any veneers should be removed from their wood core (see p.30) and stored separately in a veneer store. Any nails and screws should also be removed, partly for potential reuse if they are in good condition (see p.44) and partly as a method of preventing any unnecessary scratching from occurring. The store should be kept dry but not overly so, as excessive heat will cause the woods to warp and split.

While the majority of woods will be old, if an opportunity arises it is a good idea to buy some modern woods, such as walnut, yew or oak for renovating country-made pieces. These should then be professionally cut into boards, stacked so that air can circulate freely between them and allowed to dry and season naturally under cover.

If, however, space will not allow this storage, and modern wood has to be purchased when needed, remember that it is always better to buy air-dried rather than kiln-dried wood, as the former will be more stable in the long term.

To the untrained eye, a restorer's breaker store may look like a confused jumble of wood. The owner, however, will know all the stock that is there, even wood that was acquired years ago. When a particular grain or surface is needed, the restorer should be able to locate it almost immediately, recalling it from the day it was placed there. Next to tools, an extensive and expanding supply of breakers is one of the most important considerations for a furniture restorer.

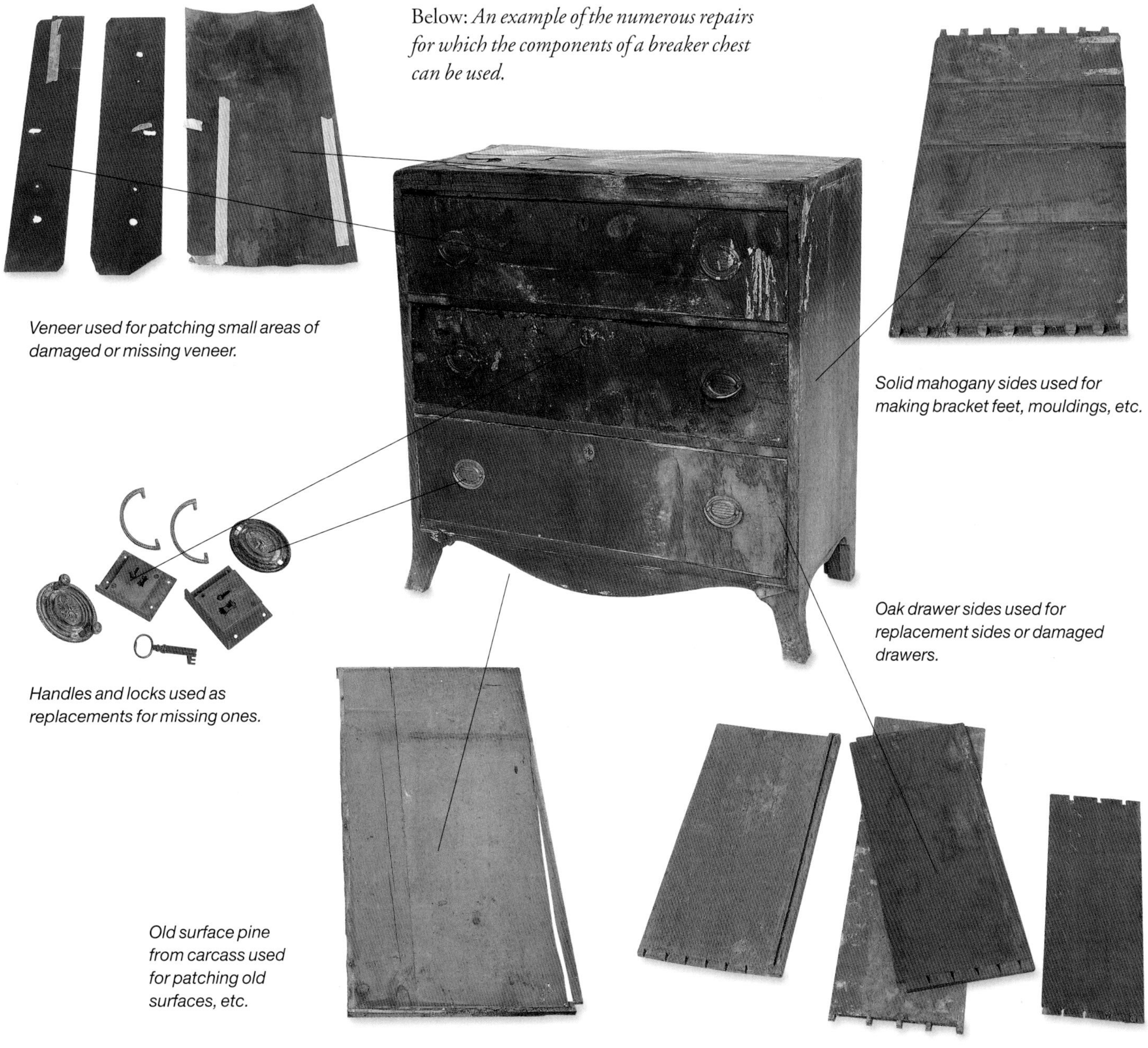

Below: *An example of the numerous repairs for which the components of a breaker chest can be used.*

COLLECTING AND STORING VENEERS

While early furniture was made using solid wood, by the late 17th century the use of veneer was becoming more widespread. Originally cut by saw, by the latter part of the 19th century thinner (and therefore cheaper) veneers were cut by peeling the log, a technique known as "knife cut", which increased their use still further. Whenever possible, a comprehensive store of used and new veneer should be stocked.

Veneers, like breakers (see p.28), are an important commodity for any serious-minded restorer. While good veneer merchants will hold a comprehensive stock of various cuts of veneer, it is still a good idea for the restorer, wherever possible, to compile a separate store in a shed or unused room. This veneer store should include not only new veneers, which may be bought in bundles, often held together with string, but also old surface veneers, which may have been removed from breakers.

With time, the colour of certain woods can alter greatly from their original colour, and for this reason the furniture restorer should aim to collect as wide a range of old surface veneers as possible.

Left: *A selection of bandings and stringings, which are often used in veneer work, are useful. They can be purchased from good veneer merchants.*

Left: *Any veneer store should be racked to allow the veneers to lie flat and be easily and quickly identified.*

Before being stored, old surface veneers will need to be removed from their core. A damp cloth is placed on top of the veneer and is then heated with an iron. The resulting steam softens the original animal glue, allowing the veneer to be gently eased off. This is done by sliding a flat-bladed knife between the veneer and the core. The old glue should be washed from the back of the veneer with hot water while it is still sticky.

The veneer should then be placed between two sheets of paper and have pressure applied to it. A hand veneer press is ideal for this, but alternatively the veneer can be placed between two flat pieces of wood with weights placed on top. This will allow the veneer to dry flat.

When the veneer is dry, it can be sorted with any other new pieces and then placed in the veneer store. Long lengths should be stored flat on slatted wood shelving, which allows the air to circulate freely. Smaller pieces, which can be used to repair cross bandings or inlays, can be placed in shoe boxes. The storage shed or room should not be allowed to become too dry, because this will cause the veneers to shrink and split. If possible, a slightly damp and cool atmosphere is best, because this allows the veneers to remain malleable. Laying cardboard on top of the veneer will also stop it becoming too dry and brittle.

Selecting a particular veneer from the store is a task best carried out by two people, one at each end of the veneer bundles, so that they can turn the bundles evenly as they search for the exact match. This method should prevent any unnecessary damage to the bundles. If, however, a veneer develops a split that starts to travel up its length, secure this with a piece of brown parcel tape.

When a piece of veneer has been removed from a shelf, the remaining pieces should be replaced in the same order as they were originally stacked. Failure to do so could result in different veneers being stacked together, which would then make selecting a particular veneer much harder in the future.

Colour and patination

Without doubt, the two most important aspects to any antique furniture are those of colour and patination. People often think that the two are the same, but in fact both are different, as each term refers to a different aspect of the finish found in antique furniture. It is the glorious colour and surface patination that furniture develops that the buyer and collector both seek. And their presence, or at times their absence, can radically alter the value of a particular piece.

Colour

The colour of a piece is found in the actual surface of the wood. This surface area illustrates how the wood has reacted over the years as many generations of natural light have affected its surface. It is interesting that for numerous reasons two pieces of the same wood, such as Cuban mahogany, can react in different ways. This can depend on the amount of light a piece has been exposed to or how dense a particular grain is. Also, a solid rounded piece, such as a chair upright, will react differently to a flat area, such as a chest top. Veneer will also change its appearance in a different way to a piece of solid wood.

Different woods can also be changed quite markedly over time, for instance kingwood and rosewood are both very purple when first cut and polished, but become a golden colour after many years of exposure. The change in mahogany, which when first polished has a very red tone, ranges from dark nutty brown to light honey colour. It is this variation that makes each piece of antique furniture unique. Unfortunately, this colour can easily be ruined by over-zealous cleaning, which allows chemicals to alter the tones, colours and hues of the wood. It is worth remembering that once altered, the original colour cannot be returned.

Patination

The term patination can best be described as the history of a piece mirrored in its surface colour and shine. Technically, it is caused by generations of oxidation of the polished surface, combined with a build-up of furniture waxes, natural grease and dust. Its appearance can be altered by many factors, including sunlight, the amount of waxing a piece has received in its lifetime, whether any solvents have been applied and the type of finish originally used when the piece was made. For example, the patination found on a piece of mid-18th-century mahogany, which would have been polished with oil, varies greatly from that found on an early 18th-century piece of walnut, which would have been finished with varnish and wax. While good patination is often present on good pieces of furniture, truly great patination is rare. When it is present, therefore, every effort should be made to maintain it.

Above and below: *These photographs illustrate the inner and outer surface of an 18th-century tea table. The inner surface, which has spent its lifetime closed and protected from the effects of light, has kept the original red colour (above). In contrast, the top of the table has mellowed and, after generations of waxing, has developed a magnificent patinated surface (below). This is an example of mahogany colour and patination at its best.*

Veneers and wood

It is the sheer variety of the woods and veneers used in their construction that makes furniture, both antique and modern, so pleasing. During previous centuries, as new woods were discovered and imported, it allowed cabinet-makers and designers to explore new techniques and designs utilizing the qualities unique to these woods. The opening up of the world in terms of trade can be directly linked to changes in furniture design over the centuries.

During the 16th century, almost all furniture was still made from solid wood. By the latter part of the 17th century, however, veneer began to play an increasingly important role in furniture making. Some changes in construction techniques followed, and in certain pieces the carcass was now little more than a framework on which to apply the veneer. Dutch, French and Italian furniture-makers experimented with marquetry and parquetry designs, while others began to use native woods such as walnut and elm – all which had formerly been used in the solid – in veneer form to gain the maximum benefit from the beauty of the grain and natural burr patterns. These same burrs, which would have been far too unstable to appear in solid wood furniture (they have a natural tendency to split and twist during seasoning after construction), could now be cut into thinner veneers and applied on to a stable core carcass of oak.

Left: *The tools used for cutting and laying veneer are fairly basic and have remained unaltered throughout the centuries.*

The first veneers were cut by hand. This was laborious and meant that the veneers were thick and fairy expensive to produce, but as quality furniture was still a luxury commodity, it mattered little. With the use of industrial machinery during the 19th century came thinner and cheaper veneers. These veneers allowed previously expensive woods such as mahogany and satinwood to be incorporated into a wider range of furniture.

How veneers are cut

To slice veneers from a log, the log is mounted in a frame that rotates or slides up and down against a sharp blade. Depending on the way the log is mounted, different sections of the figure in the grain can be displayed to their best effect.

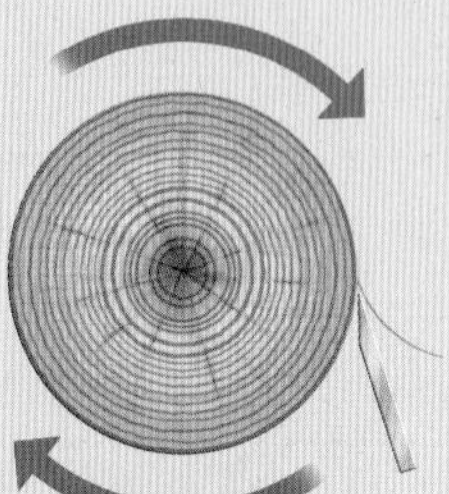

Rotary-cut veneers follow the growth rings in the log as it is unpeeled like a giant roll of paper. They are produced in large sizes.

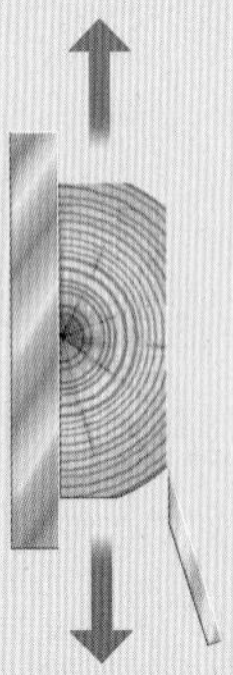

Flat-cut, or crown cut, veneers are cut parallel to the centre line of the log. Woods with distinct growth lines are best sliced in this way.

Quarter-cut veneers are cut at right angles through the rings. This displays the rays in wide bands, as in quartered oak, with its distinctive silvery "flash" rays.

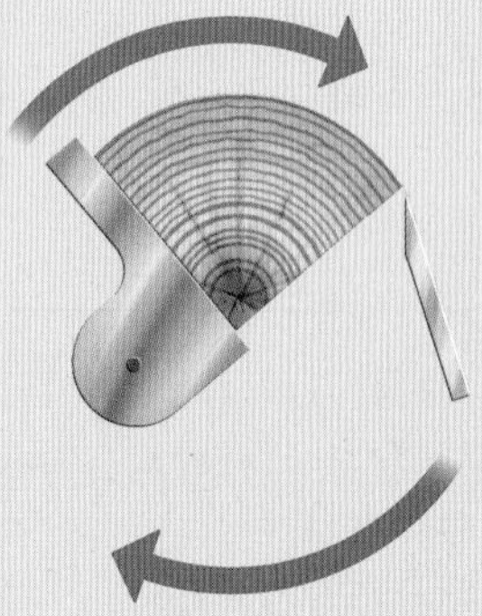

Rift cut, or comb cut, veneers are cut with the blade offset at a slight angle from the quarter position. This produces a fine parallel grain figure.

Types of veneer cuts

One advantage of using veneers over solid wood, which was quickly appreciated by the cabinet-maker, was that each individual tree as well as each species of tree could produce examples of many different types of patterns. This allowed the cabinet-maker and furniture designer to break up an expanse of wood with patterns and designs that are both unique and highly decorative.

However, although no two pieces of veneer are exactly alike, they can be categorized into broad types, depending on from which part of the tree they come from and their general pattern and form.

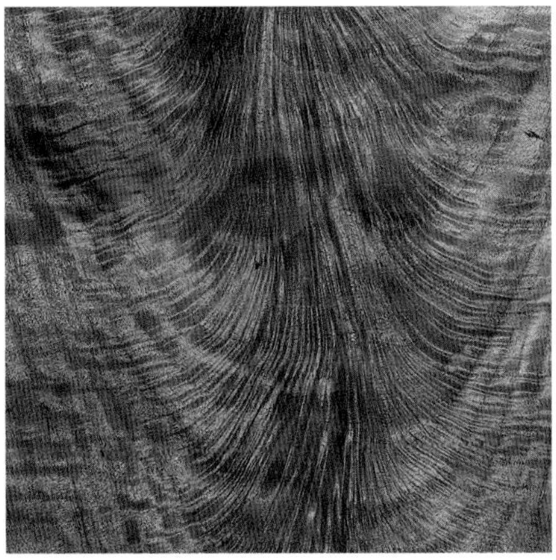

CURL VENEER

A curl veneer is obtained by cutting from the fork of the tree where the trunk divides. It gives a feathering effect, and in woods such as mahogany was highly sought after for drawer fronts and tops. Mahogany curl veneer was particularly popular during the 18th and 19th centuries.

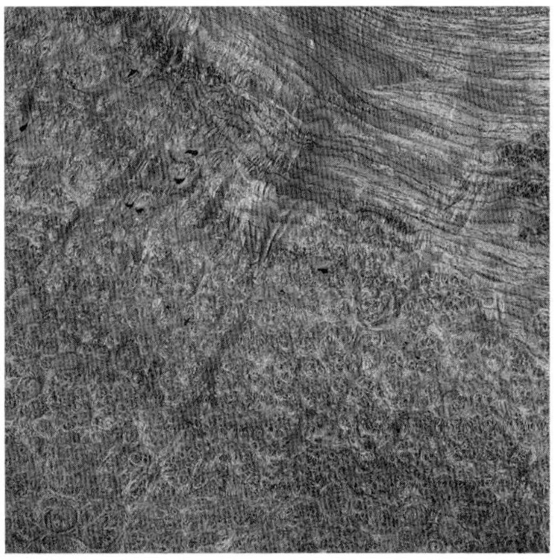

BURR VENEER

The burr is found on the side of the trunk where numerous growths have occurred. Often found near the bottom of the tree, they are sometimes known as burr clusters. Usually only available in small sections, they are unstable until glued to a stable core.

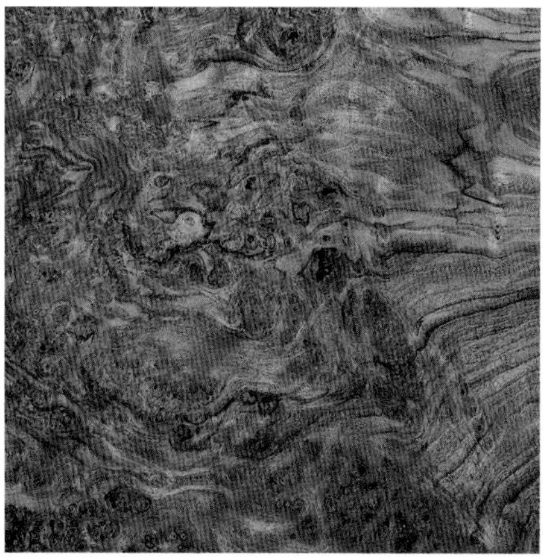

BUTT VENEER

This veneer, as the name suggests, is taken from the root, or butt, of the tree. Dense in grain, it is often wild in figure with much swirling movement.

FIDDLE VENEER

This prized veneer was used in the manufacture of violins, hence its name. It has a distinctive stripe, which usually runs at right angles to the grain, and was favoured during the 18th century with mahogany and stained sycamore, known as harewood.

FIGURED VENEER

Not as wild as burr but still with movement, this type of veneer was popular in the making of quarter-veneered tops and bookmatched ends. Various theories abound as to why some veneers are more figured than others, but it is this variety that creates uniqueness.

OYSTER VENEER

The oyster veneer, which is obtained by slicing through the branch to give distinctive rings, was popular during the 17th and early 18th centuries from woods such as olive, walnut and laburnum. It was usually then enhanced with geometric line inlays of box or holly.

Veneer treatments

Although it is possible for veneers to be simply applied in sheet form, it is far more usual for them to be laid in decorative patterns. The range of patterns is fairly small and will often be dictated by the type of cut of veneer and the origin or date of the piece. When these veneer patterns are laid, it is important that the sheets of veneer are selected from the same bundle, and indeed in the same order in which they were cut, otherwise the pattern can seem disjointed.

Quarter-veneered

As the name suggests, this is the design where the top is veneered in a quarter pattern radiating out from the centre. The most popular cut used is the figured veneer, although the use of burr is also known. Quarter-veneers were often bordered with further crossbanding to form a frame. During the 19th century, round tops were veneered in numerous curls that radiated toward the centre, but this was known as segmented veneering.

Bookmatched

The bookmatched veneer surface is obtained by taking two subsequent veneer sheets from a bundle, opening them out and laying them next to each other so that they form a counter pattern, rather like the wings of a butterfly. This is done with figured veneer and can be found on the sides or fronts of chests or bureaux, or perhaps on the top of a centre table.

Blocked

This technique was used during the 17th century, especially on the ends of marquetry chests. It allowed a patterned centre to be veneered around quickly and meant that odd cuts of a veneer could be used when a pattern would make it difficult to cut around. (Marquetry panels were laid prior to the surrounding veneer being applied.)

Feathered

In this method the veneer is cut and laid at an angle. Although quite rare, it is found on certain 18th- and 19th-century pieces of quality to give a decorative treatment to a door.

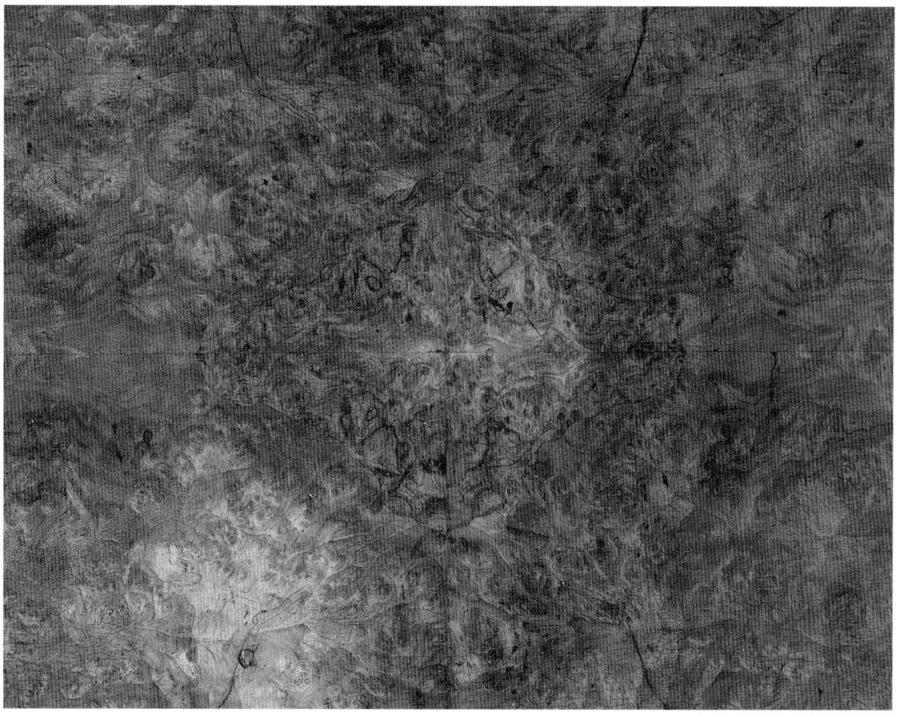

SCARF-JOINTED

This technique is used when a straight edge is not possible or desirable, for example when using burr veneers that come in small pieces. While they may be cut straight along the quartered line, the joints connecting the various pieces should remain hidden to give the illusion that each quarter is in fact one piece rather than a number of pieces joined together. A wavy cut is made that should be lost in the swirl of the grain. Over time, the veneer may shrink a little due to seasoning and the joints may become visible again.

Types of veneer

Like solid wood, veneers are affected by the action of light, polish and wax. Indeed, the range of colours found in veneer can be quite marked, and it is these colours, tones and hues that are so readily sought after today by the collector.

Although the types of woods used are numerous, and choice very much depends on the origin and date of the piece, the majority of popular antiques today use the woods illustrated in the following sections.

MAHOGANY

Numerous types of mahogany are available, but the two most commonly used for furniture manufacture during the 18th and 19th centuries were Cuban (*Swietenia mahogoni*) and Honduras mahogany (*Swietenia macrophylla*). With its rich red colour and dense hard grain, this solid wood was ideal for furniture manufacture. When cut into veneer form, the mahogany was highly decorative, especially when the sought-after curls were used in the door panels of bookcases or linen presses.

Above: *Cuban mahogany veneer prior to use and polishing.*

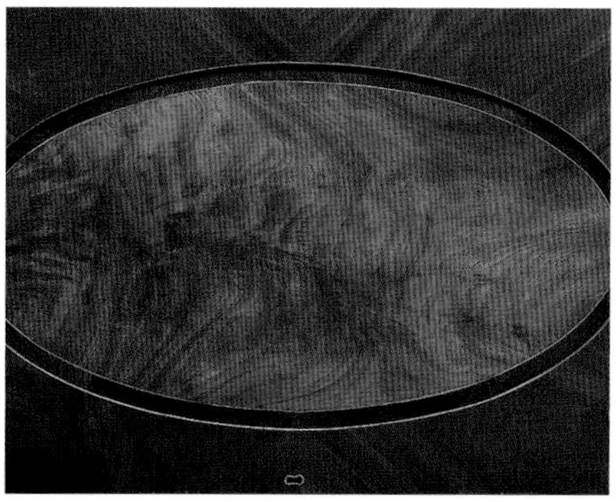

Above: *A Cuban mahogany curl veneer panel having mellowed and patinated to a wonderful surface.*

Above: *A George III linen press, c.1790, veneered in well-figured Cuban mahogany throughout and with curl veneer panels.*

WALNUT

European walnut (*Juglans regia*) was widely used for furniture manufacture from the 17th century onward, and by the end of that century its use in veneer form was increasingly fashionable for the finer pieces. Although indigenous to warmer European climates, such as France, Italy and Turkey, it was also produced in England. The Great Frost of 1709 destroyed most of the European trees, and so its export from France was banned after 1720. Its use in furniture in veneer form declined during the 18th century, but it become popular again during the mid-19th century. When first polished, it is almost orange, but it will mellow to either a honey colour or a rich nutty one.

Right: *A walnut veneer.*

Right: *A walnut veneer after 300 years of waxing.*

Above: *An 18th-century walnut-veneered bureau of excellent colour and patination.*

ROSEWOOD

This wood comes in two forms: Indian rosewood (*Dalbergia latifolia*) and Brazilian rosewood (*Dalbergia nigra*). During the 18th century, Indian rosewood was more commonly used in the solid in Indian and Anglo-Indian furniture, while Brazilian rosewood was more favoured in veneer form during the 19th century. It is often seen on table tops laid on to a mahogany core. While deep purple when first polished, rosewood mellows to a rich warm tone and on occasion can even become golden brown in colour.

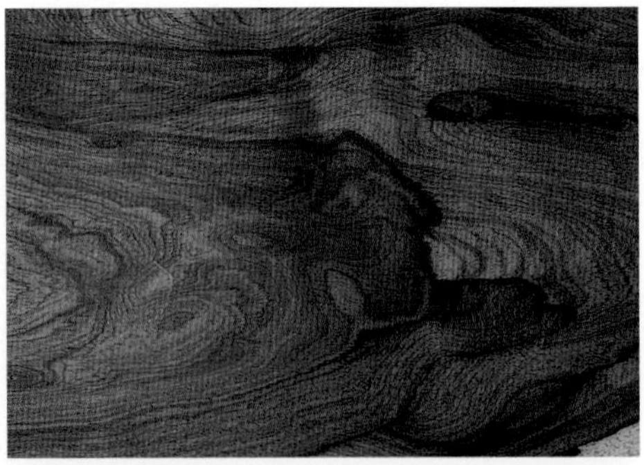

Right: *A Brazilian rosewood veneer.*

Right: *A Brazilian rosewood veneer that has developed a rich colour.*

Above: *A Regency centre table, c.1815, veneered in well-figured Brazilian rosewood and inlaid with brass.*

Satinwood

West Indian satinwood (*Zanthoxylum flavum*) originates from the Caribbean islands, while East Indian satinwood (*Chloroxylon swietenia*) comes from southern India and Sri Lanka. The wood was not in demand for furniture making until the mid-18th century. Although it was sometimes used in solid form during the latter part of the 19th century, it was mainly used in decorative veneer form. East Indian satinwood, which can be seen on later 19th-century pieces, is richer in colour than the West Indian variety and often has a characteristic ribbon stripe when the veneer is quarter cut. It is yellow when first polished, but develops a golden rich colour over time.

Right: *A piece of West Indian veneer when first cut.*

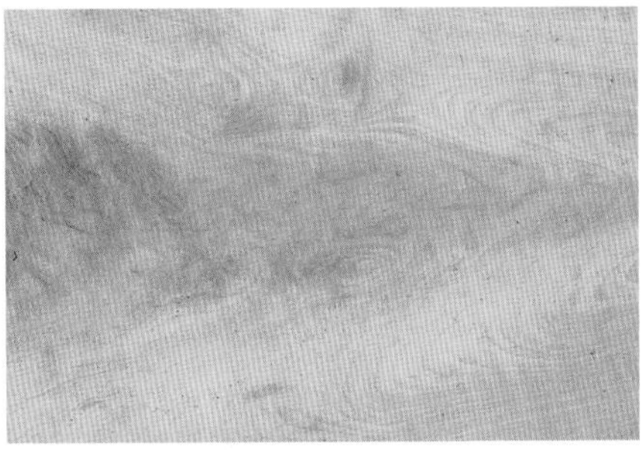

Right: *A West Indian veneer that has mellowed and patinated to a golden yellow/orange colour.*

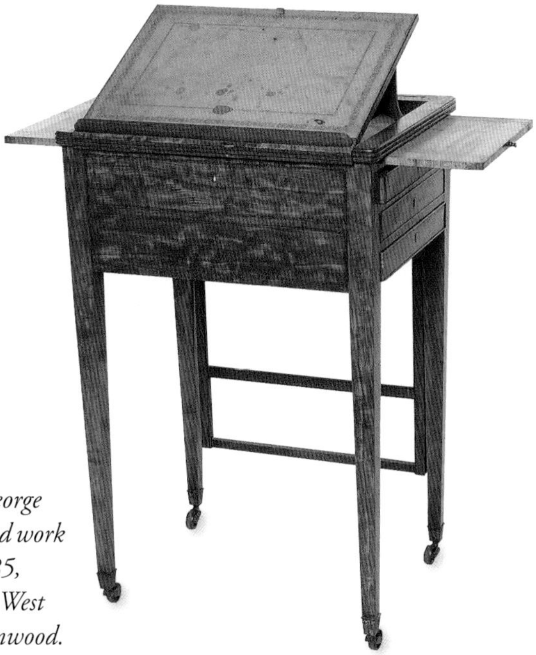

Right: *A George III game and work table, c.1785, veneered in West Indian satinwood.*

Oak

There are more than 300 varieties of oak, but European and English oak are the same species – *Quercus robur*. Until the 17th century, most furniture was made from oak. However, as the century progressed, newly imported woods became fashionable and oak was largely downgraded to either internal carcass work or country-made pieces. When first cut it is a light honey colour, and if quarter sawn it will show its distinctive, silvery, medullary ray figure, but after initial waxing it can become much darker and will continue to darken over time.

Right: *Oak when first cut with its light golden colour.*

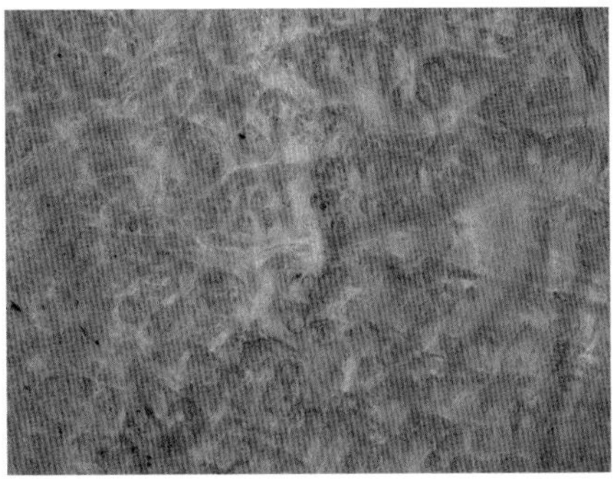

Right: *With time and generations of waxing, a rich warm tone will develop.*

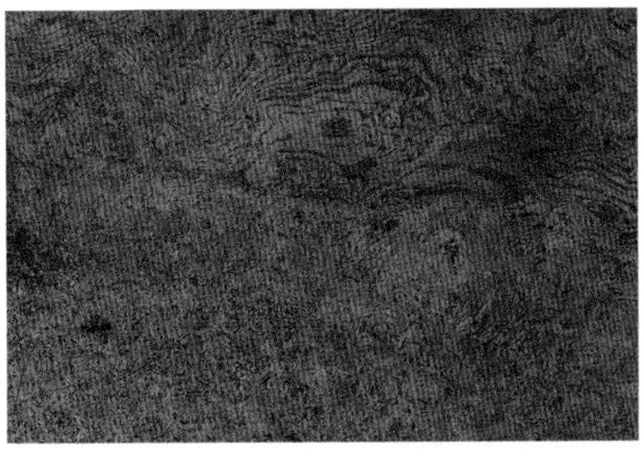

Above: *An early 19th-century sarcophagus wine cooler veneered in burr oak.*

POLISHES AND GLUES

One of the most attractive features of antique furniture is its distinctive grain patterns. It is the application of polish and waxes that, while helping to protect, feed and nourish the wood, also enhances its appearance. The polishes and techniques used today are nearly identical to those used for generations before, although the restorers of old would have had to make their own polish recipes as well as making all their own glues.

POLISHES

Ever since wooden furniture was first made, its grain has been sealed in one way or another. Waxes were used to burnish the surface, and, during the 17th century, varnishes were applied that helped to protect and enhance the wood. During the 19th century, a new technique was adopted that resulted in a shellac polish, made from the shells of lac beetles, being applied with a cotton and linen pad known as a rubber (see pp.66–67). This sealed the grain, protected the wood and brought out the pattern and figure of popular imported woods such as mahogany, satinwood and rosewood.

The polisher's basic requirements are few. The equipment involves wadding (batting) and linen or other lint-free cloth for making rubbers, a selection of various grades of wire (steel) wool, as well as a wide selection of various brushes and some mutton cloth for buffing surfaces.

The polisher's materials include shellac polish, which can be bought in either liquid form or as shellac flakes to be mixed with spirit (alcohol), and is kept in a glass or plastic bottle. Various coloured pigments to be mixed with water or spirit are needed for tinting or colouring repairs, and stopping waxes, again in various shades, are also needed. The final material is methylated spirits (methyl alcohol), which should be stored in a fire-proof cabinet. All the above equipment and materials can be obtained from a good trade supplier.

One of the main attractions of an antique piece of furniture is its colour and, hopefully, its patinated surface, so great care should be taken whenever polish is applied. The skill of the polisher is to revive a surface by gently removing the perished layers and then rebuilding the surface layer by layer. Work on small areas should be kept as localized as possible so as not to affect the surrounding areas. Patience and practice are therefore the watchwords. A good eye for colour is also needed to ensure that patches and repairs blend in with the surrounding areas. They should be practically invisible. It is also essential to have an understanding of traditional techniques and materials and to know when to clean a piece and when it is better to leave it alone. Over-zealous cleaning will not only spoil the aesthetic appearance but will almost certainly devalue the piece considerably.

Professionally, a polisher may take many years to learn the craft, and, without doubt, the polisher's role in a workshop is every bit as important as that of the cabinet-maker or restorer.

Above: *Brushes, polishes and stains are needed for nearly every restoration job. Keep a good selection to hand.*

Above: *Rubbers should be kept in an air-tight jar or tin to stop them drying out.*

Glues

Until the 15th and early 16th centuries, very little glue was used in the manufacture of furniture. Instead, the joints were held together with pegs or crude, hand-made clout nails. By the 17th century, however, as furniture construction became more complex and designs and styles more adventurous, animal glues were being employed in furniture making.

While new adhesives have been developed over the years, animal glues are still the most frequently used glues in furniture restoration. The sight and smell of the glue pot in any workshop is the same today as it was in the 17th, 18th and 19th centuries, and putting it on the fire or hot plate is still the apprentice's first task every morning.

Three main types of glue are used in the modern workshop: animal glue, PVA (white) glue and cascamite. Each has its own role and will be selected according to the nature of the required join.

Animal glue

This glue is made today as it has been for the last 300 years: animal feet and skin are boiled and the resulting liquid is poured into cold water, causing it to crystallize into small pearls. These pearls can then be mixed with water and allowed to soak overnight, before being heated in a special glue pot to melt them.

Above: *Animal glue is applied hot, using a bristle brush.*

Above: *The three most commonly used glues today (clockwise from top): animal glue, PVA (white) glue and cascamite.*

The glue pot (or gesso kettle) is an iron bain-marie pot with an inner reservoir of hot water. The pot is put on a fire or hotplate until the water boils, and it is then allowed to simmer gently, melting the glue ready for use. A top crust will appear and should be scraped off prior to use.

Great care should be taken not to allow the hot-water reservoir to boil dry. Should this happen, the glue will become too hot and its adhesive qualities will be lost. The remaining glue will then have to be discarded and a new batch prepared.

At the end of each day, the glue pot is taken off the heat and set aside until the next day, when it is simply reheated and the glue reused. A pot of glue could be cooled and then reheated day after day, but it is good workshop practice to make a fresh batch of animal glue every week.

Animal glue is ideal for furniture restoration because it allows a certain flexibility in the joints, it can be removed with hot water or spirit (alcohol) and it sets as soon as it has cooled. It can also be watered down to make a size for use on veneers and surfaces (see p.79) when a piece of furniture needs re-veneering.

The disadvantages of animal glue, however, are that it is affected by extremes of heat and cold and that a sharp blow to a joint will cause it to lose its adhesion. If such a break happens, the joint has to be taken apart, cleaned and reglued. Despite these disadvantages, however, no serious workshop would be without its glue pot.

Above: *Animal glues are heated prior to use in an iron bain-marie pot. The water reservoir should not be allowed to boil dry.*

PVA glue

Another frequently used glue is the more modern polyvinylacetate, or PVA (white), glue. It is bought in liquid form, is easy to use, needs no pre-application preparation and is unaffected by either extreme of temperature. The joint or two surfaces being joined must be brought under pressure when the glue (which is non-reversible) is applied.

When it is either impractical to have an glue pot simmering away all day, or when you are doing a small restoration job that simply does not warrant the time involved in preparing animal glue, versatile and simple-to-use PVA is the ideal workshop adhesive.

Cascamite

For projects needing an adhesive that will help to hold a shape or form, an ideal glue is urea-formaldehyde resin, or cascamite as it is more commonly known. This comes in a powder form and is mixed with water to a creamy paste. Once the glue has been applied, the two surfaces being joined should be brought under pressure with suitable clamps.

Cascamite is a versatile glue: its natural white colour can be disguised by adding coloured pigments to it, and some types are waterproof, which can be useful. The disadvantage, however, is that it is very brittle when set, making it totally unsuitable for joints, because just a knock could shatter the glue bond.

GILT AND STAINS

Gilding and staining are both methods of enhancing and disguising wood to give a better appearance. While stains are used in the main by the restorer to disguise repairs it should be remembered that during the 17th and 18th centuries inferior woods were often stained to give them the appearance of more exotic and expensive ones; for example pearwood was stained black to resemble the more sought after and expensive ebony.

GILT

The use of gilt to decorate and highlight furniture has been a part of furniture making for centuries. The two techniques used are those of oil and water gilding (see pp.73–75 for details), each of which gives a distinctive look. Some specialist materials and equipment are needed, but the most important ingredients that the gilder requires are patience and skill.

Gesso is a mixture of powdered chalk, rabbit-skin glue and boiled linseed melted in a gesso kettle, and it is used to build up the surface before gilding. A few layers can give a thick, even coat. It can have sand mixed in with it for a textured finish.

Bole is a mixture of clay and water that is available in red, white or blue and is used to form the next layer in the gilding process. Once this is dry, a size of alcohol, rabbit-skin glue and water is applied. The surface is now ready for the gold leaf to be laid gently in place.

The gold used in gilding has been rolled on machine rollers and then hand-hammered into leaves of varying levels of fineness. It can be bought in a number of different grades, depending on the carat.

Agates are used to pull together joins between the leaves and for burnishing. Originally made from dog's teeth (they are also known as "dog-tooth agates"), they are now made from synthetic materials.

Above: *During the 17th and 18th centuries metalware on the finest pieces was occasionally fire gilded (see p.45).*

Right: *The tools of the gilder have remained basically the same through the centuries, although modern plastics are now replacing dog teeth.*

Water gilding

Gold leaf cannot simply be laid on to bare wood when water gilding. Bases of gesso and then bole must be applied first, and then the gilt can be laid, evened and finally distressed.

Stains

The majority of coloured stains are either water- or spirit- (alcohol-) based, although on rare occasions a slow-drying, oil-based stain may be used. They are used to colour in repairs or to help colour out and disguise marks. Some stains can be bought in liquid form, but for the best range of tones and colours you will need to buy stains in powder form, ready to be mixed with spirit or water.

Spirit-based stains, usually mixed with methylated spirits (methyl alcohol), are quick-drying, because the spirit rapidly evaporates in air. This makes them unsuitable for use on large areas, as some areas will dry before others, causing an uneven finish. Spirit stains are usually applied after polishing. If the polish is applied on top of the stain, the spirit in the polish will dilute the stain and lighten the surface colour.

Water-based stains dry more slowly, making them suitable for large areas because they give an even finish. They are generally applied before polishing. One disadvantage, however, is that they can raise the grain, which will then need to be flattened before you can proceed any further. Both spirit and water stains can be thinned after application by adding further spirit/water.

Left: *Stains often have to be tailor-made to suit the job in hand.*

Other stains, such as coloured waxes, are not frequently used in furniture restoration. Their use is generally confined to moderating the colour of a surface slightly after it has been polished.

Stains can be applied by brush, which should be thoroughly cleaned after use with a cloth or by a dowel with some cloth wrapped around the end, known as a swab (see p.69). Alternatively, some polish can be mixed with a small amount of stain and applied not with a rubber but with a fad (see pp.70–71). This allows the whole area to be slightly tinted, and it overcomes the problem of the spirit base lightening the colour.

Below: *Stains can be purchased in colour powder form, which are then mixed with a suitable solvent.*

Mixing a spirit-based stain

1 *Aways use a clean container and a flat-bladed knife or small teaspoon for mixing stains. Methylated spirits (methyl alcohol) is an ideal spirit liquid mixer.*

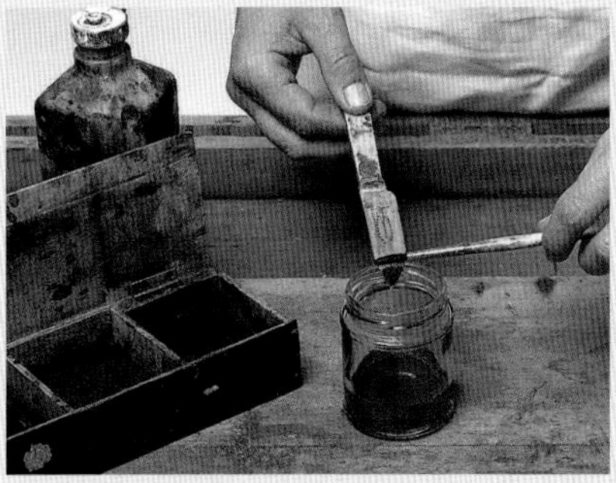

2 *Pour the required quantity of methylated spirits into the clean container. It is better to add powder to liquid rather than liquid to powder, in order to avoid unnecessary wastage. Select the correct powder required for the colour effect desired, and add a small amount at a time.*

3 *Mix with a clean brush. If a stronger stain tone is needed, simply add further powder. When you have finished with the stain, pour away the unused stain and clean all the utensils and the brush to ensure that the next coloured stain to be mixed is not tinted with any residue from this one.*

UPHOLSTERY AND LEATHER

Most restorers are more than competent to remove and undertake basic upholstery, but the actual skill of upholstering antique furniture to a good standard is a qualified trade that will take a number of years of training to master. An understanding of the methods and techniques used in upholstery is, however, essential and, like a general knowledge of leathering, will give the restorer a better understanding of his or her craft.

UPHOLSTERY

The tools for upholstery fall into two categories: those for removing existing upholstery and those for reupholstery. They can also differ depending on where the workshop is located, as styles and techniques vary from country to country. For example, in Britain and the USA the upholstered piece is raised on a bench or trestles and the upholsterer stands, while in France the general practice is to work with the piece on the floor and the upholsterer on his or her knees. Also, due to the fashion for French furniture being more rounded, especially on the edges, rounded needles are used to stitch rolled edges, while the English method, with its preference for a neater, more precise edge, requires the use of a longer, straighter needle for the stitching.

On occasion hay has been used in upholstery to stuff the seat, but horsehair is more common. Horsehair, however, is becoming increasingly difficult to source, and pigs' hair is often being used in its place. Commercial upholstery workshops will try to buy second-hand horsehair mattresses, which give a good supply of hair that can be carded (teased out) and reused. Synthetic hair is another alternative, but given the choice most qualified uphosterers prefer natural hair.

Above: *A selection of materials, including horse hair, webbing and springs, needed for reupholstering furniture.*

Another innovation is the staple gun, which is sometimes used to secure fabric instead of upholstery tacks.

Cushions should be filled with traditional down feathers rather than modern synthetic materials, which lack the weight and feel of the original. Traditionally, the down was stuffed into a goatskin suede bag around which the finish fabric was applied. This made sure that the down did not work itself through the fabric. Today, a waxed cotton jacket is adequate for the purpose. In the case of the thinner squab seats for dining chairs, good quality foam is acceptable should rubberized horsehair, which is bought in sheet form, be unavailable.

Left: *The variety of coverings and trims available is extensive.*

There are two types of webbing technique: stuff-over and underwebbing. Stuff-over gives a harder, flatter line and was used on English upholstered furniture from the 17th century onward. Continental upholsterers often favoured underwebbing, used in conjunction with internal springs, which gives a more rounded appearance. Certain styles or periods of chair may suit one method of webbing more than the other, but both are acceptable and the choice is often the client's to make.

Leather

Since the 17th century, leather has been used as a covering on desk tops and also inset into writing surfaces. Nineteenth-century leather tops are not unusual on antique furniture, and occasionally, if it has been treated carefully, you may even find a desk or table with the original leather from the 18th century. In the majority of cases, however, cracking, tearing or wear will mean that the leather surface has to be replaced.

There are basically two types of leather to choose from: skiver (sheep leather) and hide (cow leather). Skiver is found in smaller pieces and often used on davenport tops, bureau falls (the interior of a bureau, which is used as a writing surface) and writing boxes. For larger desks and writing table tops, hide is the obvious choice due to its generally larger size. Also, as a rule of thumb, hide tends to be of better quality and more suited to quality antique furniture than skiver.

When selecting the hide or skiver for use, try to find a piece that has little or no scarring to the surface and avoid leather taken from the neck area, which tends to have stretch marks. The leather will be applied to the desk or table in its natural tan colour and will be coloured when it is in situ. Also it is vital that the surface on to which the leather is going to be laid is level, with no cracks or splits, because these will become visible through the leather.

With the leather laid and coloured, the decorative bandings, known as tooling, must be decided upon. There are two basic types: gold tooling and blind tooling. Both are applied using a hot tooling wheel (see p.233), which embosses a pattern on to the leather surface. The difference between the two is that the gold tooling is applied after the top has been laid and coloured, while blind tooling is embossed into the top when the leather is still wet and uncoloured, and the deep imprint is then coloured with a suitable stain. The gold tooling effect is obtained with the tooling wheel running over a gold foil ribbon, which leaves a gold pattern. The type and style of decorative pattern used will often reflect the period of the piece of furniture, and a wide range of styles are available.

Above: *Tooling wheels are used when heated to spitting heat. Firm and even pressure produces an excellent result.*

Above: *In "blind tooling", the tooling wheel is used without the roll of gold leaf.*

Right: *A selection of patterned borders that are available on decorative tooling wheels.*

MOULDINGS AND MOULDING PLANES

From the late 17th to early 19th centuries, as furniture designs became more elaborate, mouldings of various shapes and styles began to appear on furniture. Prior to this period most planes would have been made by the cabinet-maker, but by the beginning of the 18th century the work of specialized plane-makers, such as Thomas Granford and Robert Wooding, is recorded, as the demand for more complex mouldings and planes grew.

Early moulding planes were made from either box or beech and were usually 25–28cm/10–11in long. By the end of the 18th century their size had become a standardized 24cm/9½in. The tool-maker would usually stamp his name on the end grain at the toe, but it is not uncommon to see the names of numerous other cabinet-makers, whose hands the moulding plane has passed through, also stamped on the plane.

The range and variety of moulding planes are almost limitless, and the mouldings produced from them could be anything from simple base or waist mouldings to quite complex examples, such as those used to decorate the elaborate pediments on mid-18th-century furniture. During the late 17th and early part of the 18th century, most mouldings on walnut furniture were cross-grain examples, but by the second quarter of the 18th century, with most furniture being made of the newly imported mahogany, they were being cut from long-grain wood.

Above: *Antique moulding planes were usually made from either box wood or beech and are beautiful – and highly collectable – objects in their own right.*

Making a moulding

1 *Apply your chosen wood to a pine core and glue the core to a block of wood that can be held in a vice. Draw the profile of the moulding on to one edge.*

2 *Begin to plane the wood using long, even strokes. Make sure the blade is very sharp so that it cuts through the wood without tearing the grain.*

3 *For speed and to establish depth guides, repeatedly run the moulding through a circular saw. A fence guide will create parallel lines you can work to with the plane.*

4 *Continue shaping the moulding using different planes to create various shapes in the wood. Work closely to the profile drawn on one edge.*

5 *With the shaping completed, smooth the surface with fine-grade sandpaper wrapped around overloes – wooden blocks shaped to match the profile of the moulding.*

6 *The finished moulding should accurately follow the selected profile, with sharp, clean lines.*

HANDLES AND HINGES

Handles have changed greatly during the centuries in style, decoration and the materials used to make them. They were often replaced not because the originals had worn but to keep pace with the ever-changing fashions of the period. Sometimes the replacements were out of keeping with the style of the piece. Hinges were less influenced by fashion, although some were made to be more decorative to complement other furniture hardware.

THE EARLY BEGINNINGS

During medieval times, the earliest hollowed-out coffers may have had wooden peg hinges, but it was not long before the metal strap hinge began to be used. With the arrival of the plank coffer, the use of metal greatly increased. Indeed, the box chests or coffers of the 14th and 15th centuries would often have been bound with iron bands to make them stronger and to protect against splitting. By the beginning of the 15th century, hinges were becoming more elaborate with butterfly hinges, so called because they resembled butterfly wings, being used, often embossed with punched and engraved decoration.

Handles of the period tended to be ring-like in form and, like the hinges, manufactured in iron.

Left: *This 15th-century oak coffer features the stout, metal strap hinges typical of the period.*

THE 17TH CENTURY

The major changes began during the mid- to latter part of the 17th century. By this period, the business of manufacturing hinges, handles and locks (see pp.48–49) was becoming more of a specialized field. Iron was rapidly being replaced by an alloy of copper and zinc that formed the more malleable brass. Equally, the local smith was being replaced by more specialized craftsmen, from the designer and carver of the model handle, to the moulder who cast the handle and finally to the man who would chaste (carve) any pattern or design into the surface. The handle would then have the edges chamfered and be polished with a coat of lacquering to stop any tarnishing. By the mid-18th century, fire gilding (see p.49) was used on the finest of pieces.

THE 18TH CENTURY

Until the early 18th century, brass handles had been secured to the drawer with thin iron strips, or straps as they were known. From that time on, they were replaced with cast posts, or pummels, which were attached with threaded nuts to the back of the drawer.

During the late 17th century and early part of the 18th century, plate and open plate handles, which could be plain or engraved, would be made *en suite* with

Right: *This 18th-century open plate handle and matching escutcheon are typical of their period.*

Above: *Hinges could be decorative, as well as functional, but each was designed for a specific purpose.*

▷

Left: *For the keen restorer, it is a good idea to collect antique handles and store for future renovation projects.*

matching escutcheons to give a more consistent and balanced appearance to a piece of furniture.

During the early 18th century, the hardware would in all likelihood have been made by a local foundry. From the mid part of the century the trade became more centralized. The new foundries made handles in many different styles for the home market, but handles and other brassware were also exported, most notably for use on American and Dutch furniture.

Another material used occasionally during this period was paktong. It was an alloy of copper and zinc with nickel added to make it look like silver in appearance but at a fraction of the cost. Originally imported from the Orient, where it had been used for some time previously, it was often found on export furniture or as decorative mounts on knifeboxes.

By the latter part of the 18th century, the fashion had moved once again toward plate handles. Differing from the earlier 18th-century examples, which were cast, they were often stamped out of sheet brass, which would have had a higher copper content, making the metal more malleable. Often decorative, their centres would carry designs that, like the knob handles that followed them during the early part of the 19th century, reflected the fashion and themes of the time, with the lion mask and the Prince of Wales feather plumes both featuring heavily.

THE 19TH CENTURY

By this time, the number of foundries had greatly increased and the range of published designs had also multiplied. It is interesting to note, however, that during this period the fashion for wooden knob handles took hold. Frequently, the original brassware was removed from 18th-century furniture to be replaced with large and, most would agree, unsightly wooden examples.

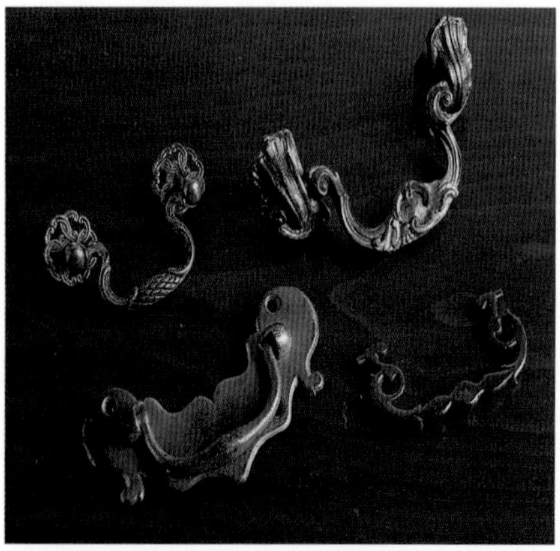

Above: *18th-century swan-neck handles in various styles ranging from plain to rococco.*

Right: *A selection of 18th- and 19th-century cast knobs and pressed plate handles.*

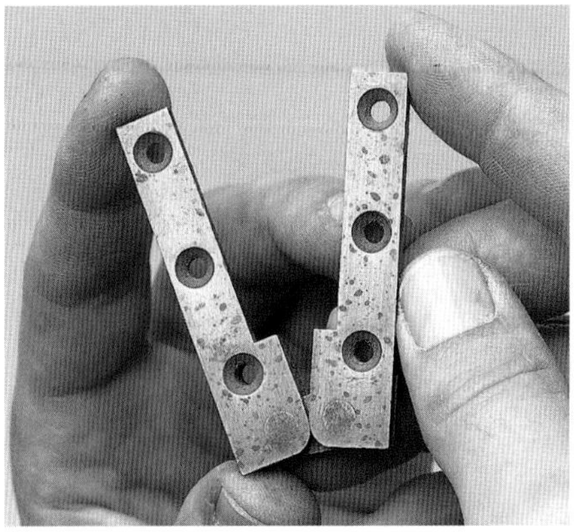

Left: *An 18th-century card table hinge, which is distinctive because it allows the top to open then sit level with the opposite side.*

Right: *When removing antique metal care should be taken as it may be brittle and can be easily damaged.*

Replacing handles

During the centuries fashion and tastes have constantly changed, and owners often replaced perfectly serviceable hardware with something more "fashionable". So, in terms of restoration, handles are frequently replaced to bring a piece back to its original state rather than to correct any damage. To select the right kind of replacement, you will need to consult reference books and study the various styles of brassware. You might also find clues by looking for marks and shadows on the furniture, which might indicate the size and type of fitting used when the piece was first made.

Frequently, replacement handles will not have been attached to drawer and door fronts in the same way. Using the Victorian wooden door knobs as an example again, these were often attached with large screws. These holes can be disguised in a variety of ways, either by selecting plate handles which cover the damage, or by patching the holes.

Occasionally, an original handle, one of a pair or a set, may be missing. There are three main options open to you in this case: you could try and find a match from another piece of furniture or from a breaker collection; order a single replacement or a whole new set from a manufacturer specializing in period handles; or commission a copy to be made by a specialist foundry, which will use the same techniques today as were used in centuries past. Copy casting involves one of two methods: sand casting and the lost-wax process, which are explained here (see box, right).

Making copies

When the profile of the item of metalware is not too elaborate, the sand-casting process will be used. This involves placing the template piece into a two-part mould, each part of which is packed with fine casting sand. The box is then carefully separated and the template removed, leaving its profile in the sand. The two halves of the mould are then rejoined and molten brass poured in. When cool, the box is opened to reveal the newly cast metalware.

The sand-casting method, while ideal for plain metalware, is unsuitable for a more elaborate design that may have undercuts or intricate patterns. These would be lost when the piece was lifted from the sand prior to casting, and so in these cases the lost-wax technique would be used.

In the example illustrated below, one of a pair of escutcheons is missing and a copy needs to be made. Because the design of the escutcheon is very intricate and detailed, the sand-casting technique would not be suitable, whereas the lost-wax process is ideal.

First, a rubber mould is made of the escutcheon. The mould is made in two parts, each with locating pins, which allows the remaining escutcheon, which is being used as a template, to be easily removed. The empty mould is then rejointed and liquid wax poured into it. This will create a perfect replica of the escutcheon, capturing all the detail of the carving.

When the mould is cool and the wax has hardened, the wax copy is removed from the rubber mould. It is then encased in a two-part plaster mould and heated, which both hardens the plaster and melts the wax, creating a perfect hollow profile of the original escutcheon. Molten brass is then poured into the plaster mould, forcing out the liquid wax.

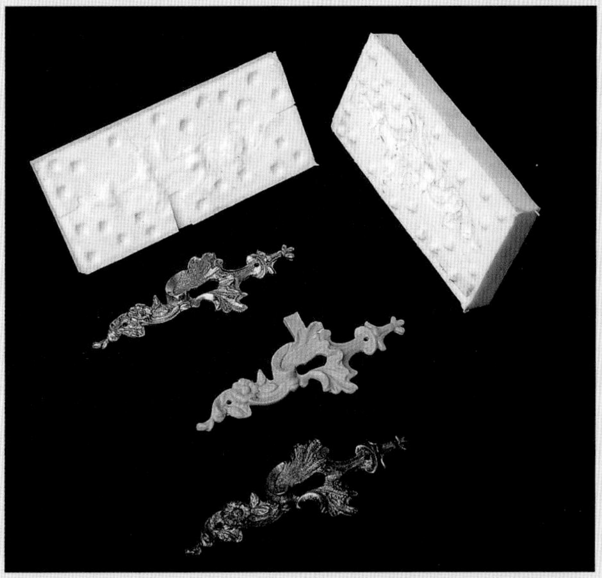

Left: *When the mould has cooled again, it is opened to reveal an excellent copy of the original escutcheon. Once cleaned, it can be coloured and lacquered to match the original.*

MOUNTS, CASTORS AND METALWARE

The range of mounts, castors and other metalware is vast and is influenced by the date, style and country of origin. In the past, such items were ordered from the local foundry when needed. Indeed, at times a strong indication of the piece's original maker can be gained simply by studying its original metalware. By the 18th century, the foundries were beginning to publish designs and you can often find their name stamped into a hinge, castor or lock.

Unlike today, when screws, nails and brass fittings are factory-made in their tens of thousands, the brassware and fixings of the previous centuries were all hand-made. Clout nails, which had roughly shaped heads, and hand-made screws, which had off-centre, hand-cut slots, were all works of art in their own right. It is a testament to their quality that, some 300 years after being made, they can be fixed back into their original locations ready to be used again.

As with the breaker store for wood (see p.28), or the veneer store for old surface veneers (see p.30), an equally important part of any restoration workshop is the brasswork store. Any old nails, screws or brassware that are removed from a piece of furniture are kept here for future use. While skilled foundries can make copies of period mounts, castors and galleries (small ornamental railings surrounding the top of a desk, table, etc.), there is still no substitute for the original. Each piece of bespoke brassware was designed for its particular role.

Above: *A selection of metalware dating from the 18th and 19th centuries, including mounts, castors and a section of gallery.*

Left: *A mid-18th-century Louis XV Japanese lacquer commode is richly embellished with ormolu mounts.*

Above: *A selection of 18th- and 19th-century brass castors, which, in spite of years of use, are still in working order.*

During the 18th and 19th centuries, there were two methods of treating brassware once it had been cast to prevent tarnishing: fire gilding and lacquering. Fire gilding was an expensive process usually reserved for the finest mounts, galleries and handles. The process involved mixing mercury with gold, applying it to the metalware and then heating it. The mercury would evaporate and the gold would bind to the metal. This gave a rich, bold finish, but, due to the mercury fumes that were constantly being given off, the life of the mercury gilder was a short one. The second method, lacquering, gave a similiar, if not quite as rich, appearance to fire gilding. Unfortunately, the use of abrasive solvents for cleaning over the years means that the majority of handles have lost their original finishes, but when fire-gilt and lacquered finishes are still largely intact, they should be cleaned with care (see p.61). For the most part, they need little more than an occasional wipe with a damp cloth.

Blunting a nail

1 *Knocking a large nail into a hard piece of wood, such as oak, can cause splitting. This is due to the fact that the sharp point is acting as a wedge.*

2 *An easy step to counter this is to blunt the point of the nail prior to use.*

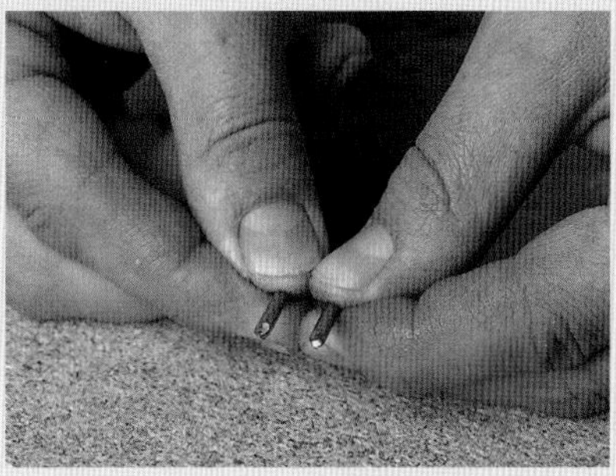

3 *Just one or two taps with the hammer are needed to gain the desired effect.*

4 *With the tip now blunted, you can hammer the nail through the wood without it splitting.*

Removing a nail

1 *When a nail needs to be removed from a polished surface, the pliers should not touch the wood as illustrated here.*

2 *The pressure caused by the pliers bearing down on the wood can often cause bruising and marking to the surface polish.*

3 *The preferred method is to place another layer between the pliers and the polished surface. In this instance, a cabinet scraper is being used. Equally acceptable is a thin piece of wood, etc.*

LOCKS AND KEYS

The range of types of key is vast, and all workshops should keep as many as possible. Often the more simple lock can be operated with a replacement key that may require little or no alteration. These antique keys can be sourced in many locations ranging from junk shops to local bric-à-brac markets. Replacement blanks, which can be cut to fit locks, are also available and can be sourced from suitable specialist suppliers.

Left: *It is important to carry a wide selection of locks and keys salvaged from breaker chests and cabinets.*

The earliest known locks date from the Egyptian times, around 2000 BC, and the Romans also manufactured and used them. Their use continued through the ages, and by the 14th century locks were not uncommon on English furniture. Indeed, examples from the 14th and 15th centuries are to be found, with their distinctive feature of a flush face plate and sunken movement, both making sure that they could not be prised open. By the latter part of the 15th century, locks were becoming more decorative and their use increasingly widespread. In these periods, it was not only gold and valuables that required safe keeping but equally so correspondence, as a letter swearing allegiance to the wrong party could result in an untimely end.

By the late 17th century, elaborate locks were still in use, but the increasing manufacture of chests and other cabinet furniture meant that a plainer steel lock was being used, often with a simple throw mechanism. As furniture designs became more elaborate, so the need for a more tailored lock increased. Bureaux required angled face plates to mirror the fall, cupboard locks could be designed to throw either left or right and, where extra security was required, such as with an escritoire, three- or four-pin locks were used, which made their forcing open very difficult. On continental locks, one often finds a double throw movement, which increases the length the bolt is extended into the lock housing, thereby helping to strengthen the security of the lock.

During the 18th century, brass began to be used on the better-quality locks, although cheaper locks were still made from iron. Their manufacture began to be more elaborate, and, in 1778, a major watershed was reached when Robert Barron designed a revolutionary lever system that, unlike previous locks, which had operated on a ward system and relied on a single tumbler, operated with two tumblers, meaning that in order for the lock to throw open, the tumblers had to be lifted both back and up to a precise height. This lever system still exists in today's locks.

The lock was further developed during the 18th century by Bramah, who, in 1784, patented a system that incorporated a tube-like key with notches on the end that fitted into a lock fitted with springs, meaning that the key had to fit precisely into position in order for the lock to work. Even a slight variation would mean that the lock did not throw, and therefore a very specific key had to be used with each lock. If the key was lost, cutting a new one was a specialist task that required a trained locksmith.

It is rare that a maker would use only one specific lock or key in his furniture making, although one such exception is that of the 18th-century designer and

Right: *A selection of Bramah locks with their distinctive patent pattern mark.*

furniture-maker Thomas Chippendale. The use of the S key and corresponding escutcheon, while not proved to be exclusive, is widely accepted by academics and collectors alike as a mark of a piece made by Chippendale. Documented examples are to be found on pieces at Brocket Hall, Harewood House and Nostell Priory, all of which are Chippendale commissions.

While general servicing and key replacement should be able to be carried out by a competent restoration workshop, it should be remembered that some locks are very elaborate, and these more complicated examples are better dealt with by a specialist locksmith or restorer.

Above: *During the 18th and 19th centuries, a variety of locks were developed each with a specific role or task to perform.*

Servicing a lock

1 *Over the years working locks can collect all kinds of debris, such as dust, wax and even insect remains, that will eventually make the lock less efficient. A quick service is all that is needed.*

2 *Remove the lock and place it flat on a clean surface. Unscrew the retaining screws from the back plate. Take care not to misplace the original screws.*

3 *Slide the screwdriver carefully between the face and back plate and gently ease it off making sure not to damage either piece. You will now be able to see if there is any debris collected in the lock's workings.*

4 *Gently remove any debris with a soft brush. Check for any other damage while the back plate is off. If there is any rusting or parts have broken away, restoration must be carried out by a specialist locksmith.*

5 *When the lock is clean, lubricate the internal workings using a dry silicon lubricant spray. Do not use oil-based lubricants as they will quickly attract dust and cause the same problem over time.*

6 *Check that the lock works freely, then replace the back plate using the original screws. Check the lock again before placing the lock back in its original position.*

Surfaces and finishes

Two of the most important aspects of any piece of antique furniture are its colour and surface patination. Exposure to light, plus years of waxing, causes the original wood to develop a wide range of tones and also a surface skin, or patination, which is highly valued by collectors and restorers.

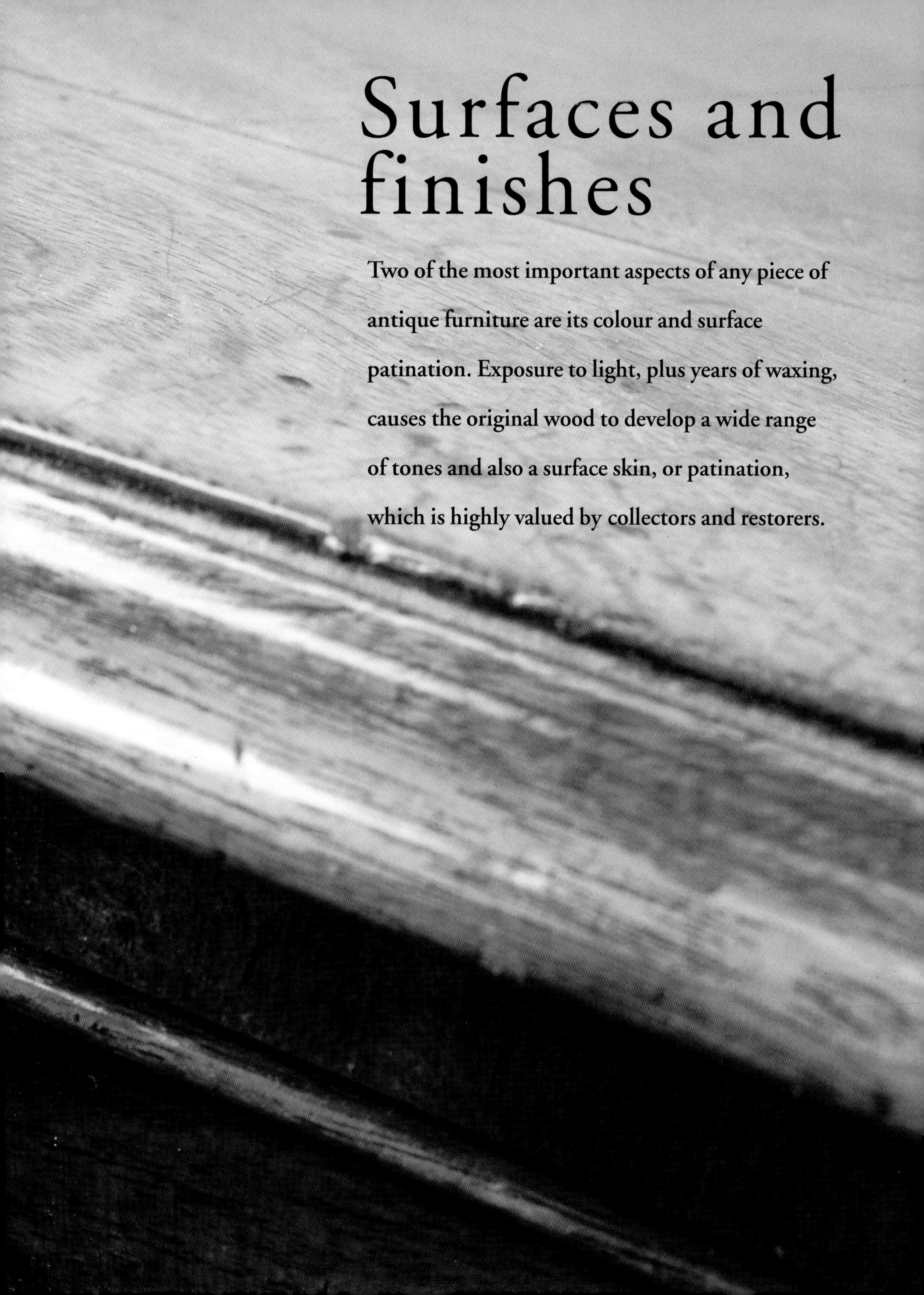

RESTORING DAMAGED SURFACES

There are a great variety of surfaces associated with antique furniture and there are equally numerous ways in which they can be affected by excessive heat, water, moisture, grease, dirt or oxidation, to name a few. To remedy these problems each surface may need treating in a different way. Great care must be taken in the process, as a badly restored piece of furniture will not only look unsightly but be radically decreased in value.

The types of damage found on the surfaces of veneers, solid wood furniture, gilt, marble or leather fall mainly into two categories. That caused by accidental damage and that which has simply been a result of the passing of time and the action of normal wear and tear.

In some cases the damage can be corrected by little more than a light clean and a rewax, but occasionally the existing finish will have to be stripped and replaced. In the case of a gilt finish, for example, this will not be too much of a problem (the vast majority of gilded pieces have been regilded at some point). With polished surfaces, however, only the minimal amount of work should be undertaken and the work confined to the localized area of damage.

There is also the question of whether to restore a surface or leave it alone. When the damage has been caused recently, it is obvious that attention is needed. When the surface damage is old, the stain, dent or mark might have been covered with numerous generations of waxing so that it forms part of the "character" of the piece. The decision is whether to remove an unsightly mark or leave an otherwise excellent patinated surface well alone. The skilled restorer and polisher should be able to remove any localized damage successfully. The amateur restorer should not attempt this type of work on good coloured and patinated pieces. Often collectors and furniture owners alike would rather leave a mark and retain the overall integrity of a piece.

Blisters

When the glue bonding a veneered surface to its core perishes due to heat or water damage, or simply because the glue has deteriorated through age, blisters will form. The solution is either to apply hot blocks or fresh adhesive.

Water marks

Caused by either the direct or indirect action of water on a polished surface, water marks are characterized by the appearance of white patches, known as blooming. This is usually treated with new applications of polish and wax, although occasionally the surface will need to be washed back and refinished.

Spirit and water stains

Should spilled water or spirit be left to penetrate through a polished surface into the wood beneath, the result will be a black or dark stain. This can sometimes be treated with mild bleach, which will improve if not always completely remove the mark. This is, however, a specialist procedure best left to the professionals.

Dents

If dents occur on legs they can be largely ignored; if they appear on a flat, top surface they need attention. If the dent is not too deep the most common method is to try and remove it with the action of steam, which raises the grain.

Burns

The most common type of burn damage is that caused by cigarettes. A considered view should be taken to restore or not, but a burn is easier to correct on a veneered surface than a solid one. However, it is a specialist job best left to the professionals.

Scratches

Scratches are one of the most common forms of damage found on antique furniture. Light scratches that only affect the polished surface can be waxed out, while deeper ones will need to be filled and coloured out with stain.

Sunlight

The action of direct sunlight will often have an adverse effect on a polished surfaces, causing the polish to dry out and the surface to change colour. If the overall change in colour is aesthetically pleasing, it can be left; if the damage is patchy then localized areas may need to be coloured to match the rest of the surface.

Above: *Burn damage.*

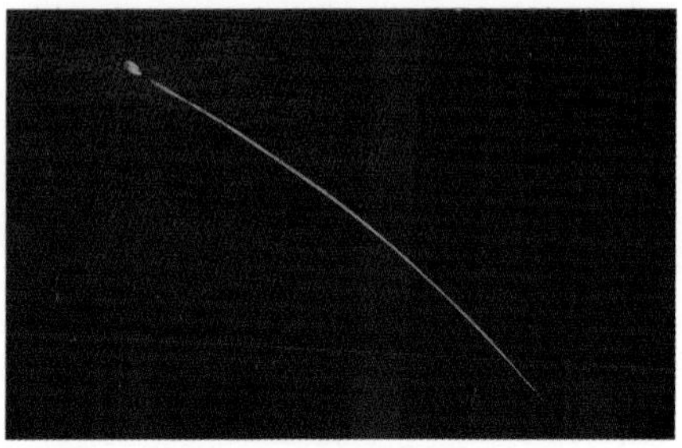

Above: *Scratch.*

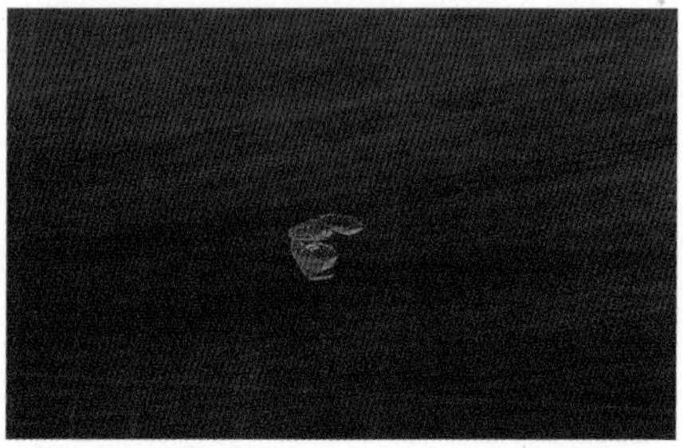

Above: *Dent.*

Removing a blister

The figured walnut veneer on the top of this Regency chiffonier has blistered badly. The first solution to try is to apply a hot block in an attempt to soften the glue beneath the veneer so that it will re-adhere (see p.78). If that is not successful, the alternative is to introduce new adhesive through a cut in the veneer, but without marking the finish.

MATERIALS AND EQUIPMENT
- sharp knife
- PVA (white) glue
- clean white paper
- wooden block
- G-clamp
- rubber
- polish
- wax
- cloth (cotton rag)

1 Using a sharp knife, make small cuts in the blistered veneer to the core underneath. Follow the grain of the veneer to disguise the cuts.

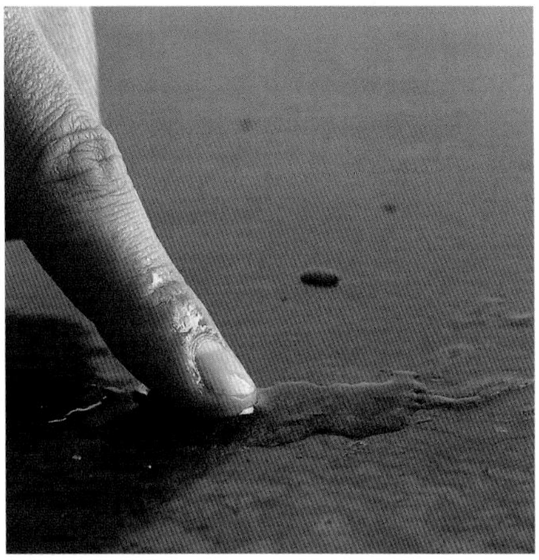

2 Spread a little water on top of the cut blister; this will penetrate the incisions.

3 Spread some PVA (white) glue on top of the blister and work it in with a finger in a circular motion. The water under the veneer will draw the glue through the cuts and into the space between the veneer and core.

4 Wipe away the excess glue and place a sheet of clean white paper over the blister. Lay a hot block (heated on a hot plate or an iron, see p.78) on top and clamp it firmly in place. The paper will protect the block from the glue. Leave overnight so that the veneer can rebond with the core.

5 Remove the block and paper; carefully wash off any paper that has been stuck with excess expelled glue. If there are any minor heat marks from the hot block, charge a rubber with polish and apply a thin layer to the surface, before waxing to finish (see pp.66–67).

Above: *Once polished, no trace of the blister remains.*

Removing a water mark

The photograph below shows a common problem found on polished surfaces: a water mark caused by hot or wet items being placed directly on to a surface. In this instance, a wet vase has been placed on the table and has marked it. Fortunately, it has penetrated only the top layers of polish and not stained the actual wood. The solution is to remove the damaged polish and carefully build up the finish with fresh polish and wax so that it matches the surrounding finish. The top is quarter veneered, which means that the grain is split in four directions, so the wax must be applied in a circular motion.

MATERIALS AND EQUIPMENT

- methylated spirits (methyl alcohol)
- cloths (cotton rags)
- rubber
- polish
- wax

1 Gently wash just the affected area with a cloth (cotton rag) dipped in methylated spirits (methyl alcohol). This will remove the perished polish.

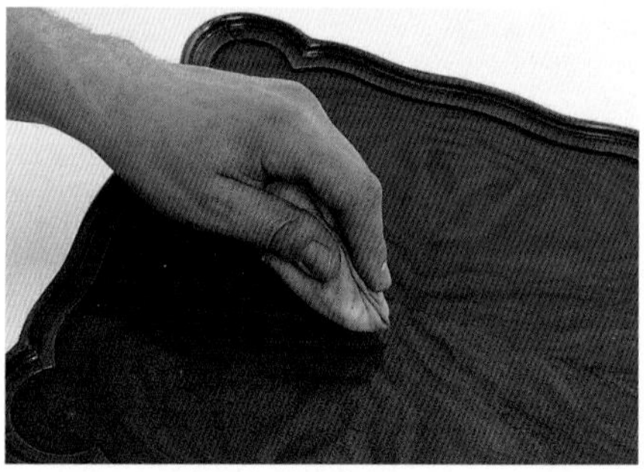

2 Charge a rubber with polish (see p.66) and apply a light layer to the washed-off area to build up the surface. Then give the whole top a rubber of polish to produce a uniform appearance (see p.67).

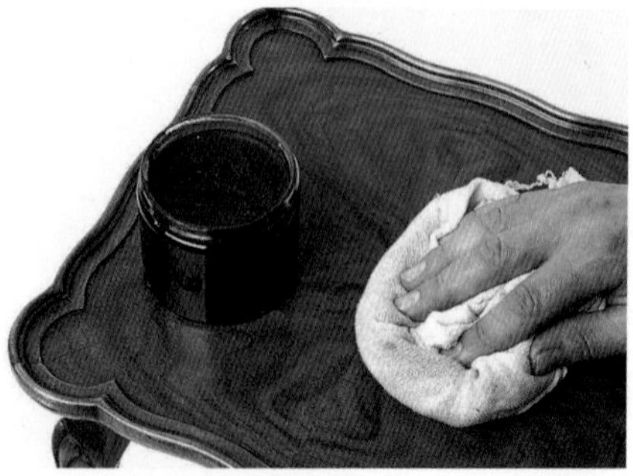

Above: *The water mark has now been removed without touching or altering the table's colour or patination.*

3 Allow the polish to harden, then treat the surface with a dark wax (see p.68), using circular movements.

Raising a dent

Dents and bruises are common problems with polished furniture, often caused by something being dropped on to the surface or the surface being damaged in transit. Most dents can be lifted with steam and then made invisible with polish, as shown here, but some dents are more difficult to remove. If they are not in a central position or on an otherwise unblemished surface, it is best simply to leave them alone and regard them as part of the history and character of the piece.

MATERIALS AND EQUIPMENT
- cloths (cotton rags)
- iron
- fine wire (steel) wool
- methylated spirits (methyl alcohol)
- fine-grade sandpaper
- fine brush
- spirit-based (alcohol-based) stain
- rubber
- polish
- wax

1 Place a wet cloth (cotton rag) over the dent and press the tip of a hot iron on top. This will generate steam, which will lift the bruised wood fibres. Take care to use only the tip of the iron in order to keep the steamed area as localized as possible.

2 The dent has been raised, but the steam has caused some localized damage. Use fine wire (steel) wool and methylated spirits (methyl alcohol) to wash off the areas of damaged polish.

3 The grain of the wood will have been raised by the heat. Using fine-grade sandpaper, lightly sand the repair until the wood is smooth.

4 Mix a spirit-based (alcohol-based) stain to match the colour of the table (see p.41), then carefully apply this to the restored area, disguising the raised grain. Charge a rubber with polish and seal the area by rubbing in circular motions until it is covered (see pp.66–67). Leave the polish to harden.

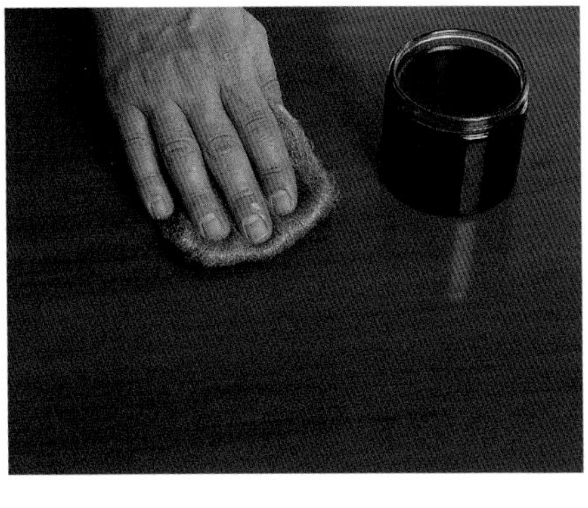

5 Wax the affected area using fine wire wool, then wax the rest of the surface with a soft cloth until the repaired area blends in.

Right: *When finished, all evidence of the dent should be removed and no trace of the restoration remain.*

Disguising a scratch

A deep single scratch is not uncommon on an otherwise unmarked surface, and the aim is to try to disguise the scratch as best as possible without disturbing the rest of the polished area. If the scratch runs parallel to the grain, the task will be that much easier. If, as in this case, it runs across the grain, it will be very difficult to disguise the damage completely, although filling wax, polish and stain can produce remarkable results.

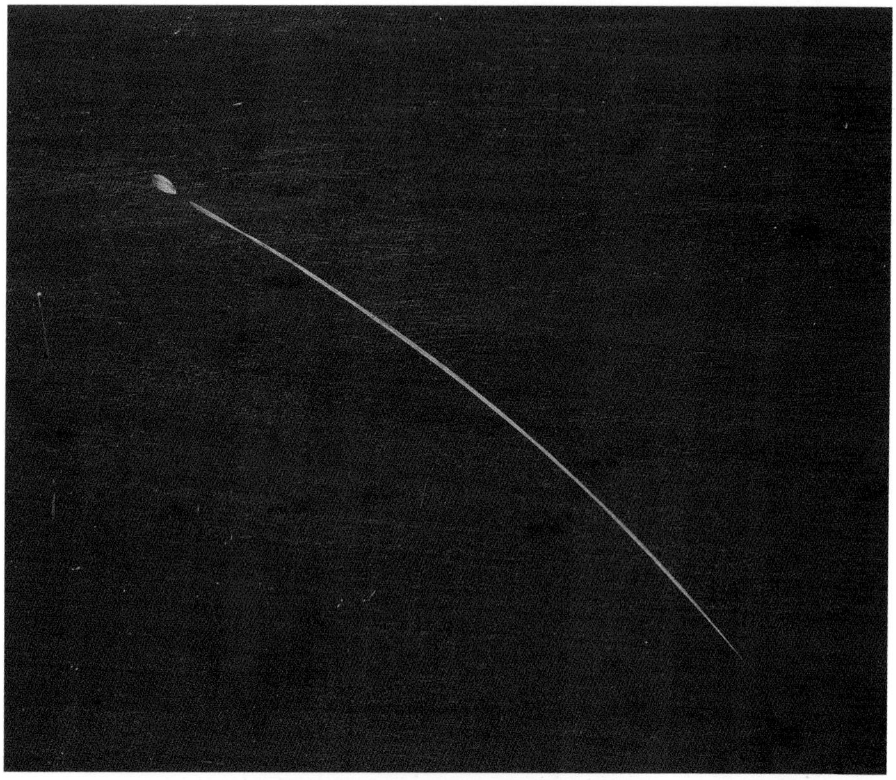

MATERIALS AND EQUIPMENT

- fine wire (steel) wool
- filling wax
- flat-bladed knife
- fine-grade sandpaper
- rubber
- polish
- spirit-based (alcohol-based) stains
- fine brush
- cloth (cotton rag)
- clear wax

Tip

Good craft stores should stock a range of coloured wax blocks for use in furniture restoration.

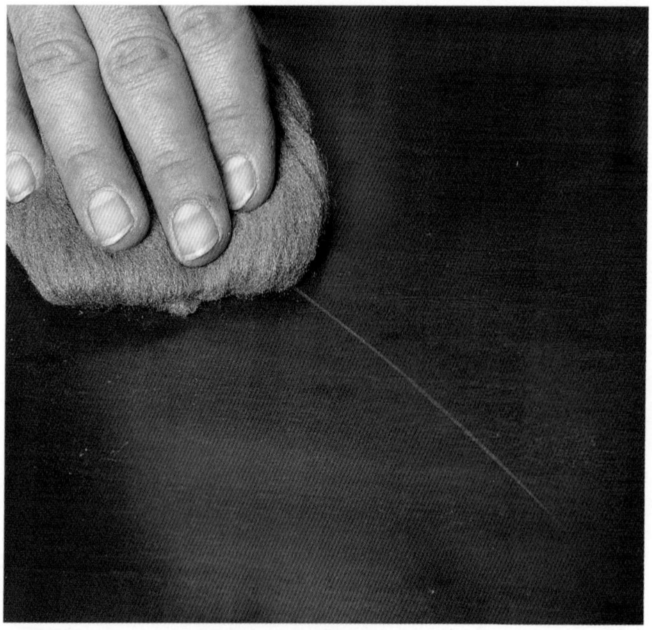

1 Rub the area around the scratch lightly with fine wire (steel) wool to remove the surface wax.

2 Choose a filling wax that is as close a match in colour to the table as possible. Fill the scratch with wax using a flat-bladed knife.

◁ **3** Allow the wax to harden, then gently scrape away the excess wax with a flat-bladed knife. Take great care not to mark the surface of the wood with the blade.

▷ **4** Remove the last traces of the surface filling wax with fine-grade sandpaper. Take care to avoid marking the existing polish.

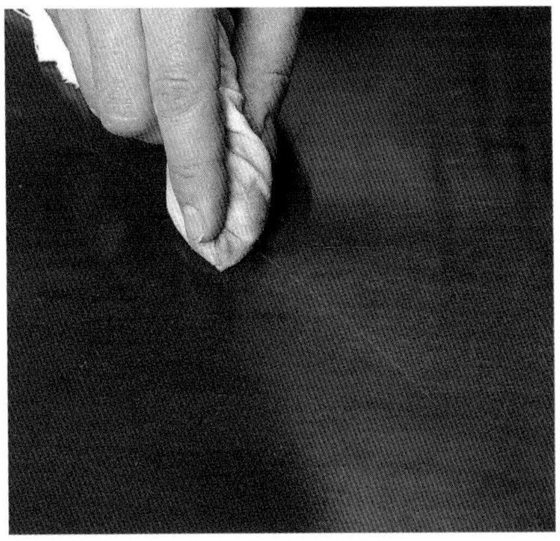

5 Charge a rubber with polish and apply a layer over the scratched area to seal in the wax and blend the repair into its surroundings (see pp.66–67).

6 Mix a spirit-based (alcohol-based) stain to a colour slightly darker than the polished wax (see p.41), and apply it to the scratch with a fine brush. When the stain is dry, seal the surface with another rubber of polish.

7 Now mix a spirit-based stain to match the original surface, and apply it to the scratch with a fine brush to blend the repair into the surrounding area. Leave to dry, then seal with a rubber of polish.

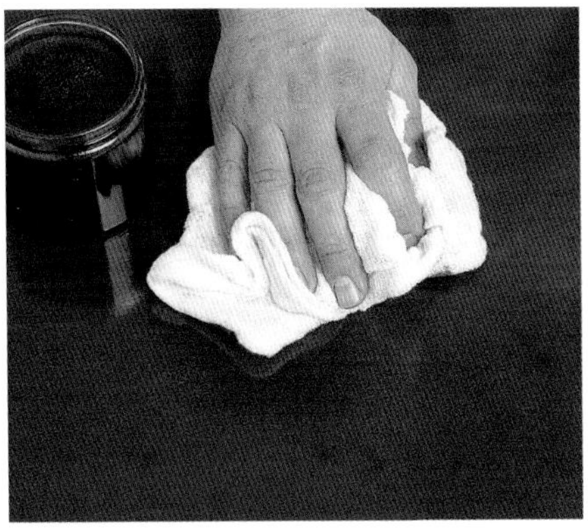

8 Once the polish has dried, apply a wax coat to the whole table top. Allow the wax to dry, then buff it to a shine (see p.67).

Right: *Although the scratch has not disappeared completely, it has been disguised and looks a lot less unsightly. Most importantly, the surrounding polished area has not been altered by the repair.*

CLEANING AND REVIVING

By its very nature and with the period of time that passes, surfaces become oxidized or coated with dust, waxes and natural greases that combine to form a surface coating. While this is desirable with wood, other materials such as metal, marble and leather may on occasion need to be cleaned or the surface revived. Different materials will require different methods, but the one common theme is to clean a little at a time to enable the desired effect to be reached and not overdone. If you are over-zealous when cleaning, the result may look rather artificial.

There are a number of steps that can be taken to help keep the need to revive or clean a surface down to a minimum. The one measure that will apply to most materials is to wax on a fairly regular basis. The wax will nourish and feed both timber and leather.

Marble, it must be remembered, is porous and to help prevent stains on the tops of tables, for example, light waxing with clear wax should be regularly applied. As well as protecting the surface, the wax will help it to develop a lustre. Regular dusting will also help to avoid the build-up of a surface coating. Dusting should be done with a dry cloth (cotton rag) – home recipes, such as the application of a harsh vinegar and water solution, should never be used. The following techniques will help to clean and revive the surfaces listed.

Cleaning marble

Over a period of years, there can be a build-up of dirt, grease and grime on marble tops. In fact, marble, like wood, often develops a warm surface patination over the years. While this can sometimes add to the colour and character, there comes a point when it will need to be cleaned. This piece of marble from an antique table is in good condition; it simply requires cleaning and sealing.

MATERIALS AND EQUIPMENT
- soda crystals
- clear wax
- cloths (cotton rags)

▷ **1** Dissolve approximately a handful of soda crystals in 4.5 litres (1 gallon) of warm water in a bowl. Use this solution to give the top a light clean, using a cloth (cotton rag) to lift off the surface dirt. Take care not to remove too much, as the natural character of the marble is part of its charm.

2 Using a clear wax, apply a thin coat with a cloth, rubbing with a circular motion, and allow it to harden.

3 When the wax has hardened, buff it to a soft sheen. Repeat the process until a warm patination returns to the marble.

Tip

Marble can sometimes have an unseen fault line in it, which can crack under its own weight. When carrying a piece of marble, therefore, turn it on its side to minimize any possible risk of breakage. Remember that marble is very heavy, so enlist a helper if you have to move a large piece.

Cleaning metal

Some metal fittings, usually brass, are gilded, while others have a lacquer coating to stop them oxidizing and the brass tarnishing. The cleaning of brass is very much a personal affair: some people may be happy to leave brass fittings completely tarnished, others may prefer to have just the highlights brightened, and others still may like to see the brass shining brightly like a soldier's buttons. If traces of the gilt or lacquer finish remain, surface grease and dirt should be removed without touching the finish underneath. In this example, two pieces of an early 19th-century cast brass moulding, known as a gallery, will be cleaned: one by a gentle method of washing with diluted soda crystals, the other using a stronger proprietary cleaning agent. The original finish on the gallery is fire-gilded.

MATERIALS AND EQUIPMENT

- soda crystals
- soft toothbrush
- de-greasant agent
- protective gloves

Tip

When cleaning mounts, mouldings, galleries or handles, it is best to remove them from the piece of furniture, if possible, to prevent any damage to the polished surface. If this is done, make a note of their location to enable them to be refitted correctly.

1 The least severe method of cleaning is to use a solution of soda crystals and water. This will gently ease off the dirt and grease without removing the finish below. Dissolve a handful of soda crystals in 4.5 litres (1 gallon) of warm water in a bowl large enough to take the metal item.

2 With a soft toothbrush, gently scrub away the residue. As this is quite a mild form of cleaning, you can leave areas of dirt in the background to give the cleaned brass a softer look. If the host piece of furniture is of good colour and patination, this is often the best and most desirable finish.

3 If you want to remove all the dirt and grease and return the gilt as closely as possible to its original state, then a strong de-greasant is recommended. Leave the brass to soak in the cleaning agent for some minutes, then scrub it with a soft toothbrush. It is advisable to wear protective gloves to prevent your skin from being stained.

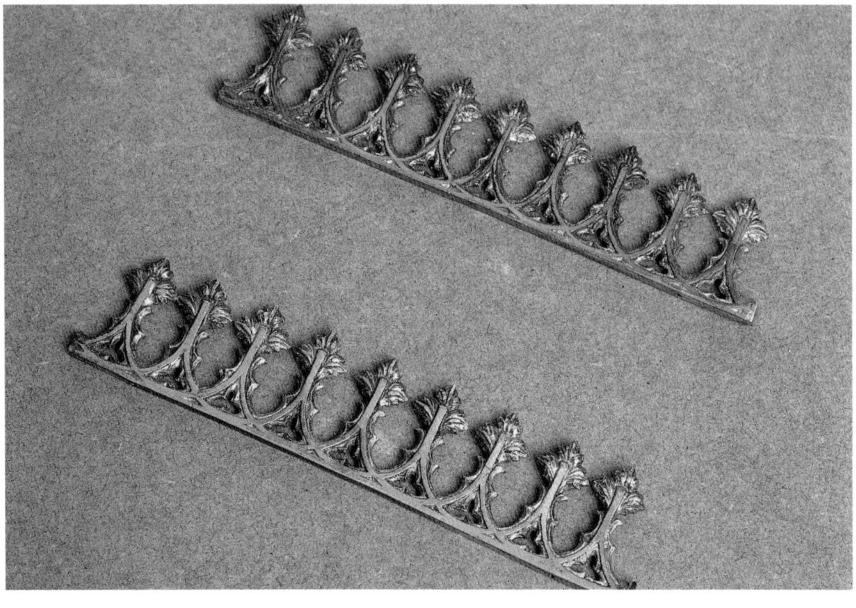

Above: *The top section of gallery has been cleaned with soda crystals, giving a softer, still slightly tarnished look, while the bottom length has been cleaned with a proprietary cleaning agent, producing a brighter, harder appearance.*

Reviving leather

Leather was often used to cover writing surfaces as well as act as an upholstery material in antique furniture. Due to its nature, however, leather tends to become dry and brittle, and so usually has a shorter life than that of the piece of furniture it adorns. During the life of a piece of leather-topped furniture, therefore, the leather may have been replaced a number of times, and on occasion it may simply have been renewed because the owner wanted a colour change. Even so, a worn and textured leather surface can often enhance the character of a piece of furniture, and the surface can be revived. On this leather surface, you can see clearly where a blotter, which offered protection to the central area, has been laid. The outer, unprotected borders of the leather have become faded, worn and dry and so need to be revived.

MATERIALS AND EQUIPMENT

- brush
- clear wax
- leather-reviving cream
- rubbers
- polish
- spirit-based (alcohol-based) stain
- fine wire (steel) wool
- soft cloth (cotton rag)

1 First, brush a coat of clear wax over the whole piece of leather. This will feed and nourish the leather and provide a protective coating. Coloured wax should not be used, as it could change the overall tone. In addition to the wax, a leather-reviving cream could be applied to the piece.

2 When the wax is dry, charge a rubber with polish and apply a thin layer to the surface (see pp.66–67). This will help to seal the grain, as well as giving a protective layer in readiness for the stain. If the grain is not stained first, certain areas will absorb more stain than others, giving a blotchy look.

3 Charge a rubber with a spirit-based (alcohol-based) stain mixed to the required colour (see p.41), and apply a thin layer. This must be done in an even manner, working from the top downward. This will not disguise the worn areas totally, but it will blend them closer to the colour of the less-worn areas. When the stain is dry, apply a thin layer of polish to seal in the colour.

4 When the polish is dry, cut it back with fine wire (steel) wool with wax on it. The wax ensures that the wool does not cut back the top too much. Finally, buff to a soft sheen with a soft cloth (cotton rag).

Right: *The leather is now revived and fed. All that is necessary in future is to wax it along with the rest of the piece.*

Reviving a polished surface

General wear and tear causes most items of furniture to become discoloured and marked over time. Water marks, light scratches and stains will penetrate only the first layers of polish, allowing surfaces with this type of damage to be revived rather than completely repolished (see pp.56 and 58–59). The process of revival requires care, patience and sensitivity, but with the right application the blemishes can be erased, and the original colour and sheen will be revealed.

This top from a Georgian chest of drawers has a variety of water marks, stains and scratches. Although they are numerous, it is immediately apparent that none of the blemishes penetrates beneath the top layers of the polish, so a systematic revival of the surface is all that is required. A variety of techniques are required for this, and, when used with care, these can produce quite dramatic results, as you will see on the following page. However, as mentioned previously, any restoration work should be carried out with great care, as the idea is to attend to existing damage and not cause further problems.

MATERIALS AND EQUIPMENT
- flat-bladed knife
- fine wire (steel) wool
- linseed oil
- polish
- linen cloth
- wadding (batting)
- methylated spirits (methyl alcohol)
- fine brushes
- oxalic acid
- spirit-based (alcohol-based) stain
- rubber
- coloured wax
- soft cloths (cotton rags)

1 First remove any lumps and bumps, such as candle wax, by dragging a flat-bladed knife at a 45-degree angle across the surface. Be careful not to add any further scratches.

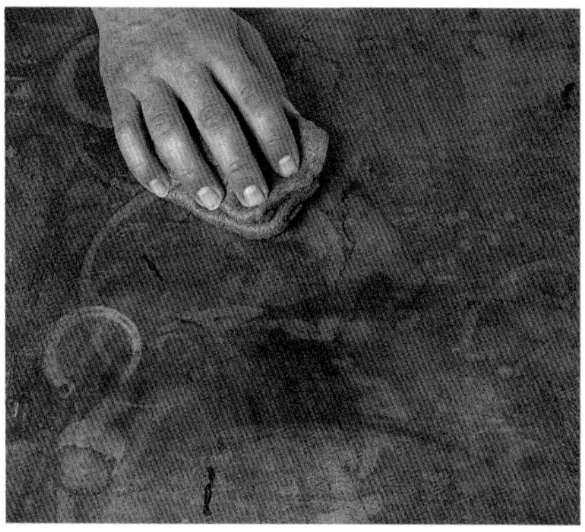

2 Rub the surface with fine wire (steel) wool, following the line of the grain. Failure to follow the grain could result in numerous tiny scratches, which will be difficult to remove at a later stage. Apply only very light pressure at this stage.

3 Apply linseed oil and polish to a piece of linen and rub gently in a circular motion. This will soften the top layers of polish, allowing the new colour and polish to bind to the existing surface.

4 Lightly moisten a piece of wadding (batting) with methylated spirits (methyl alcohol), and wipe it over the surface to remove any remaining traces of oil.

5 Paint over the dark inside and outside edges of the ring marks and stains using a fine brush and oxalic acid. Paint only the edges, which are always the darkest areas of ring marks and stains.

▷

Reviving a polished surface...continued

6 Mix a spirit-based (alcohol-based) stain to match the surface colour (see p. 41) and apply it with a fine brush. Try to blend the blemishes with the surrounding area rather than masking the stain with solid colour. Leave to dry.

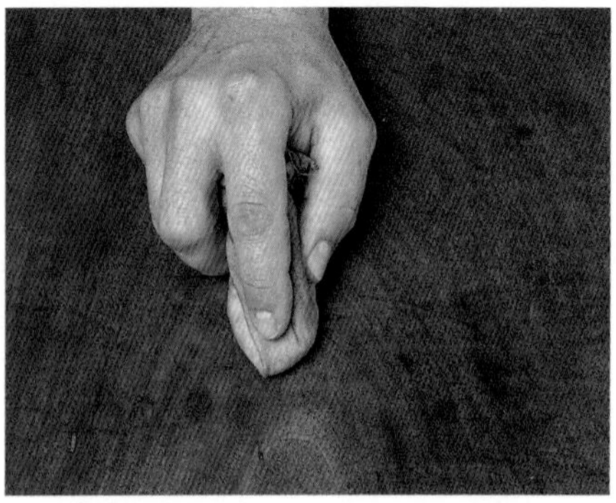

7 Charge a rubber with polish and apply a layer of polish over the surface in even strokes (see pp.66–67). Allow to dry, then repeat until you have replaced the layers of polish removed by the linseed oil.

8 Cut back the surface by gently dusting with a piece of fine wire wool, following the grain. The idea is to even the surface and remove the glossy finish.

9 Select a wax to match the colour of the wood, and use a soft cloth (cotton rag) to apply it, rubbing with a circular motion. Leave to harden for approximately an hour.

10 Buff the surface lightly with a soft cloth, following the grain. Work carefully, because the underlying polish will still be soft, and over-enthusiastic buffing will simply cause unsightly streaking.

Above: *The finished surface is now free from marks and blemishes, and the original grain, colour and patination have been revived.*

POLISHING AND COLOURING

The term "polishing" is used to describe the overall method of filling the grain and enhancing the figure of any piece of wood using shellac polish. The vast majority of polishing work today is commonly known as French polishing, which involves the use of shellac polish combined with oil – often linseed oil – and applied to the wood with a linen rubber.

Within the history of antique furniture, however, there are two very distinctive methods of finishing: varnishing using oil or spirit varnishes, and French polishing, which was introduced only in the 19th century. Both methods create distinctive appearances, and it is the effects of light, oxidation and time that make these polished and waxed surfaces so sought after by today's collectors.

The principles involved in polishing a new surface or repolishing an old surface remain the same: numerous thin layers are built up to form a combined surface. When completed, the polish should have a translucent quality that allows the colour and figure of the wood beneath to be seen. On occasion it may be necessary to tint the polish in order to adjust the final colour. This method of colouring is different from staining with spirit, water or oil, which is the process by which the actual wood tone is changed rather than simply colouring or tinting the polish.

When removing polish from a piece of furniture, it must be done a layer at a time to minimize any damage to the colour and surface of the piece. When the damaged areas have been carefully lifted, further polish can again be applied, a layer at a time, until the required surface appearance is obtained. If too much polish is applied the surface will have a treacle-like appearance; if too little polish is used the grain in the wood will look open and "hungry", resulting in a blotchy effect once the surface has been waxed.

French polishing

Prior to the early 19th century the methods of finishing furniture were mainly the application of varnishes or oils such as linseed and various wax compounds. These were usually applied, often by brush or cloth (cotton rag), after the grain had been sealed with ground brick dust or pumice powder. They served to protect the wood and could be burnished to a soft lustre finish.

In 1820 a new practice, imported from France, came to favour. It was the use of shellac, which comes from the shells of the lac beetle. The shellac, which was dissolved in spirit, was applied layer by layer, giving a hard, glossy finish. Over the years, and with the application of wax, the hard, glossy surfaces mellow, and depending on the style and period of the piece, the surface finish can range from hard and glossy to a soft, almost matt appearance.

MATERIALS AND EQUIPMENT

- wadding (batting)
- linen
- polish
- fine wire (steel) wool
- methylated spirits (methyl alcohol)
- soft cloth (cotton rag)
- shellac
- linseed oil
- clear beeswax

Left: *This Regency table has become severely damaged on its polished surface and must be repolished.*

▷

Making and charging a rubber

A rubber is an essential tool for applying a French polish finish and is easy to make. All you need is some wadding (batting) or plain unmedicated cotton wool and a square of linen or similar lint-free cloth. The rubber acts in the same manner as a sponge, absorbing a quantity of the polish (known as charging), which is squeezed out on to the surface being polished when you apply pressure to it. A rubber can also be used to apply a stain to wood.

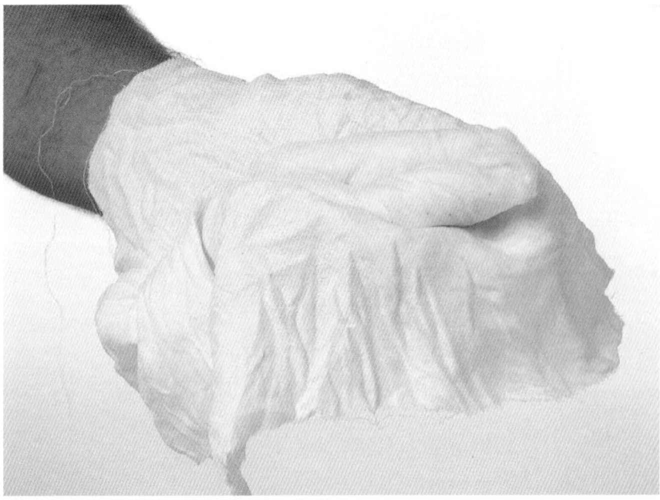

▷ **1** Lay a 15cm/6in long piece of wadding (batting) on the centre of a piece of linen the size of a large handkerchief.

2 Fold the ends of the linen inward and grasp them in the centre of your palm.

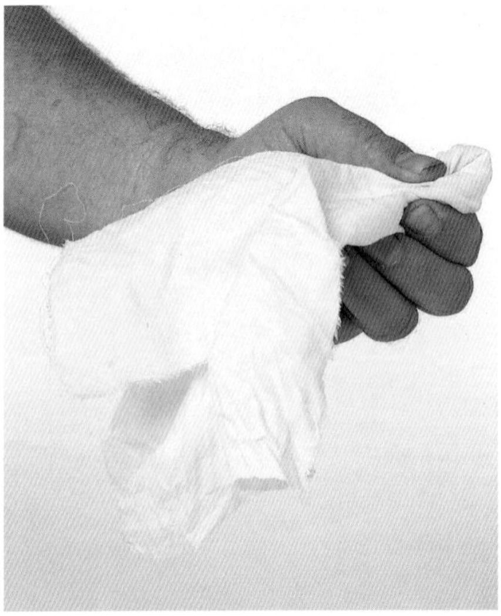

3 With all the outer edges gathered together, twist the ends of the linen to form a tail.

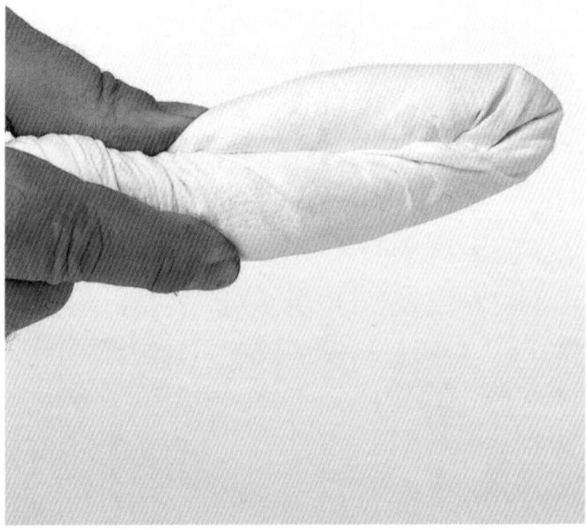

4 The rubber is complete when the tail is completely twisted. For a smaller, more intricate, polishing job, make a smaller rubber to suit.

◁ **5** To charge the rubber, open out the linen to expose the wadding, then pour a small amount of polish on to the wadding. With practice, you will be able to judge the correct quantity. Note that if the rubber is too dry it will not run smoothly over the surface; if it is too wet it will simply lay the polish on the surface.

▷ **6** Refold the linen around the wadding. Squeeze the tail to apply pressure to the wadding, to force the polish through the linen. The more you tighten the tail, the more polish will emerge. After polishing, you can store the rubber for another day.

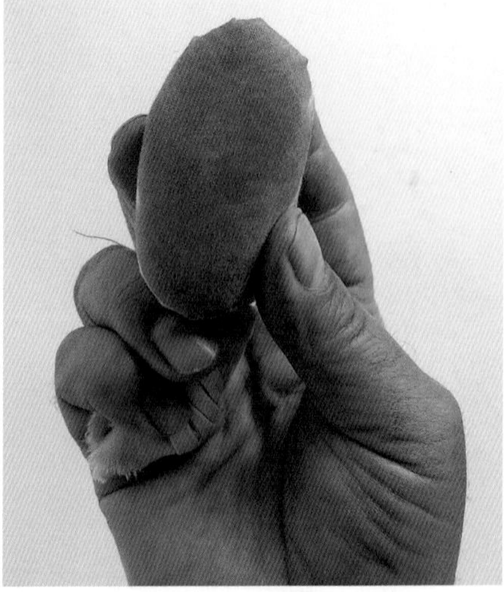

Applying the polish

If the damage to a surface is extensive, it will have to be stripped back with methylated spirits (methyl alcohol) before repolishing, as shown here. New wood is polished in much the same way, except that the grain is first filled with pumice and polish, then sanded flat with very fine or broken down sandpaper.

Once the rubber has been charged, the polish can be applied. This process takes time, and the finish must be left overnight for the polish to harden before it can be buffed to a high sheen or cut back to produce a matt finish.

1 Remove the old polish and wax surface with fine wire (steel) wool and methylated spirits (methyl alcohol).

2 Once the old polish and wax have been removed, wash off the surface with a soft cloth (cotton rag) and methylated spirits.

Tip

When polishing with a rubber (step 3) the idea is to "body up" or fill the grain. This is done by first applying the polish in straight continuous strokes along the grain (below top). The polish is then applied in circular motions (below centre) and finally with wider figure of eight movements (below bottom).

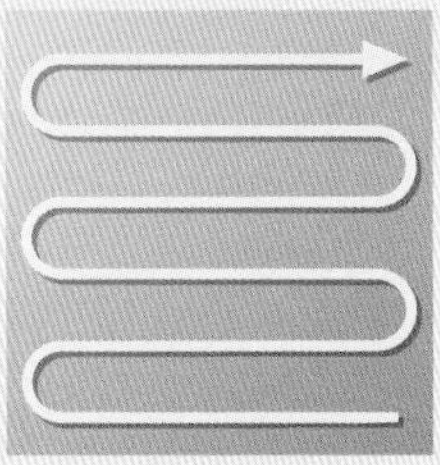

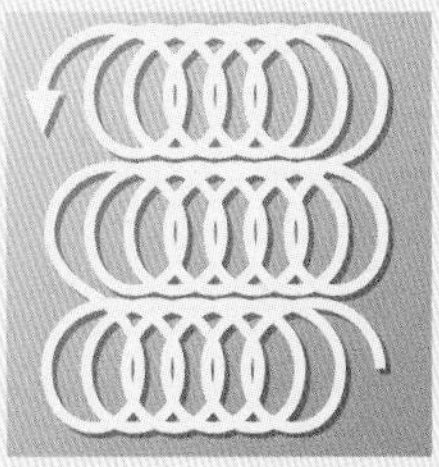

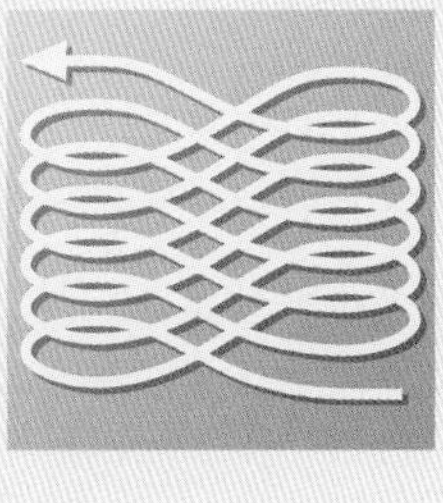

3 Polish the surface using a rubber and shellac (see Tip). Linseed oil can be dripped on to the surface to help lubricate the rubber. This technique, known as "bodying up", fills the grain. Leave for at least 24 hours to harden.

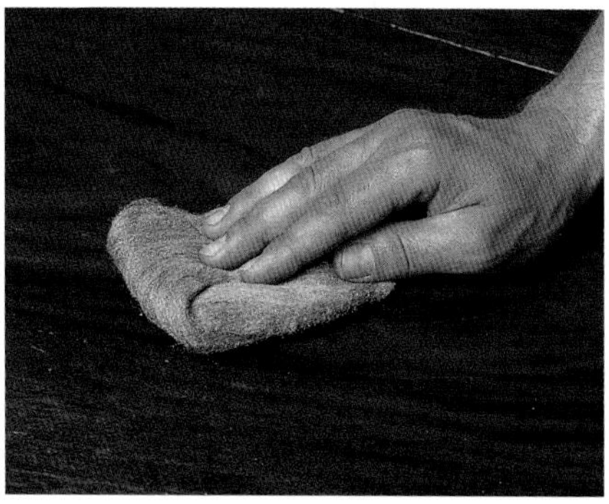

4 When the polish has hardened, cut it back lightly using fine wire wool and working in the direction of the grain. Use light strokes to remove any raised nibs of polish. This also produces a higher gloss finish.

5 Finally, apply a coat of wax. Use light strokes as the polished surface will still be delicate. Allow to stand for a week before use to allow the polish to fully harden.

Right: *When polished, the scratches become invisible and the table has an even, soft sheen that should last for years.*

Waxing

All antique furniture will require waxing during its lifetime. Waxing feeds, protects and nourishes the wood. It is the combination of waxes with natural grease and oxidation that forms the surface patination that is so desirable. Over the generations, various types of wax have been used, with workshops producing their own secret recipes.

One of the most common misconceptions is that the more frequently a piece is waxed, the fuller the finish will be. Over-waxing will result in smeary surfaces, since wax softens wax. The only remedy for this is to remove all the wax and begin afresh. It is far better to wax at sensible intervals and apply only a very thin layer. Use only natural wax-based products.

MATERIALS AND EQUIPMENT
- clear wax
- soft brush
- soft cloths (cotton rags)
- brush

Waxing a flat surface

1 Apply a thin layer of wax using a soft cloth (cotton rag) impregnated with the chosen wax. Never apply too thick a layer, as this will simply make the rubbing up more difficult and time consuming.

2 Even out the wax using a soft brush. Take care not to mark the surface and make sure you work along the direction of the grain. Use long, steady strokes, working from one side of the surface to the other.

3 Allow the wax to harden for a few minutes, then buff the surface vigorously with a soft cloth, working in the direction of the grain. Finally, use a clean cloth to give the surface a final burnish.

Waxing a carved surface

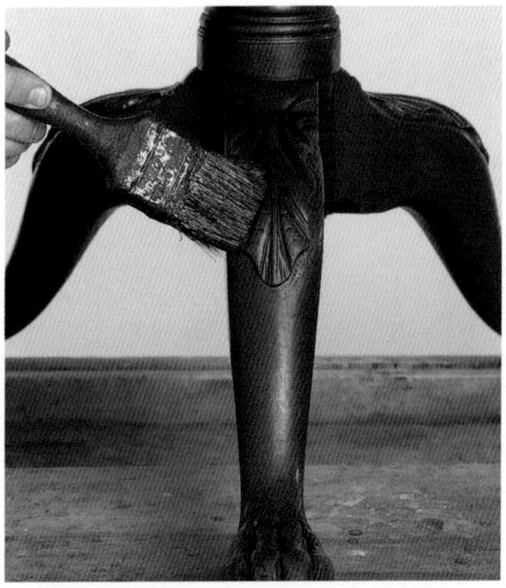

1 Due to the nature of the hollows and relief, it is better to apply a thin coat of wax with a soft brush, making sure that it is neither too hard nor too soft.

2 Allow the wax to harden for a few minutes, then gently burnish the carving with a soft brush. This will remove any surplus wax and even out what remains.

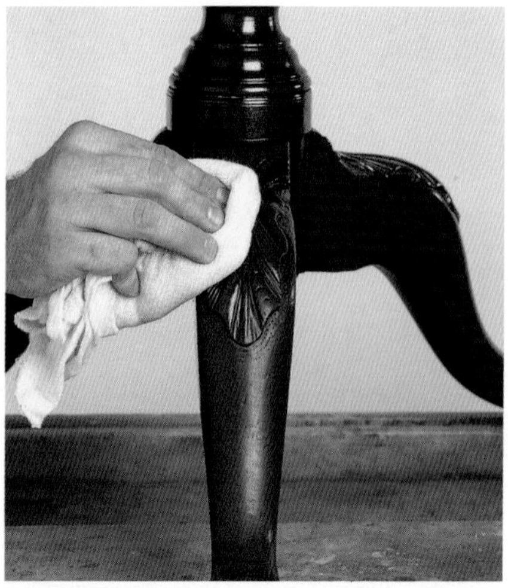

3 Finally, buff the highlights using a soft cloth (cotton rag). Mutton cloth, which is available from most trade suppliers, is ideal for this role.

Staining

Paints and varnishes adhere to the surface of the wood, but stains penetrate it, changing its colour permanently. For this reason, stains are favoured by the restorer. They can enrich dull-looking wood or change the colour of new wood so that it blends in with the rest of the piece of furniture. This bureau has had a new piece of wood added to it that must be stained and polished so that it matches the rest of the piece.

MATERIALS AND EQUIPMENT

- spirit-based (alcohol-based) stain
- cloth (cotton rag)
- wooden dowel
- fine brush
- rubbers
- polish
- methylated spirits (methyl alcohol)
- soft brush
- wax

1 Use a spirit-based (alcohol-based) stain mixed to match the colour of the furniture. For a small area like this, wrap a piece of cloth (cotton rag) around one end of a dowel and use this to apply the stain to the new piece of wood. If staining a large area, use a brush to apply the stain. Continue until the colour is even, then leave to dry.

2 Check again that the stain is even. If necessary, add another layer, or draw in the grain with a fine brush (see p.72). When you are satisfied with the colour of the dried stain, charge a rubber with polish and apply a layer to the stain, and also to the rest of the bureau to blend in the stained area (see pp.66-67). Allow the polish to dry.

Tip

Spirit-based (alcohol-based) stains, thinned with methylated spirits (methyl alcohol), are the best stains to use, because they dry very quickly. However, they are harder to obtain and more difficult to use. This is because they can leave obvious overlap marks. Solvent- and water-based stains are available ready mixed and are easier to apply.

3 Cut back the polish with a rubber charged with a little methylated spirits (methyl alcohol). The new wood should now be indistinguishable from the old.

4 Use a soft brush to apply a thin coat of wax to the new wood, and the rest of the piece of furniture, to give a soft, even sheen. Leave to dry.

Above: *Now stained and polished, the new wood blends seamlessly with the old.*

Modifying the colour

The room for which a table was initially commissioned will often not be the one in which it spends the majority of its life, and in the case of larger tables not all the original leaves will be used. An extra leaf may well be stored under a bed or in a cupboard, where it will keep its natural colour while the rest of the table will fade and mellow in colour. When the time comes to set the table up to its full size, it will be necessary to modify the colour and tone of the unused leaf to match the rest of the table.

This mahogany table shows how the two ends have been used together for most of the time – they have a warm, even colour and wax patination – but the middle leaf has had almost no use and remains much darker than the other leaves. The technique for lightening the darker section requires that the original polished finish be removed with a weak solution of paint stripper, after which the wood can be made paler with a solution of oxalic acid or bleach.

MATERIALS AND EQUIPMENT

- protective gloves
- weak paint stripper
- brush
- flat-bladed knife
- coarse wire (steel) wool
- cloths (cotton rags)
- methylated spirits (methyl alcohol)
- oxalic acid
- mutton cloth
- bleach
- acetic acid
- dowel
- rubber
- polish
- spirit- (alcohol-) based stain
- fine wire wool
- dark wax

1 Apply a weak solution of paint stripper with a brush in 30cm/12in squares. The reason for using a weak stripper is that it is required to remove only the top layers of polish and wax. Under no circumstance should it be allowed to bite into the wood.

2 Once the stripper has been applied, the polish will begin to glaze and congeal. At this point, use a flat-bladed knife to gently scrape away the dissolved polish and wax, taking great care not to mark the wood.

3 With coarse wire (steel) wool, remove any residue of polish and wax. The wire wool should simply be slid over the surface and not applied with any pressure, as this would cause unnecessary and unsightly damage.

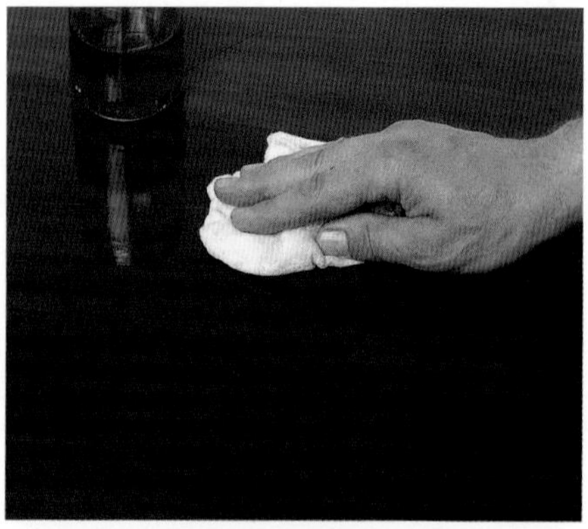

4 Use a clean cloth (cotton rag) to wipe methylated spirits (methyl alcohol) over the table top. This will neutralize any residue of the stripper. Make sure that you apply it evenly across the whole surface.

5 Having removed all the polish and wax, you now need to colour the wood to match the desired shade. The first method to try is to mix one part oxalic acid with ten parts hot water and apply the mixture with a pad of mutton cloth.

6 In this case, the oxalic acid was too weak to lighten the leaf to the desired tone, so you will need to try another method, this time using bleach.

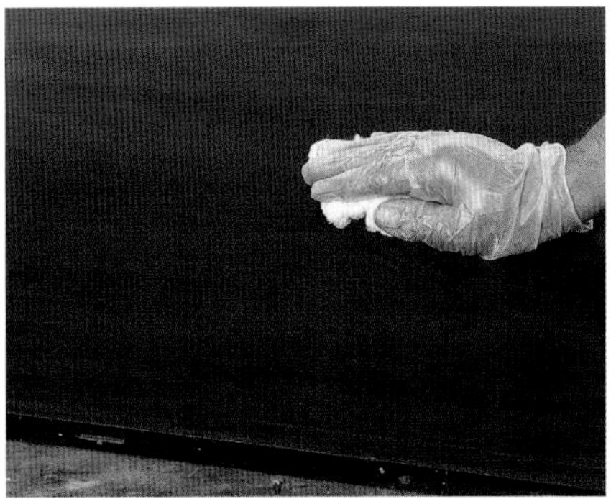

7 To lighten the table further, apply bleach with a cloth. Wear gloves to protect your skin. Initially, treat the wood with a solution of one part bleach to three parts water. If this is unsuccessful, treat the wood with one part bleach to one part water.

8 When completed, neutralize the bleach by applying acetic acid using a cloth or a dowel with cloth wrapped around the end. The leaf is now ready to be polished and coloured to match the rest of the table.

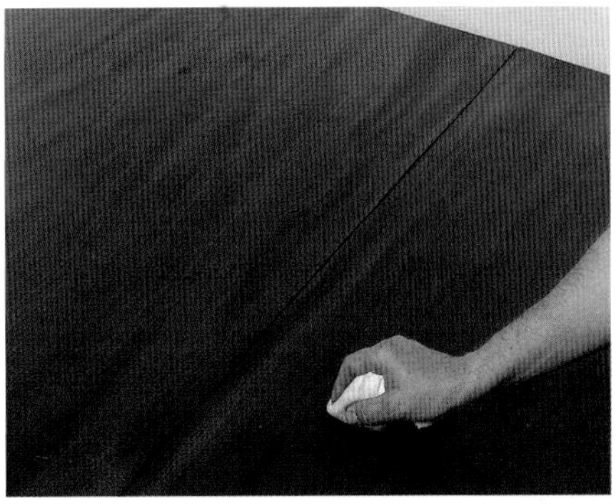

9 Lay the bleached leaf beside one of the end leaves to see if the correct tone and colour cast have been obtained. Charge a rubber with polish and apply a thin layer to the lightened leaf to indicate its final colour.

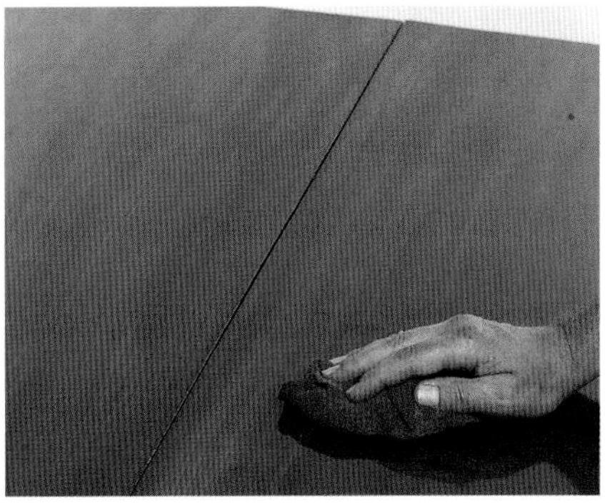

10 If the colour and tone need further adjustment, mix a spirit-based (alcohol-based) stain to the colour required (see p.41) and apply it to the whole leaf or just localized areas, using a cloth.

Left: *After applying the coloured stain, you will need to add several rubbers of polish (see pp.66–67). Allow each layer of polish to sink in before applying the next. It is advisable to allow the last layer of polish to settle for a couple of days to ensure that the grain has been filled completely. After the top has hardened fully, cut it back lightly with fine wire wool, then apply a thin coat of dark wax using a soft cloth (see p.67). When cutting back and waxing, make sure that you work in the direction of the grain.*

Graining

During the late 18th and early 19th centuries, rosewood was imported from India, South America and the West Indies for use in the manufacture of furniture. It was an expensive wood, and so only the finest pieces of furniture were made from solid rosewood; other pieces were made from beech, which was a hard-grained, easily workable, cheap native wood. The beech was "grained" with a paint finish to give the appearance of rosewood. Over time, the areas of graining wear away, revealing the beech underneath, as has happened with this Regency chair. In this case, it is necessary to simulate the rosewood graining while also giving it a patinated, antique look. The techniques for distressing are varied and include using smooth stones, fine wire (steel) wool and homemade tools. These should be practised and perfected before use.

MATERIALS AND EQUIPMENT

- light brown spirit-based (alcohol-based) stain
- fine brushes
- screwdriver
- rubber
- polish
- dark brown spirit-based stain
- wax
- cloth (cotton rag)

Above: *An area of the graining has worn away on the chair leg to reveal the beech wood underneath.*

1 Apply a base coat of a light brown stain mixed to match the base colour of the rest of the chair (see p.69). Leave to dry. Charge a rubber with polish and apply a thin layer.

2 Apply a dark brown stain mixed to match the grain of the simulated rosewood, using a fine brush to replicate the pattern. If no residue of graining is left, use a piece of patinated rosewood veneer as a pattern.

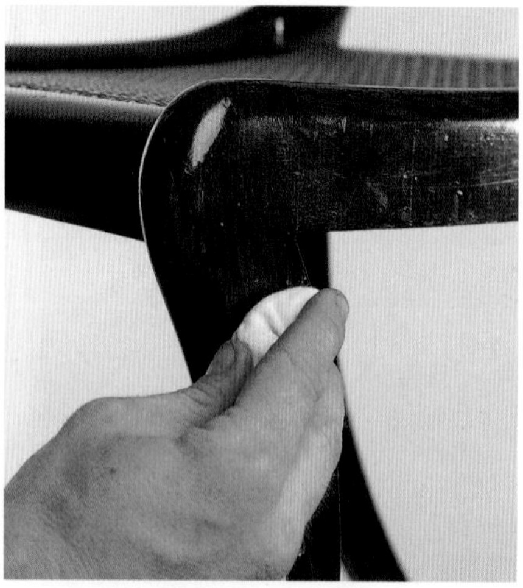

3 When the graining is dry, distress the graining effect using a screwdriver, if necessary, to match the original. Give it another rubber of polish to seal in the effect, then wax the chair using a cloth.

Above: *The grained beech chair, on the right of the picture, now looks very similar to the solid rosewood chair on the left. Both these chairs are dining chairs, made c.1810.*

Gilding

Water gilding requires great patience and an extremely delicate touch. Leaves of hand-beaten gold, beaten to a thickness of 0.025mm (0.001in) thick, are expensive, so it is wise to practise with metal leaf, which is much cheaper, until you are confident.

This 18th-century carved wood and gilt frame had been weakened by worm, which led to it becoming detached from its wire hooks and falling to the floor, causing considerable damage. Fortunately, most of the pieces had been kept together.

MATERIALS AND EQUIPMENT

- animal glue
- two-part epoxy resin
- wood carving tools
- gesso and gesso kettle
- soft brushes
- fine-grade sandpaper
- bole
- size
- fine brush
- gold leaf
- suede pad
- blunt knife
- gilder's fitch or good-quality artist's brush
- agate

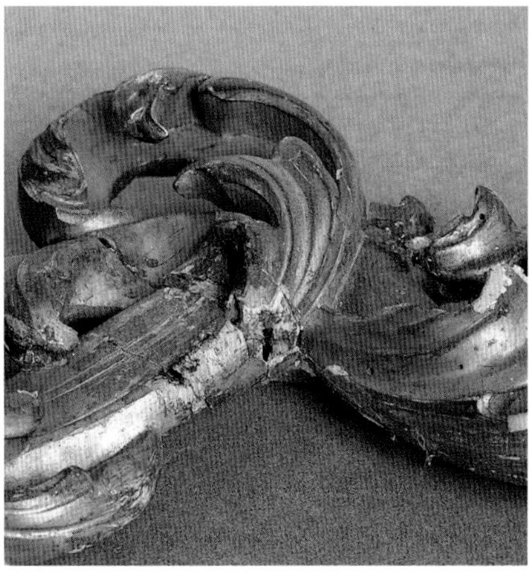

1 Place the frame on a flat surface and glue the separate parts together. Leave to dry.

2 Fill the missing areas with two-part epoxy resin. This useful substance offers strength as well as malleability. It will bond easily with the damaged parts.

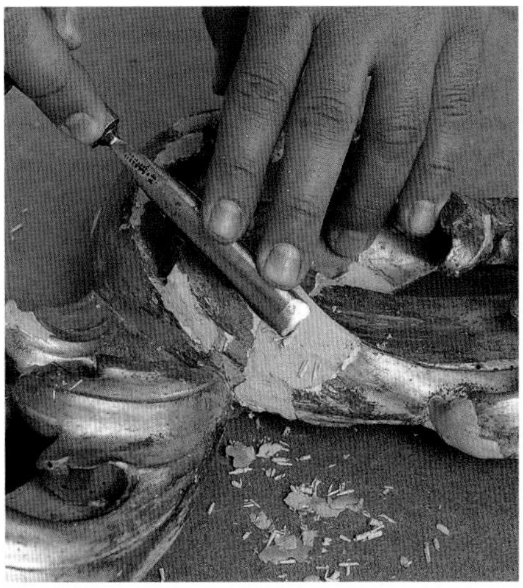

3 After the resin has hardened, carve it to follow the line of the existing frame using normal wood carving tools.

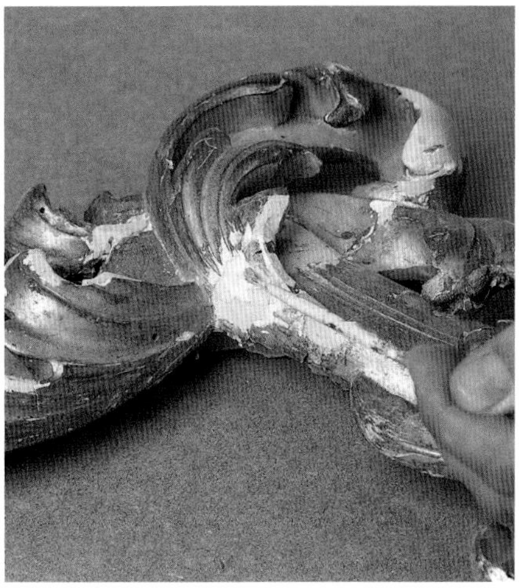

4 Heat a quantity of gesso in a gesso kettle to the consistency of double (heavy) cream. Apply it to the frame with a soft brush. Continue applying layers until you obtain the desired thickness. Leave to dry.

▷

Gilding...continued

5 Shape the gesso with carving tools and cut in any detailing. It is always the gesso that is carved, rather than the wood, which is why many intricate mirrors with carved decoration appear quite ordinary when stripped back to the wood prior to regilding.

6 Give the gesso the lightest of sandings with very fine-grade sandpaper. The purpose of this is simply to remove any raised nibs and to smooth the sweeping curves.

◁ **7** Paint a thin layer of bole on to the gesso. Red bole is being used here to match the original bole colour of the mirror. Following the method used with the gesso, warm the bole and apply it with a soft dry brush. When dry, smooth lightly with fine-grade sandpaper.

▷ **8** Place a sheet of gold leaf on a suede pad edged with stiff card for protection, and peel off the backing. Take care when handling gold leaf, since even the lightest of draughts will blow it out of line.

9 Cut the gold leaf into a number of small sections with a flat-bladed, blunt knife; only the lightest of pressures is required. Note how the unused scraps (offcuts) of gold leaf are left at the back of the pad to be used for faulting (filling in any small areas).

10 Apply a coating of size to the frame with a fine brush. Apply it to small areas at a time, followed by the immediate application of the pre-cut gold leaf.

11 The leaf is so light that it can prove difficult to handle. One of the best techniques is simply to use static electricity. Rub a clean gilder's fitch or artist's brush against your skin to build up a little static.

12 With the fitch or brush charged, simply touch the bristles to the gold leaf to lift it from the pad and place it on the frame.

13 Lay the leaf on the sized area. The size will pull it down on to the various contours. Repeat this process until all the areas of bole have been covered. This requires patience, and rushing will affect the final finish.

◁ **14** After gilding a significant area, dust over with a large soft brush, called a mop. This will remove any loose and excess gilt, exposing any uncovered areas. Use the gilt scraps saved for faulting to fill these gaps.

▷ **15** With the frame now fully gilded, use an agate to burnish the surface. This will give an even finish and tone to the gilt throughout. Take care not to remove the delicate gilt surface.

Above: *The fully restored frame is now ready to be fitted with its mirror plate. All evidence of the extensive damage has now been removed.*

Oil gilding

Oil gilding is a much simpler process than water gilding. After the gesso has been applied, the area to be gilded is painted with a special oil gilt size. The gold leaf is then laid directly from the sheet, held into place by its own backing. Oil gilding can even be used straight on to a wood surface. Unlike water gilding, the gilded surface is not burnished after application, so the carat of leaf used dictates the finish.

VENEERING

During the history of furniture making, the introduction of certain new techniques has radically altered the design and form of furniture. The skill of veneering, where thin layers of wood are laid on top of a different base wood, was introduced in the 17th century and this resulted in furniture taking on a much more flamboyant appearance. Woods that had previously been used in the solid could now be hand cut into thin sheets and laid to display the distinctive patterns of the wood, thereby greatly enhancing the look of furniture.

Highly decorative burrs and pollards, which had been too unstable to use in the solid, could now be cut and laid on to stable cores. It was indeed a giant step forward in the history of furniture construction.

The use of veneer in furniture construction became more popular during the latter part of the 17th century and the 18th century; prior to this it was used sparingly in decoration but more in a marquetry or parquetry form. Veneer was preferred over the solid during this period as it enabled a more decorative appearance to be achieved. For this reason it is common to find quarter-veneered tops or bookmatch drawer fronts from this period. Indeed, during the latter part of the 18th century, it was usual to find expensive decorative veneer such as mahogany laid on top of an equally expensive, but plainer, mahogany core.

This reflects the philosophy of this time when the use of veneer was more about aesthetics than economy. The quality of an individual's furniture was also seen to reflect the wealth of its owner and their position in society. However, by the 19th century, with the ability to cut wood mechanically, combined with the increasing demand for furniture by the merchant classes, the use of veneer enabled cheaper furniture to be made that could still be covered by the fashionable and expensive imported woods such as mahogany and satinwood.

Above: *A selection of old surface veneers.*

Above: *A late 17th-century bureau veneered in walnut rather than made from the solid.*

Above: *A George III linen press veneered in figured mahogany throughout.*

Above: *A Regency period drawer front veneered with figured rosewood and burr amboyna, and inlaid with brass decoration.*

Above: *A walnut bookmatch veneered end.*

Removing veneer

On the whole, veneer does not need to be removed. Either it will be loose, in which case it can be heated and clamped back into position (see p.78) or it will be missing. In some instances, however, a previous repair may have to be removed because it was not done professionally. In the example here, the veneer patch is rectangular and can easily be seen. Had it been cut to follow the pattern of the grain, it would have blended in with the rest of the piece more successfully. The old piece of veneer must be removed completely before the new patch can be cut in.

MATERIALS AND EQUIPMENT

- fine wire (steel) wool
- methylated spirits (methyl alcohol)
- metal rule
- utility knife
- masking tape
- chisel
- iron
- veneer
- PVA (white) glue
- clamping blocks
- G-clamps
- rubber
- polish

1 Wipe over the veneer patch with fine wire (steel) wool soaked in methylated spirits (methyl alcohol) until the polish comes off the patch. This allows you to see exactly where the patch meets the rest of the veneer.

2 Use a metal rule and a utility knife to score along the edges of the patch, making sure you cut all the way through the veneer.

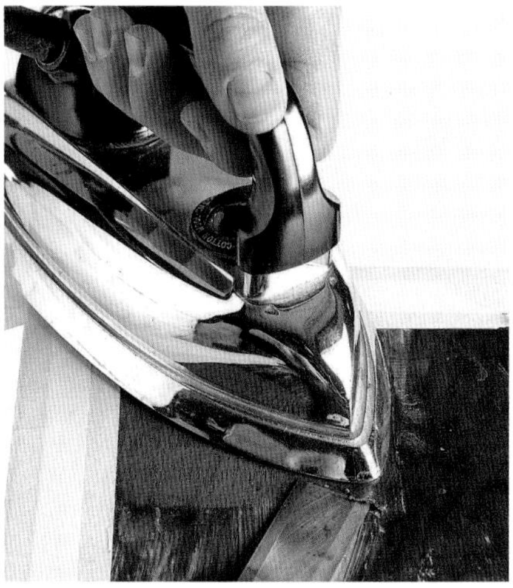

3 Push a chisel under the veneer patch and place a hot iron on top. Lift and remove the veneer patch in sections, continuing until it is all gone. Be careful not to put the iron on any of the original veneer.

◁ **4** Select a veneer that has appropriate graining and pattern, and cut out a piece, following the pattern, that is slightly larger than the area to be patched.

▷ **5** Place the new veneer over the area to be patched and use a utility knife to cut a new patch to fit the shape. Glue it in place with PVA (white) glue, apply clamping blocks and leave to dry. Stain and colour the veneer patch to blend with the surrounding wood (see p.69). Some graining may need to be added, too (see p.72). Finally, polish the patched area (see pp.66–67) and wax to finish (see p.68).

Laying veneer sheets

Small areas of veneer are simple to glue and clamp into place; the difficulty is in selecting the correct veneer. Larger areas of veneer cannot be clamped; instead, they are sealed with a different glue and a veneer hammer, which is a rather complicated procedure. To veneer curved surfaces, a counter-core must be made, which allows the clamps to exert even pressure on the drying veneer. Corners and edges of veneer will often be missing or split after years of use.

MATERIALS AND EQUIPMENT

- MDF (medium-density fiberboard)
- iron
- screwdriver
- paper
- clamping block
- G-clamps
- utility knife
- veneer
- PVA (white) glue
- ebony stringing
- masking tape
- rubber
- polish

Laying small areas of veneer

This bracket clock is veneered in Cuban mahogany. The veneer is loose, and parts of the veneer and the ebony stringing have been broken off and lost. It is not necessary to re-veneer the loose areas of veneer as they can simply be rebonded to the core.

1 Veneer is secured with animal glue, which means that heat and pressure can often be enough to rebind the veneer. Heat a piece of MDF (medium-density fiberboard) on an iron for approximately 5 minutes.

◁ **2** Remove the base section, taking care not to lose the screws. Place a piece of paper on the upper side of the veneer, and a clamping block below, to prevent damaging the carcass. Clamp the hot MDF into place, then leave until cool.

▷ **3** Cut a piece of veneer slightly larger than the missing piece. Cut the damaged area to the size of the new piece, then glue the new veneer in place. Clamp it until the glue dries, using a clamping block.

◁ **4** Select a new length of ebony stringing (see p.83). Cut this to size, glue it in place and secure with masking tape. (Note that there is no need to soak the stringing because it does not have to be shaped.) Reattach the base. Charge a rubber with polish and apply a thin layer over the whole carcass (see pp.66–67).

Right: *A good match for the original veneer was found, making the repair to this clock completely invisible.*

Laying large areas of veneer

There is little call to lay new veneer in most antique furniture restoration, but in some circumstances, such as extreme fire or water damage or if large areas of veneer are missing, this may be needed. The tools used are almost identical to those utilized by cabinet-makers over the past 200 years.

MATERIALS AND EQUIPMENT

- **fine wood filler**
- **putty knife**
- **smooth toothing plane**
- **short, thick brush**
- **animal glue**
- **newspaper**
- **veneer**
- **veneer hammer**
- **cloth (cotton rag)**
- **flat piece of wood**
- **utility knife**
- **steel straightedge**
- **cabinet scraper**
- **medium fine-, fine- and very fine-grade sandpaper**
- **sanding block**

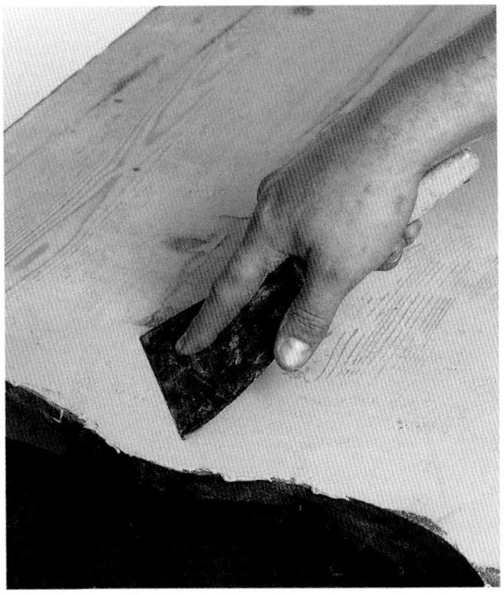

◁ **1** First, prepare the base wood by filling any splits or dents with a fine wood filler. If these are not filled, they will show through the veneer when it is laid.

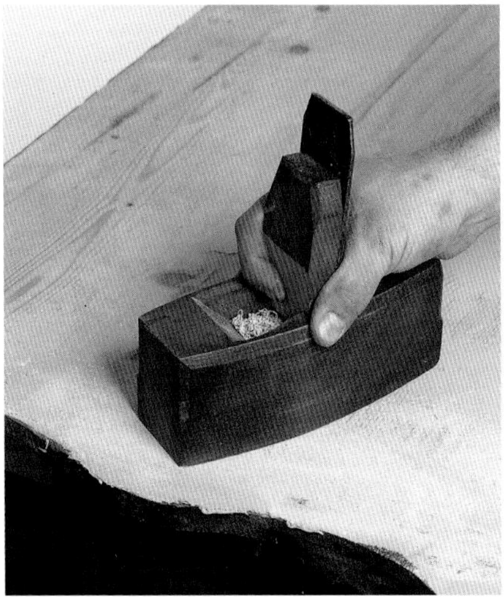

▷ **2** When the filler has hardened, level it using a smooth toothing plane. This will also key the surface for the veneer and adhesive.

3 Brush a size made of animal glue and hot water over the surface of the carcass. This will fill the grain and ensure that when the animal glue is applied prior to veneering, it will produce an even layer. Failure to do so can result in blisters in the veneer. Protect the rest of the carcass with newspaper.

4 Veneering half the surface at a time enables you to work while the glue is still malleable. Coat half the surface liberally with animal glue, then lay the veneer and use a veneer hammer with a firm pressure to expel all the excess glue. Dip the hammer into a mixture of glue and hot water to help it glide easily.

5 When half the surface is covered, wash off the surface of the veneer with a hot, wet cloth (cotton rag) to remove any traces of animal glue.

▷

Laying large areas of veneer...continued

6 Trim the excess veneer by placing a flat piece of wood against the edge and scoring around the shape of the carcass with a utility knife. The wood will prevent the veneer from splitting.

7 Repeat the veneering process on the other half. To obtain a perfect join, overlap the first piece of veneer with the second. Lay a steel straightedge over both pieces and cut through them with a utility knife.

8 Lift away the trimmed strips from both sections of veneer, leaving a perfect join. Run the veneer hammer along this join to make sure the edges lie flat. Leave to dry overnight.

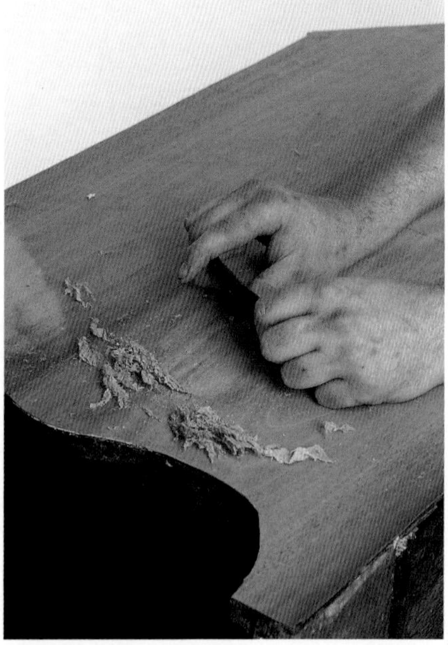

9 When the glue is dry, go over the newly veneered section with a cabinet scraper. This will level the veneer and flatten the grain, which will have become raised with the application of hot water.

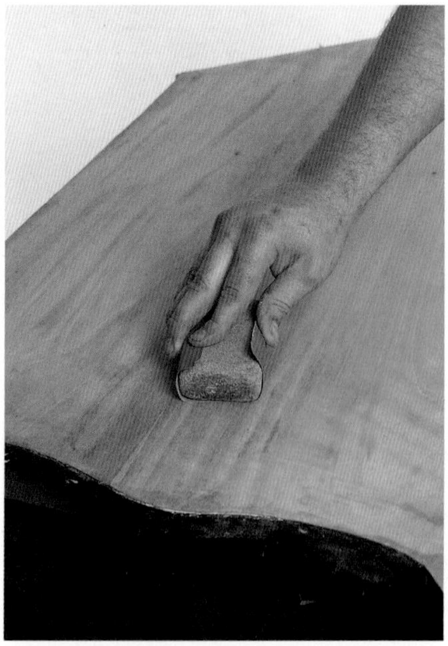

10 Finally, use three grades of sandpaper (graduating all the time to the finest grade) wrapped around a sanding block to remove all scraper marks and prepare the veneer for polishing.

Laying curved veneer

On occasion, you may need to make or replace a missing veneered part for a piece of furniture that is shaped. For example, a moulding may have lost its veneer, or, as in this case, a piece of furniture has lost its cornice, so a replacement cornice (known as a core) needs to be made and then veneered to match.

MATERIALS AND EQUIPMENT

- **pine or mahogany**
- **band saw**
- **moulding plane**
- **veneer**
- **brush**
- **animal glue**
- **G-clamps**
- **utility knife**
- **curved cabinet scraper**
- **fine-grade sandpaper**

1 Cut the core and also a counter-core, which follows the internal curve of the core or original moulding, out of pine or mahogany using a band saw or spoke shave. Shape both pieces with a moulding plane. Select a length of veneer that is wider than the core or moulding.

2 To make the veneer malleable so that it does not crack or split when applied, soak it in water until pliable. An old tin bathtub is often best for such a task, as it allows veneers of a good length to be soaked. Change the water if you plan to use different veneers, to prevent staining.

3 Remove the veneer from the bath and, while it is still wet and pliable, brush animal glue evenly over the core or moulding, and press the veneer firmly on to it.

4 Place the counter-core on top of the veneer and clamp it tightly. Make sure that an even pressure is applied throughout to ensure that no blisters result. Leave the veneer to dry overnight.

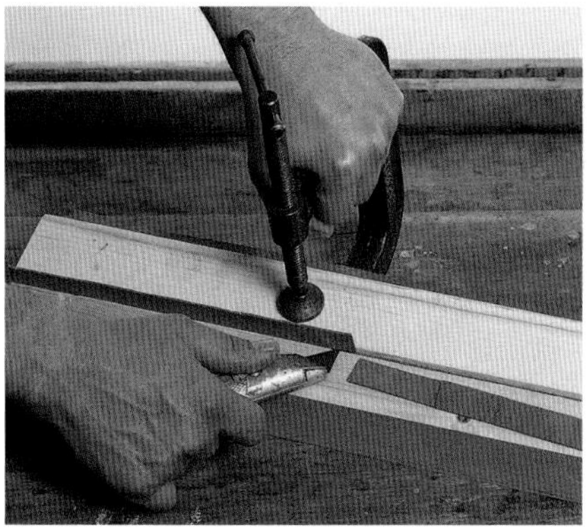

5 When the glue is dry, remove all but one of the clamps, but leave the counter-core in place while you trim off the excess veneer with a utility knife. The remaining clamp acts as a useful handle.

◁ **6** Remove the final clamp and the counter-core. Clean up the veneer with a curved cabinet scraper, applying an even pressure. The idea is to remove fine shavings and not to tear the grain.

▷ **7** Go over the veneer with fine-grade sandpaper. A section cut from the counter-core, which will fit into the shape of the moulding or core, makes a suitable sanding block for this purpose.

Replacing bandings

Decorative veneer inlays situated around the edges of tables, chests and cabinets are known as bandings. They are usually cut from the same veneer as the main body veneer, but across, rather than along, the grain to distinguish them from the body veneer. Their position makes bandings vulnerable to knocks, and they are often the first piece of veneer to break off. This table has lost part of its banding.

MATERIALS AND EQUIPMENT
- veneer
- utility knife
- dividers
- PVA (white) glue
- clamping blocks
- G-clamps
- chisel
- fine-grade sandpaper
- spirit-based (alcohol-based) stain
- cloth (cotton rag)
- wooden dowel
- rubber
- polish

1 Cut out the chosen veneer with a utility knife into lengths of approximately 10cm/4in. If the table is curved, place a length of veneer under the edge or, in this case, the flap, and draw around the edge.

2 Scratch the width of the missing banding on to the veneer, using a pair of dividers. Remember to mark across, rather than along, the grain. Cut out the banding.

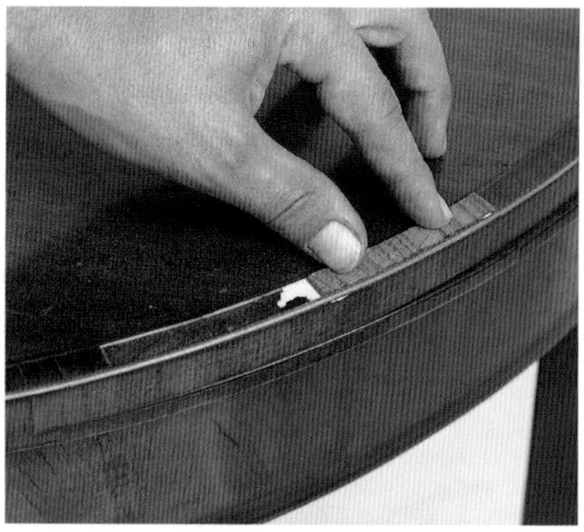

3 Make sure that the area to be veneered is clean before applying a thin layer of PVA (white) glue. Lay one piece of veneer on the glue and press it down. Clamp using G-clamps and blocks and leave for a few hours.

4 When the glue is dry and the bond secure, remove the clamps and blocks and level the veneer with a chisel. Take care not to damage the main body of veneer.

5 Repeat with the remaining veneer, then smooth with fine-grade sandpaper. The new banding should sit flush with the old and follow the curve of the table exactly.

Above: *Once it has been stained and polished (see p.69 and pp.66–67), the new banding should blend seamlessly with the old.*

Replacing stringings

Very thin, string-like pieces of veneer, usually cut from boxwood, are also used as decorative veneer inlays. Stringings are often situated next to bandings, and are just as likely to be knocked, as was the case with this table, which has lost part of its stringing. For this project the stringing is soaked and applied wet as it needs to be malleable in order to bend around the curved shape of the table.

MATERIALS AND EQUIPMENT
- utility knife
- stringing
- PVA (white) glue
- masking tape
- chisel
- fine-grade sandpaper
- spirit-based (alcohol-based) stain
- cloth (cotton rag)
- wooden dowel
- rubber
- polish

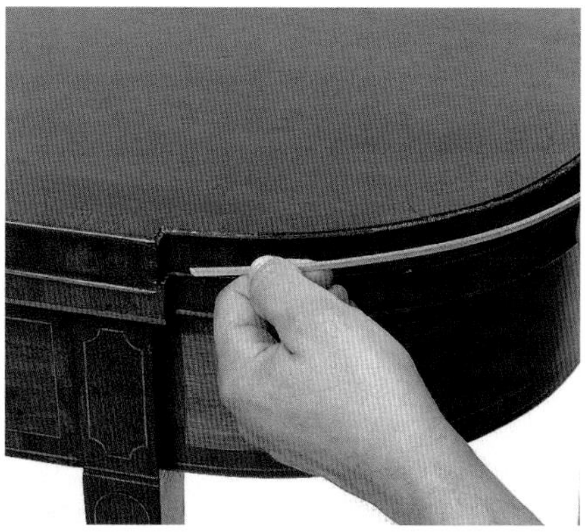

1 Using a utility knife, cut a length of stringing from a piece that matches the original in dimension and colour. Soak the stringing in some hot water to make it more malleable.

2 While the stringing is still wet, glue it in place with PVA (white) glue. Tape it down with masking tape and leave to dry.

3 When the stringing is dry, level the top and sides with a chisel. Take care not to damage the existing veneer.

4 Smooth the stringing with fine-grade sandpaper. Continue until the edges are blunted and the veneer is level.

Left: *Once stained and polished (see p.69 and pp.66–67), the new stringing is indistinguishable from the old.*

Marquetry repairs

Intricate veneer inlay in the shape of flowers, leaves and other natural objects is known as marquetry. This table is Dutch in origin and was made c.1740. It is veneered in walnut with marquetry panels of box, sycamore and walnut laid on to an oak core. It is of good colour and patination, but there has been some shrinkage to the oak carcass, which in turn has damaged the marquetry panels. Closer inspection reveals that previous losses of veneer and marquetry have been disguised with coloured filler.

MATERIALS AND EQUIPMENT

- fine wire (steel) wool
- small chisel
- tracing paper
- veneer
- fret saw
- PVA (white) glue
- masking tape
- fine brush
- spirit-based (alcohol-based) stain
- rubber
- polish

1 First, expose the old coloured-out parts by rubbing off the entire surface colour from the filler with fine wire (steel) wool.

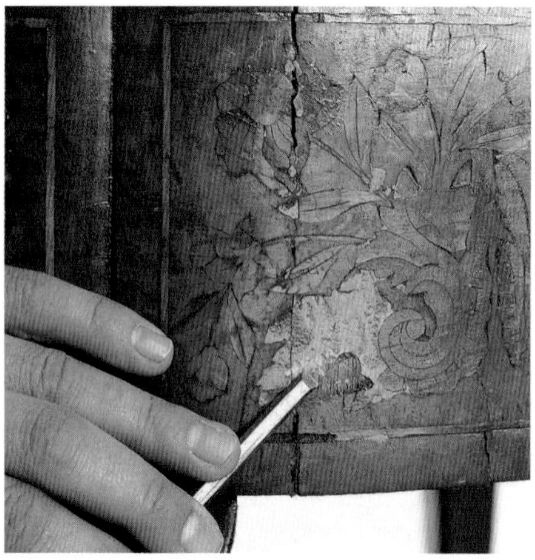

2 The areas of missing marquetry will now be visible. Remove the old filler with a small chisel, taking care not to dig into the core.

3 Determine the style and shape of the missing marquetry by looking for corresponding areas of marquetry that are undamaged. Trace their shapes carefully.

4 Offer up the tracings to the areas of missing marquetry and carefully position the copied patterns to ascertain which designs need to be cut.

5 Cut the veneer with great care, using a fret saw. Once each piece is cut, stick it in place with PVA (white) glue, then tape it into position and leave to dry.

Above: *Once all the missing pieces of veneer have been replaced, the area needs to be stained and polished (see p.69 and pp.66–67). The table should then look as it did in 1740.*

Parquetry repairs

Intricate veneer inlay in geometric shapes, such as diamonds and squares, is known as parquetry. It often utilizes differently coloured and grained veneer to give a three-dimensional effect. Some areas of the parquetry on this cabinet have worn away and must be replaced.

MATERIALS AND EQUIPMENT

- veneer
- sliding bevel gauge
- utility knife
- small chisel
- PVA (white) glue
- masking tape
- small blade
- spirit-based (alcohol-based) stain
- cloth (cotton rag)
- wooden dowel
- rubber
- polish

1 Select a replacement veneer that has a similar grain and can be polished to the same colour as the existing veneer.

2 Cut the veneer to size using a sliding bevel gauge and a utility knife. This will make sure that the angles are correct so that you can achieve an exact fit.

3 Remove the damaged veneer with a small chisel, making sure that you remove complete shapes from damaged areas. Do not touch the surrounding veneer.

4 Glue the new pieces in place with PVA (white) glue and tape them down with masking tape. When the glue is dry, scrape the new pieces with a small blade until they lie flush with the other pieces.

Left: *Careful choice of veneer needs to be followed by expertly applied stain and polish (see p.69 and pp.66–67) to ensure that the restored diamond shapes echo the distinctive grain and patina of the original parquetry.*

Project: rosewood pole screens

Pole screens began to appear at the beginning of the 18th century. They were designed to protect women's faces from the heat of the fire. With the advent of coal-fired boilers in the late 19th century, their manufacture all but ceased. These items of furniture make interesting decorative pieces in their own right, however, and are worth restoring. They are likely to have suffered from a variety of ills.

Assessing the project

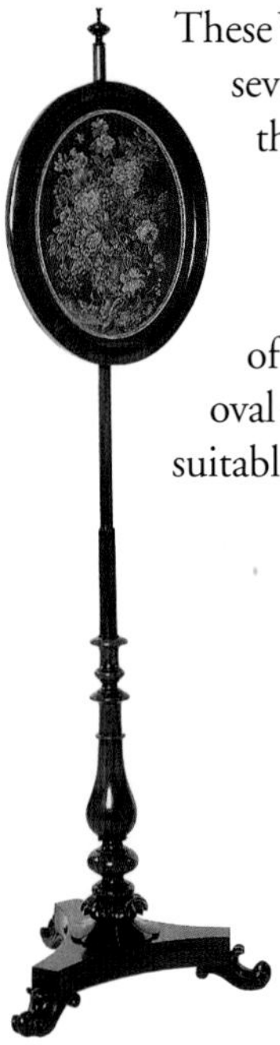

These William IV rosewood pole screens have several areas of damaged veneer and wood that need to be repaired or replaced. Most importantly, both frames for the screens are missing, so these will have to be built from scratch. Research into the history of the pieces shows that they ought to have oval frames, and the owner has chosen some suitable material to fit.

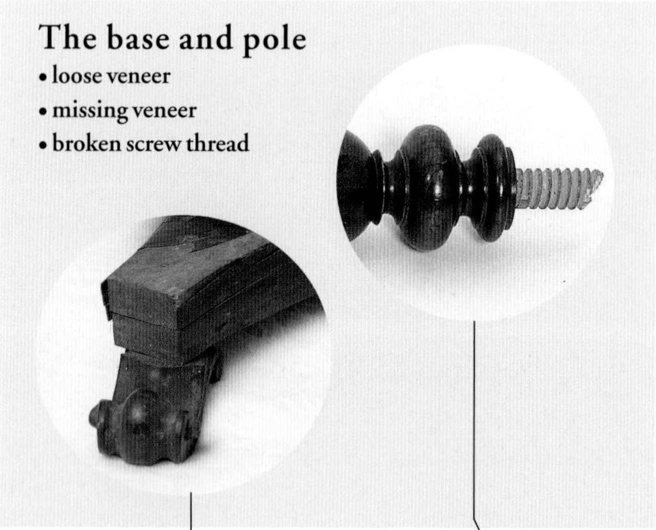

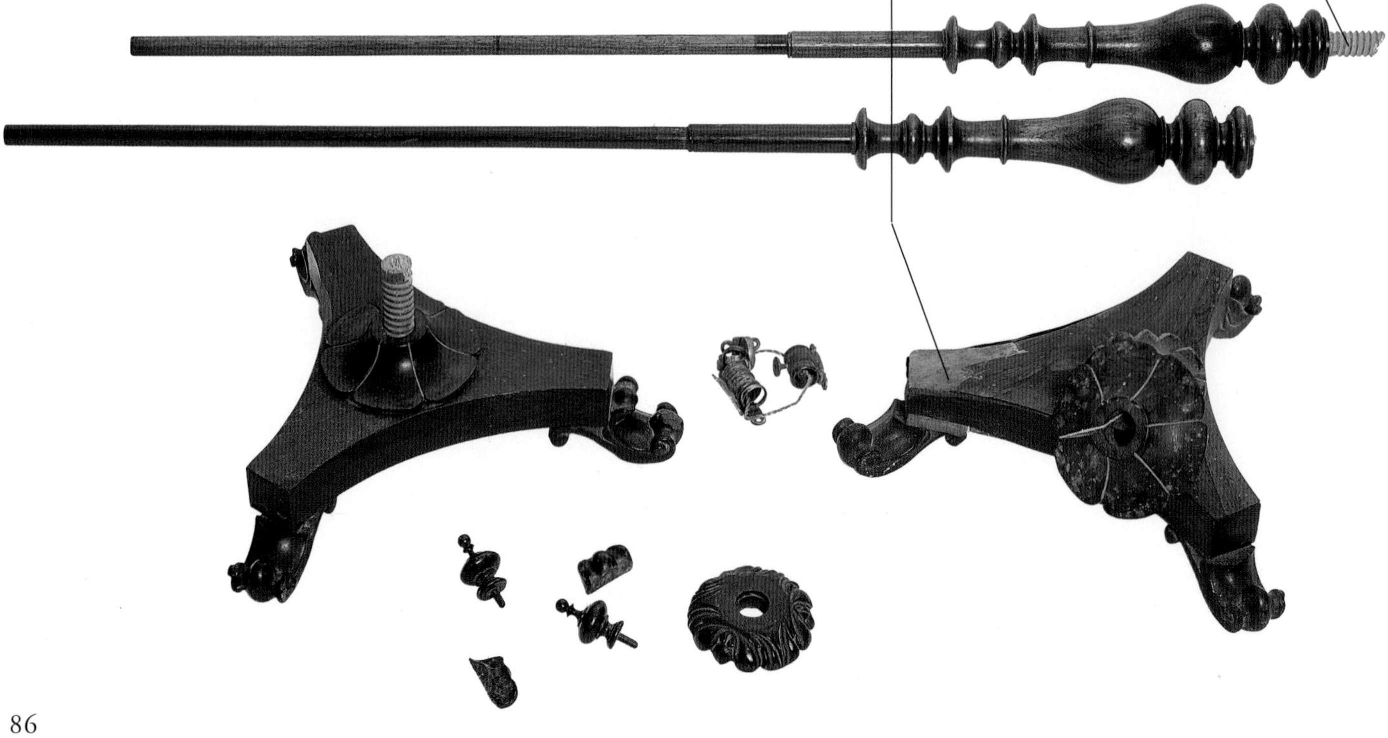

Repairing the base and pole

Damp had caused the glue joining the veneer to the core to perish, allowing the veneer to become detached and, in some areas, to break off completely. The glue joining the main body of the feet to the scrolling top sections had also perished, and while some of the pieces could simply be reglued, others were missing and would have to be recarved. Each pole was joined to the base by a wooden screw. One of these had sheared off and needed to be replaced.

MATERIALS AND EQUIPMENT

- PVA (white) glue
- snap clamp
- flat-bladed knife
- brass pins (tacks)
- hammer
- pliers
- softwood
- band saw
- moulding plane
- sash clamp
- pincers
- utility knife
- chisel
- masking tape
- G-clamps

SECURING AND REPLACING VENEER

Securing loose veneer is a straightforward procedure, but replacing veneer is a more complicated process, mainly because care needs to be taken to find a good match. To secure the veneer to a curved area, a piece of softwood will need to be cut and shaped to fit the curve, in the same way as a counter-core was cut on p.81. This shaped piece is known as a jig.

1 Place the base section on a workbench. Apply PVA (white) glue to any cracks and insert slivers of wood if they are wide. Apply a snap clamp and leave to dry.

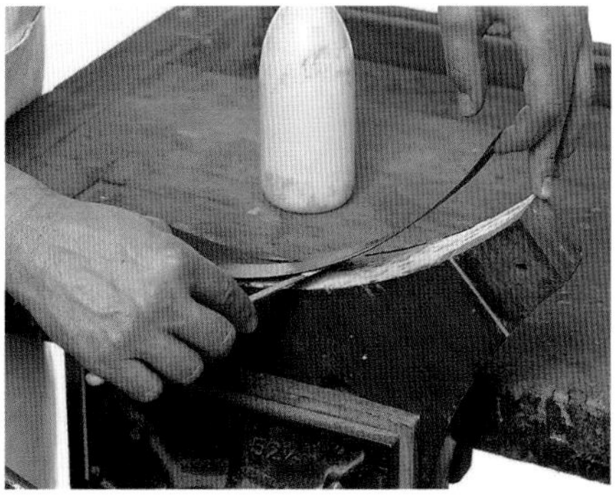

2 Reattach the loose veneer by pulling it up gently and applying PVA glue to the core using a flat-bladed knife.

3 Tap in two or three small brass pins (tacks) to hold the veneer in place, then snip off the ends with pliers, leaving enough showing to allow their removal with pincers later.

4 Prepare a jig to fit the concave area. Place newspaper between the jig and the veneer to prevent any excess glue bonding them together. Secure with a sash clamp and leave to dry for a few hours, then remove the clamp and jig. Pull out the pins with pincers.

5 Replace the missing end pieces of veneer first, as these must be laid over the top edge. Cut the replacement veneer to size with a utility knife and apply PVA glue to the core. Place the veneer on the glue,use the sash clamp and jig to secure it, and leave to dry.

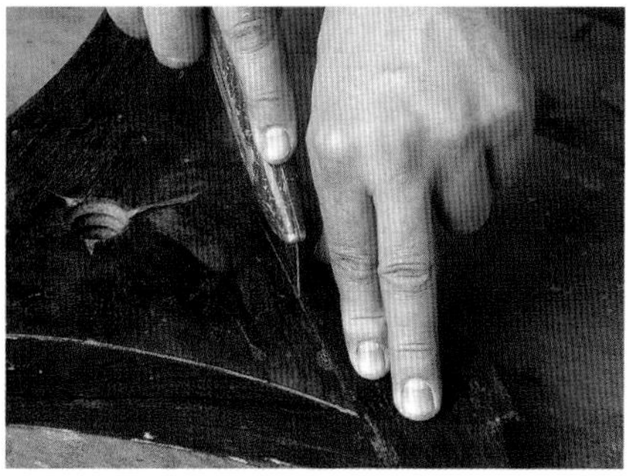

6 Lay the replacement veneer for the top of the base over the damaged area. Ascertain how much of the old veneer will have to be removed in order to provide a straight line for the new piece to butt up to (meet). Cut along this line with a utility knife.

▷

Securing and replacing veneer...continued

7 Remove the splintered edge of the old veneer by sliding a sharp chisel between the veneer and the core. Tape the new veneer in place and turn the base over.

8 Mark the shape of the concave base on the new veneer with a pencil. Turn the base back over, remove the veneer and cut along the pencil line with a utility knife.

9 Glue the veneer in position and tap in two or three brass pins. Snip off their ends, apply G-clamps and glue blocks, and leave to dry. Remove the clamps and the pins. Repeat this process for all loose and missing veneer.

Repairing the Feet and the Pole

The carved knurl feet are made up from two pieces of wood, which was typical of this type of foot construction. The top section has become detached and lost, and so a new scrolling top part must be carved. The feet are made from rosewood, but walnut, if stained, makes a suitable substitute. The pole needs a new screw thread to attach it to the base, and this must be turned using a box of a suitable size.

MATERIALS AND EQUIPMENT

- **well-figured walnut**
- **PVA (white) or animal glue**
- **carving tools**
- **fine-grade sandpaper**
- **screwdriver**
- **fine wire (steel) wool**
- **polish**
- **fine brush**
- **rubber**
- **well-seasoned beech**
- **large gouge**
- **callipers**
- **chisel**
- **box**
- **soft cloth (cotton rag)**
- **wax**

1 The knurl feet comprise two sections. The first is the actual foot that rests on the ground and the second is the rolling scroll at the top. A number of these scrolls are missing from the feet.

2 The knurl feet, like the pole screen, are made from rosewood, but since rosewood is difficult to source, a suitable piece of well-figured walnut has been chosen instead. Glue the walnut block to the damaged foot.

▷ **3** Sketch out the shape of the missing scroll, then, using the appropriate carving tools, shape and carve it to match a scroll on another foot. When it is finished, clean it up using fine-grade sandpaper. Repeat this process for the other damaged feet.

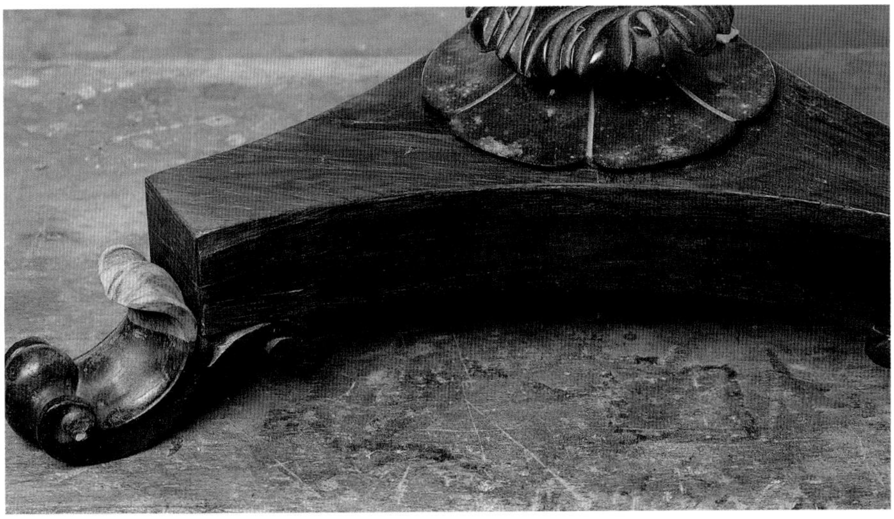

4 Screw the repaired feet temporarily in position on the newly restored base to make sure that everything fits correctly prior to being glued.

5 ◁ Remove the loose surface dirt and wax using fine wire (steel) wool prior to polishing. This will enable the fresh polish to bind to the exisiting finish.

6 ▷ The repaired feet can now be removed again to aid the process of polishing. Apply polish to the surface using a fine brush. Charge a rubber with further polish and apply to the feet to give an even finish all over (see pp.66–67).

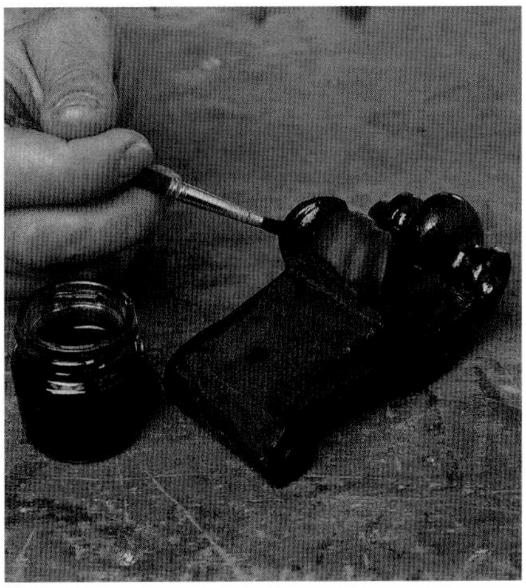

Screw threads

The construction method used to attach the pole to the base is a screw thread. On one of the pole screens this has broken and so a new one must be turned and then cut using a box cutter (see p.25 and below). Hard beech is the best wood to use as it will be both strong enough for the repair and hard enough to maintain a good edge on the thread.

7 Turn a new screw thread for the pole (see box left) out of well-seasoned beech, then fit the pole to the base. Charge a rubber with polish and apply a layer to the pole. Cut back the finish with wax to complete the work (see p.67).

Above: *The finished, polished and restored pole screen base.*

▷

Making a frame

The new oval frame is constructed on a template (pattern) made from MDF (medium-density fiberboard). This template is used for both the frame and rim, which is made of strips of veneer and pieces of cross-grain rosewood. A tailor-made band clamp, fashioned from a steel tape, is used to secure the several thin layers of veneer that make up the rim. The moulded front of the frame is constructed from numerous pieces of solid rosewood, meticulously shaped and then attached to the rim. So that the frame has the same patina and colour as the base of the pole screen, the same rosewood veneer was used for the base and the outside of the frame. However, walnut veneer, which is cheaper than rosewood, could be used for the inner parts of the laminate.

MATERIALS AND EQUIPMENT

- plywood
- jigsaw (saber saw)
- fabric
- MDF (medium-density fiberboard)
- steel straightedge
- dividers
- hammer
- oval nails
- string
- pincers
- band saw
- steel band
- centre punch
- drill
- metal drill bit
- countersunk drill bit
- hardwood blocks
- screws
- screwdriver
- file
- clamp
- veneer for core
- facing plane
- depth gauge
- utility knife
- block plane
- masking tape
- large board
- newspaper
- brush
- PVA (white) glue
- small pieces of wood
- rosewood veneer
- scotch glue
- sponge
- cabinet scraper

Making the rim

The moulded front of the frame will be attached to the rim, while the glass, fabric and backing board will sit within it, so it needs to be both strong and regular in shape. It is made by layering veneer around a template, fixing it with glue and clamping it with a band clamp made specially for this project.

1 Prior to making the new frame, ascertain the correct diameter of the oval to suit the chosen fabric. To do this, cut a plywood oval with a jigsaw (saber saw) and place it over the material. This avoids the costly mistake of making a frame that is too small.

2 Cut a piece of MDF (medium-density fiberboard) with a jigsaw to a size just bigger than the frame, and place it on the bench. Draw two lines bisecting the MDF into quarters using a steel straightedge.

◁ **3** Divide the height and width of the oval frame in half. Mark each half-length on corresponding arms of the cross by scribing them with dividers.

▷ **4** Set the dividers to half the length of the oval. Place one point of the dividers on the mark indicating the width of the oval and scribe a line through one length line. Repeat this along the other length line.

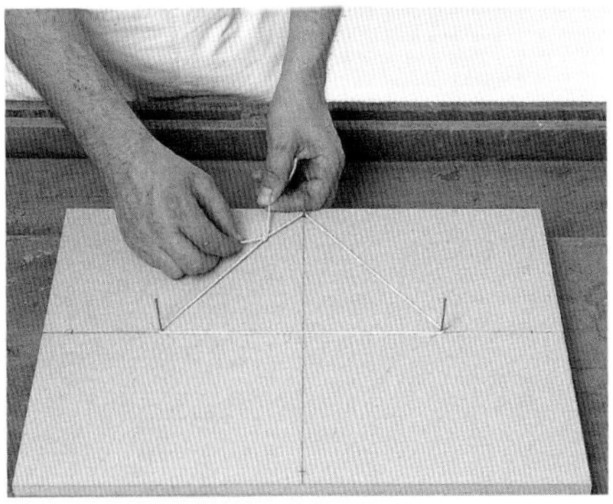

5 Hammer an oval nail into each of the scribed marks on the length line and the outer mark on the width line. Tie string around the nails, allowing no slackness. Remove the nail from the width line.

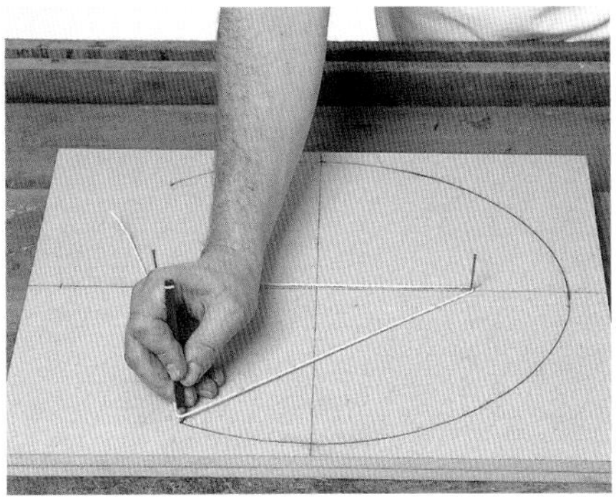

6 Hold a sharp pencil inside the string and draw around the two nails, keeping the tension on the string at all times.

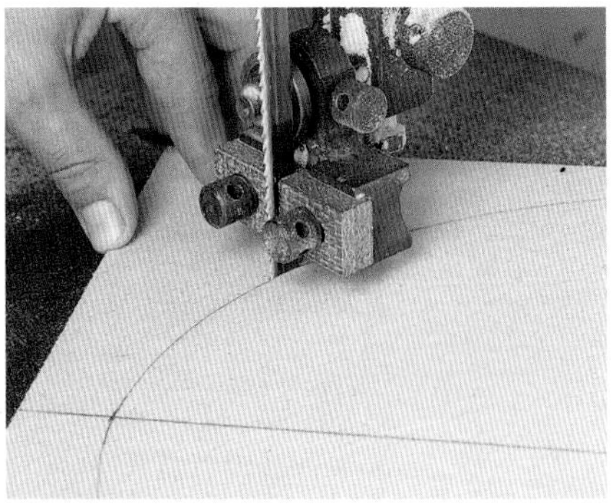

7 Cut along the line with a band saw. The resulting oval shape will match the chosen size of the frame and will be used as the template (pattern) for making the frame.

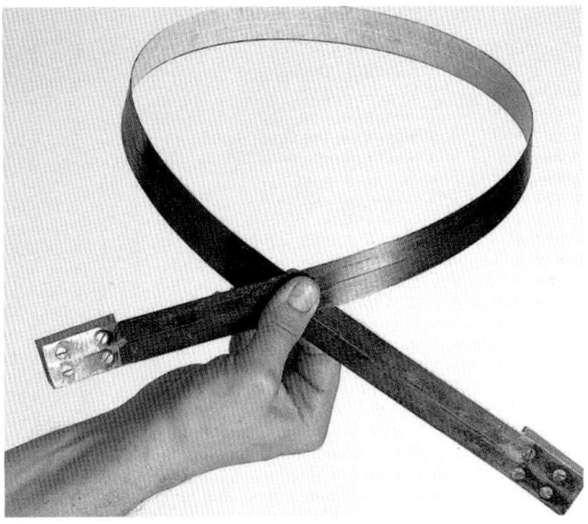

8 Make a band clamp following the instructions on p.21. Band clamps have to be tailored to the rim they are going to fit, and therefore they must be custom made for the job and cannot be bought.

9 Select enough sheets of the cheaper veneer that is being used for the core to make five or six layers around the edge of the template. Place the veneer on the workbench and rough the surface with a facing plane.

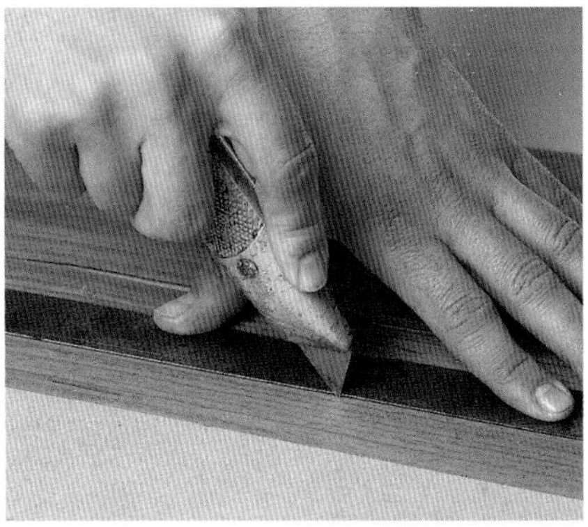

10 Set a depth gauge to slightly wider than the template edge. Place the veneer on a flat surface and run the gauge along it. Use a utility knife to cut the veneer, along the gauge marks to a length slightly longer than the template rim.

11 Score and cut five more strips of veneer. Taper one end of two of the lengths of veneer with a block plane. These will be the first and last lengths to go around the rim, and paring them down prevents a step from forming on the rim.

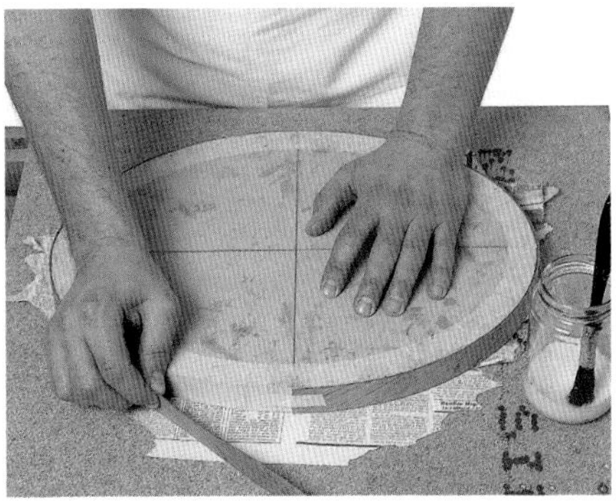

12 Cover the edge of the template with masking tape and screw it to a large board covered with newspaper. Tape one of the planed-end strips of veneer to the template, wrap the veneer around the template and mark where it overlaps the secured end.

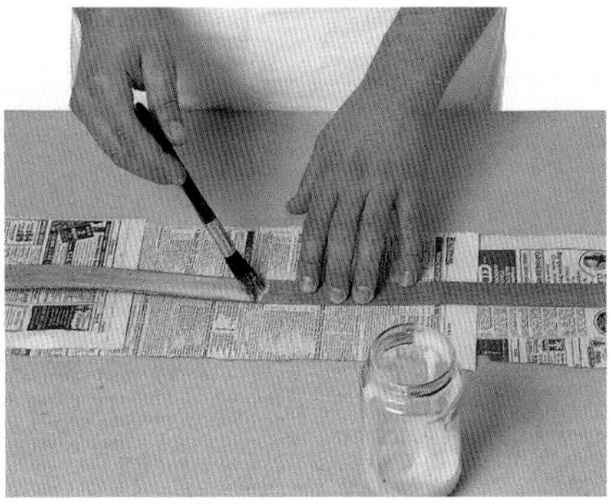

13 Remove the veneer strip from the template and brush PVA (white) glue on to the underside of the overlapping section only. Wrap the veneer strip around the template again and press it firmly to stick the overlapping ends together.

Making the rim...continued

14 Add the remaining strips of veneer, applying glue to the previous layer before butting up the next strip. Use masking tape to secure the end of one strip to the start of the next. Finish with the planed-end strip.

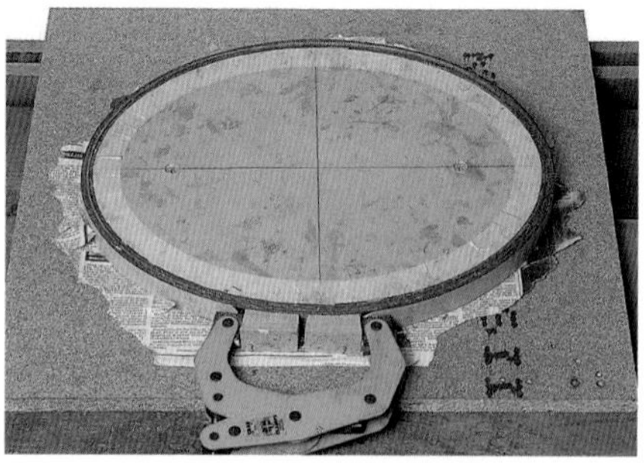

15 Apply the band clamp and clamp the hardwood blocks to create the tension. Leave to dry for at least 12 hours, then remove the band clamp.

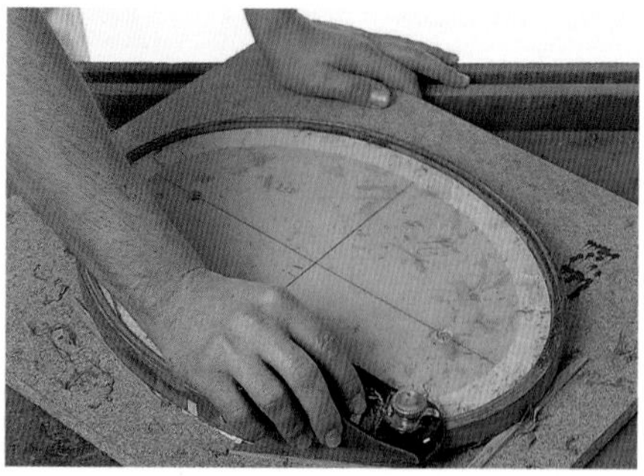

16 Raise the rim clear of the template , resting it on small pieces of wood, then use a block plane to smooth the rim edge. Turn the rim over, and plane the underside. Remove the rim and unscrew the template.

17 Cut a strip of rosewood veneer to the same height as the rim and long enough to go around the rim once exactly. Cut the ends square. Coat the inner surface of the strip thoroughly with scotch glue.

18 Place the veneer on the rim, joining the ends exactly. Place the rim on the template, secure it in a vice and use the back of a hammer to press the veneer into place. Dip the hammer into hot water to stop it sticking.

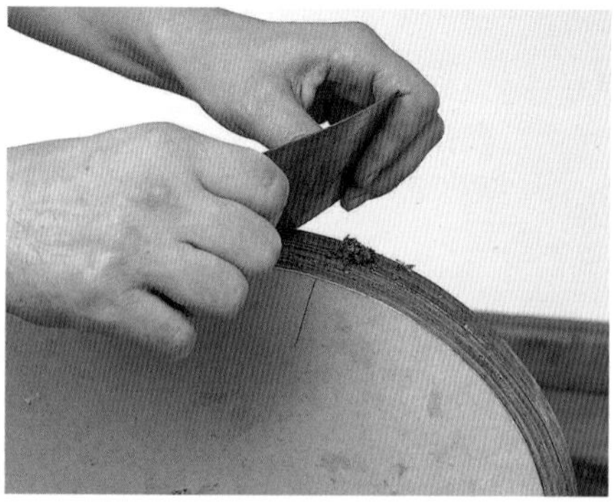

19 Leave the veneer to dry in the vice then lightly clean up the surface of the outer veneer with a cabinet scraper. Remove the rim from the template, which will be used for making the frame moulding.

Making the Frame Moulding

The moulded front of the frame is made from rosewood that matches the rosewood veneer. Pieces of cross-grain wood need to be cut to fit the rim, then planed into shape.

MATERIALS AND EQUIPMENT

- rosewood
- dividers
- band saw
- rim template
- utility knife
- jigsaw (saber saw)
- masking tape
- chisel
- PVA (white) glue
- G-clamps
- spokeshave
- depth gauge
- snap clamp
- drill
- fine-grade sandpaper
- cork block
- flat-bladed knife
- hammer
- roughing plane blade
- scotch glue
- sealer
- rubber
- shellac polish
- clear beeswax
- soft cloth (cotton rag)
- glass
- plywood
- coloured silk
- small screws
- screwdriver
- brass brackets
- laminated walnut strip
- black water stain
- steel panel pins (tacks)

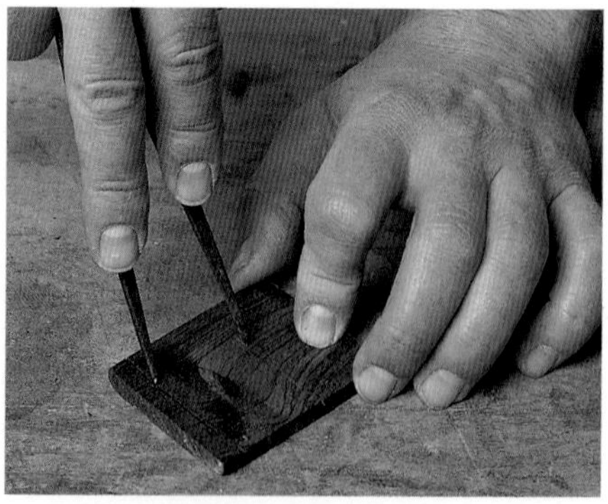

1 Cut the rosewood into small sections of the desired thickness. Use a pair of dividers to mark the approximate width of the frame, allowing extra for shaping (see step 8). Cut the rosewood into the required cross-grain size with a band saw.

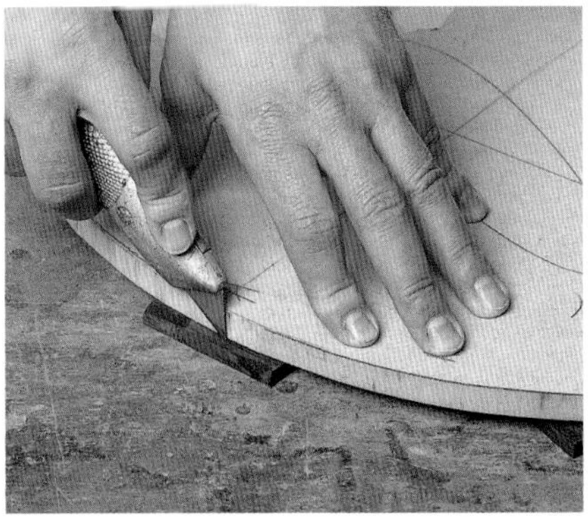

2 Place the rosewood underneath the template, with the area left for shaping protruding. Score the rosewood around the template curve with a utility knife. Cut this line with a band saw.

3 After each piece is cut, hold it next to the preceding piece and make a pencil line to provide a smooth joint.

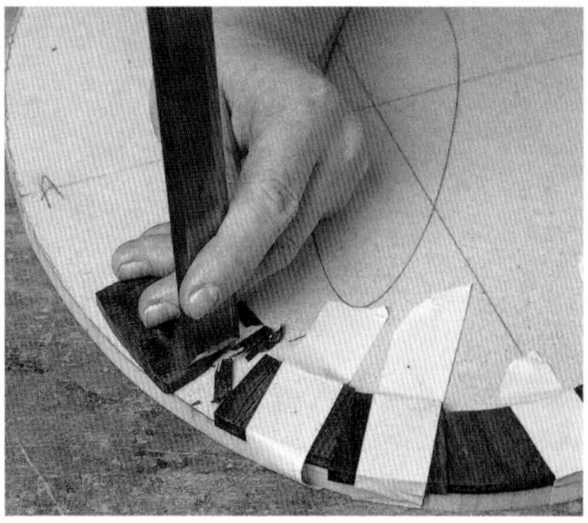

4 Cut along the pencil line with a sharp chisel to make sure that the ends of the pieces butt up (meet) exactly. Tape the new piece in place. Repeat this process until the entire frame is complete.

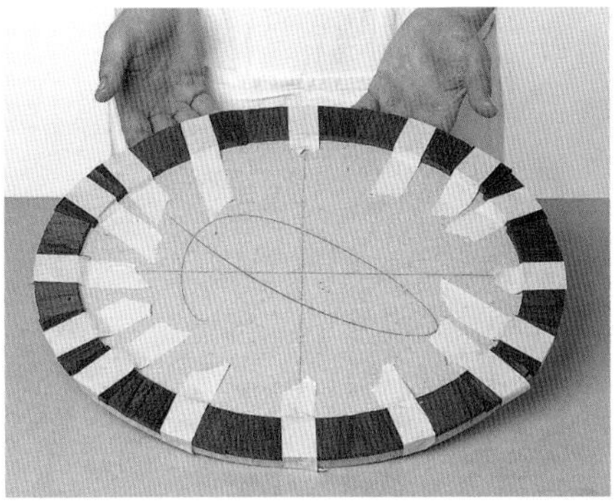

5 The frame is now ready to be glued. Make sure that there are no gaps between the rosewood pieces at this stage.

6 Cut some newspaper to the same size as the rosewood pieces and glue a piece to the underside of one of the wood sections with PVA (white) glue, to stop the frame sticking to the template. Apply glue to the edges of the wood, and a small amount to the paper.

7 Flap back the other pieces out of the way, then place the first piece of rosewood in position on the template and secure it with a G-clamp. Follow this method for the remaining pieces of rosewood, gluing the joints together at their edges. Leave to dry.

8 Remove the clamps, put the template and frame in a vice, and plane the outer edge with a spokeshave. Out of the vice, set a depth gauge to the frame width and score a line around the inner edge of the frame.

9 Clamp the template to the workbench so that part of it overhangs the edge. Drill a pilot hole in the template, against the inner edge of the frame, then use a jigsaw to cut around the scored line in sections.

10 Put the frame, still attached to the MDF, back in the vice and clean up the inner edge with a spokeshave until the surface is completely smooth and flush with the scored line.

▷

Making the frame moulding...continued

11 Clamp the frame and MDF layer to the workbench. Use the spokeshave to mould a convex shape on the front of the frame.

12 Remove the frame and MDF from the clamp. Continue shaping the frame by sanding it with fine-grade sandpaper wrapped around a cork block. The frame must be smooth and even.

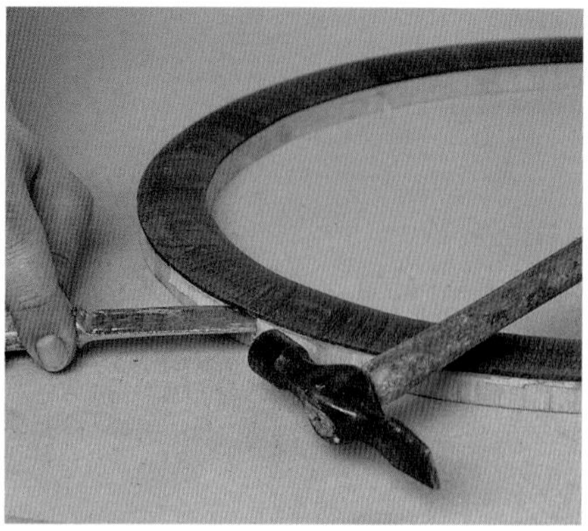

13 Place the frame and MDF on a level surface and insert a flat-bladed knife between the two pieces. Lightly tap the edge of the blade with a hammer until the frame comes away, probably in pieces.

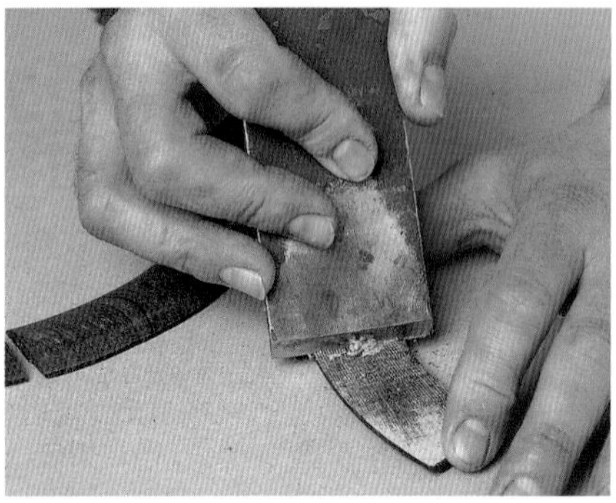

14 Place the pieces of frame in the correct order on the flat surface. Use a blade from a roughing plane to remove any remaining traces of glue or newspaper from the underside of the rosewood.

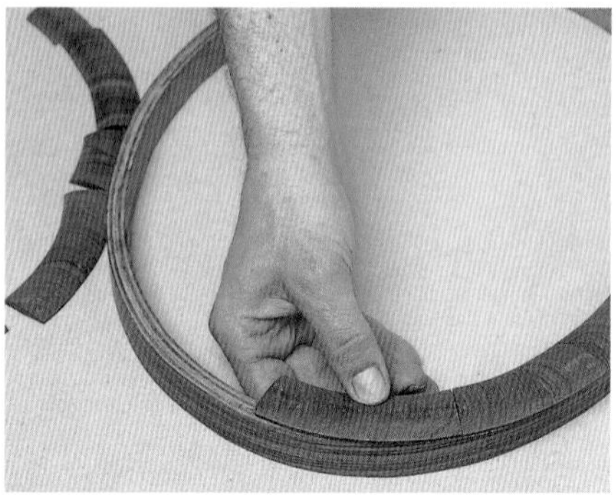

15 Apply scotch glue to the underside of the outer half of each frame section, and place the pieces on the rim, making sure that each piece goes back into the same position it was in on the template. Leave to dry.

16 When the rim is dry, sand it with fine-grade sandpaper and apply some sealer with a brush. This seals the grain before it is polished. Charge a rubber with polish and apply layers to the frame (see pp.66–67).

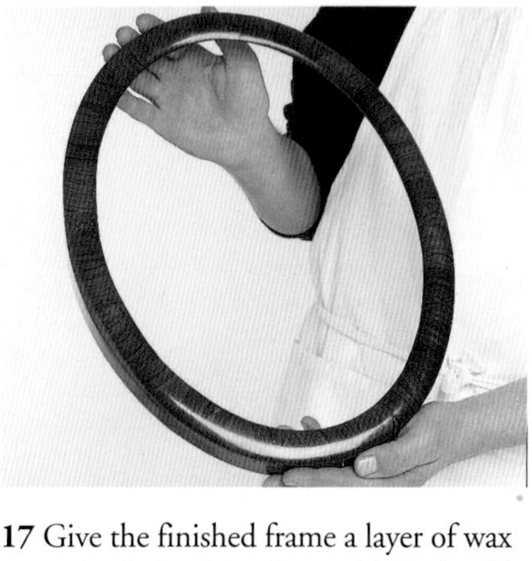

17 Give the finished frame a layer of wax to cut back the shine (see p.67). It should now match the base of the pole screen in colour, grain and finish.

18 Cut a piece of glass (or take it to a glazier) and a piece of 3mm (⅛in) thick plywood to fit inside the rim, and another small piece of plywood for the bracket mounting plate.

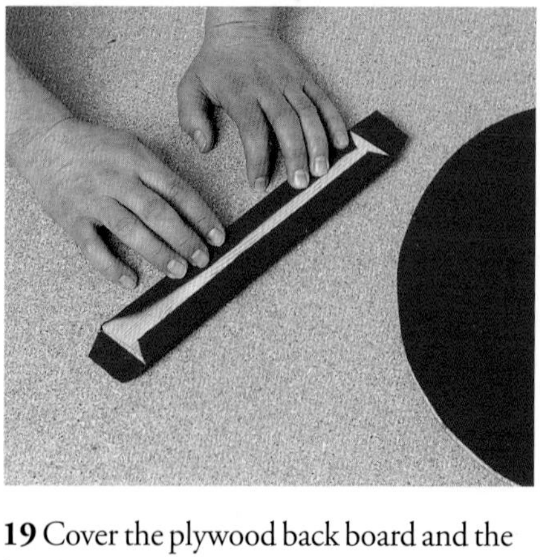

19 Cover the plywood back board and the bracket mounting plate with a suitable coloured silk and join them by screwing them together from the inside.

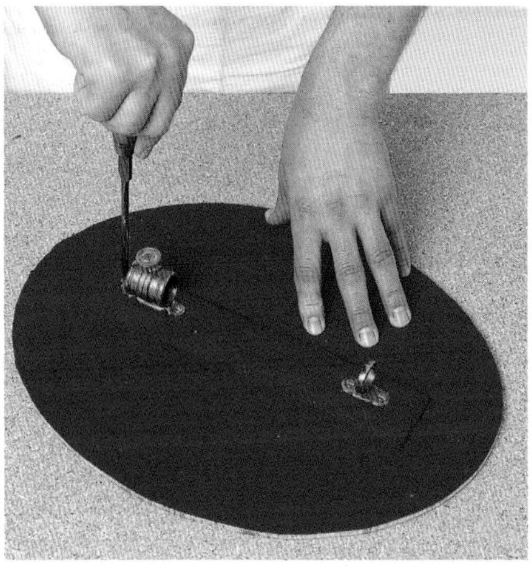

20 Screw either the original or suitable replacement brackets into place. Make sure that they are in the correct position on the back and not upside down. Fit the glass, the piece of fabric and the back board.

21 The back is held in place by a laminated walnut strip. Shape this by feeding it into hot water until it is pliable. Use the reservoir pot from the scotch glue for this process.

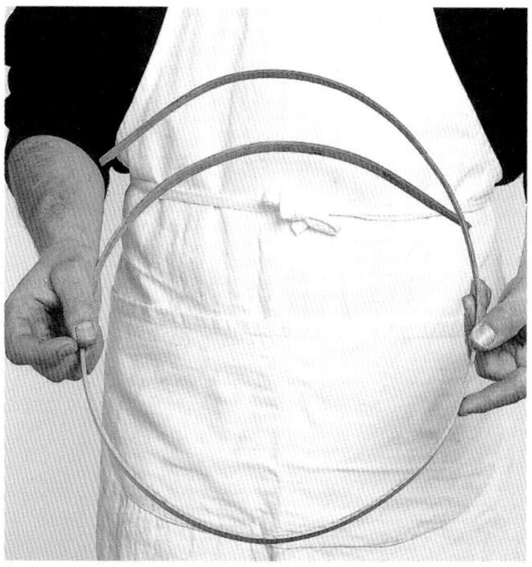

22 When it is wet and pliable, the walnut strip has shaped itself and is suitable to be fitted on to the inside of the rim. Leave it to dry naturally.

23 Fit the walnut strip, now shaped into a curve, inside the frame, trimming it to size with a utility knife. Remove it and apply a black water stain to match the rim (see p.69).

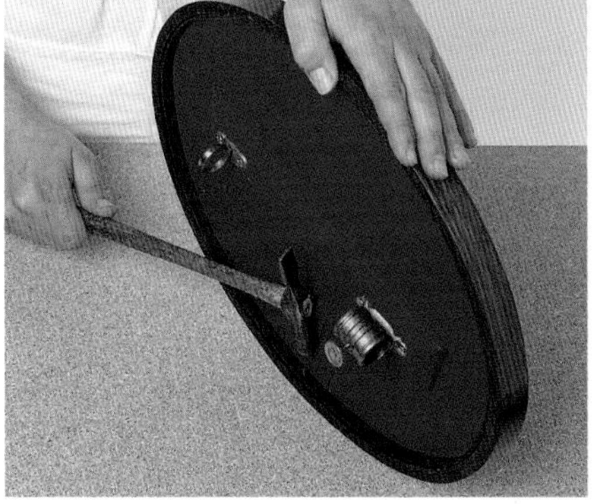

24 Tap the walnut strip back into place , and fix it with steel panel pins (tacks). Attach the frame to the stand using the brass brackets. Repeat for the other screen.

Above: *A pair of rosewood pole screens, sympathetically restored to their original condition.*

Chairs

Of all the types of furniture, chairs often endure a hard life, which can take a toll on their structure. Over the years, the joints become weakened, fine-shaped backs and legs can suffer from breaks, delicate carving can be damaged or lost and upholstery will become worn or simply out of style.

HISTORY OF CHAIRS

One of the most imposing symbols of authority throughout history has been the chair. It was the throne upon which the monarch sat when dispensing justice, and the term "chairperson" still refers to a person in a position of authority. While the material, style and design of the chair have all changed, its basic construction has remained constant, and, whatever its origin, the finest examples are still highly sought after by collectors all over the world.

The chair was one of the scarcest items of furniture to be found in the large halls of medieval Europe. Its use would have been reserved for the master, with the rest of the household sitting on stools or benches. Indeed, the 1594 inventory of Gilling Castle, Yorkshire, England, notes that the great chamber contained 28 stools but only one chair.

There were several styles of chair during the Middle Ages and latter part of the 15th century. Box chairs probably developed from early coffers (see p.204), which had had the back and front posts continued to form supports for the back and arms. Indeed there are examples dating from the late 15th and early 16th centuries in which the seat lifts to give a storage area below, like a coffer. Such examples, known as close chairs, were often elaborately carved to emphasize the importance of the user, and, for comfort, were supplied with a down cushion covered in the finest velvet. The next step was the development, or rather removal, of the boxed section below the sitter, with bold turned legs, joined by low stretchers, replacing the uprights. As with the majority of furniture of this period, the construction was of oak.

During the first part of the 16th century, a second important style of chair emerged and became popular throughout Europe. This was the Italian X-frame chair, which was descended from the ancient Roman high-status curule chair – an upholstered folding seat with curved legs. The X-frame chair consisted simply of webbing strung between side frames to form a seat. The side frames were often covered with expensive velvet or gold cloth, and a cushion was placed on the webs for greater comfort. It is unusual for these chairs to survive, because they were often made of beech, which is prone to infestation. Their development is important, however, as they were the first properly "upholstered" chairs.

Left: *A 17th-century oak box-seat armchair showing how storage was combined with seating from the 15th century to the 17th century.*

A third type of early chair was the back stool. In its simplest form, and as its name suggests, this was a stool with an added back. Its chief characteristic was that its back legs descended vertically from the seat level to the floor. Interestingly, it was called a back stool because all chairs before the late 16th century had arms.

A final category of chair, less elaborate and much easier to make, was the thrown chair, which was usually made from ash, elm or yew. It was constructed of interlacing struts and rails, heavily turned (or "thrown" as it used to be called) with knob and ring decoration. Rather than the mortise and tenon joints found on the X-frame or box chair, the joints would consist of tapering dowel joints. Country craftsmen produced thrown chairs following designs that were handed down from generation to generation, and early examples may be seen in illuminated manuscripts from the 13th and 14th centuries. It is from these earliest designs that, during the 17th and 18th centuries, many regional variations of chair evolved throughout Europe and America. Perhaps the most famous of these rural

Left: *A prime example of how during the late 17th century decorative walnut was used both in the solid and veneer and covered with fine needlework.*

chairs is the Windsor, with its solid wooden seat, turned legs and stick back. The design of thrown chairs has remained remarkably consistent since the 18th century, although features such as cabriole legs, pad feet and pierced back splats have been incorporated from time to time. They were then, and have remained, the chairs of the masses.

The box chair, however, underwent numerous changes, often taking more than one direction in its evolution. The French caquetoire, or gossip chair, became fashionable toward the middle of the 16th century. It had a seat that narrowed toward the tall, narrow back and splayed arms. By the end of the century, a simple chair known as the farthingale evolved. Named after the whalebone-hooped petticoats that supported the large skirts then fashionable, the farthingale chair allowed a lady to sit without becoming wedged between the arms (it had none).

During the mid-17th century, armchairs would often have had elaborate carved uprights, stretchers and backs, the backs being combined with cane, velvet or leather. Oak remained a popular wood, but walnut – which was cheaper and could be more easily turned and carved – was becoming increasingly popular.

Comfort was also playing an increasingly important role in chair design: the angle of the back became less upright, and fully upholstered backs and seats were introduced. The walnut show wood was, on occasion, being replaced on the finest chairs with gesso, which was then carved, painted and gilded. While during the 15th and early 16th centuries chairs had been produced by coffer-makers, by the late 17th century a new breed of cabinet-maker, including Thomas Roberts and Daniel Marot, became closely associated with designing chairs. Marot was largely responsible for promoting the new Anglo-Dutch style. The early part of the 18th century saw the introduction of a new and distinctive type of walnut chair. It had a wide, shaped back, centred by a veneered or carved vase-shaped splat, above a curved seat, and would stand on cabriole legs often finished with pad feet. The earliest examples were strengthened with stretchers, but these were later abandoned in favour of a cleaner line. Later ball and claw or lion's paw feet were favoured in place of pad feet. It was from this point that the true diversity of style and function can be seen. Armchairs covered in needlework or velvet were designed to sit beside open fires, salon chairs were destined for the drawing room and shaped veneered back chairs, with their drop-in seats, were designed to be used at the dining table.

The Palladian movement of the early to mid-18th century, which reflected a revival of interest in classic Roman styles, coincided with the increased use of Cuban mahogany in furniture making in response to a French embargo on the export of walnut. Mahogany, with its dense grain, was ideally suited to the rich carving demanded by this architecturally inspired movement, and there developed a new type of chair, the Gainsborough, to adorn the galleries, libraries and drawing

Right: *By the mid-18th century, the finest mahogany Gainsboroughs were festooned with foliate carving.*

▷

Left: *By the early 19th century, Greco-Roman and Egyptian themes were influencing chair designs.*

rooms of elegant country houses. Later in the century, with the emergence of designers and furniture-makers such as Thomas Chippendale (1718–79), William Ince (d.1804) and John Mayhew (fl.1758–1804), combined with the need to illustrate one's wealth, wonderfully carved sets of dining chairs, heavily influenced by the rococo and French style, began to emerge.

The next significant change in fashion was the emergence of neoclassical designs and influences during the second half of the 18th century. The architect and furniture designer Robert Adam (1728–92) oversaw the introduction of a lighter, more classical look, and the use of gilt decoration with delicate carved foliate and Greek mythology themes began to prevail. The requirement for a finer, more elegant impression toward the end of the 18th century, as championed by Thomas Sheraton (1751–1806), led to chairs also being decorated with japanning, paint and gilt.

During the early 19th century, the trend toward a finer line of construction began to be reversed, with chair designs being more affected by the growing interest in other cultures and histories. In Europe, Greco-Roman and Egyptian themes were rapidly adopted, while in France these same ancient cultures provided the inspiration for the Empire furniture encouraged by Napoleon, himself an emperor.

Designs were varied and, during the 18th and 19th centuries, a number of new types of chair emerged. These included the bergère, a chair with a mahogany or rosewood frame supporting a canework back and seat panels, the hall chair, with its solid mahogany back and seat, and the reading chair, with its unusual design allowing it to be sat on in reverse and, on the finest examples, an arrangement of trays, candle slides and reading slopes.

With the emergence of the merchant classes during the mid- to late 19th century, chair production was vastly increased. Mahogany, now cheaper to import, was more commonly used. With the emphasis on function rather than fashion, chairs become bolder and more robust in design. Outside the main stream of commercial development, however, completely different thoughts about furniture were being expressed. William Morris (1834–96) was one of those in the Arts and Crafts movement who championed traditional handcrafting methods over the poor quality of much machine production. In France, the natural, curving forms of the Art Nouveau movement, led by such makers as Emile Gallé, gave a completely new look to chairs.

In the 20th century, a fresh approach to design emerged, with the Art Deco movement using old and new techniques of furniture decoration – from lacquering to covering in mirror glass – to produce pieces that looked thoroughly modern. Later in the century, new materials, including chrome and laminates, were experimented with, producing landmark pieces such as the American designer Charles Eames's classic rosewood laminated chair of the mid-20th century. With the rapid increase in communication networks compared to the 18th and 19th centuries, designs went in and out of fashion much more rapidly than in previous historical periods and reached a more global audience.

Above: *A mid-20th-century, laminated birch dining chair designed by Charles and Ray Eames.*

CHAIR CONSTRUCTION

All antique chairs were individually made and so subject to minor variations. These variations can be accounted for not only by the chair's date of origin but also by its place of manufacture; they can even point to a particular cabinet-maker. For this reason, prior to any restoration, a close inspection should be made of a chair's construction so that any repairs can be carried out in as close a style as possible to the original cabinet-maker's work.

Unlike modern chairs, an antique chair can incorporate numerous construction methods. As a general rule, the earlier the chair the simpler the construction will be. For instance, the thrown chair dating from the medieval period has simple tapering dowel joints holding the legs and arms to the seat. At the same period, an early settle or framed chair will incorporate mortise and tenon joints. For extra strength, these will have a dowel drilled through and fitted into the tenon. By the late 17th century, most quality chairs have a mortise and tenon jointing the legs to the frame. During the 19th century, dowel peg joints often replaced the traditional mortise and tenon.

Corner blocks also altered over the centuries. These blocks, known as webs, were cut into rebates in the seat frame in the 18th century. However, on a chair with a drop-in seat, they can simply be small solid corner blocks that help to secure the corners of the seat rail and act as supports for the seat. By the mid- to late 19th century, the blocks were larger, solid triangles and were screwed to the inside of the frame.

Stretchers are another construction detail to look for. Again, like all the other features, the date of manufacture of the chair often dictated their form. Their use declined generally by the 19th century.

Varying designs of backs have been used, ranging from plain stick backs on perhaps a thrown chair or Windsor to the most fabulous carved interlace backs on the finest of Chippendale's chairs. If the seat was a stuff-over example, then a "shoe", which is basically a shaped cover piece, would have been placed over the upholstery. The shoe was designed to hide the holding tacks at the back of the seat frame.

Right: *The illustration shows the basic components of a chair with a classic drop-in seat.*

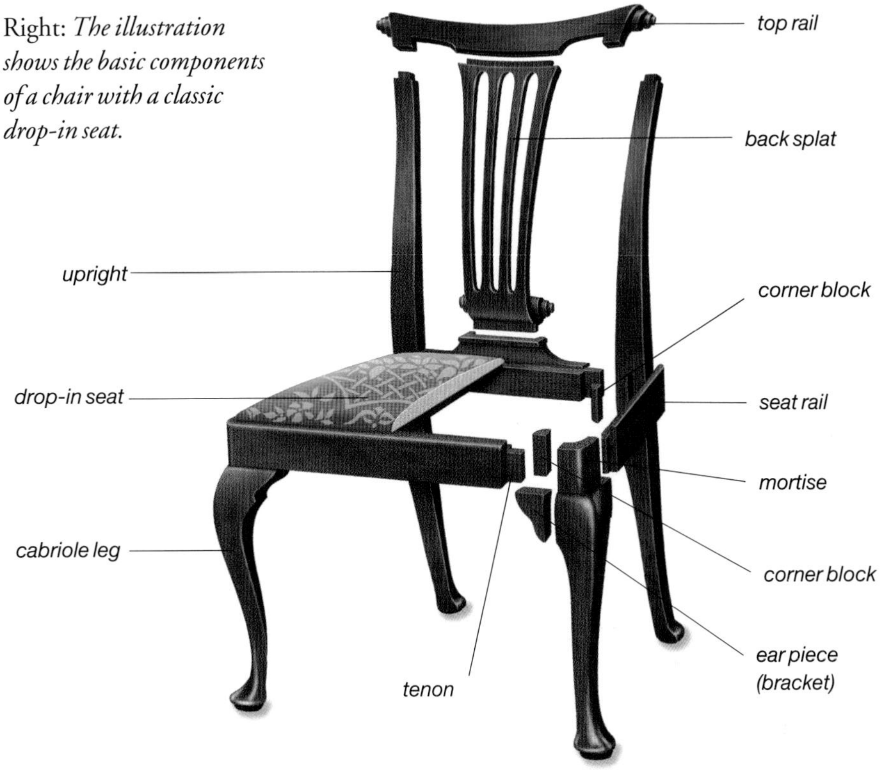

Right: *With a stuff-over seat, certain constructional changes are made in the manufacture of the chair.*

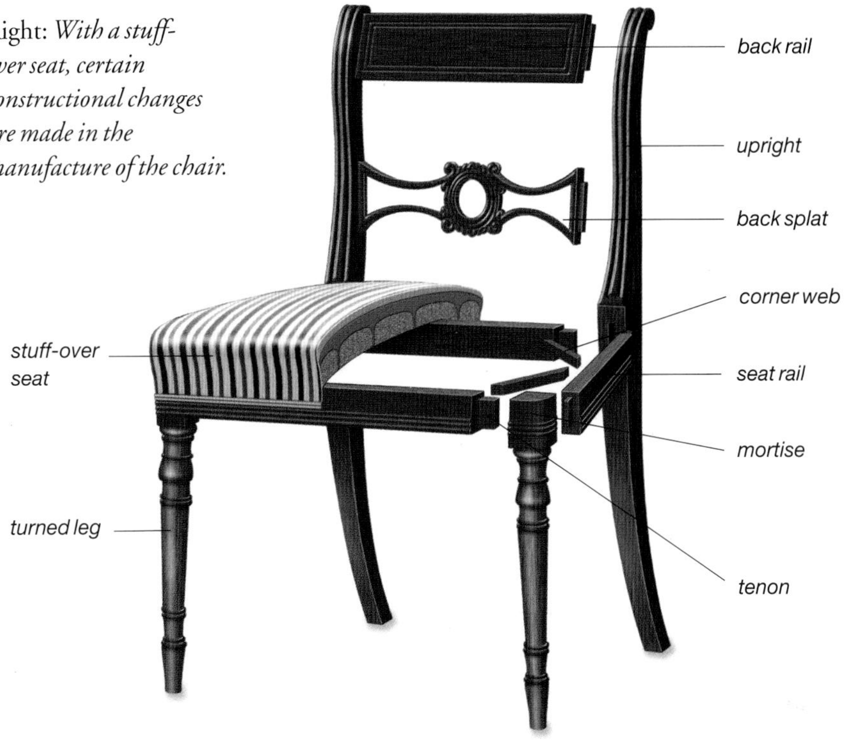

Dismantling and reassembling chairs

Learning how to dismantle and reassemble chairs is an important skill for the furniture restorer. One of the most common problems in chairs is loose joints, and the easiest way to rectify this problem is to dismantle the whole chair, reglue the joints and reassemble the chair. Other damage, such as to the frames and backs of chairs, may require a chair to be dismantled only partly before the restorer can start to put the problem right.

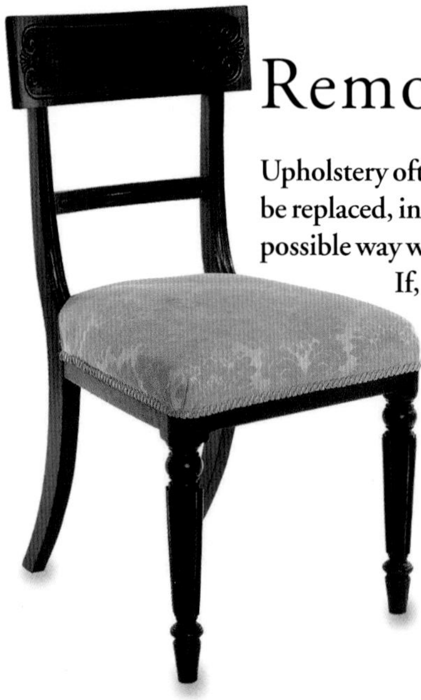

Removing upholstery

Upholstery often sustains the most damage and may need to be replaced, in which case it can be removed in the quickest possible way without regard for any damage that it may suffer. If, however, the upholstery is in good condition, it should be removed carefully so that it can be replaced once the frame has been repaired. The upholstery on this single Regency dining chair is in good condition, but it must be removed so that the damage to the back can be repaired. A careful and methodical approach must be employed to ensure that the upholstery is not damaged and remains in a suitable condition to be reused, if wished.

MATERIALS AND EQUIPMENT

- **tack remover**
- **heavy mallet**
- **ripping chisel**
- **narrow, flat-bladed tool**
- **pincers**
- **utility knife**

1 Place the chair upside down on a protected workbench (a blanket can be spread over it) and remove the tacks from the dust cover with a tack remover and heavy mallet. The latter is used because its weight will ensure that a gentle wrist action will knock out the tacks. Work along the grain, not across it, to avoid splitting the seat rail.

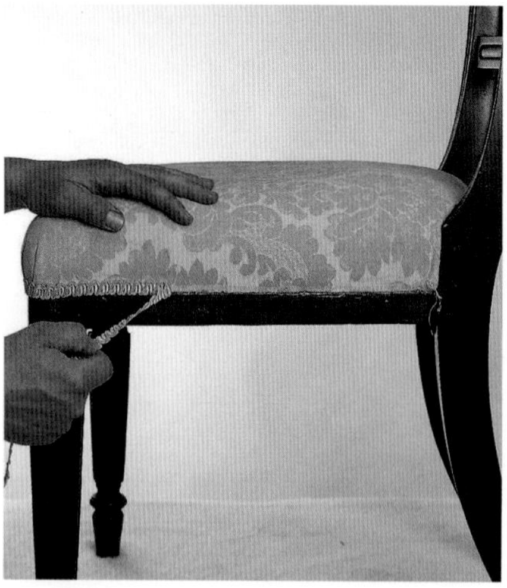

2 Decorative braid is often held in place by glue and a few gimp pins, as is the case here. Remove the pins with a ripping chisel,then pull the braid off. Alternatively, the braid may simply be glued on. If the chair is close-nailed, the nails can easily be knocked out with a tack remover and mallet.

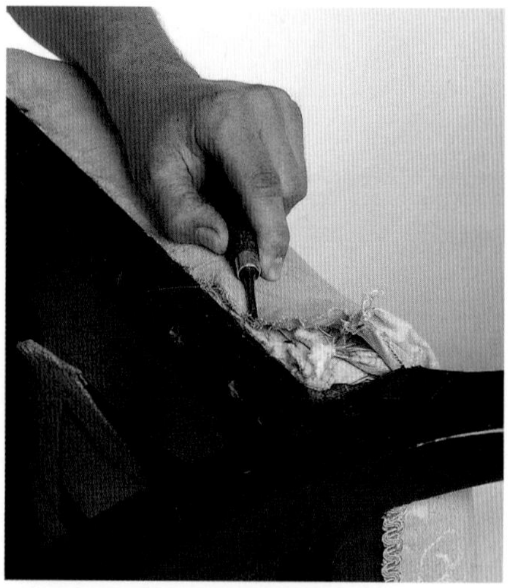

3 Turn the chair on to its side to remove the top cover. Handle the fabric carefully because it may be refitted after the chair is repaired. Remove the upholstery tacks with a tack remover, as in step 1, and remove any staples by slipping a narrow, flat-bladed tool between the staples and frame to lift them, before pulling them out with pincers.

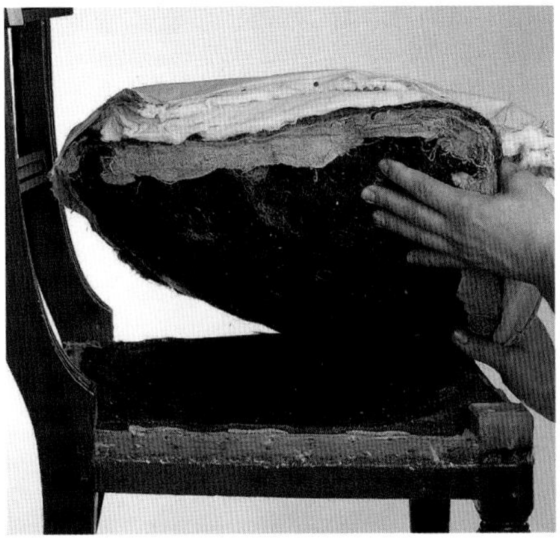

4 With the top cover removed, you can detach the various layers of material and stuffing from the seat. Do this with a tack remover and a heavy mallet. If necessary, remove each layer separately. You may need to use a utility knife to cut through some of the layers of upholstery.

5 Once you have removed all the tacks, lift away the top cover. Keep the horsehair and other stuffing materials safely together.

6 Finally, remove and discard the webbings. These will often be attached with the largest tacks found on the chair, which will require strong blows with the mallet. Make sure that the chair is secure on the bench; if possible, ask someone to hold it for you.

Knocking the chair apart

The majority of restoration techniques, regardless of the style or type of chair, will require the chair to be partially or completely dismantled. As the term "knocking apart" suggests, the chair will be taken to pieces with the aid of a mallet and/or hammer. This should be done with care and patience, however, to make sure that further damage is not caused in the process. The frame of this chair is in quite good condition, so care must be taken when knocking it apart to ensure that no damage is caused to the joints.

MATERIALS AND EQUIPMENT

- masking tape
- pincers
- hardwood block
- hammer
- screwdriver
- drill
- wood drill bit
- metal drill bit

1 First, label all the parts of the chair. With a single chair, the various components will be obvious. If more than one chair is being repaired at the same time, however, parts can easily be confused, causing a major problem when you try to reassemble them.

2 Check to see if the corner blocks have been nailed to the frame. If they have, remove the nails with pincers. Once the nails are removed, or if no nails were used, place a block of hardwood against each corner block in turn to protect it from bruising, and give a firm hammer blow. Remove the blocks.

3 Next, unscrew any metal brackets. These are often found where a chair has been broken and repaired in the past. While these solve a problem in the short term, at a later stage the repaired joint will work itself loose again.

Knocking the chair apart...continued

4 Make a quick inspection of the chair to look for any tenon pegs and screws that may have been put through the mortise and tenon joints to strengthen them. If you find any, drill them out.

5 Knock the side seat rails apart from the back uprights. Lift the back clear of the workbench and apply a series of firm blows to the back near the joints, protecting the uprights with the hardwood block.

Tip

If a joint is particularly tight, it may help to inject methylated spirits (methyl alcohol) into it. This will soften the glue and aid dismantling.

6 Follow the same process with the other seat-rail joints at the front of the chair. If some joints are very tight and cannot be knocked apart without causing damage, try the Tip (top right) or leave them as they are.

7 Finally, knock the back seat rail, back support and top rail away from the back upright. Note that for many chair repairs the knocking apart can stop before this stage, with the back left intact.

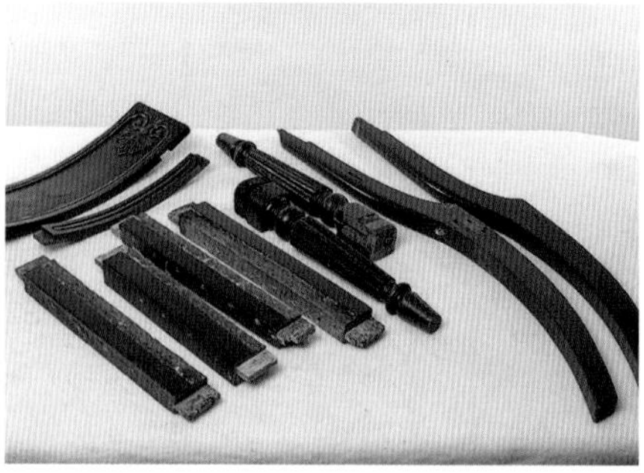

8 Once the chair is knocked apart, double-check that all the components are present before you begin restoration work.

Reassembling the chair

Once any necessary repair work has been undertaken, the chair can be reassembled. While chairs come in various styles, shapes and woods, the steps necessary to reassemble them remain fairly consistent. The process of gluing the chair joints together during reassembly will cure many problems, such as wobbly legs and creaking.

MATERIALS AND EQUIPMENT

- **toothbrush**
- **rasp or file**
- **PVA (white) glue**
- **sash clamps**
- **clamping blocks**
- **gauge sticks**
- **hardwood block**
- **hammer**

▷ **1** Clean all the joints using either a toothbrush and hot water, which will dissolve the animal glue, or, if this is not successful, a rasp or file. Be careful to remove only the old glue and not any of the wood itself, because any reduction in tenon thickness results in a sloppy joint.

2 Glue the front legs and seat rail together and secure them with a sash clamp and clamping blocks. Check that the legs are parallel by measuring the gap at the top and bottom. Leave to dry overnight.

3 Glue the back uprights together, making sure the back support is inserted at the same time as the back seat rail. As with the front legs, ensure that the uprights are parallel. Clamp to secure and leave to dry overnight.

4 Remove the sash clamps and fit the side seat rails to hold the chair together. Stand the chair on a flat surface while doing this to ensure that it sits level and does not rock. Apply sash clamps.

◁ **5** Before the glue is dry, check that the seat frame is square by comparing both diagonals with pointed gauge sticks held firmly together. If any adjustment is needed, loosen the clamps, ease the joint(s) slightly, retighten the clamps, then check again.

▷ **6** When the glue has dried, add the corner blocks, tapping them lightly into place and using a block of wood to prevent bruising. Leave the sash clamps in place while doing this to make sure that the tapping does not loosen the joint.

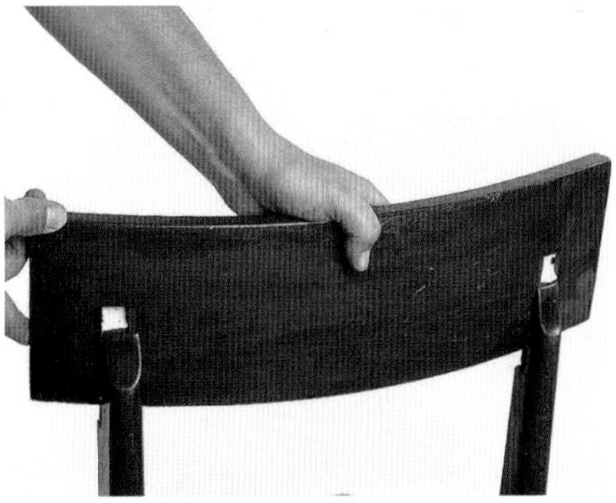

7 Now you can fit the back top rail. This chair has sliding dovetails for the joints, and so the top rail is fitted last. In chairs where the back top rail is mortised and tenoned, however, it should be fitted when the two back uprights are glued together.

8 Clamp the bowed back in place under light pressure, using clamping blocks to ensure that no bruising occurs.

Right: *Once the reassembled chair has been re-upholstered (see pp. 129–133), it should last for years before needing further repair.*

Repairing arms and legs

The arms and legs of chairs are particularly vulnerable to damage and suffer all manner of problems. The most common of these is scuffing to the feet, which is inevitable and, in severe cases, can lead to the wearing away of the feet until eventually they must be cut off and replaced. Chairs are often not treated properly, with users leaning back on them too hard or balancing on the rear two legs, which puts tremendous strain on the structure, leading to failure of the joints or breakages of the frame. Even the worst damage can, however, be put right.

Restoring a scuffed foot

Everyday wear and tear takes its toll on most items of furniture, and chairs in particular. This claw and ball chair is more prone to scuffed feet than most because its feet are quite pronounced. Some of the scratches and dents on this foot are quite severe, but they are part of its history and do not need to be repaired. Sympathetic restoration should improve the condition of the item but care, as always, should be taken not to remove any existing colour and patination. The repairs to the surface should be blended in to match the existing finish.

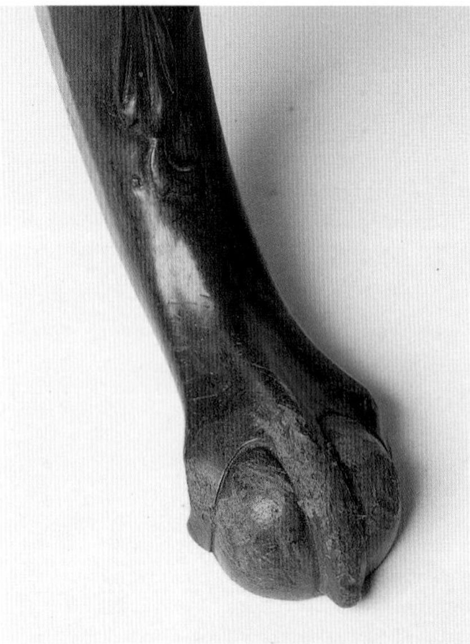

MATERIALS AND EQUIPMENT
- **fine-grade sandpaper**
- **brush**
- **spirit-based (alcohol-based) stain**
- **rubber**
- **polish**

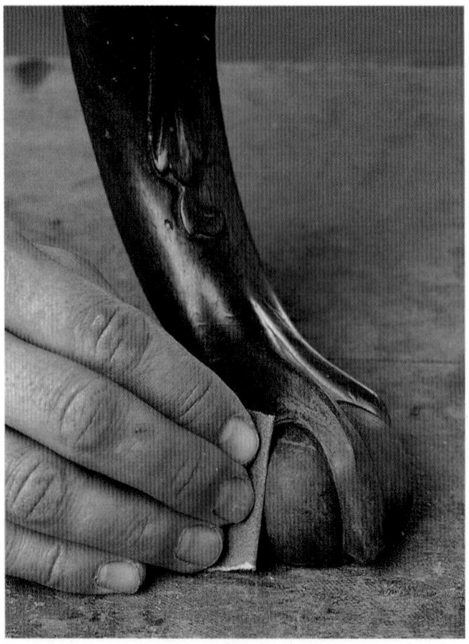

1 Place the chair on a workbench and go over the scuffed area with fine-grade sandpaper until you have removed the old polish and any other debris.

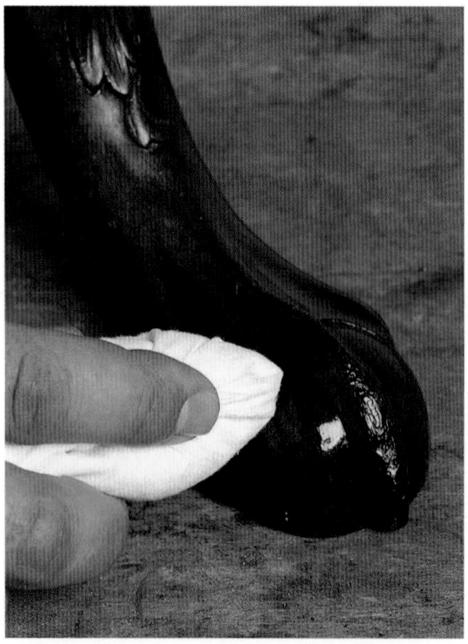

2 Mix some stain to the required colour (see p.41) and brush this over the foot, then use a rubber to polish the foot to match the rest of the chair (see pp.66–67).

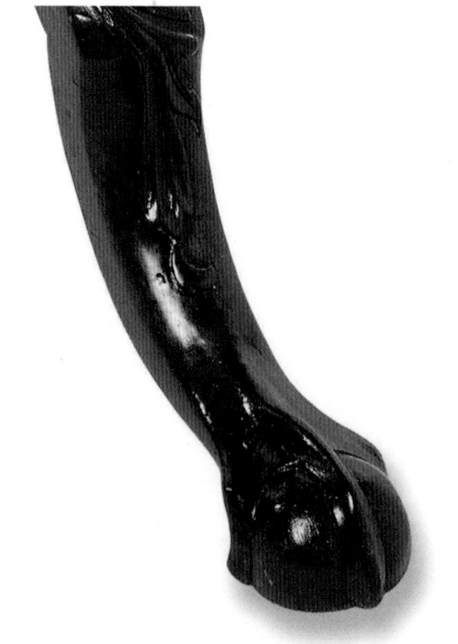

Above: *The restored foot has not been made to look brand new, which would make it stand out from the rest of the chair, but has simply had its colour and sheen restored.*

Replacing a chewed arm

Some dogs and cats have a propensity for gnawing, chewing or sharpening their teeth on wooden furniture. Sometimes the damage inflicted is just a few scratches, but in other cases the furniture needs substantial rebuilding. This 18th-century Cuban mahogany child's rocking chair has had its arm and leg almost completely chewed off by the family dog. Before the arm and leg can be rebuilt, some of the damaged wood must be removed.

MATERIALS AND EQUIPMENT

- Cuban mahogany
- PVA (white) glue
- sash clamp
- coping saw
- spokeshave
- fine-grade sandpaper
- brush
- spirit-based (alcohol-based) stain
- rubber
- polish

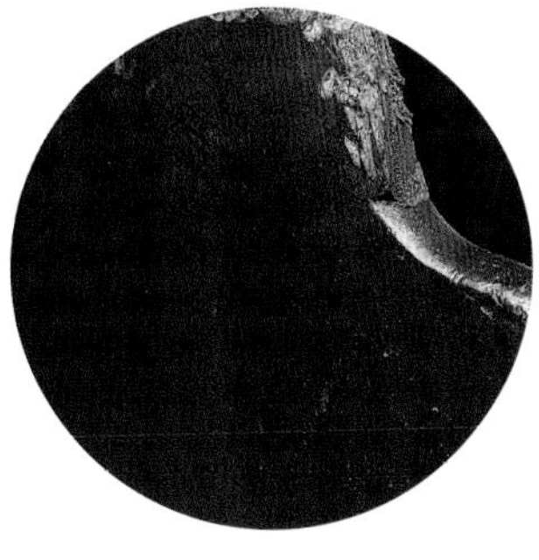

Above: *The chewed-off arm.*

1 Select appropriate replacement mahogany pieces and build up the rough shape of the arm in layers, using PVA (white) glue, and starting on the inside surface. Make the rebuilt arm slightly larger than the original.

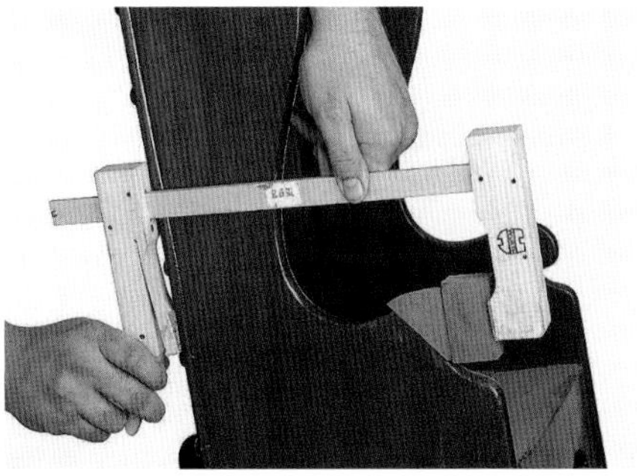

2 Glue a single block of mahogany to the outer surface, and a larger block to the front of this. Then clamp the rebuilt arm in position. Leave the sash clamp in position until the glue is dry.

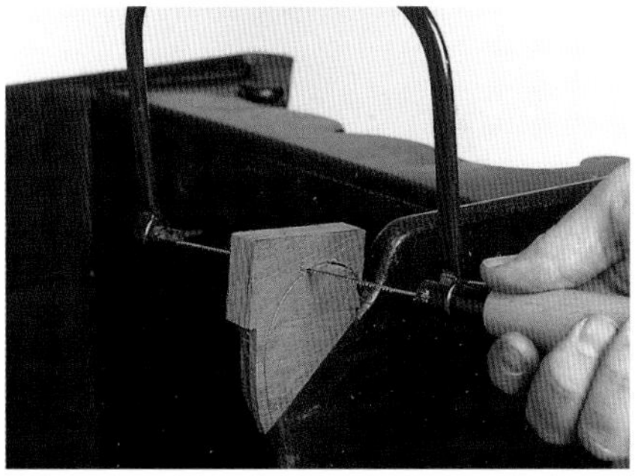

3 Remove the clamp and draw the shape of the arm on the new wood, slightly larger than the original. Cut along this line with a coping saw.

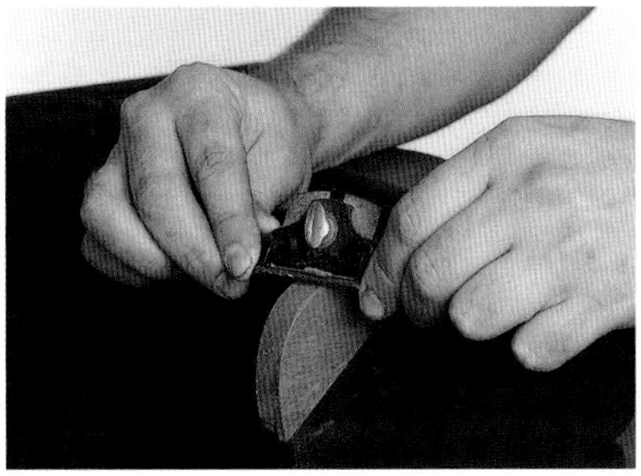

4 Shape the surface with a spokeshave, copying the contours of the other arm. Continue until you have an exact match. Repeat this process for the damaged leg.

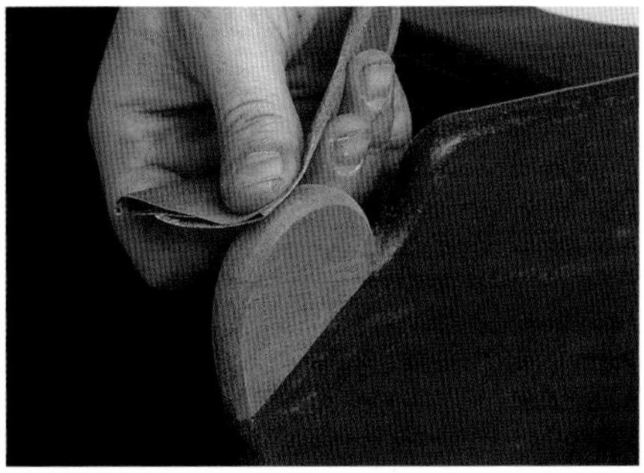

5 Smooth both repairs with fine-grade sandpaper. Mix some stain to the required colour (see p.41), brush this over the repairs, then polish to match the rest of the chair.

Right: *Once polished, the repairs become invisible, restoring the chair to its former state.*

Repairing a cabriole leg

This 19th-century Victorian walnut balloon-back chair has a typical break to its leg. The curved shape of the cabriole leg, combined with the inherent weakness of walnut along the grain, means that this type of chair design is particularly vulnerable to damage, especially if misused.

Although this leg has a clean break, simply regluing it would not give it enough strength. Instead, a dowel must be inserted into holes drilled in both parts of the leg, which are then glued together to give a strong and lasting repair. The technique is quite straightforward, the most critical stage being the alignment and drilling of the dowel holes in the two broken pieces. Fortunately, there is a simple method of achieving this, using nothing more than a nail.

MATERIALS AND EQUIPMENT

- hammer
- 25mm (1in) nail
- snips or cutters
- pliers
- drill
- wood drill bits
- dowel
- thin chisel
- wood glue
- snap clamps
- fine-grade sandpaper
- rubber
- polish

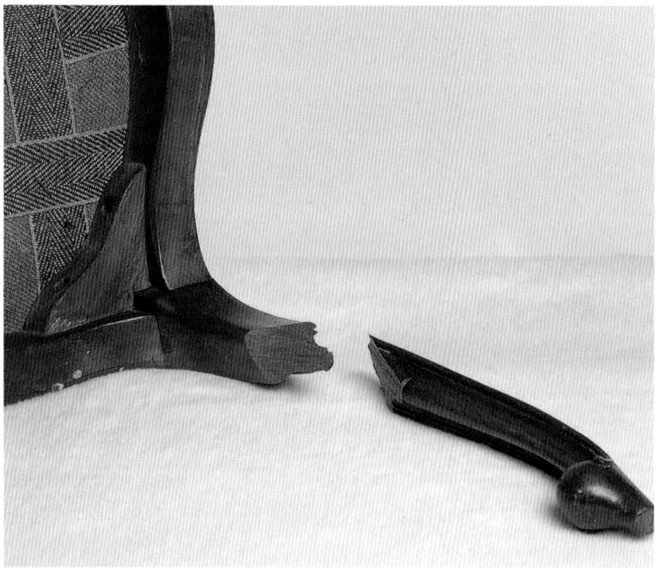

▷ **1** Place the chair upside down on a protected workbench. Hammer a 25mm/1in nail halfway into the centre of the upper section of the leg to provide a means of marking matching dowel hole positions on both pieces of the leg.

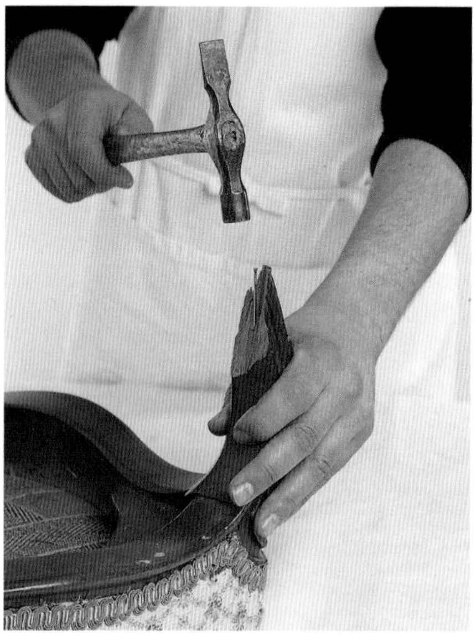

2 Cut the nail to a short, sharp point using a pair of snips or cutters.

3 The projecting piece of nail will now be used to mark the centre of the lower section of the leg.

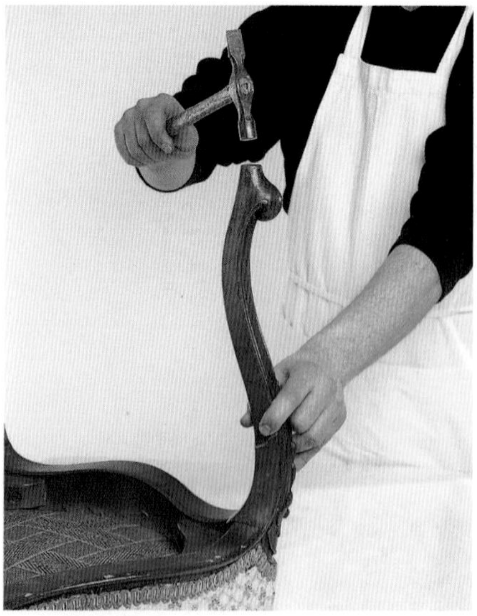

4 Bring the two sections of the leg together and tap the lower section down so that the nail leaves an indentation on its broken surface. Remove the lower section and pull out the piece of nail with a pair of pliers.

5 Drill a small pilot hole in both sections of the leg, using the indentations left by the nail as guides.

6 Select a dowel that is about a third of the width of the leg and about 75mm/3in long. Use a drill bit of the same size as the dowel to drill holes about 38mm/1½in deep in both sections of the leg.

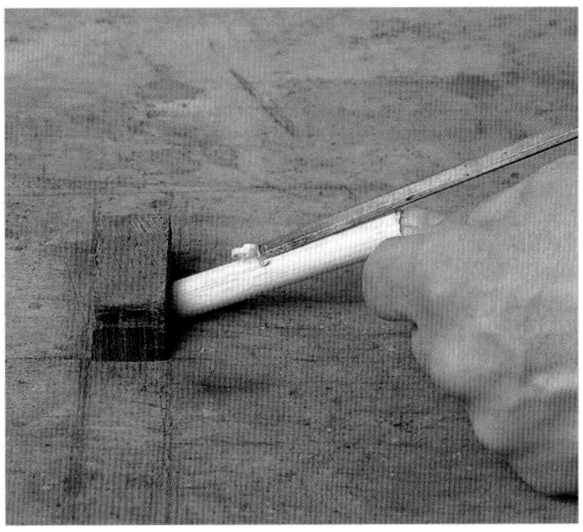

7 Rest the dowel against a block fixed to the workbench, and use a thin chisel to cut a narrow sliver along the length of the dowel. This will allow excess glue to escape.

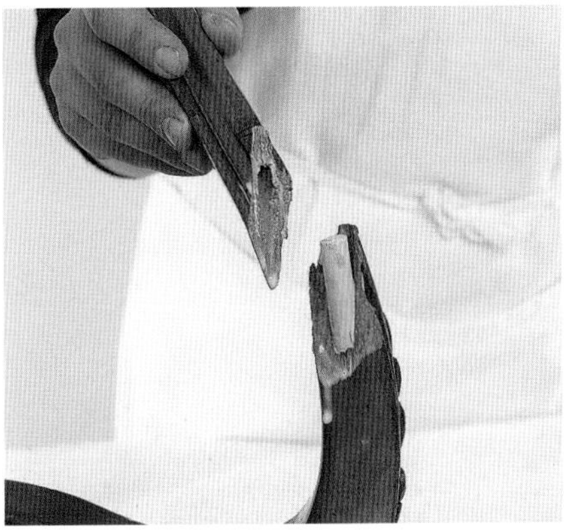

◁ **8** Apply glue to both matching faces and the dowel, then insert the dowel into the upper section, tapping it down with a hammer if necessary, and bring the two parts together.

▷ **9** Make sure that the edges are flush, then clamp the leg sections together with snap clamps and leave the glue to dry.

10 Remove the clamps and stand the chair upright. Sandpaper the area of repair, then polish it so that it matches the rest of the chair (see pp.66–67).

Right: *Once polished, the repair should not be visible, while the strength of the chair leg will have been increased significantly.*

Repairing a broken upright

This Georgian chair shows a common problem: the user has sat back perhaps a little too heavily and broken the chair at the weakest point, along the long grain, just above the seat level.

In this instance, a previous repair had been carried out and the break had followed the line of the old damage. This illustrates how make-shift repairs are only temporary measures. To create a more permanent repair, a new piece of wood must be inserted to enable the two parts of the broken upright to be secured properly.

MATERIALS AND EQUIPMENT

- white cardboard
- profile gauge
- tenon saw
- plane
- scissors
- mahogany
- band saw
- PVA (white) glue
- G-clamps
- clamping blocks
- spokeshave
- sash clamps
- fine-grade sandpaper
- fine brush
- stain
- rubber
- polish

1 Place the chair on a protected workbench, remove the upholstery (see pp.102–103), then knock the chair apart following steps 1–5 on pp.103–104. Place the undamaged upright on a large piece of white cardboard and use a profile gauge to trace its outline. This is the template (pattern) for the new piece of wood.

2 Now knock the back uprights apart from the stretcher, back seat rail, back support and back top rail.

Tip

When marking out a template on a shaped upright, a simple workshop-made profile gauge is best. Join an upright to a face plate at right angles and drill a hole through that allows the refill from a ballpoint pen to be inserted.

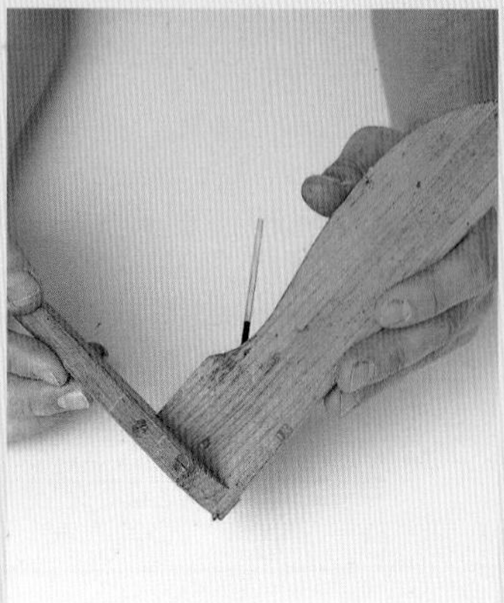

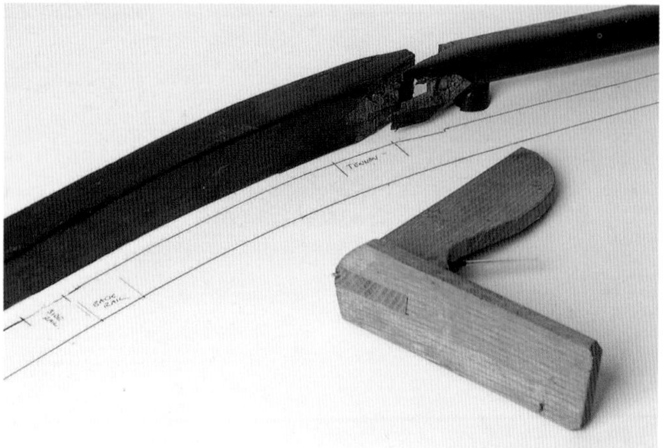

3 Compare the broken upright to the traced outline.

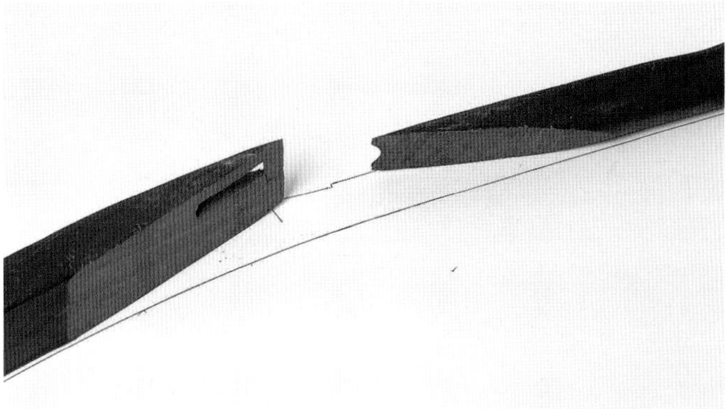

◁ **5** Cut out the cardboard template. Place it on a matching piece of mahogany, then mark the correct shape. Cut along this line with a band saw.

4 Cut away the damage with a tenon saw and plane the edges of the two parts flat. Lay the parts on the pattern in the correct position. The gap will indicate the size of the new part to be inserted.

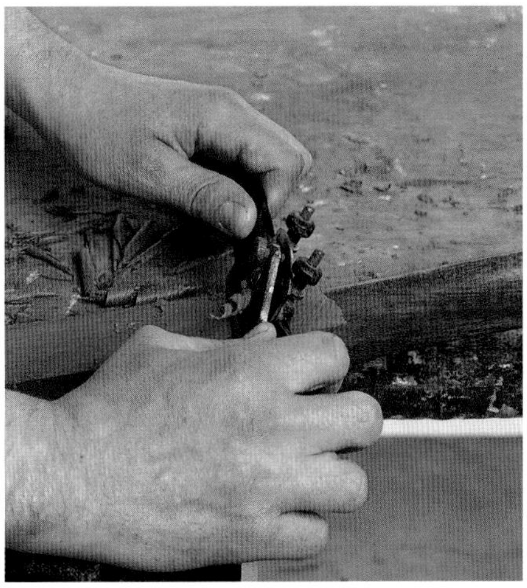

6 Glue the matching piece of mahogany securely into position between the two pieces of the upright. Clamp it securely and leave to dry overnight – this will ensure a secure bond.

7 Form the correct shape with a spokeshave, using the undamaged upright as your guide. Cut three new mortises (see p.119) in the upright to house the tenons of the side and back seat rails and the back support.

8 Reassemble the chair back and clamp until dry. Remove the clamps, then finish shaping the new wood with fine-grade sandpaper.

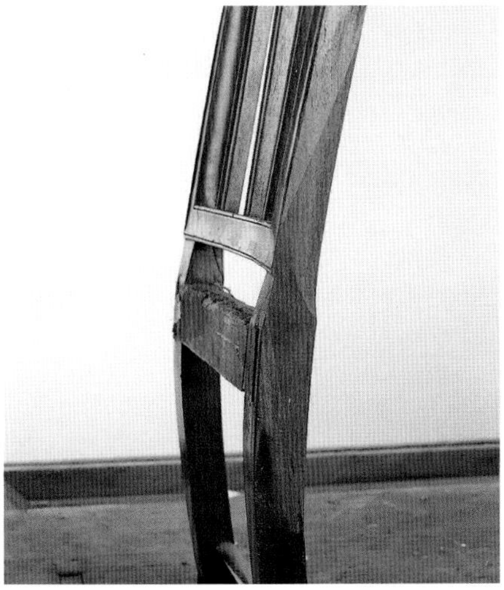

◁ **9** The final shape should now match the other upright exactly. Stain the replacement mahogany (see p.69) and polish the repairs to match the existing chair (see pp.66–67) before reassembling the whole chair (see pp.104–105). Replace the upholstery (see pp.129–133).

Right: *The new joint on the restored chair should be almost invisible.*

Repairing a broken arm

Almost all arms on chairs have two points of fixing: one on a back upright, the other against a seat rail. Some are housed with a tenon or dovetail joint, while others may simply be placed flush and held with large screws. When faced with a damaged arm, as with all other restoration work, the first step is to examine the damage and ascertain the construction methods used in the piece. With this information, the correct procedure and techniques can then be determined.

The arm of this maple chair had become loose against both the seat rail and the back upright. This could have been caused by any number of events, including being dropped or knocked, or being picked up by the arms rather than by the seat. The arm must be removed and assessed before being reassembled.

MATERIALS AND EQUIPMENT
- screwdriver
- hammer
- hardwood block
- chisel
- toothbrush
- PVA (white) glue
- G-clamp
- snap clamps
- clamping blocks

1 Place the chair on its side on a workbench, and loosen and remove the two large screws that hold the arm support to the side seat rail. The screws, which are fixed from the inside of the rail, are usually hidden by the drop-in upholstered seat. Keep the screws for reattaching the arm support.

2 Gently ease the arm tenon out of the mortise in the back upright, so that the whole arm structure is now detached from the chair. The dowel peg joint between the arm and arm support is also found to be loose. Place the arm on the workbench and tap off the joint using a block of hardwood and a hammer.

3 Remove any lumps of old glue from the joints using a sharp chisel, taking care not to mark any polished areas. If a crystalline residue is present, then an animal adhesive has been used; remove this with an old toothbrush and hot water. The water will soften and dissolve the glue, but make sure that it does not run and cause marks.

4 Check that all the joints are tight, then reglue them and reattach the arm and the support to each other and to the chair. Use a G-clamp to secure the support to the seat rail and snap clamps to secure the arm to the back upright and the arm to the arm support. Use clamping blocks at all clamping points; if the chair upright is bowed, you will need to pre-shape a clamping block to fit.

Left: *Once the glue has dried and the clamps have been removed, the chair should be as sturdy as when first made.*

Removing a broken screw

If a screw has remained in a piece of furniture for many years, perhaps even hundreds of years, it may have become weak, and when you try to remove it, the shank may break. If this happens, there are three possible solutions.

You may be able to make a new, temporary screw from the damaged one by cutting a new slot in the broken shank (see steps).

Alternatively, you could drill a hole, slightly larger than the screw shank, down the side of the screw, then tap it sideways into this hole with a screwdriver. This will allow you to remove it with a pair of long-nose (needlenose) pliers. You will have to plug the hole with a glued-in wooden dowel before reusing it.

Finally, you could simply drill out the screw with a metal drill bit of the same size, or slightly larger; but again you will have to plug the resulting hole in order to be able to reuse it.

1 *If the shank of a screw breaks when you try to remove it, leaving a stub proud of the surface, cut a new slot in the end of the shank with a hacksaw.*

2 *Remove the screw simply by undoing it in the normal fashion. The metal will be weak, so use a screwdriver that fits snugly into the slot.*

Reeding a turned chair leg

During the 18th century, reeded decoration on turned legs came into fashion. The legs were tapered, and so the reeding also had to taper from top to bottom, as well as being equally balanced around the leg. In order to do this work, a scratch box is used (see below). The scratch box has parallel sides and adjustable centre points at each end to allow a shaped reed cutter to be applied to the turned leg. In this instance, one leg from a Sheraton chair, c.1790, has been broken and lost, so a replacement is needed.

MATERIALS AND EQUIPMENT

- callipers
- wood
- lathe
- turning tools
- dividers
- band saw or scraper
- rat-tail file
- scratch box
- try square (combination square)
- back bent chisel
- cabinet scraper
- fine-grade sandpaper
- gouge
- fine brush
- stain
- rubber
- polish
- wax

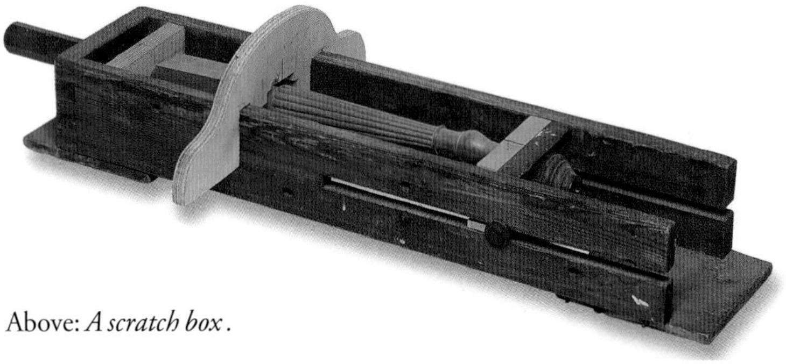

Above: *A scratch box.*

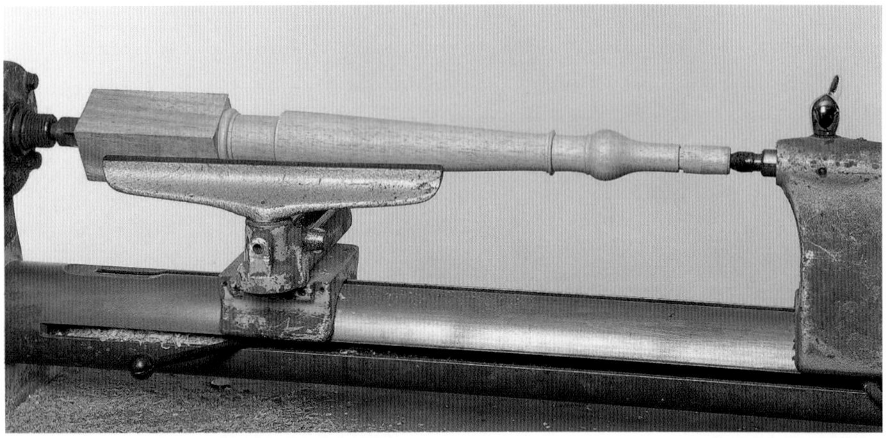

◁ **1** Take the measurements for the template (pattern) leg from the original leg, using callipers for the circumference. Make sure that enough wood is left to allow for the reeds to be scratched. Turn the template leg on the lathe.

◁ **2** Using a pair of dividers, measure the width of the reed. When set, transfer the dividers to the template leg and mark divisions at the top of the leg corresponding to the original.

3 Now cut the reed cutter to the correct size and profile using an old band saw or scraper. As the blade will scrape and edge rather than cut it, make sure the edge is at a 90-degree angle to the side.

◁ **4** Fit the leg to the scratch box just below the height of the sides. To ensure that it is set parallel, measure the distance from the height of the sides both at the top and bottom of the leg with a try square (combination square).

▷ **5** Pass the cutter back and forth to scratch the reed into the leg. This should be done with an even pressure. When the reed is scratched, revolve the leg to the next division mark and scratch the next reed.

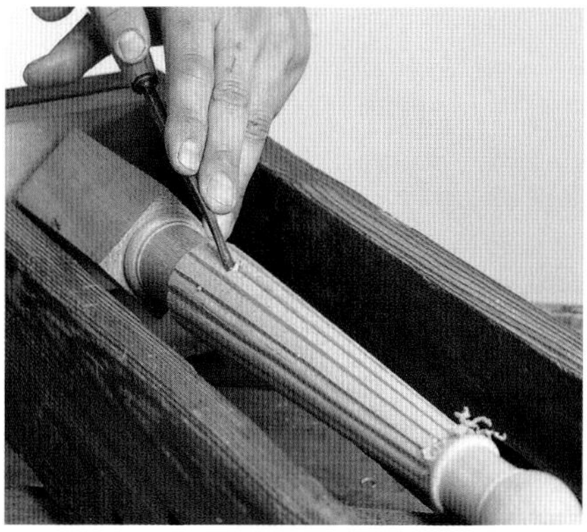

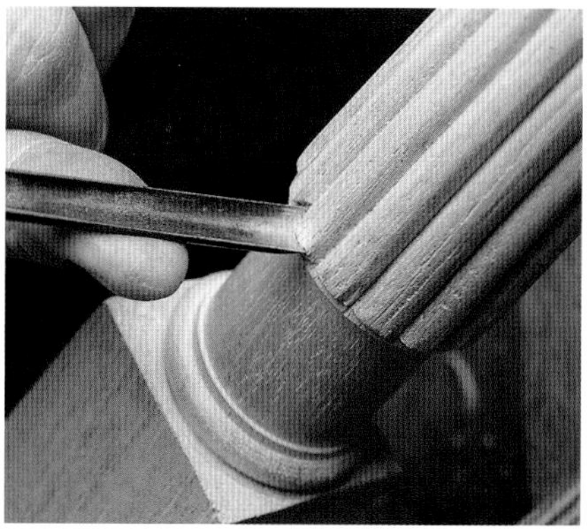

6 The scratch blade in the cutter will scratch a V shape. However, you can round it using a back bent chisel if you want a more rounded shape.

7 Use a cabinet scraper to clean the reed again. This will give a clean finish, as it is the same shape as the actual reeds. Then use fine-grade sandpaper with an overloe.

8 On certain reeded legs the top is not square but rounded. If you want to create this effect, use a gouge.

◁ **9** When finished, compare the new leg against the original to ensure that they are a good match. Note that enough wood is left at the top to allow a new mortise to be cut and joined to the seat rails.

Right: *The new leg can now be stained, polished and waxed (see pp.66–69), and any necessary distressing may be applied to make it match the patina of the other legs.*

Repairing backs and frames

The most common fault found in chair frames is joint damage, such as broken mortise and tenon or dowel joints. Top rails are liable to break at the weak short grain at the end of each rail. Repairs can necessitate fairly major surgery on the broken parts, but the results can be very effective. Dowel joints are easiest to fix, since the broken dowels can simply be drilled out and replaced with new ones. Broken tenons, however, are more difficult, as their strength comes originally from being an integral part of the piece being joined. The answer is to replace the broken piece by gluing a wooden tongue into a slot cut in the frame piece.

Cutting in a tenon joint

The protruding piece of wood on a side seat rail is a tenon; the recess it slots into in a back upright is a mortise. This is the standard joint found on frame chairs, but on occasion the tenon can break. The tenon on this mahogany Regency chair has snapped off completely and been lost.

To make a repair, a new piece of wood must be cut to size and glued into a slot cut into the seat rail, before being shaped to fit snugly within the mortise. The mortise itself does not need repairing. When sanded and polished, the repair will not be noticeable.

MATERIALS AND EQUIPMENT

- mortise gauge
- tenon saw
- mortise chisel
- heavy mallet
- mahogany
- PVA (white) glue
- clamping blocks
- G-clamp
- square rule
- spokeshave
- bench hook
- block plane
- fine brush
- stain

1 Knock the chair apart following steps 1–5 on pp.103–104. Set a mortise gauge to the width of the mortise in the upright, then run it over the broken end of the side seat rail and 10cm/4in down its underside.

2 Place the damaged side seat rail in a vice. Cut along the lines made by the mortise gauge with a tenon saw. It is important not to cut beyond the marks made by the mortise gauge.

3 Remove the mahogany from between the cut lines with a mortise chisel and a heavy mallet. It is important to cut to a reasonable depth in the rail to ensure that the new joint will be sufficiently strong.

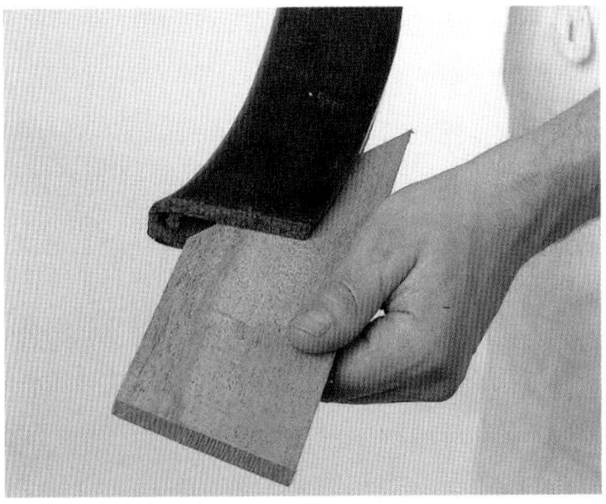

4 Cut a piece of mahogany to fit in the new slot in the side seat rail, allowing about 15cm/6in to protrude.

5 Apply PVA (white) glue to the new wood and insert it into the side seat rail. Clamp the side seat rail between two clamping blocks and leave to dry.

6 Remove the clamp and blocks. Place a square rule against the cut end of the side seat rail and draw a pencil line to mark out the upper end of the tenon. Repeat for the lower end and the top, which should match the depth of the mortise.

7 Cut along the pencil lines with a tenon saw, then use a spokeshave to remove the excess wood from the bottom of the rail.

8 Place the side seat rail on a bench hook (see Tip below) and use a block plane to make the tenon the correct width. Check the fit of the tenon in the mortise repeatedly during this procedure to ensure a tight fit.

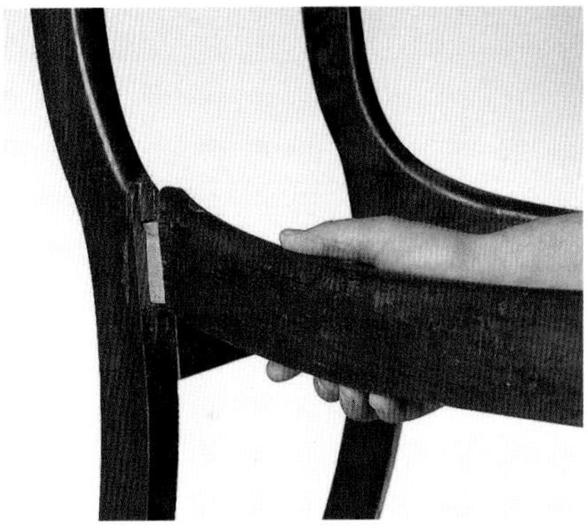

9 Once the tenon has been planed to fit exactly in the mortise, reassemble the chair (see pp.104–105) and leave to dry.

Right: *When the glue has dried, the clamps can be removed, and the underside of the tenon in the side seat rail stained to match the rest of the chair (see p.69). The new joint should last for many more years.*

Tip

A bench hook comprises a board with a batten at each end, one of which butts against the edge of the bench top, while the other provides a stop for the workpiece to hold it securely. To make one, use a piece of 2.5cm/1in thick board, about 25cm/10in long and 17.5cm/7in wide. Cut two lengths of batten about 2.5cm/1in square and 12.5cm/5in long. Glue one of these flush with one end and the left-hand edge of the board. Turn the board over and glue the remaining batten to the other end, again flush with the left-hand edge.

Replacing a mortise and tenon joint

The mortise and tenon on this George III mahogany chair frame have both been damaged. An earlier repair was badly executed, so a new mortise and tenon will have to be cut and fitted. This involves cutting away the damaged wood, splicing in new pieces of similar material and forming the two halves of the joint. The result will be as strong as the original joint.

MATERIALS AND EQUIPMENT

- tenon saw
- mahogany
- PVA (white) glue
- G-clamp
- spokeshave
- try square (combination square)
- utility knife
- medium- and fine-grade sandpaper
- paring chisel
- drill
- wood drill bit
- mortise chisel
- carving tools
- mortise gauge

1 Knock the chair apart following steps 1–6 on pp.103–104, and place the side seat rail in a vice. Cut away the existing repair wood with a tenon saw to leave a flat surface for the new wood to adhere to.

2 Cut a piece of mahogany for a replacement tenon. Apply PVA (white) glue and attach the new piece to the seat rail. Clamp until dry, then shape the wood to follow the rail's curve with a spokeshave.

3 Using the undamaged side seat rail as a guide, transfer the measurements of the tenon on to the new wood with a try square (combination square) and utility knife. Cut the tenon.

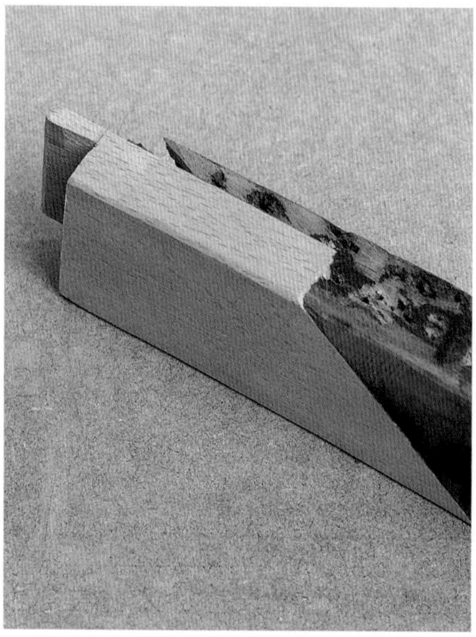

◁ **4** Smooth the new wood, including the newly cut tenon joint, with sandpaper.

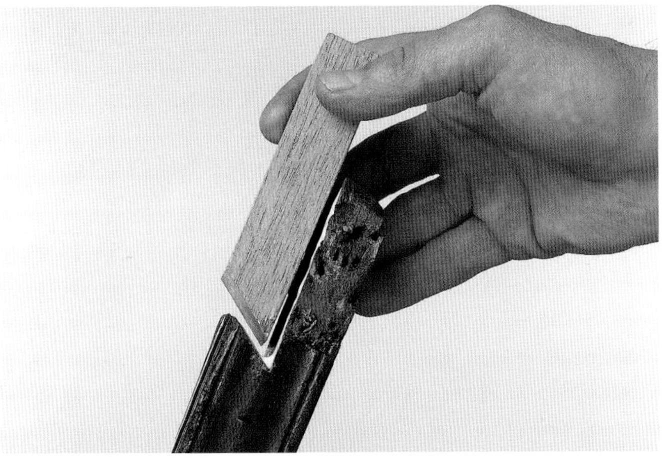

5 Cut out the damaged wood and the old repair from the leg with a paring chisel, leaving a wedge-shaped cut-out. Shape a piece of new wood to fit this and glue it in place. Clamp until dry, then remove the clamp.

6 Remove the remains of the side seat rail tenon, which is lodged in the mortise joint, by first drilling access holes, then using a mortise chisel to clean out the remaining wood.

7 Place the leg in a vice and cut the new wood to size. Use carving tools to shape it to match the rest of the leg. Finish by sanding it smooth with medium-grade sandpaper.

8 You now need to cut a new mortise into the new wood. Use a mortise gauge to mark the correct width of the mortise and then a mortise chisel to remove the wood.

◁ **9** Smooth the joint with fine-grade sandpaper, then check that the tenon fits snugly into the mortise. Make any necessary final adjustments using sandpaper to ensure a perfect fit.

Above: *The restored mortise and tenon joint will have the strength of the original. The chair can now be reassembled.*

Dowel joint repair

While the most common type of joint used in furniture construction during the 17th, 18th and 19th centuries was the mortise and tenon, by the mid-19th century, due to the increase of furniture production and the need for less time-consuming construction techniques, the dowel joint was being used in certain furniture manufacture. Although similar to the mortise and tenon joint in purpose, the dowel joint employs inset dowels to connect two pieces together. Like the mortise and tenon, however, it does, on occasion, break and have to be replaced.

The dowel joints of this mid-19th-century Victorian balloon-back chair had broken. An earlier repair between the frame and back upright, utilizing a metal bracket, was not successful, and the joint needed to be repaired properly. Once the upholstery had been removed and the chair knocked apart (steps 1–5 on pp.103–104), the extent of the damage could be ascertained. The dowels in one joint had broken off and needed removing from the back upright, while the dowels in the other joint had been removed and covered with a mahogany patch; new holes would need to be drilled into this patch.

MATERIALS AND EQUIPMENT
- drill
- wood drill bits
- tenon saw
- dowels
- PVA (white) glue
- hammer
- panel pins (brads)
- pincers
- sash clamps
- clamping blocks
- masking tape
- hand drill
- chisel
- rubber
- polish

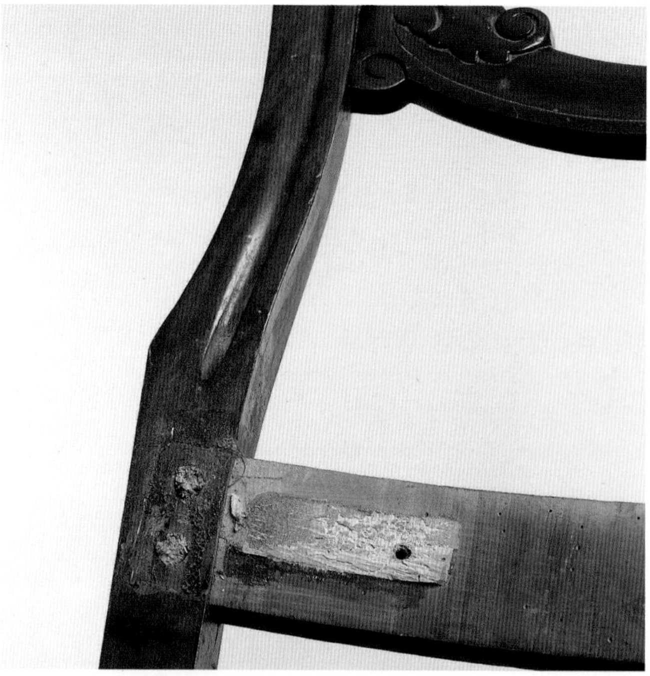

◁ **1** Place the left-hand upright in a vice and drill out the remaining dowel pieces. The auger bit used must be the same diameter as the dowels. Also drill out the remaining dowel pieces in the corresponding side seat rail, then cut and glue new lengths of dowel into these seat rail holes.

▷ **2** Turning now to the problem of the patched upright, place the other side seat rail in a vice. Fit a length of dowel into each of the two seat rail dowel joint holes. Do not glue them in, but cut them flush with the shoulder of the joint.

3 Hammer a panel pin (brad) into the centre of each of the dowel pieces (known as location pegs), and cut back the ends with pincers to leave sharp points standing proud of the surface.

4 Position the seat rail correctly against the back upright and use a sash clamp to pull it into place. Clamp the other side seat rail to keep the frame square. Hold the clamping blocks in place with masking tape.

5 Release the clamps and remove the front and side seat rail structure. The location pins will have marked the correct positions of the new dowel holes in the mahogany patch.

6 Hand drill pilot holes into the pin marks, opening them up to the size of the dowels with an auger bit. Drill at an angle that is square to the back seat rail, so the shoulder of the joint pulls up flush with the upright.

7 Remove the location pegs by gripping the pins and pulling them out. Use the location pegs to determine the correct length of the new dowels required.

8 Cut and glue the new dowels into the joint, then cut channels into the dowels with a chisel. These grooves allow any excess glue to escape from the joint. Reassemble the chair (see pp.104–105).

Right: *After the glue has dried and the clamps have been removed, give the chair a rubber of polish (see pp.66–67). At this stage, it is ready to be re-upholstered (see pp.129–133). The joint is now as strong as it was when the chair was first constructed.*

Repairing a broken back

A common problem with chairs is that they can break along their top rails. This can be caused by a diner leaning back too hard or a chair being knocked over and the joints shattering. Many breakages of this type require extensive repair work.

In this instance, the top rail of a George III Cuban mahogany dining chair has become broken, and, unfortunately, one of the tenons was smashed beyond repair. An added complication was the fact that the chair retained its original horsehair upholstery, and it was considered wisest to leave the seat ***in situ*** during restoration. This meant that extra care had to be taken when making the repair.

MATERIALS AND EQUIPMENT

- masking tape
- tenon saw
- Cuban mahogany
- coping saw
- PVA (white) glue
- G-clamp
- clamping block
- mortise gauge
- chisels
- hammer
- nails
- spokeshave
- band clamps
- fine-grade sandpaper
- flat-bladed knife
- stopping wax
- brush
- stain
- rubber
- polish

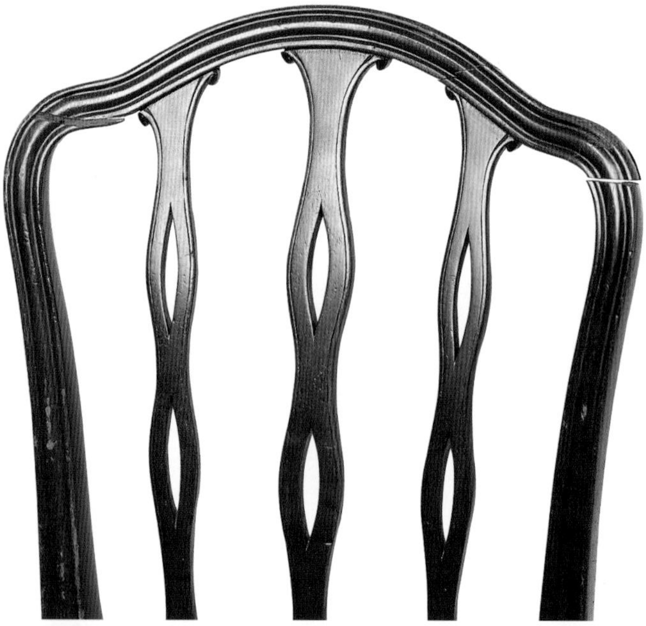

▷ **1** Remove the top rail and vertical back supports, which will all be joined by mortise and tenon joints. In this instance, the top rail split into three parts on removal. Label the different parts with masking tape (see p.103).

2 A new tenon must be cut to replace the smashed one, but first a section of mahogany must be let into the back upright. Line the vice with old baize and cut out the damaged section with a tenon saw.

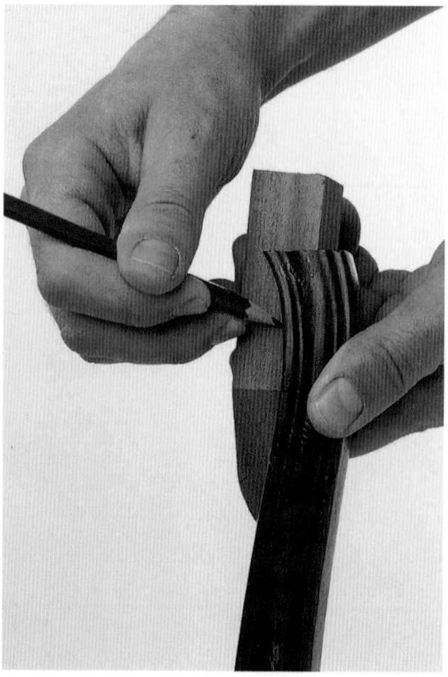

◁ **3** Having removed the damaged section from the right-hand upright, select a suitable piece of matching Cuban mahogany. Holding it in position, draw the outline of the back upright on it. Cut along this line with a coping saw.

◁ **4** Glue the mahogany insert into place. Clamp it into position with a G-clamp and clamping blocks and allow the glue to set. This insert will form the new tenon joint.

◁ **5** Measure the tenon on the opposite side upright with a mortise gauge. Transcribe this dimension to the new wood.

6 Cut the new tenon with a tenon saw. Make it slightly wider than the scored lines so that you can pare it down later to produce a really tight and accurate fit.

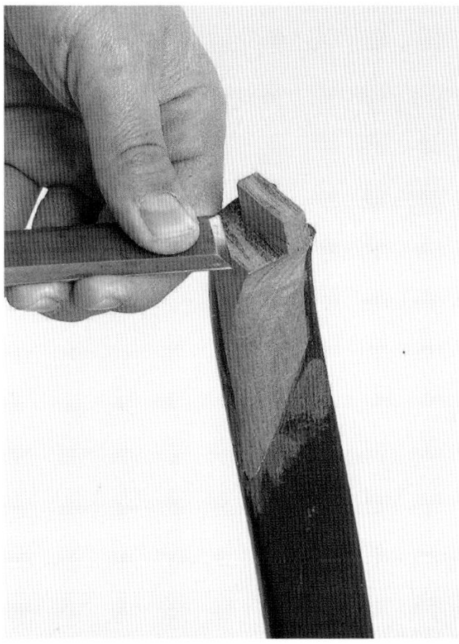

◁ **7** Clean up the joint using a sharp paring chisel. Check the measurement repeatedly against the top rail mortise to ensure a tight fit.

8 The mortise on the left-hand side of the top rail has broken away. Glue back any large sections, pinning the joints together with nails for extra strength. Countersink the heads of the nails.

9 Replace the badly smashed piece from the top rail with sections of Cuban mahogany, trimming it roughly to shape with a chisel.

▷

Repairing a broken back...continued

10 Continue shaping the new piece of wood on the top rail with a spokeshave, but do not shape the insert at the joint until the chair has been reassembled. This will allow it to be blended into the upright.

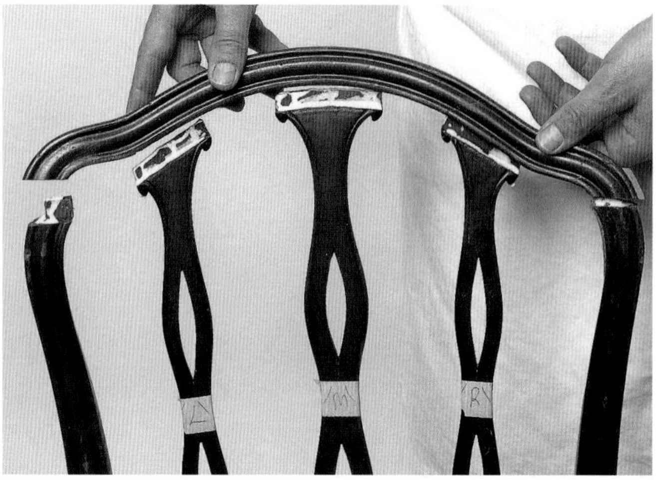

11 Reglue the vertical supports to the top rail and the back seat rail, then reglue the back uprights and top rail together. Note that the rail insert (right) has not yet been shaped.

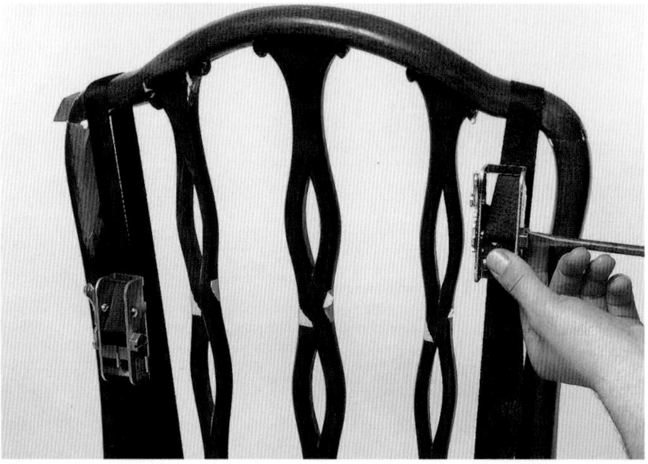

◁ **12** Use nylon band clamps to apply pressure. These are made from nylon straps fitted with ratchets that allow an even pressure to be applied. Band clamps are ideal for gluing shaped chair backs. When the glue has dried, remove the clamps and shape the mahogany inserts to follow the line of the back upright and the top rail. Finish the repair by smoothing it with fine-grade sandpaper. Using a flat-bladed knife, fill the countersunk nail holes (see step 8) with stopping wax.

Right: *Stain (see p.69) and polish (see pp.66–67) the repairs to match the existing surface. By remaking the smashed parts of the joints, rather than simply gluing them back together, you will have restored the strength of the chair completely.*

Repairing a top rail

The top rail of this 19th-century Regency mahogany chair has become loose due to a break in the stopped dovetail joint. It is old damage, and at some point a temporary repair had been made using a dowel to strengthen the joint, but this did not stop it breaking a second time.

The joint now needs to be repaired properly. The process will involve splicing out the damaged areas from the upright and the top rail and remaking both parts of the joint.

MATERIALS AND EQUIPMENT

- tenon saw
- Cuban mahogany
- plane
- PVA (white) glue
- G-clamp
- spokeshaves
- fine-grade sandpaper
- chisel
- sash clamp

1 First remove the damaged area of the upright using a tenon saw. Cut away an angled splice to ensure that the new joint will be strong and less noticeable.

2 Cut a suitable piece of Cuban mahogany roughly to size with a tenon saw. Plane one side flush and glue to the upright. Apply G-clamps overnight. When the joint is tight, roughly shape the new wood using a spokeshave.

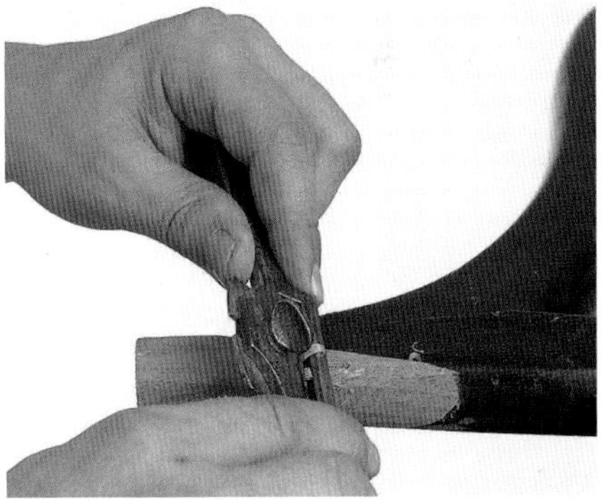

3 Using a finer spokeshave, shape the new wood, carefully copying the profile of the intact upright. The repair should blend seamlessly with the original. Finish with fine sandpaper.

4 To repair the top rail, remove the damaged areas of wood with a sharp chisel. To make a good joint, ensure that the edges are clean and crisp.

5 Glue together the upright and top rail using PVA (white) glue. Apply sash clamps overnight to ensure a strong joint.

Above: *When the joint is tight, the new wood is stained to match the original wood and then polished. The restored area should be almost invisible.*

UPHOLSTERY

The majority of antique seating furniture, ranging from stools to settees, will need to be upholstered in one form or another. The choice of fabric used will be a personal one, but you should always endeavour to match the style and method of upholstery to the relevant period, since the construction of the chair, stool or settee will reflect the original cabinet-maker's choice of upholstering. To alter this will not only spoil the aesthetics of the whole piece but can also devalue the chair. Also, for authenticity, use tacks rather than staples when reupholstering.

The earliest recorded mention of upholstery was during the 15th century. However, during this period it was the beds and state canopies that received lavish fabric treatments, with seating being confined in the main to squab or loose cushions. These chairs would have been filled with down or horsehair, but by the 16th century the X-frame chair was in use, often covered with velvet or silk damask (see p.98).

Upholstery rapidly became more fashionable, and by the 18th century there were numerous types and styles of upholstery, ranging from the simple squab seat, to be used with a cane seat, to elaborate wing chairs, which were fully upholstered with only their show-wood legs showing.

The techniques and materials used can alter depending on the origin of the chair, but although modern materials are now available, traditional ones should be favoured whenever possible.

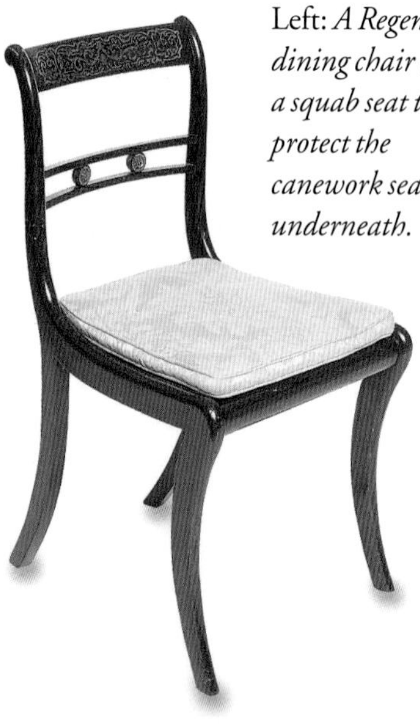

Left: *A Regency dining chair with a squab seat to protect the canework seat underneath.*

Right: *A George III dining chair with a drop-in seat.*

Above: *An elegant Queen Anne wing chair with fully upholstered back and arms and a down-filled loose cushion.*

Left: *A Regency bergère chair with deep-buttoned leather squab seat.*

Right: *A George II dining chair with a stuff-over seat and close nail decoration.*

Caning

Cane seating can be found in various patterns and styles, although the most common design found on antique furniture is the traditional six-way pattern shown here. Cane is actually rattan, which grows in tropical areas of the Far East, and to obtain the cane, strips are cut from the outside of the rattan, then reduced to various widths, which are classified on a scale of 0 to 6. This outer part of the rattan is used for seating, while the inner parts are employed for basketwork. The tools required are few, and it is very much a technique that requires patience and care. The most common examples of canework are chairs, stools and bed heads.

The method used in chairs is known as open caning, which describes the technique of interweaving long lengths of cane to form a strong, flexible platform on which a squab seat is usually placed. Prior to beginning work, remove all the old cane, including the pegs. The best method of doing this is to drill them out with a drill bit that is slightly smaller in diameter than the holes. Also make sure that the seat frame is tight, since caning a loose or rickety chair is pointless.

MATERIALS AND EQUIPMENT

- cane
- cloths (cotton rags)
- rattan pegs
- shell bodkin
- secateurs (pruners)
- hammer
- stain or wax

1 The first stage, or first setting as it is known, is to thread damp cane (see Tip) through the holes from side to side. Hold the cane in place with a rattan peg, then pull the cane across the frame and thread it down through the opposite hole. After securing it with a temporary peg, thread the cane up through the adjacent hole from the underside and repeat the process.

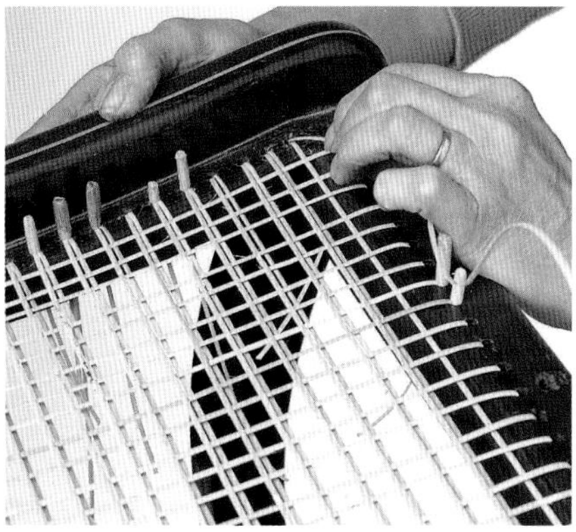

2 Change direction and lay cane at right angles to the first setting, i.e. from front to back. This is the first weaving. Now thread a second row of cane through the same holes as the first setting, but slightly to the right to form a double-width band. This is the second setting.

Tip

Although the cane can be worked dry, the task will be easier if it is soaked in water for a minute or two first and kept wrapped in a damp cloth to mellow while the seat is being worked. Do not make it too wet or keep it damp for too long, because either of these conditions will cause the cane to deteriorate.

Caning...continued

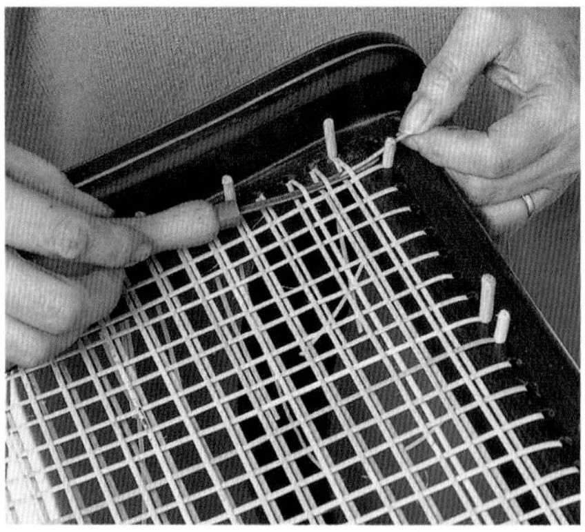

3 The second weaving, which involves laying a second strand of cane from front to back, differs from the first weaving in that this strand is woven over the second setting and under the first setting, which interlocks all four cane bands. Use a shell bodkin to help thread the cane through the various stages of weaving.

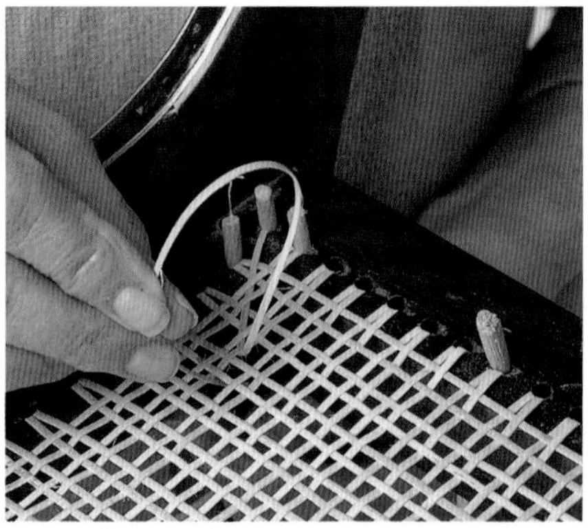

4 For the first diagonal weave, or first crossing as it is known, you need to thread cane over the settings and under the weavings, i.e. over the double cane bands set from side to side, and under those woven from front to back.

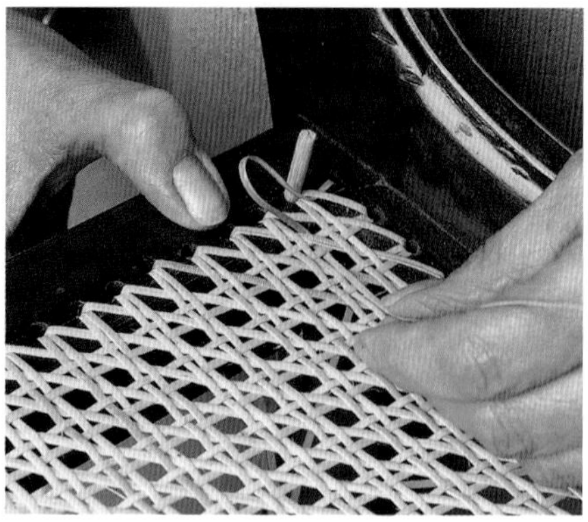

5 Repeat the process across the other diagonal. This second crossing involves weaving the cane under the settings and over the weavings. This is the opposite to the first crossing. The cane should slip neatly into the corners between the first weaving and the second setting.

6 Hold the cane securely in place by inserting rattan pegs in the holes, cutting them flush with a pair of garden secateurs (pruners). No glue is used, you just hammer the pegs home with a gentle tap.

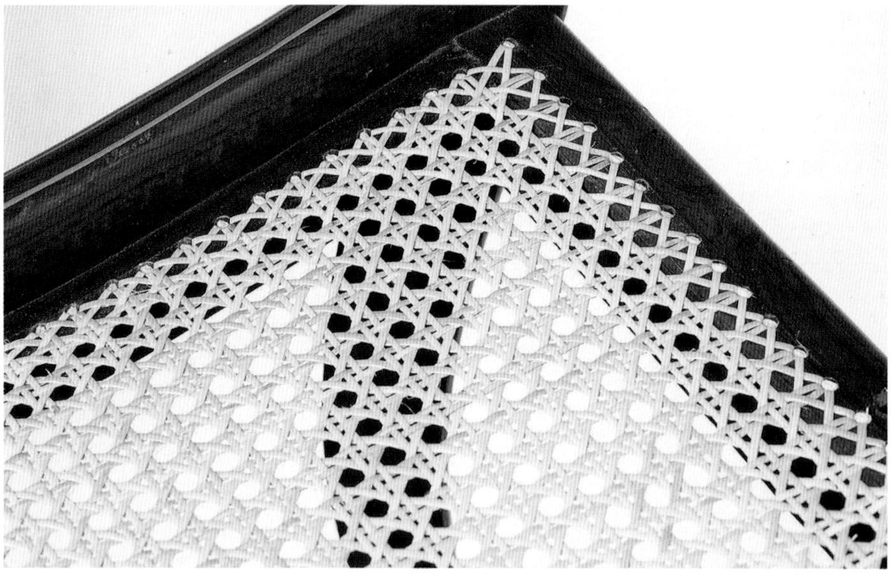

Above: *When completed, the seat should exhibit an evenly woven geometric pattern that will give strength and flexibility. You can leave the cane in its natural state, but it is often better to apply some stained wax or a water-based stain (see pp.68 and 69).*

Beaded finish

Prior to 1850 a pegged finish (as shown above) was generally used. After this date a decorative beaded finish was favoured (see right). Always select the finish that fits with the period of the chair you are restoring.

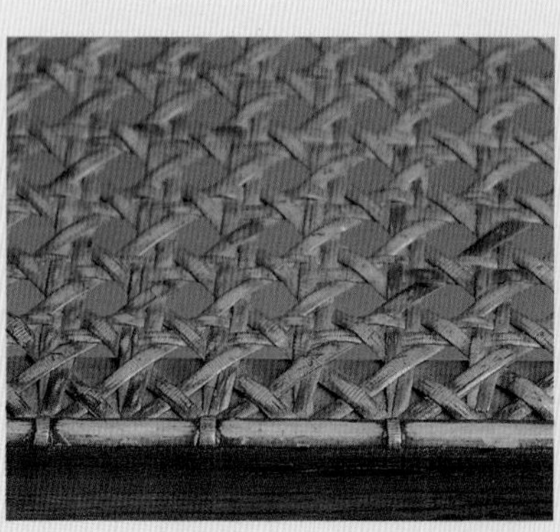

Upholstering a stuff-over seat

There are several ways to upholster a chair. The style and method employed will be dictated by the period and design of the chair, but the most common method in most 18th- and 19th-century furniture is that of over webbing. If carried out correctly, the chair will have an even, flat line that will be comfortable and durable and, most importantly, will show off the lines of the chair to their best effect.

Today, the staple gun is often used alongside the traditional tack and hammer in the upholstery workshop, but while the staple gun undoubtedly saves time, the tack and hammer are always the choice of the quality restoration workshop.

This chair will be upholstered using traditional methods and tools. Although you may already possess some of the tools – such as the mallet, pincers and scissors – the more unusual items will need seeking out from specialist tool suppliers and stores that stock furnishing materials. Alternatively, look out for traditional examples in car boot sales and second-hand stores.

MATERIALS AND EQUIPMENT
- webbing
- tacks
- hammer
- web stretcher
- mallet
- pincers
- scissors
- hessian (burlap)
- twine
- upholstery needles
- horsehair
- calico
- upholstery pins
- skin wadding (batting)
- top fabric
- gimp pins
- braid finish
- superglue
- tack hammer

1 Fold over the ends of four lengths of webbing and tack them to the back of the chair frame at equal intervals. Stretch the webbing across to the front of the frame using a web stretcher, fold over the ends and tack them down. Repeat across the sides of the frame, interweaving the lengths of webbing as shown.

2 Cut a piece of hessian (burlap) slightly larger than the seat frame. Place it on top of the webbing, fold the edges over and tack it down to secure.

3 Stitch several lines of large, looping stitches around the edge of the hessian and across the centre using an upholstery needle. These loops will be used to keep the horsehair in place.

4 Starting from the middle of the seat and working outward, place handfuls of horsehair on the hessian and tease it under the twine loops to secure. Continue until the horsehair sits evenly.

Upholstering a stuff-over seat...continued

◁ **5** Cut a second piece of hessian and drape it over the horsehair. Secure the hessian with temporary tacks along the chair frame. Stitch further twine loops through the seat with a long needle; these are used to pull the seating flat as well as to hold the horsehair in place.

▷ **6** Remove the temporary tacks with a mallet and tack lifter. Trim the hessian to size, then tack all the way around the seat, taking particular care at the corners. Mistakes at this stage will be very difficult to rectify later.

7 Stitch more ties through the seat, then use the long needle to apply a blind stitch just above the tack line, and also on the top edge, about 2.5cm/1in above the tack line. This begins the process of making the finished edge and will hold the horsehair in place for the next stage.

8 Use the ties to readjust the stuffing, flattening it as much as possible, then blind stitch around the top edges once more, just outside the existing stitches, paying special attention to the corners. When completed, the seat should be flat with the edges held firmly in place.

9 Place another layer of horsehair on the hessian and tease it to fit the dimensions of the seat exactly, producing a slightly domed shape.

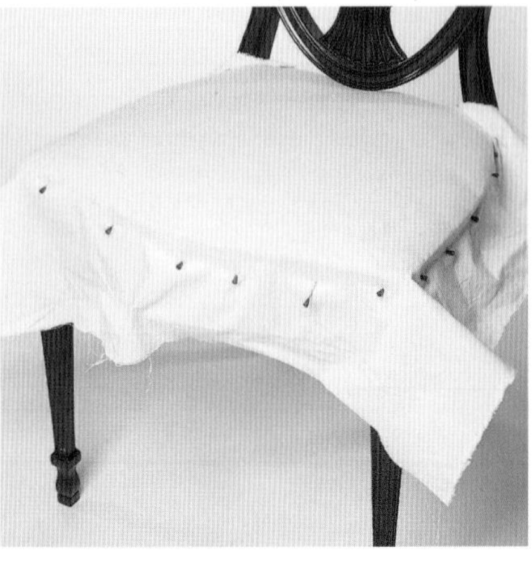

◁ **10** Cover the horsehair with a piece of calico. Pull the calico tight and secure it with upholstery pins. The seat should be smooth and regular in shape.

▷**11** Fold in the corners of the calico and cut to fit. Tack the calico in position and remove the upholstery pins.

12 Cut a piece of skin wadding (batting) to double the length of the seat, fold it in two and place it on the seat. This will prevent the coarse horsehair from coming through.

13 Lay the top cover on the wadding. Fit temporary tacks to the underside of the seat rails so that you can check that any pattern is aligned and the fabric is not overstretched.

14 Adjust the temporary tacks as necessary. Secure the fabric by hammering more tacks into the underside of the seat rails. Trim the corners and fold them away, making sure the folds are on the outside edge.

15 Use small gimp pins hammered in with a tack hammer to hold in the corners, if necessary. The top cover should look smooth and even.

16 Apply the braid finish with superglue and snip off any loose threads.

Left: *The newly upholstered seat should enhance the overall design of the chair, be comfortable to sit on and, most importantly, last for many years.*

Finishes

There are several ways of finishing the upholstery of a chair. These include applying attractive finishing techniques to the seat itself and adding various types of decorative edging around the seat rail. The latter have a practical purpose, too, since they are used to provide a neat finish to the edges of the top fabric.

Space nailing

This technique involves applying a braid with superglue, then hammering in large-headed nails at regular intervals. It is suitable for late 18th-century and Regency styles.

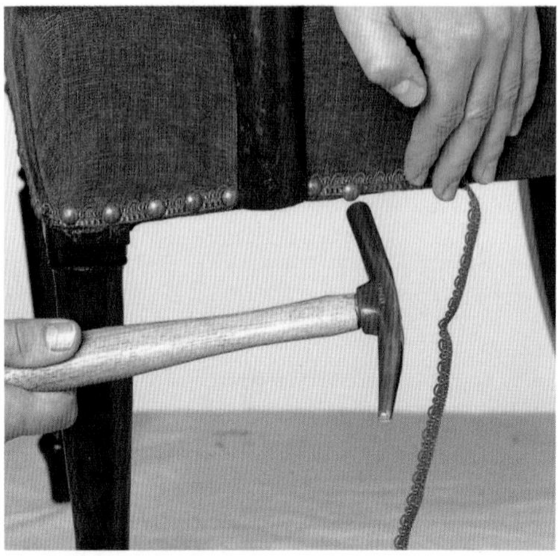

Close nailing

This technique, as the name suggests, involves forming a border of closely spaced nails tacked into the seat rail. It is suitable for tapestry fabrics and a mid-18th-century look.

Braid

There are numerous braids to choose from, in all colours, tones and styles. They are usually applied with superglue and can be employed with any suitable fabric.

Rope and piping

Rope and piping finishes are used to emphasize the edges of cushions and seats. When used on upholstered seats they are known as "self piping" and give a sculptured look to a seat.

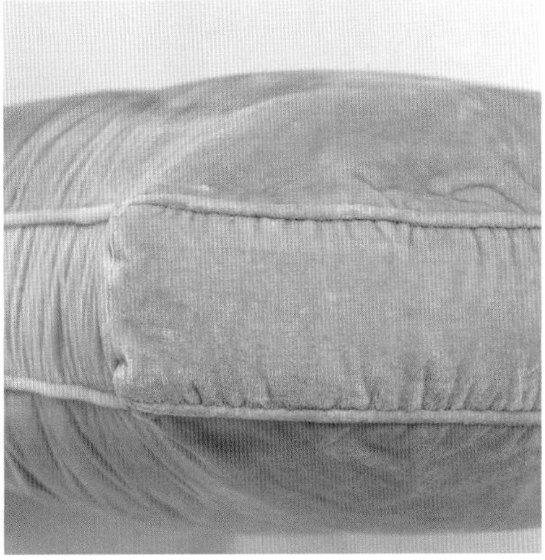

Floating buttons

The use of five floating buttons, combined with space nailing on a braid border, gives a smart, stylish finish. The technique of fitting the buttons is shown below.

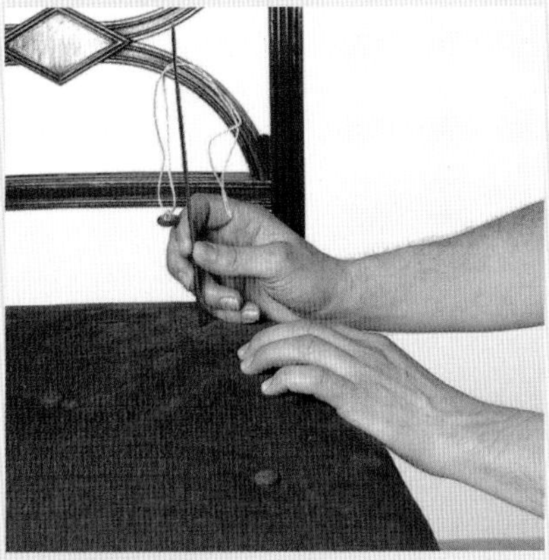

1 *Pass some upholstery thread through a button, then use a long needle to pass the double threads down through the seat.*

2 *Guide the button into position while pulling the threads taut underneath. The button should form a gentle dip in the seat.*

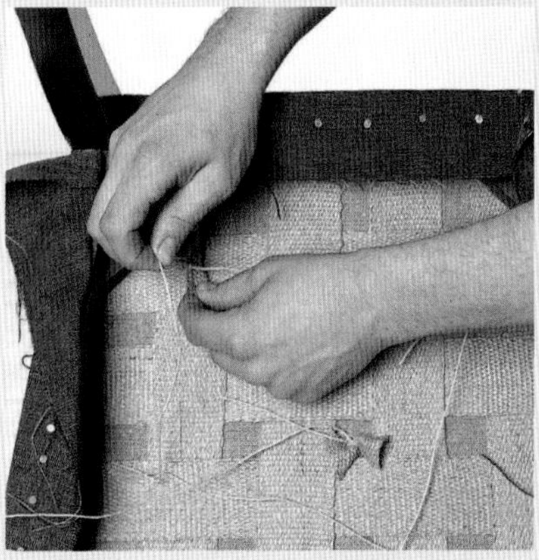

3 *Tie off the threads from the underside of the seat, using a scrap (offcut) of webbing to spread the pressure. Repeat for the other four buttons.*

PROJECT: RAYNHAM CHAIR

The age of this chair was unknown when it was bought from an auction house. The material, Cuban mahogany, the style of the internal seat rails and the carving indicated that it was a mid-18th-century piece and almost identical to a number attributed to Thomas Chippendale or William Vile for the Marquess of Townsend at Raynham Hall, Norfolk. As such, it could be an important piece and would require sympathetic restoration to bring it back to its original condition. It needed a considerable amount of work to the frame to overcome the ravages of time, including the replacement of parts that were missing with new Cuban mahogany. However, with a great deal of patience and careful work, it was possible to re-create the beauty of the original craftsmanship.

ASSESSING THE PROJECT

This chair was in need of comprehensive restoration. On removing the upholstery (which revealed original hay stuffing), it became clear that the seat frame was worm-eaten and loose, and new wood would be needed to strengthen it. Furthermore, the legs appeared to be too short for the height of the chair, and they were missing areas of carving. The feet looked as though they had been cut down and they did not have castors.

The seat frame
- loose
- worm-eaten wood

The feet
- wrong shape
- castors missing

The legs
- incorrect height
- areas of carving missing

Repairing the seat frame

The seat frame was found to be loose and, in areas, the rails were extensively damaged by woodworm. As with all restoration projects, it is important to keep as much of the original material as possible, so the seat frame must be knocked apart carefully and then restored sympathetically. The method used is to remove the core from the original wood and fill the space with a core of new wood. In this way, the strength of the chair can be restored with the new strong core, while the retained exterior of original wood helps to confirm the age of the piece. Chairs that have been completely rerailed can be substantially devalued.

Right: *Woodworm damage.*

MATERIALS AND EQUIPMENT
- tack lifter
- hammer
- hardwood block
- masking tape
- circular saw
- beech
- PVA (white) glue
- clamping blocks
- G-clamps
- tenon saw
- fine brush
- spirit-based (alcohol-based) stain

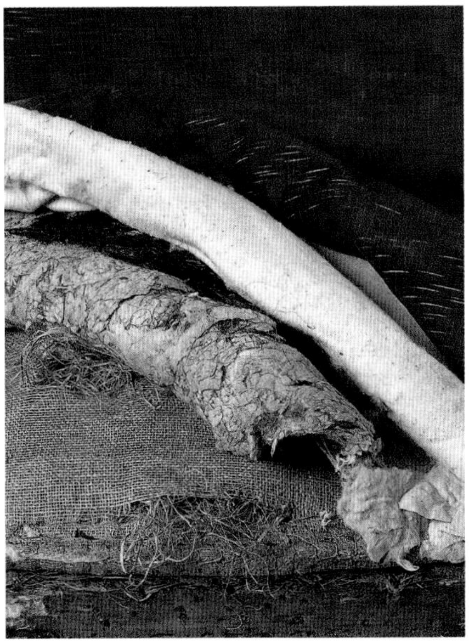

1 Remove the upholstery and set it aside (see pp.102–103). Note that the chair still has hay as part of its stuffing, indicating that it was last fully re-upholstered in the 19th century. With the upholstery removed, it could be seen that the seat rails were original throughout.

2 Use a tack lifter to free the ends of the now-revealed webbing and strip it away. The springs, which are stitched to the webbing, can be seen beneath the webbing.

3 Knock the chair apart completely (see pp.103–104) using a hammer and a hardwood block. The block ensures that an even pressure is applied and that no damage is caused to the mahogany surface.

▷

Repairing the seat frame...continued

◁ **4** Label the individual parts as you remove them. Although it would be difficult to confuse the pieces with just one chair, this could easily happen if there were more than one, so it is good workshop practice to label everything.

5 One of the seat rails has been radically attacked by woodworm and must have a new core inserted. Cut through the length of the seat rail using a circular saw, removing the inner core. Note that for the sake of clearer photography the safety guard has been removed.

▷ **6** Cut a central core from a piece of beech to the same dimensions as the one removed. The original face wood from the rail, which is quite damaged, will serve little more than a cosmetic role, so the beech insert, which will provide the strength, should be a good piece of wood, free from any knots or faults.

7 Glue the three lengths of wood together, with the beech (which will form the tenon) in the middle. Position some newspaper (to protect against leaking glue) and some clamping blocks, then clamp the three parts together and leave to dry. Cut a tenon joint (see p.117).

◁ **8** Although the other seat rails do not need new cores, they do have worm-damaged areas that need to be patched with new beech. It is important, however, to retain as much of the original seat rails as possible. Make sure that any joints that need to be restored still fit prior to the chair being reglued. Continue until all the seat frame damage is repaired, then stain the repairs to match the original wood.

Repairing the feet

Now that the seat frame has been repaired, attention can be given to the problem of the shortened legs. At some stage in their history, their length has been reduced by about 4cm/1½in, almost certainly because of damage. This gives the chair an unbalanced appearance. The answer is to glue mahogany blocks to the legs and to shape them to fit in with the overall design. Damaged areas of moulding around the bottom of the old legs are replaced with new wood, which is then carved and shaped to match the undamaged areas.

MATERIALS AND EQUIPMENT

- tenon saw
- Cuban mahogany
- PVA (white) glue
- sash clamps
- clamping blocks
- G-clamps
- chisels
- spring clip
- fine-grade sandpaper
- utility knife

◁ **1** Cut four 4cm/1½in blocks of Cuban mahogany. Saw through the bottom of each of the existing feet to produce flat, square surfaces. Apply glue to the bottom of each foot, then, in the case of the front legs, clamp each block in place with a sash clamp.

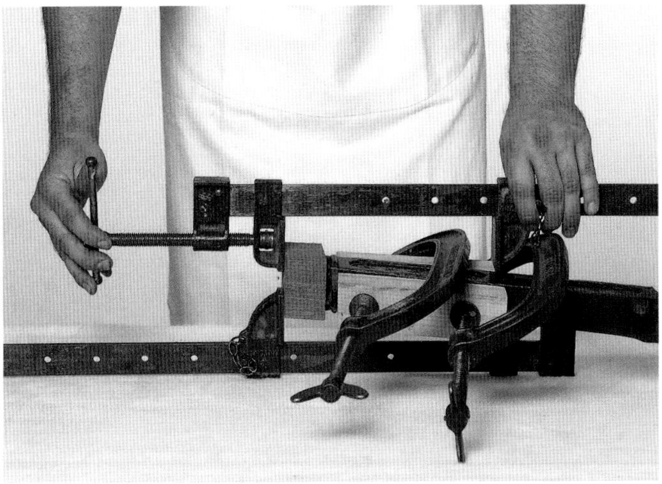

2 When clamping the back legs, you will need to compensate for their angle by adding clamping blocks to the sides of each leg with G-clamps. These will provide a purchase for the sash clamps that hold the new wood in place.

◁ **3** When the glue has dried, remove the clamps and start work on one foot by shaping the block with chisels so that it follow the lines of the original foot. Mark the indents carved on the original foot with a pencil.

▷

Repairing the feet...continued

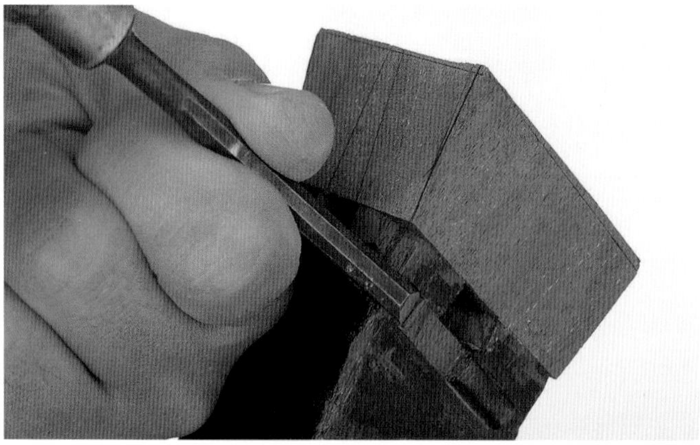

4 Cut any damaged areas of moulding on the foot flat and parallel with a chisel so that new wood can be glued on and later carved.

◁ **5** Cut small pieces of matching Cuban mahogany to size. Apply PVA (white) glue to the new wood and the existing foot, and press the new wood down firmly.

6 The replacement moulding covers a very small area, which means that a G-clamp is not suitable. The best method of holding this wood in place while the glue dries is to use a spring clip (see p.215).

7 When the glue has dried, remove the spring clip. Shape the moulding to match the undamaged areas on the other feet with a bevel-edged chisel.

▷ **8** Finish off the shaping with fine-grade sandpaper. Repeat this process for the mouldings on the other feet.

9 Score along the pencil lines on the foot with a utility knife. This will act as a guide when sawing out the indentations.

◁ **10** Cut along the V-shapes in the foot with a tenon saw. Do not cut too deeply – about 1cm/⅜in should be enough.

11 Begin paring out the V-shape with a narrow chisel. Take care to follow the shape accurately, because any mistakes you make at this stage cannot be corrected.

12 Continue to pare out the V-shape until it matches the depth in the old foot. Try to achieve as smooth a finish as possible.

◁ **13** The restored feet should closely resemble the original ones. The shape of the new feet was determined by researching the various styles of the period in reference books. The feet will be stained and polished once the repairs on the legs have been completed.

Repairing the legs

The legs are worn, and in some areas the carving has been lost completely. Because carved detail can be quite delicate on furniture, it is vulnerable to knocks and scrapes. Over the years, little bits can be broken off. The solution is to glue on new blocks of wood and carve them to shape to reproduce the missing detail. The new wood then needs to be stained and polished to blend it into the original wood. The important requirement is to have some form of reference so that the carvings can be reproduced. Fortunately, in this case it was possible to copy the detail from one leg to another.

MATERIALS AND EQUIPMENT

- chisel
- tenon saw
- Cuban mahogany
- PVA (white) glue
- carving tools
- fine brushes
- bichromate of potash
- polish
- pumice powder
- cloths (cotton rags)
- rubber
- methylated spirits (methyl alcohol)
- wax

1 Trim the groundwork level using a sharp chisel. Cut a piece of straight-grained Cuban mahogany so that it is slightly bigger than the area to be carved, then glue it in place.

2 Using the surviving carving from one of the other legs as a guide, shape the new mahogany roughly to the correct profile with a chisel.

3 Following the design and, more importantly, the style of carving, recarve the missing parts. The skill of the carver in restoration work lies in being able to mimic the hand of the craftsman who originally carved the decoration.

◁ **4** The natural colour of mahogany is redder than is usually desired, so once the carving is complete, brush the new wood with bichromate of potash. This is a chemical stain that will react with the tannin in the wood to produce a more desirable brown.

5 Apply the first layers of polish in thin coats, using a fine brush. This will ensure that all parts of the carving will be polished.

6 Put some polish on a cloth (cotton rag) and sprinkle some fine pumice powder on it, then use this to work the polish into the grain. This process is called fadding. Repeat until the grain is full.

◁ **7** Charge a rubber with polish for the final coats (see pp.66–67) and blend the new work with the existing surface on the legs. Use a cloth to give the original polish a clean using methylated spirits (methyl alcohol), then polish it to revive the surface. Follow this with a dark wax to finish (see p.68). Repeat this process for any other damaged legs.

▷

Rebuilding the chair

Reassembling the chair frame is a straightforward process, but care must be taken to ensure that it is square.

MATERIALS AND EQUIPMENT
- chisel
- PVA (white) glue
- sash clamps
- clamping blocks
- battens
- gauge sticks
- G-clamps

◁ **1** With the new feet glued on and shaped and the legs repaired, the chair can now be rebuilt. Begin by removing any lumps of old glue from the mortise and tenon joints with a chisel. Take care not to reduce the tenon size, as this will result in sloppy joints.

2 Glue the front legs and seat rail together and secure them with a sash clamp and clamping blocks. Check that the legs are spaced correctly by measuring them at top and bottom.

3 Repeat this process for the back legs, then glue the front and back assemblies to the side seat rails to form the seat frame. When clamping the seat frame together, stand the chair on a flat, level surface. Check that the side seat rails are at the same angle by placing a batten of the same size on each and then sighting across them. Their edges should be parallel if the rail angles are the same.

◁ **4** Check that the seat frame is square by measuring the diagonal dimensions with gauge sticks. You can make these from two lengths of wood with the ends cut to points. Hold the rods together so that the points touch diagonally opposing corners. Then, without allowing the rods to shift in your hand, position them between the other two corners. If both dimensions are the same, the seat frame is square. If any adjustment is needed, loosen the clamps, ease the joint(s) in question slightly, then retighten the clamps and check the diagonals again. Leave to dry.

◁ **5** Now glue together the four pieces of the chair back and secure them with sash clamps and clamping blocks. Check the frame for squareness using the gauge sticks. Leave to dry overnight.

6 Apply a generous amount of glue to the area where the back legs meet the seat back upright. This is a particularly fragile area that is easily damaged if the chair is mistreated.

▷ **7** Clamp the back legs and the seat back together, using a G-clamp and clamping blocks. Leave to dry overnight.

▷

Fitting the Castors

Castors were used on 18th-century furniture as a means to lift the pieces slightly and to give an impression of lightness. Their use for moving furniture was less important. This chair was missing the original castors, so suitable alternatives had to be sourced and fitted.

MATERIALS AND EQUIPMENT

- castors
- drill
- wood drill bits
- chisel
- fine-grade sandpaper
- fine brushes
- stain
- polish

1 Try to find castors from a similar period; otherwise select good reproductions from a furniture restoration parts supplier.

2 Find the centre of the foot and drill a clearance hole for the castor spindle. Put the castor on the foot and draw around it. Make sure that the castor sits exactly in the centre.

3 Bore a hole with a diameter that matches the width of the castor base plate, making it almost as deep as the castor and base plate. The wheel should only just be visible when the castor is fitted.

4 Pare around the edge of the hole with a chisel. Continue until the hole is wide enough to accommodate the wheel.

5 Drill a hole for the castor spindle in the centre of the foot, matching the size as closely as possible.

◁ **6** Finish the recess by smoothing it with fine-grade sandpaper, then screw the castor in place. Repeat this process with the other three feet. Finally, use fine brushes to stain and polish the feet to match the rest of the chair.

▷ **7** When the feet have been polished, they can be distressed slightly so they are not so obviously new. The castor likewise can be toned down.

Fitting the brackets

This chair had curved brackets fitted between the seat rails and legs. These were secured originally with glue and dowels. The old dowels have been drilled out and the holes plugged, so the new ones have a secure fixing. The same method of fixing will be employed to refit them, requiring new holes to be drilled in the core wood and new mahogany dowels to be made to match the holes in the brackets.

MATERIALS AND EQUIPMENT
- **drill**
- **wood drill bit**
- **tenon saw**
- **mahogany**
- **hammer**
- **steel plate**
- **PVA (white) glue**
- **chisel**
- **fine-grade sandpaper**

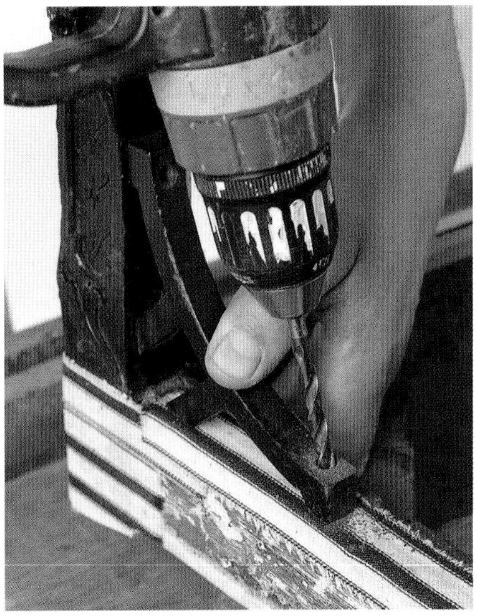

1 Hold the brackets in place and, using a closely matched bit, drill through the dowel holes into the legs and the new core wood or plugged dowel holes of the seat rails.

2 Cut strips of mahogany for the dowels. Hammer them through a hole in a steel plate to round them off and make them the correct diameter.

3 Glue the brackets in place, then knock the dowels through them into the seat rails and legs. Cut down the dowels with a tenon saw, then pare off the remainder with a sharp chisel. Sand them smooth with fine-grade sandpaper.

Right: *Once the chair has been re-upholstered (see pp. 129–133) and polished (see pp. 66–67), it will look as good as new and should last for another 250 years.*

Project: Windsor chair

This 19th-century Windsor chair, made from beech and elm, had been found in a garage. Long forgotten and in a sorry state, it was in need of complete restoration. This required a variety of techniques, since there was a range of damage to be put right. Although such chairs are quite simple in appearance, they are still handsome pieces of furniture and it is worth making an effort to bring them back to their original condition. If the work is done correctly, the result will be a sturdy, good-looking chair that will give many years of service.

Assessing the project

The most obvious damage is that one arm had broken off. Upon further inspection, it was also discovered that the arm joints in the back upright and shaped seat had broken away and would need replacing. Moreover, the back legs had been reduced in height to give the chair a more reclined feel. This had, however, put an unequal strain on the other legs and stretchers, causing them to become loose. The back legs will therefore need to be removed and returned to their original height. Finally, the seat, unusually for a Windsor chair, had split, and will need to be glued and secured with butterfly keys.

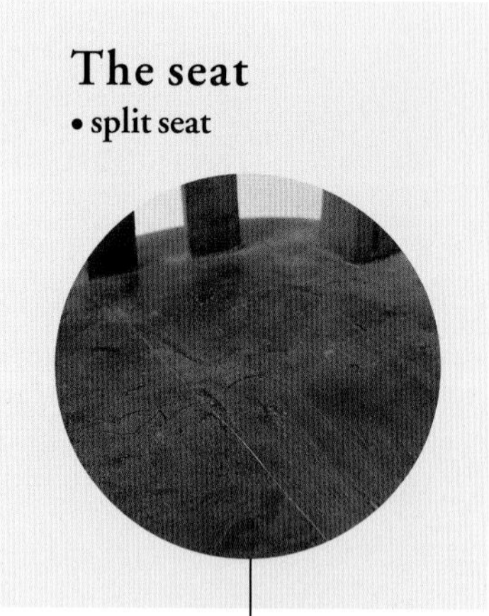

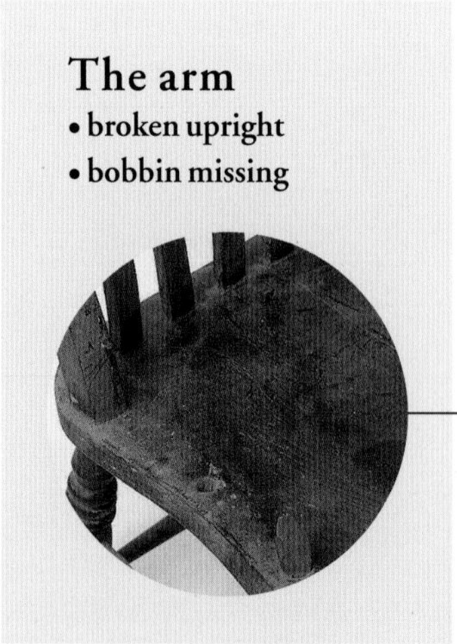

Repairing the seat

The split in the seat had probably been caused by a combination of misuse and climatic changes. Windsor chairs are very robust, and so splits in the seat are relatively uncommon. Fortunately, they are not difficult to repair. The application of glue and butterfly keys will produce a strong seat that will last for many more years to come. There is no need to match the wood of the seat for the butterfly keys; softwood will suffice, and it can be stained to blend in with the original material. You will need a router to cut the recesses for the keys, and, since the chair has a slightly curved surface, a routing guide to provide the router with an even surface to work on.

MATERIALS AND EQUIPMENT

- tenon saw
- softwood
- router
- PVA (white) glue
- sash clamps
- clamping blocks
- plywood
- hammer
- nails
- plane
- water-based stain
- brush

1 Cut four butterfly keys from a piece of softwood (see p.230). Remove all the legs, which, due to their condition, should involve no more than simply easing them out. Turn the seat over. Set the stop depth on a router to slightly less than the thickness of the keys.

2 Glue the crack, then clamp the seat together using sash clamps and clamping blocks. Cut a plywood routing guide slightly larger than the butterfly keys. Nail this to the underside of the seat where the first key is to be inserted (the waist of each key sits on the crack).

3 Cut the remaining three recesses then glue all the butterflies into position. The crack is now secured.

Repairing the seat...continued

4 Allow the glue to dry. Plane the butterfly keys until they are level with the seat base, then remove the clamps.

◁ **5** Mix a water-based stain to match the wood colour then brush it over the keys. Once the top of the seat has been cleaned and waxed, the crack will be all but invisible.

Repairing the arm

The arm support had broken off at its base. It could not simply be reglued, as the joint would not be strong enough to hold it. A new section would therefore have to be made and fitted.

The bobbin linking the arm to the chair back had been broken off and lost, so a replacement would need to be turned on a lathe.

Repairing the Support

The arm support was cylindrical in shape and tapered to a narrow point that fitted into a hole in the seat. This shape could not be turned on the lathe, but had to be formed by hand.

MATERIALS AND EQUIPMENT

- **drill**
- **wood drill bit**
- **beech**
- **tenon saw**
- **plane**
- **paring chisel**
- **PVA (white) glue**
- **snap clamp**
- **spokeshave**
- **fine-grade sandpaper**
- **hammer**

◁ **1** Remove the broken part of the upright that still remains in the seat by drilling it out from the underside. Choose a drill bit that matches the diameter of the existing hole.

2 Plane the support at an angle and draw a corresponding line on a piece of beech that is slightly bigger than the support.

3 Cut the beech along the line. Plane the end of the longer piece of beech until it is smooth and fits snugly against the support.

4 Glue the support to the centre of the planed end of the beech, and clamp it in position. Leave to dry then remove the clamp.

5 Place the support in a vice and roughly shape the beech with a spokeshave. Continue until it is cylindrical and tapers to a size that will fit in the hole in the seat.

6 Smooth the support with sandpaper. Continue until it matches the support on the other arm of the chair, comparing the two often so that you do not remove too much material.

◁ **7** Fit the upright in the chair seat. Check its height against the upright on the other side. If necessary, continue sanding until the correct height has been reached.

▷

Repairing the support...continued

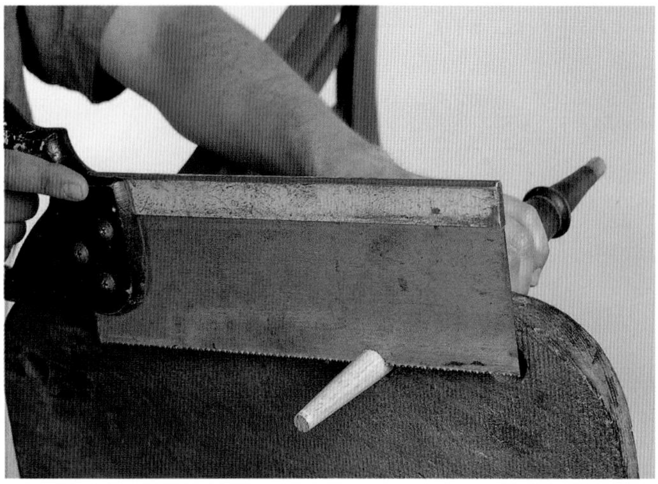

8 With the suppot inserted in the seat, saw off the excess wood so that it protrudes slightly from the seat.

9 Place the arm support in a vice and use a saw to remove a narrow wedge, about 2.5cm/1in deep, from the bottom of the support.

▷**10** Fit the support back into the seat and apply glue to the wedge-shaped slot. Cut a beech wedge that is marginally larger than the wedge cut out of the support, and hammer it into the slot. This will expand the end of the support, giving a tight joint. When the glue is dry, make the support flush with the underside of the seat using a plane or a paring chisel.

Turning a Bobbin

To replace the missing arm bobbin, a new bobbin, with the same dimensions as the bobbin on the undamaged arm, must be turned. This requires skilful lathe work.

MATERIALS AND EQUIPMENT

- drill
- wood drill bits
- beech
- lathe
- turning tools
- dividers
- callipers
- very fine-grade sandpaper
- bench hook
- tenon saw
- PVA (white) glue
- sash clamps
- clamping blocks

◁ **1** Drill out the remainder of the spigot that joined the original bobbin to the back upright. Use a drill bit that corresponds to the diameter of the original hole.

2 Turn a piece of beech to the approximate diameter of the bobbin on the other arm. It is always best to be cautious at this stage; if you over-turn the wood, you will have to start again.

3 Use a pair of dividers, set to the width of the existing bobbin, to mark the new bobbin's position on the rough-turned beech.

4 Use a paring chisel to cut into the wood on each side of the bobbin outline, in preparation for forming the spigots.

5 Continue turning the spigots until they approach the correct diameter, making frequent checks with callipers set to the size of the spigots on the existing bobbin.

◁ **6** Check that the diameter of the spigots is slightly larger than the spigot hole on the arm. This will ensure a good fit and make the joints stronger. Take care, though, that the larger size does not change the balance or proportions of the original piece.

7 Use an angled chisel to turn the bobbin to the correct shape. There is no easy way to do this except with patience and experience. If a mistake is made, the whole process has to be started again. ▷

Turning a bobbin...continued

8 Having turned the bobbin, cut a series of shallow grooves into the two spigots with a turning chisel to give any excess glue somewhere to escape to when the joint is glued. (A joint with too much glue in, and no space for it to escape to, will split the surrounding wood.)

9 With correctly sharpened tools and the proper technique, there should be very little need for much cleaning up, but a final sanding with very fine-grade sandpaper will finish off the turned bobbin. Do not sand the two spigots.

10 Remove the length of beech from the lathe, hold it firmly on a bench hook and cut away the ends with a tenon saw. Make sure you leave enough spigot material to ensure a snug fit in both the back upright and the arm.

11 Use a drill to clean out the spigot hole in the arm. Use a drill bit that corresponds to the size of the new spigot.

12 Glue one spigot into the arm and the other into the back upright. The arm can now be glued to the new support and clamped until dry.

Repairing the legs

The back feet had been reduced in height, making the legs too short, so it is necessary to build them up to make the chair level again. They had been cut off at an angle, so it is not possible simply to glue on extra pieces without them being obvious. The best solution is to replace the whole foot section with a longer version, joining at the old ankle, so that the joint is cleverly disguised. The front original feet can act as a guide to both style and size.

MATERIALS AND EQUIPMENT

- beech
- tenon saw
- steel rule
- drill
- wood drill bits
- lathe
- turning tools
- callipers
- fine-grade sandpaper
- bench hook
- centre finder
- PVA (white) glue
- sash clamps
- fine brush
- spirit-based (alcohol-based) stain
- rubber
- polish
- cloth (cotton rag)
- wax

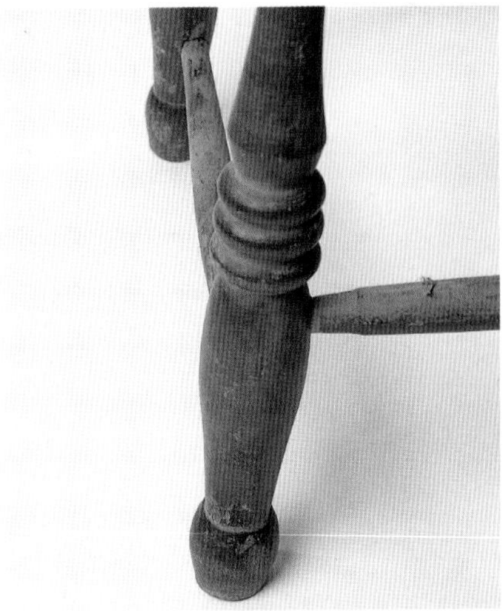

◁ **1** Select a piece of beech to match the rest of the leg, and cut it to a suitable length and a width larger than the diameter of the foot. Mark the centre of the block on each end with a steel rule and drill a hole about 1cm/⅜in deep at each end.

▷ **2** Cut a shallow groove along a cross-mark at one end with a tenon saw. This drilled and grooved end will house the head stock of the lathe and the end with just the hole will house the tail stock. Both stocks are used to rotate the wood. Measure the existing foot with callipers.

3 Mount the beech in the lathe, then, using a large gouge, roughly turn the wood to the diameter of the widest part of the foot. Do not push the gouge too hard or at too acute an angle, as this could cause it to be "snatched" by the square edges of the wooden block.

4 Use the callipers to mark out the end of the foot and a turning chisel to cut a shallow groove. Then turn a spigot, which will be inserted into the leg.

▷

Repairing the legs...continued

5 Mark a line from which the bulbous shape will be turned, then shape the foot using a skew chisel. Place the bevel against the wood and, after it has been raised and begun to cut, turn it with a smooth rolling action. This will give the required shape.

6 Finish off the shaped foot by gently applying fine-grade sandpaper to remove any tool marks. Cut the excess from the bottom and cut the spigot to the correct length.

7 Place the leg on a bench hook and cut off the shortened foot flush at the ankle. This will mean that the new foot will be attached at a natural joint line, disguising the fact that it is a later replacement.

8 Mark the centre of the leg using a centre finder. This is a useful tool that will enable you to determine the centre of any round item.

9 Drill out the centre of the leg to a diameter that matches the spigot at the top of the new foot. Make sure that the drill is held in line with the leg; it can be helpful to have someone watch you to make sure that the drill does not wander off line.

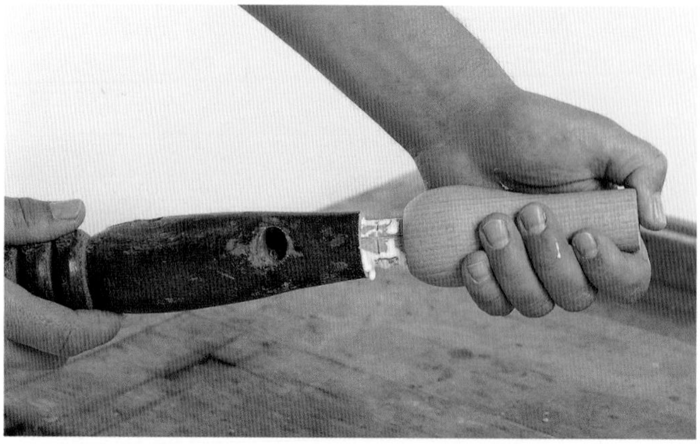

10 Glue the foot to the leg and use a sash clamp to apply pressure. By attaching the foot in this way, the strength of the joint will be as good as if the leg and foot had been turned from the same piece of wood. Leave to dry, then remove the clamp.

11 Make and attach another foot in the same way, then clean out all the leg and stretcher holes before gluing the joints and reassembling the chair legs and stretchers.

12 Mix a spirit-based (alcohol-based) stain to match the original wood (see p.41), then brush this over the two new feet.

13 Finally, charge a rubber with polish and apply a layer over both new feet (see pp.66–67). Then wax the entire chair so that the repairs blend in (see p.68).

Left: *The restored chair is as good as new and will now sit at the angle originally intended by the maker. The chair will require no further maintenance other than the occasional waxing.*

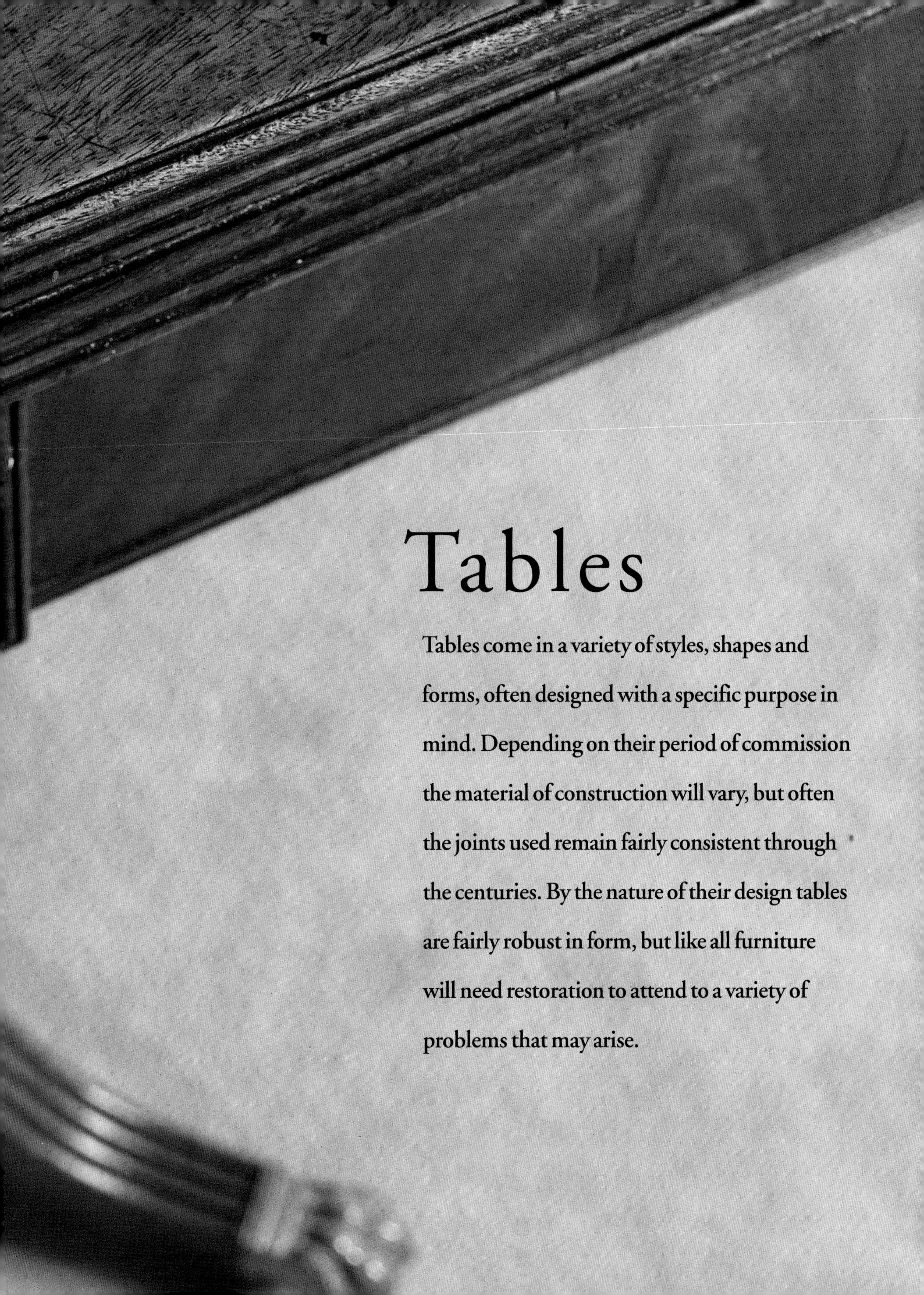

Tables

Tables come in a variety of styles, shapes and forms, often designed with a specific purpose in mind. Depending on their period of commission the material of construction will vary, but often the joints used remain fairly consistent through the centuries. By the nature of their design tables are fairly robust in form, but like all furniture will need restoration to attend to a variety of problems that may arise.

History of tables

The table has to be one of the most varied types of furniture in existence, with its role over the centuries being developed to suit numerous requirements ranging from business to functional to aesthetic. To trace the table's history one has to delve back to a much earlier period when furniture was scarce and great importance was placed on what little there was. While the earliest examples were basic in their design, they rapidly evolved.

Left: *A late 17th-century oak gateleg table designed to seat eight people.*

During the medieval period, the dining table would be found in the great hall of the manor. There would usually be a dormant table at which the master and mistress plus any family members or favoured guests would sit. This table, often massive in size, would consist of a thick-planked top with a jointed underframe supported on large, bluster-turned legs, themselves joined by low stretchers. The room might also have further tables with planked tops, but these were of trestle construction and could be dismantled with the removal of pegs holding the supports in place to allow for dancing after the meal.

An interesting development during the 16th century was the draw table, where pull-out leaves were added to the basic refectory table design. Smaller tables that could be drawn up to the fireplace in winter, known as cricket tables, were also being used, and, like the refectory tables, were made from oak. They were basic in their construction, with a round top supported on three turned legs. With the exception of variations to the carved decoration, the basic model of the refectory or draw table remained fairly similar through to the 17th century.

During the latter part of the 17th century, dining in the great hall went out of fashion. New manor houses were being built with smaller, more intimate rooms, and these demanded a new style of table. The gate-leg table, designed to seat between eight and ten people, had a

Left: *The planked-top refectory dining table with its heavy carved base was popular from medieval times through to the 17th century.*

rectangular top similar to the refectory table but with two rounded flaps, which were hinged on one side and allowed the table to be folded down when not in use. Usually made from oak, but sometimes from walnut, these tables rapidly overtook the refectory, which was now made on a smaller scale and demoted to a buffet or side table. Other small tables were also produced to act as side or perhaps writing tables; their appearance owed much to the refectory table.

In European furniture, elaborate and gilded tables began to appear in the finest stately houses and palaces. Tables covered in gesso and carved detail were much prized, but it was not until the mid- to late 17th century that tables designed for a particular role began to develop their own distinctive style and character.

Left: *As gambling became an increasingly popular pastime from the late 17th century onward, elaborate gaming or card tables were made by the cabinet-makers of the period.*

Cards were introduced to Europe during the 15th century, and gambling with dice was then also commonplace, but it was not until the late 17th century that specific tables for playing cards and gaming were made in any great numbers. The earliest card tables were usually veneered in walnut, with fold-over tops supported on single or double gates. Their evolution developed through the 18th century, with the only variations being the wood used and the type of embellishment added. Early tops were lined in velvet or needlework, but by the early 18th century baize was more popular. The main stylistic change came during the 19th century, when the gate-leg frame was replaced by four separate legs or a central column standing on a platform base on which the top would revolve before being supported on the carcass frame.

The introduction of the use of mahogany in furniture making during the early 18th century prompted another stylistic change. Underframes became much lighter, stretchers were removed and legs, following the trend of the time, became more cabriole in profile, with carved lion paw or pad feet. With the increasing size of the country house and the fashion for entertaining on a larger scale, longer tables were now made. At first these were supported by numerous legs, but this soon gave way to the pedestal table, which was more elegant and user-friendly. These tables, sometimes able to seat 20 people, developed in the same form through the 18th and 19th centuries, with only the style and form of the bases changing to match the fashions.

Left: *With the increased fashion for entertaining on a large scale, three-, four-, or five-pillar dining tables were commissioned for the large country houses of the 18th century.*

At the same time, another style of rectangular table evolved. This was designed to suit the fashion for smaller town houses and could be reduced in length to accommodate a varying number of diners. Various techniques were used to support the table tops, with concertina and pull-out bearers being incorporated. By the mid-19th century, however, numerous legs had been replaced by only four, and the weight of the table tops was supported by a central threaded metal draw bar operated with a winch-like handle inserted into the end.

As well as the larger dining table there was, of course, a need for smaller tables, known as breakfast tables. Originally designed so that the family could enjoy an intimate breakfast together rather than feel lost around a large pillar table, they quickly developed, especially during the latter part of the 18th century, to suit the growing number of smaller town houses.

Above: *A superb example of an 18th-century kettle stand.*

One interesting table is the Irish wake table. Made during the mid-18th century, this was a long oval with a narrow central section on to which twin hinged flaps were attached. During a wake, the coffin would be laid in the centre of the table, with the food and drink for the mourners placed on the raised flaps on either side.

A blossoming of interest in the arts, business and entertaining promoted the evolution of a whole range of tables from the 18th century onward. A ceremony that probably inspired more furniture-makers than most was the taking of tea, which became the social highlight of the day during the 18th century and was seen as an opportunity to flaunt one's wealth and social position. A wide range of tables connected to the tea ceremony sprang up, including kettle stands, often richly carved, on which the silver kettle would stand; urn tables with delicate legs on which the urn would sit; and silver tables, with their open-fret galleries, pierced brackets and elegant stretchers, which would sit central in the drawing room and on which the silver tea set would be placed. The tea table, similar to the card table but with a veneered interior rather than a baized one, would be ideal for sitting at, and small tripod tables with round tops would be placed beside the settees and chairs.

In the mid-18th century, small flap-tables began to appear; these had hinged brackets rather than gate-legs supporting the flaps. Known as Pembroke tables, they were used to breakfast on or as ladies' writing tables. Another new appearance was the drum table, with a circular top and number of built-in drawers, which furnished offices and libraries.

In the drawing room, large pier tables, evolved from the earlier card and side tables, were placed on either side of windows or fireplaces with the new fashionable pier glasses above them. Behind settees sat elegant sofa tables, which were longer, rectangular versions of the Pembroke table. In short, tables were designed and commissioned for almost every use in the 18th century. Their overall designs remained fairly unaltered throughout the 19th century, although more decorative inlays and woods were used, the main difference being the gravitation toward a more robust style.

Above: *Although English in style, this outstanding 18th-century tripod is in fact American in origin. This illustrates how designs were carried across the Atlantic.*

During the early years of the 20th century, furniture-makers such as Charles Rennie Mackintosh (1868–1928) showed a wide virtuosity in table design, but it was not until the 1920s that function finally took precedence over form. Over the century, the emphasis on eating together faded, and the dining table became less central to the home. More meals were being eaten in the kitchen and the dining table was reserved for more formal occasions and entertaining. In its place sprang up coffee tables and, more recently, computer desks. Where once oak, mahogany or walnut were the only choice, now laminates, steel, chrome and plastic are all incorporated into the modern table.

TABLE CONSTRUCTION

Antique tables dating from medieval times to the early 20th century come in all manner of forms, each designed and made to undertake a particular role. The construction principles remain the same, however, although the joints used and degree of construction detail may vary. The earliest forms of refectory table, for example, consisted of little more than a planked top fixed to a trestle base, but over the years the aesthetics of the piece rapidly developed.

From the 15th century onward, table bases were held together with dowelled tenons, which were the strongest type of joint. When better adhesives appeared, the dowel in the joint was used less often.

When smaller gate-leg tables became fashionable, a new type of joint known as the knuckle joint was devised. This allowed part of the underframe, which was attached to the gate leg, to swing out, away from the main frame, and support the hinged part of the top.

When the sofa table first appeared later in the 18th century, it had twin end supports joined by a central stretcher. This stretcher gradually became lower as the bases became heavier. By the early 19th century the twin ends had often been replaced by a central column, which sat on smaller splay legs.

The legs of central column tables are fixed to the column with dovetailed tenons to ensure that the weight does not collapse the base. As an extra precaution, there will often be a metal strengthening bracket as well. With drum tables the column may pass through the underside of the top to allow it to revolve, and it is usually fixed with a birdcage movement – a removable wedge that allows the base and top to be disconnected.

Decoration became more important from the late 17th century onward. For instance, 18th-century open-fret galleries surrounding the tops of tea tables were there to prevent the service being knocked off. Their construction was one of the earliest forms of laminating, with three layers of veneer, each at right angles to the next layer to give added strength. The fret would be cut out from this laminate, and the gallery would be joined with small foxtail mitres, which involved using slithers of veneer as joining pieces.

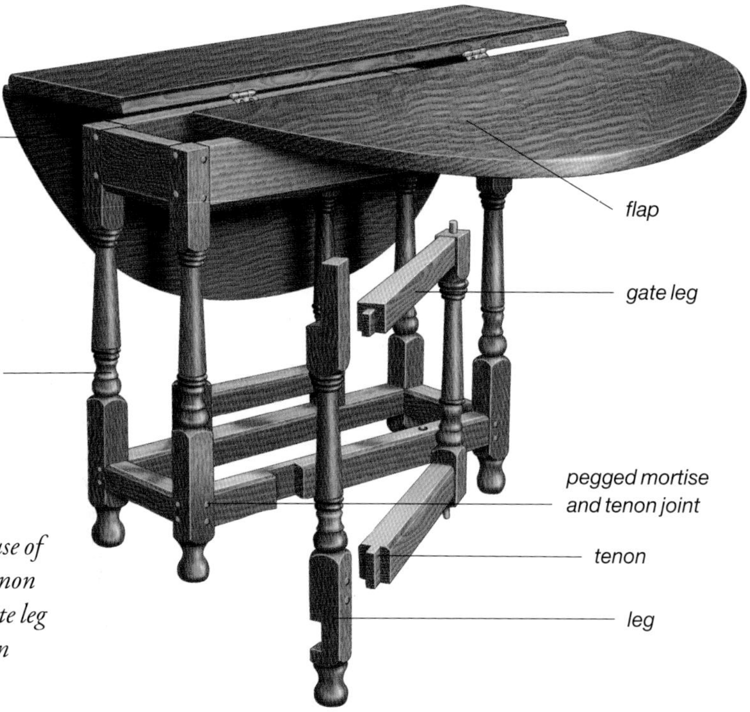

Right: *The use of the pegged tenon joint and gate leg was typical in early tables.*

Right: *The tripod table has a birdcage block and wedge, which allowed the top to be removed from the base.*

DISMANTLING AND REASSEMBLING TABLES

Although tables come in many styles, their basic construction remains the same and the method required to knock them apart remains fairly consistent. The dismantling procedure must be followed in a logical step-by-step manner, and particular care must be taken to identify the types of joint employed. Failure to do so could result in smashed joints and unnecessary further damage. Once the table has been taken apart, you can inspect the components and carry out any necessary restoration or repair work before reassembling it.

Dismantling the table

This table is a George III, c.1800 drop-leaf Pembroke table made from Cuban mahogany. Over a period of time, its joints have become loose, but before any necessary repair work can be done, the table needs to be dismantled.

MATERIALS AND EQUIPMENT

- **chalk or masking tape**
- **screwdriver**
- **hammer**
- **hardwood block**
- **toothbrush**
- **rasp**

1 Label the various parts of the table, either with chalk or by applying marked masking tape, which will not mark the polish.

2 Turn the table upside down and lay it on a protected workbench. Remove all the screws from the frame, which will release the top.

3 Now unscrew any metal brackets that may have been added to the table in the past to strengthen any damaged joints.

Tip

If a screw is difficult to remove, fit the blade of an old screwdriver into the screw slot, tap the handle firmly with a hammer and tighten the screw slightly. This should break the bond, allowing the screw to be removed.

◁ **4** Examine the construction of the joints to decide the best method of knocking apart without causing further damage.

◁ **5** Disassemble the various components, taking care not to cause structural damage to the joints. Failure to do so will result in smashed joints that will need to be restored prior to the table being reassembled. Use a hardwood block to prevent bruising by the hammer.

6 When separating the side frame from the legs, use the hardwood block again to guard against bruising by the hammer. Direct the blows as closely as possible to the actual joint.

7 Now knock the legs apart from the remaining frame, using the same technique and making sure you put a piece of hardwood between the hammer and the leg to prevent any damage.

8 Remove all traces of glue with a toothbrush and hot water. Where animal glues have crystallized, use a rasp to clean the joint. Take care not to file away any of the tenon, as this will result in a sloppy joint.

9 Carefully check the various parts of the table once it is dismantled, before carrying out any necessary restoration work.

Reassembling the table

When all the necessary restoration work has been carried out, the table can be reassembled. PVA (white) glue and animal glue are the best adhesives to use.

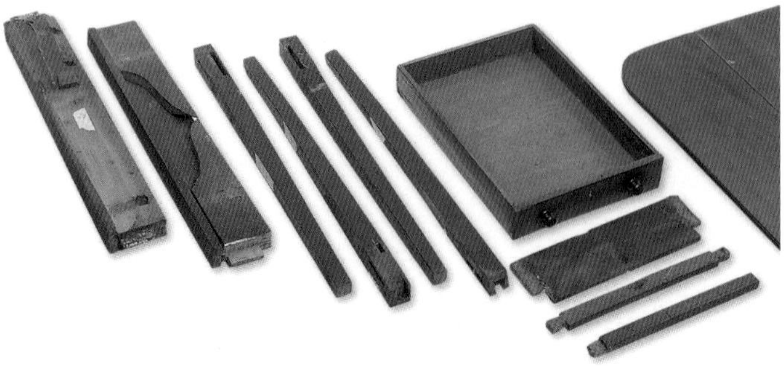

MATERIALS AND EQUIPMENT

- PVA (white) or animal glue
- sash clamps
- clamping blocks
- hammer
- hardwood block
- masking tape
- drill
- flat-bottomed grain plug drill bit
- grain plug cutter
- mahogany
- chisel
- fine-grade sandpaper
- hand drill
- wood drill bit
- screwdriver
- screws
- flat-bladed knife
- stopping wax
- cloths (rags)
- methylated spirits (methyl alcohol)
- spirit- (alcohol-) based stain
- brush
- rubber
- polish
- wax

1 Glue the front legs and the front frame together. Apply pressure with a sash clamp, using clamping blocks to protect the polished surface, and leave to dry. Repeat for the back legs and back frame.

2 Now complete the table frame by gluing both pairs of legs together, using the bottom rail at the drawer end and the side frame at the other end. Stand the table on a flat, level surface to do this. Make sure that the frame is square by measuring across the diagonal corners. Clamp as before.

3 This top rail is secured by dovetail joints, so it should be glued back into position at this stage. Tap the dovetails into their recesses with a hammer and a hardwood block. If the rail had mortise and tenon joints, it should have been fitted at the same time as the bottom rail.

◁ **4** Before the glue has set, fit the drawer to ensure that the table is square. If the drawer sticks or rubs, you may need to make small adjustments. Leave the glue to dry overnight. When it is dry, remove the clamps.

▷ **5** Beneath the top, there was evidence that the previous screw fixings had been pulled out and the hinge moved to try to get a better purchase. Since the top will be reset in its original position, the old screw holes can be plugged.

6 Follow steps 1 and 2 on p.177 to enlarge the existing screw holes. Cut small plugs of wood to fill them, and then glue the plugs in place.

7 When the glue is dry, use a chisel to level the plugs off flush with the underside of the table, then sand them with fine-grade sandpaper. There is now a smooth surface for the screws to be set into.

8 Now turn the top upside down and put it on the protected workbench. Put the frame back in the correct position. Since the old holes have been plugged, drill pilot holes to locate the positions of the screws.

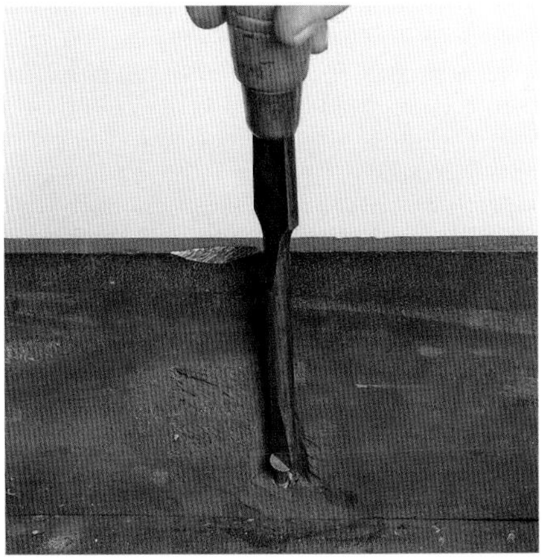

◁ **9** If you are using the old screws, screw them into the new holes. If you are using replacements, check that they are the right length and will not go through the table top and mark the surface.

▷ **10** Using a flat-bladed knife, fill the screw holes made by the metal brackets removed earlier with stopping wax in a similar colour to the mahogany.

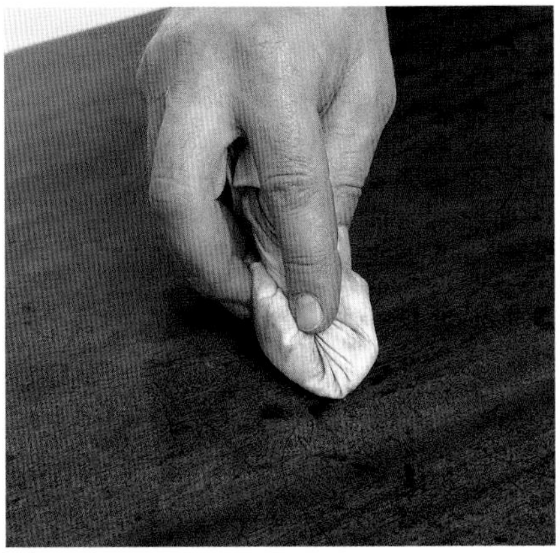

11 Stain the repairs to match the wood. Wash the surface off with methylated spirits (methyl alcohol). Charge a rubber with polish and revive the surface. Apply wax and buff the wood to a warm lustre.

Left: *Reassembled and polished, the table has been restored to its former glory and is ready to give many more years of service.*

REPAIRING CARVING

Carving as a form of decoration on furniture has been in existence since medieval times, but by the 17th century its use was becoming more widespread.

When restoring or replacing carving, it is important to select a similar-grained piece of wood. It is often advisable to make an initial test cut with a carving tool to ensure that the wood is suitable to work with. This is because some wood will have a grain that is too "wild", which means that you may tear rather than cut the wood. Alternatively, the wood might be too soft, which could result in the wood simply crumbling when being carved and unable to keep a crisp edge.

Carving a damaged bracket

During the 17th and 18th centuries, carved and shaped legs had brackets, or ears as they are commonly referred to, that were applied separately rather than being part of the leg. As a result, if the animal glue perished, the bracket could become detached and even lost.

This table had lost a bracket from one of its swing legs, so the leg needs to be removed and a replacement bracket made. A profile of the carving on the other swing leg bracket needs to be taken so that it can be used as the basis for the new carved decoration, which can then be stained and polished to match the other legs.

MATERIALS AND EQUIPMENT
- tenon saw
- Cuban mahogany
- spokeshave
- animal glue
- modelling clay
- mallet
- indelible ink
- marker pen
- carving tools
- screwdriver
- fine brushes
- bichromate of potash
- polish
- pumice powder
- cloths (cotton rags)
- rubber
- colour
- fine wire (steel) wool
- wax
- large soft brush

△ **1** Cut a profile bracket out of Cuban mahogany and shape it with a spokeshave. It should be similar to the missing bracket but slightly larger to allow the carving to be undertaken, otherwise it will end up too small. Glue it into place.

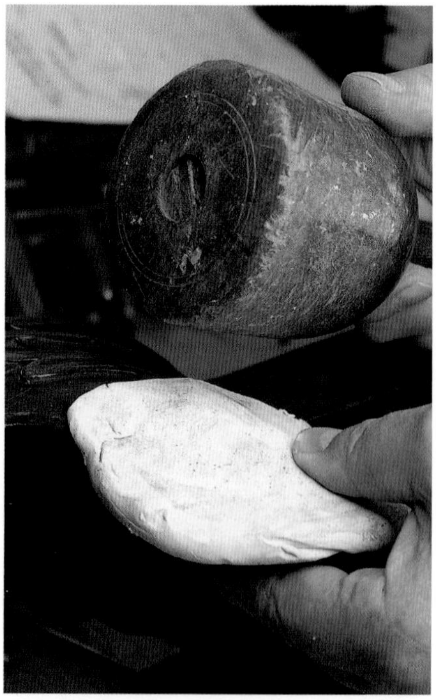

△ **2** To obtain the correct profile of the missing carving, lay a piece of modelling clay over the matching bracket on the other swing leg. Tap it lightly with a mallet, then gently peel it away.

3 Turn the clay over and use your thumb to cover the profile of the carving with indelible ink. Then lay it gently on the replacement bracket to leave the outline of the carving on the wood.

4 Remove the clay then thicken the outline with a marker pen, making sure the lines flow into the carving on the rest of the bracket.

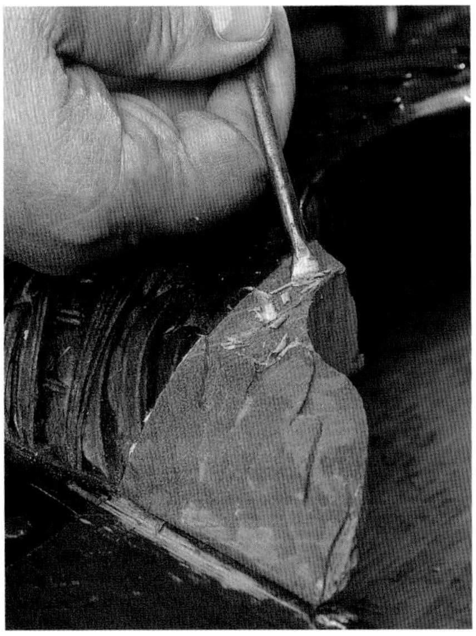

◁ **5** Having established the outline of the carving, remove the groundwork using grounders. This technique, known as grounding out, establishes the depth of carving.

◁ **6** When the outline of the carving has been set, carve the detail into the relief, using either veiners or modellers. There should be no need to clean up the carving, as the razor sharpness of the tools should give a perfect finish.

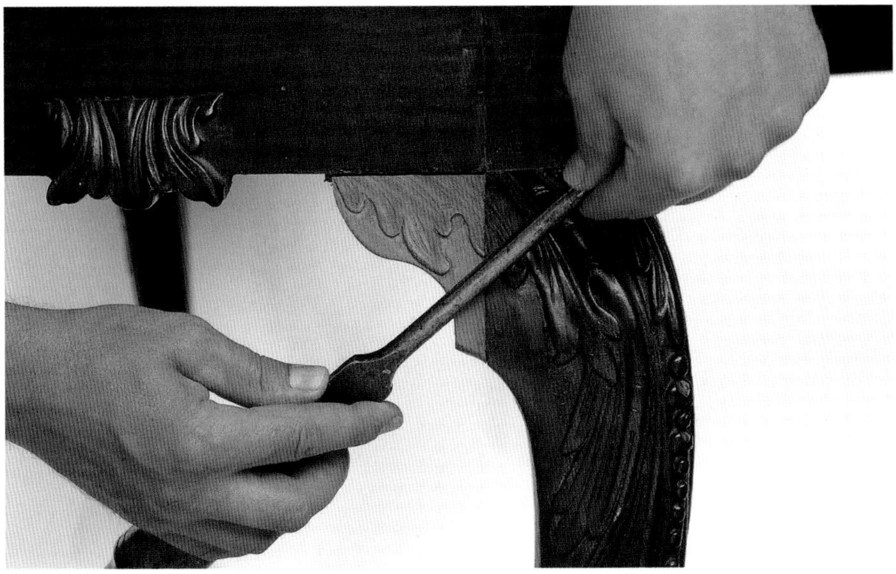

◁ **7** Reattach both swing legs to the table and round off the sharp edges of the new bracket using the shank of a screwdriver or some similar tool.

▷

Carving a damaged bracket...continued

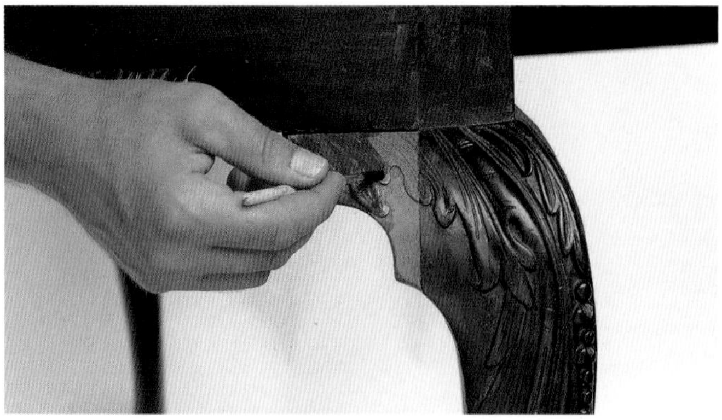

8 In its natural state, mahogany is a red colour, but over the years it patinates to a brown tone. To mimic this colour, apply bichromate of potash, which, being a chemical stain, reacts with the tannin in the wood to turn the natural red tone into a more suitable brown.

9 Apply the polish with a brush, painting it on evenly. The idea is just to fill the grain, so do not use too much, otherwise streaks and runs may occur.

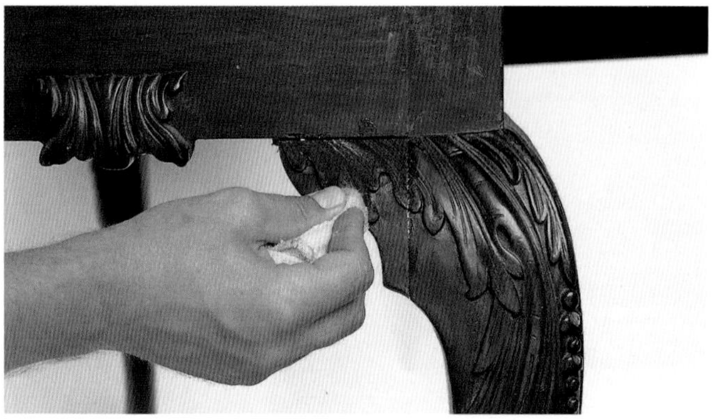

10 Put some polish on a cloth (cotton rag) and sprinkle some fine pumice powder on it. Use this to work the polish into the grain. Do not round over the edges or break through highlights to reveal wood.

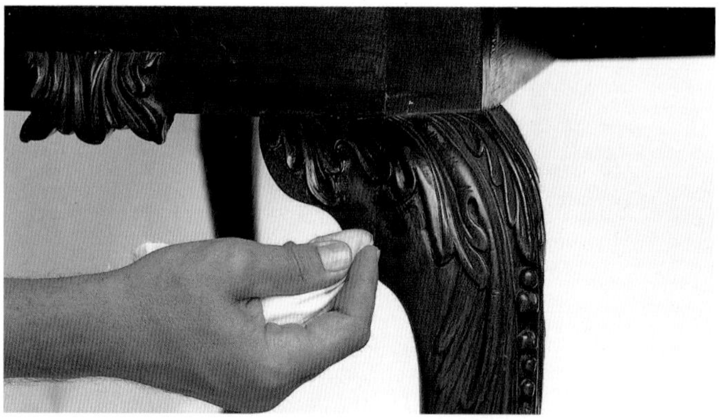

11 With the grain filled, use a rubber to apply further polish mixed with some colour until the bracket tone blends in with the leg and matches the original bracket (see pp.66–67).

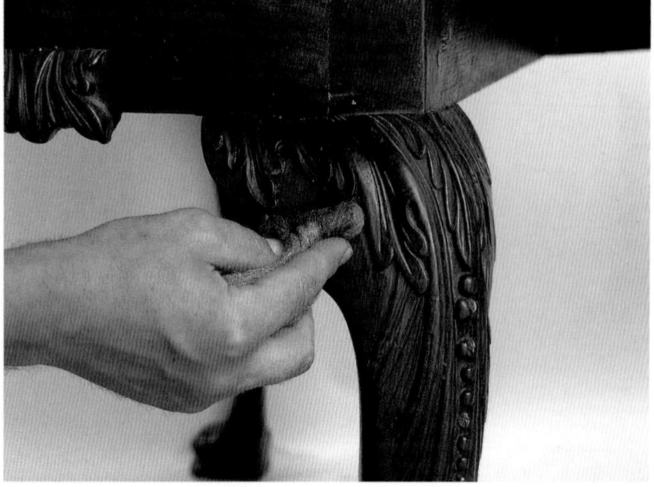

12 After the polish has hardened, cut it back with fine wire (steel) wool, then wax the bracket (see p. 68).

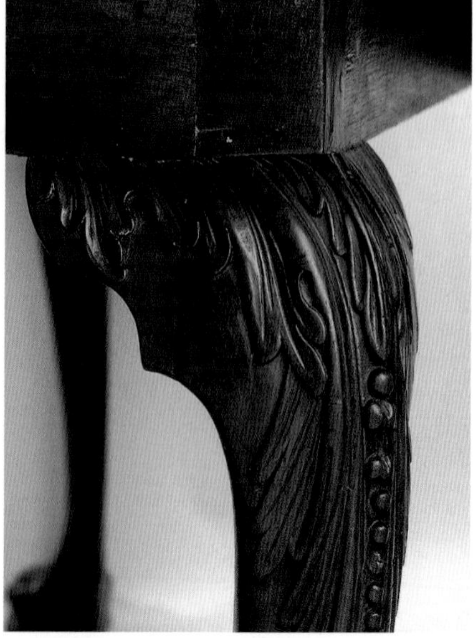

Right: *After the bracket has been polished and waxed, it will look original. It is worth noting the amount of distressing on the bracket you have taken a profile from and trying to mirror it on the replacement. However, be careful not to overdo this and give the bracket a "fake" look.*

Carving small pieces

The previous technique covered replacing a completely missing carved section, piece or bracket; on occasion, however, you may need to replace only small pieces of carving. The method or technique used for this is different to that of replacing a complete section, because your aim is to fill in the small areas that are missing with pieces of wood, and then to carve them to match the original. The pieces cannot be carved and then glued into place, as the detailed carving needs to be flowing and the replacements undetectable. This carved foliate bracket has many sections of leaf and vine missing.

MATERIALS AND EQUIPMENT
- mahogany
- fine-bladed fret saw
- animal glue
- carving tools
- fine brushes
- stain
- polish

1 Hold a new piece of mahogany against one of the missing areas and roughly sketch out the profile in pencil.

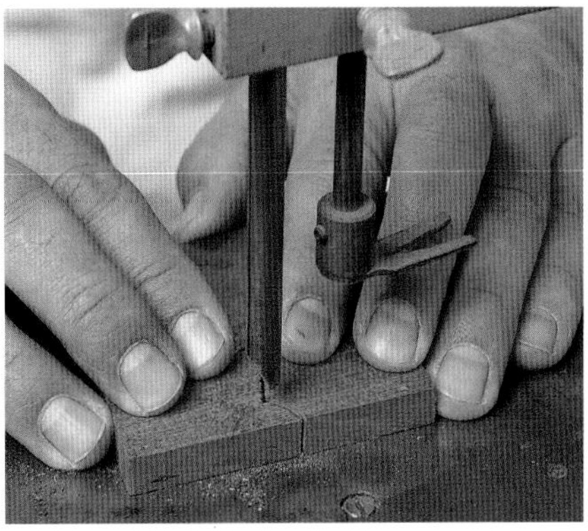

2 Use a fine-bladed fret saw to cut the wood to the approximate size. Repeat steps 1 and 2 for all the other missing pieces.

◁ **3** Glue the pieces into place and leave them to dry. Draw in the outlines of the missing pieces to give a guide for carving, although the majority of the work will be done by eye.

◁ **4** After roughing out the outlines, carve the chosen shapes and patterns. Use tools that are razor sharp, otherwise the new pieces may break off. Should this happen, glue them back into position. Finally, add the details, matching the original carver's style.

Above: *When completed, the newly carved areas should be stained and polished to match the rest of the bracket. The highly carved surface demands that a fine brush be used for both techniques.*

REPAIRING TOPS

The top is subject to more general wear and tear than other areas of a table. Scratches, dents and stains are commonplace, and methods of restoring tables with these problems are covered in Surfaces and Finishes (pp.54–85). Other common problems that can occur with table tops are warping, splitting and damaged decorative edges. By using the correct restoration techniques, however, it is possible to make good all of these defects and to bring a damaged top back to the condition it was in when the table was made.

Restoring a damaged table edge

This Cuban mahogany Georgian tripod table is missing a section of its decorative edge. A new piece of wood needs to be cut, glued in place and shaped to fit, before being stained and polished to match the table top. This technique can be used on all moulded edges, including pie-crust tops.

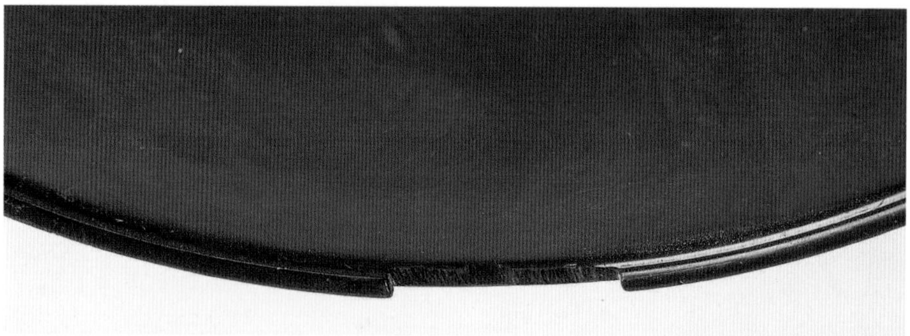

MATERIALS AND EQUIPMENT

- screwdriver
- mahogany
- jigsaw (saber saw)
- tenon saw
- chisel
- PVA (white) glue
- spring clip
- plane
- carving tool
- spokeshave
- fine-grade sandpaper
- brush
- stain
- rubber
- polish

◁ **1** Remove the table top from the frame by undoing all the screws (see p.162). Turn the table top upside down and lay it on a protected surface. Put a piece of mahogany, slightly thicker than the decorative edging, underneath the top, and draw around the edge with a pencil. Slide the mahogany farther out by an amount slightly greater than the width of the decorative edging, and draw another curved line.

2 Cut the mahogany along the pencil lines using a jigsaw (saber saw), then turn the table top right side up again. Cut through the damaged edging on either side of the missing area with a tenon saw.

3 Remove the damaged wood underneath the missing edging with a chisel. Continue working until you have a flat, level surface.

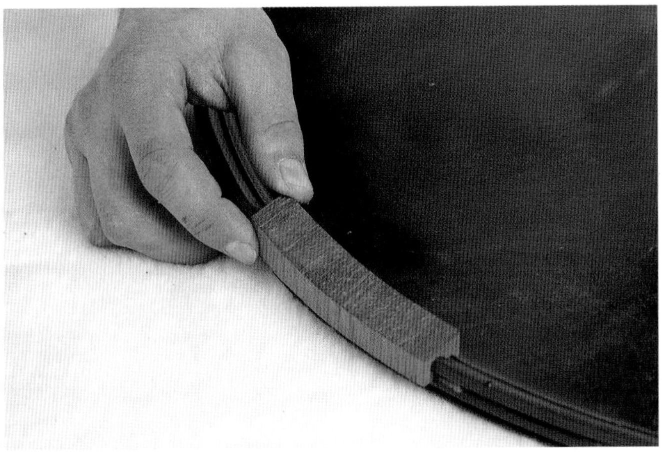

4 Check that the piece of mahogany fits in the allotted space. Apply PVA (white) glue and secure it with a spring clip (see p.215). Leave to dry, then remove the spring clip.

5 Plane the mahogany down until it is level with the rest of the edging. Make small strokes to avoid damaging the table top.

6 The inner ledge on the table must be shaped with a suitable carving tool. Again, avoid damaging the polished mahogany.

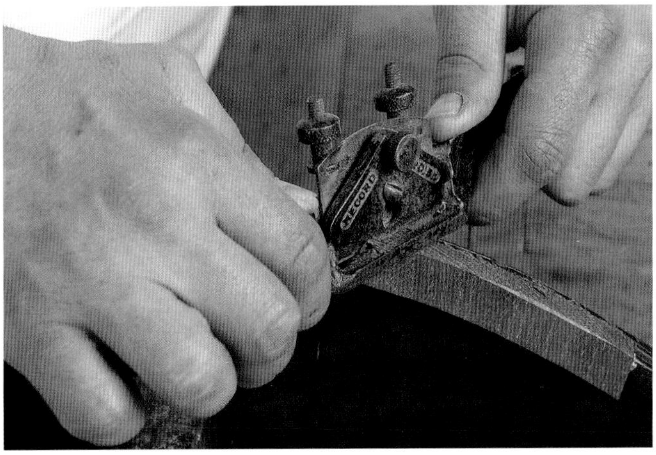

7 Use a spokeshave to shape the curve along the edge of the top. It is easier to obtain a more delicate shape with a spokeshave than a plane.

8 Smooth the top of the restored area with fine-grade sandpaper. Fold a small piece of the sandpaper in half and hold it with your thumb and forefinger for accuracy.

Above: *Once the detailed shape of the edging has been formed with sandpaper, stain (see p.69) and polish (see pp.66–67) the repaired edging so that it is invisible.*

Repairing a rule joint

The rule joint is commonly found on drop-leaf tables. It allows for a leaf to be raised and supported along its length. On occasion, it can become damaged, as shown here, where part of the rule joint has broken away, allowing the hinge to be seen from the top. This could have been caused by the leaf having been raised too high, putting too much pressure on the hinge and joint.

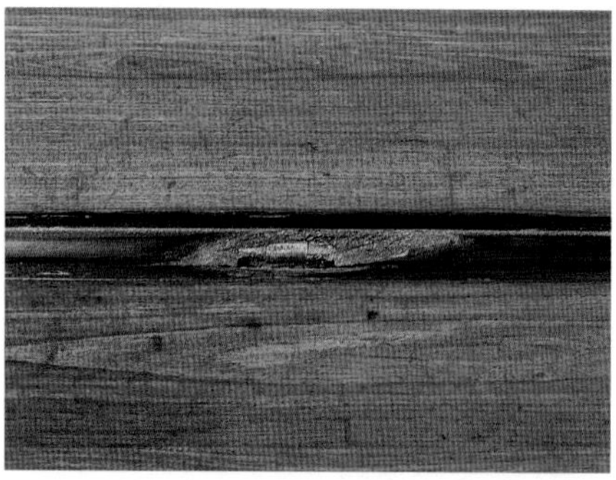

MATERIALS AND EQUIPMENT

- tenon saw
- mahogany
- PVA (white) glue
- spring clip
- chisel
- fine-grade sandpaper
- fine brush
- stain

1 Trim away the damaged area of moulding with a tenon saw. Cutting the ends at angles will help to disguise the repair when it is finally polished.

2 Cut a piece of mahogany to the length of the gap and a little wider, and glue it in place. Clamp it using a spring clip (see p.215), which is ideal for this type of small repair, and leave to dry. Remove the clip.

3 Shape the wood with a chisel and fine-grade sandpaper so that it continues the lines of the existing wood, otherwise the flap may not open properly. Stain it to match the existing moulding.

Drilling out damaged screws

The photograph shows a very common problem: after the screws had been put into this card-table hinge, their heads were filed flat to remove the slots. The flap of this table needed routing out, which meant that the screw heads had to be drilled out so that both hinges could be removed.

MATERIALS AND EQUIPMENT

- centre punch
- hammer
- drill
- metal drill bit
- screwdriver
- long-nose (needle-nose) pliers
- Cuban mahogany
- PVA (white) glue
- chisel

△ **1** First hammer a centre punch into each screw head as accurately as possible.

▷ **2** Drill out the heads of the screws taking care not to drill the actual holes in the hinges any larger than they already are. This will leave countersunk holes, which will be filled by the replacement screws when the hinges are refitted.

3 Using a small screwdriver, carefully ease the hinges clear, being careful not to bend the flaps of the hinges out of shape.

4 Removing the hinges will expose the shanks of the screws, which will still be embedded in the table edge. Drill small holes on each side of, and as close as possible to, the embedded screw shanks.

5 To remove the screws, insert a pair of long-nose (needlenose) pliers into the freshly drilled holes, grip the shank of each screw in turn and pull it out.

◁ **6** The holes must be filled before new screws can be inserted. Cut wedges of Cuban mahogany and glue them into the holes. Trim them flush with a chisel when dry.

Right: *Once the table has been repaired, the hinges can be refitted.*

Repairing fretwork

The illustration shows the damaged open-fret gallery from a Georgian silver table, c.1760. The silver table, as the name suggests, would stand in the drawing room and have the silver tea service placed upon it. Such tables were designed to be elegant and often had open-fret galleries, made from three layers of veneer for strength.

The gallery on this silver table has been damaged and small areas have broken away and been lost. As much as possible of the damaged fretwork will be glued back into place, and the missing areas within this will be filled with pieces from a new section of gallery made specially for the purpose.

MATERIALS AND EQUIPMENT

- superglue
- paper
- wood block
- clamping blocks
- G-clamps
- Cuban mahogany
- band saw
- toothing plane
- cascamite glue
- pigment
- brushes
- hammer
- veneer pins (tacks)
- pincers
- plane
- drill
- wood drill bit
- fine-bladed fret saw
- paring chisel
- tweezers
- fine file
- spirit-based (alcohol-based) stain
- polish

△ **1** The first step in the restoration process is to put back as much of the damaged work as possible, gluing it into place with superglue. The quick-drying nature of this glue allows the gallery to be held in the correct position while the glue sets.

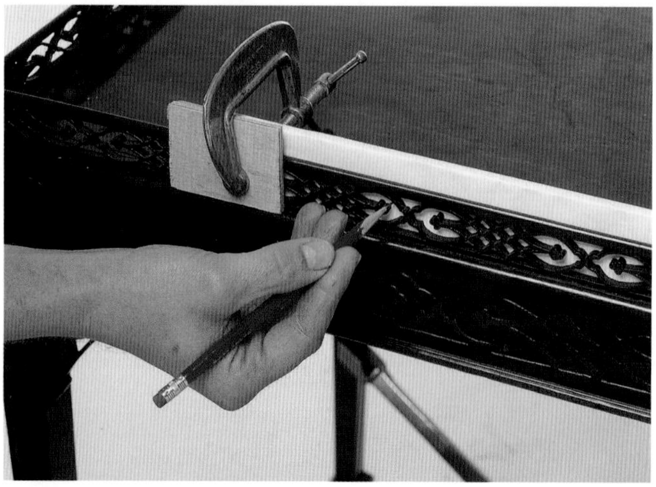

2 To make a new section of gallery for the repairs, wrap a piece of paper around a long block of wood and then use G-clamps and some clamping blocks to hold it against a section of gallery that matches the damaged area. Draw the outline of the fretwork very carefully. Release the clamps and blocks and remove the piece of paper.

3 Cut three lengths of Cuban mahogany with a band saw, roughly the length of the damaged fret area, and, using a toothing plane, plane one side only of two lengths and both sides of the third length. This will aid the purchase of the mahogany when the three layers are glued together.

4 Cut one length into pieces of the same length as the width of the remaining two lengths. These will be the inner core pieces that will give strength to this new section.

5 Cascamite glue, while suited to this job (see p.39), could show as a white line on this gallery, so add a small quantity of pigment to the powder prior to mixing it with water.

6 Coat the planed side of one length of mahogany with cascamite glue then place the short pieces on top to form a second layer. Coat these short pieces with glue.

7 Place the second length on top, planed side down. Tap in two or three small veneer pins (tacks) to prevent the newly formed laminated section slipping when it is clamped up.

8 Place paper strips on either side of the section then put clamping blocks in place. The paper will ensure that any excess glue does not bind the two together. Clamp the section under pressure and leave to dry. The pressure must be even along the whole length.

9 Remove the clamps and blocks, then pull out the veneer pins with pincers. Failure to remove the pins could result in damage to the fret saw when the fret is being cut.

10 Place the gallery in a vice and plane the long edges level with a jack plane.

11 With the laminated section now ready, glue the paper template (pattern) made in step 2 on to it.

Repairing fretwork...continued

12 Drill holes in each area that needs to be fretted out. This will allow the fret saw blade to be put into position.

13 Using a fine fret blade, cut out the open fret, following the design. Work slowly and take great care not to spoil the work already done. Scrape off the remains of the template.

14 Before restoring the glued fretwork, cut any splintered breaks flush using a sharp paring chisel. To protect the fragile fret, place a block of supporting wood behind it.

15 Cut out the sections from the new fret needed to fill the gaps with a fret saw, and carefully insert and glue them in place.

16 Use a fine file to smooth the edges flush where the old and new pieces join, taking care not to alter the open-fretted shape.

17 Repeat until all the damage is repaired. Finally, stain and polish the new portions of fret to match the existing gallery.

Right: *With the fretwork restored, stained and polished, this silver table can once again be returned to the drawing room of the large country house from where it came.*

Filling screw holes

Over the years, a piece of furniture may be subjected to a number of repairs that relied on brackets or reinforcing plates being screwed on. During restoration, these will be removed, leaving the screw holes behind. Fortunately, it is easy to fill these holes with wooden plugs.

MATERIALS AND EQUIPMENT
- masking tape
- drill
- flat-bottomed grain plug drill bit
- grain plug cutter
- wood
- PVA (white) glue
- chisel
- fine-grade sandpaper
- brush
- stain

1 Mark the required drilling depth on the flat-bottomed grain plug drill bit with some masking tape (see Tip), then drill a hole larger than the old screw hole.

2 Use a grain plug cutter to cut a plug from matching wood, making it slightly longer than the hole's depth. Glue it into the hole.

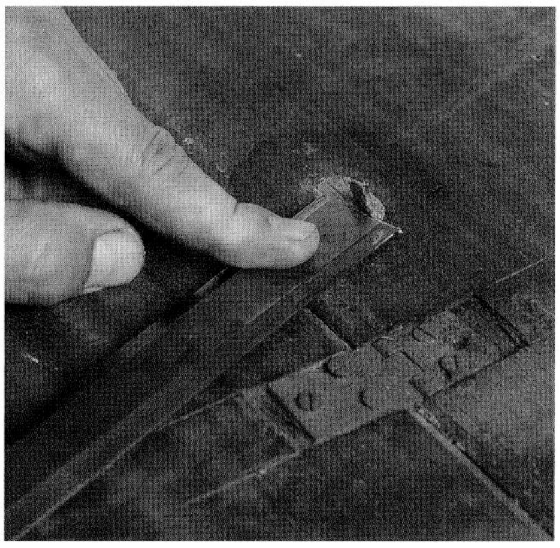

3 When the glue has dried, pare off the projecting portion of the plug with a sharp chisel, then sand it smooth.

Above: *The finished repair is now ready to be stained.*

Tip

If a drilled hole must not penetrate all the way through a piece of wood, it is vital to know how far you can drill before this will happen. First ascertain the required depth of the hole by holding the drill bit against the edge of the wood, then mark this level on the drill bit with a piece of masking tape. When drilling into the wood, stop as soon as the masking tape touches the surface. The hole will then remain invisible from the other side.

Correcting a warped card table

A dry level of humidity is the most common cause of warping. The flaps of veneered card tables, and other types of flap-over or drop-leaf table, are more prone to warping than frame tables for two reasons. First, they are usually relatively thin (for ease of handling), and second, they are free-standing, secured to the base only by their hinges.

The flap of this mahogany card table is significantly warped. Fortunately, the veneer has not split, which means that the core material can be removed from the baize-covered side, and then replaced with a new, flat MDF (medium-density fiberboard) interior. Finally, a new baize cover can be added without disturbing the veneered upper surface.

MATERIALS AND EQUIPMENT

- flat-bladed knife
- screwdriver
- 5cm/2in masking tape
- padded packaging
- cloth (cotton rag)
- iron
- board
- scraper
- marking gauge
- chipboard (particle board)
- saw
- softwood
- drill
- wood drill bit
- chipboard screws
- MDF (medium-density fiberboard)
- router
- gouge
- smoothing plane
- jigsaw (saber saw)
- fine-grade sandpaper
- PVA (white) glue
- large pieces of wood
- G-clamps
- rubber
- shellac polish
- wood filler
- baize
- utility knife
- tooling wheel

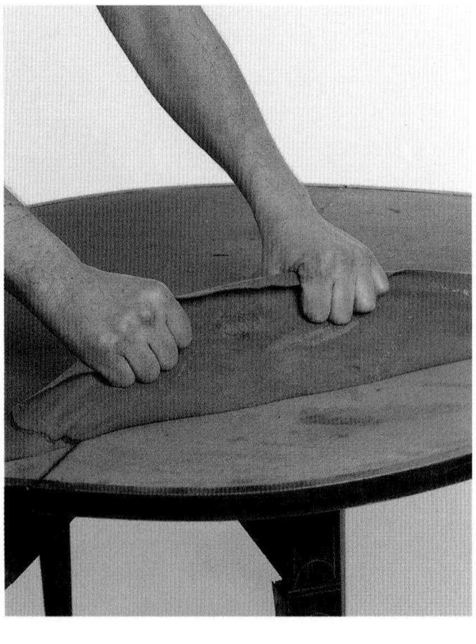

1 Lever the edge of the baize away from the table with a flat-bladed knife. Grip the baize firmly with both hands and pull it off with one continuous movement. Unscrew the hinges linking the flap to the table.

2 Place the flap, veneer side up, on a protected workbench. Cover the surface with strips of masking tape. This will hold together the veneer, banding and stringing on this side until a new core is inserted.

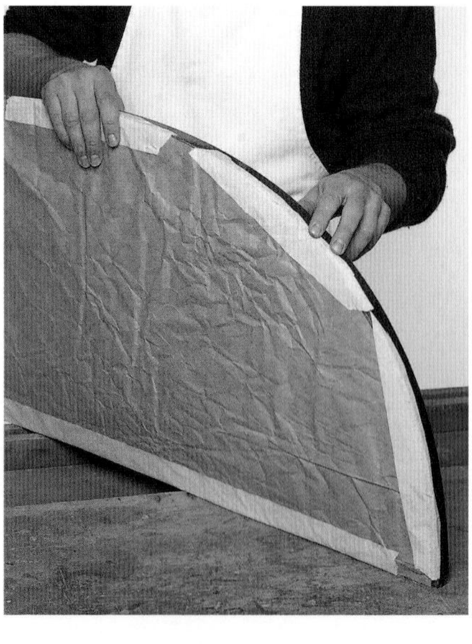

3 Cut a semicircle of padded packaging to fit the flap. Secure it over the veneered side with masking tape for extra protection. Turn the flap over so that the stripped side is uppermost.

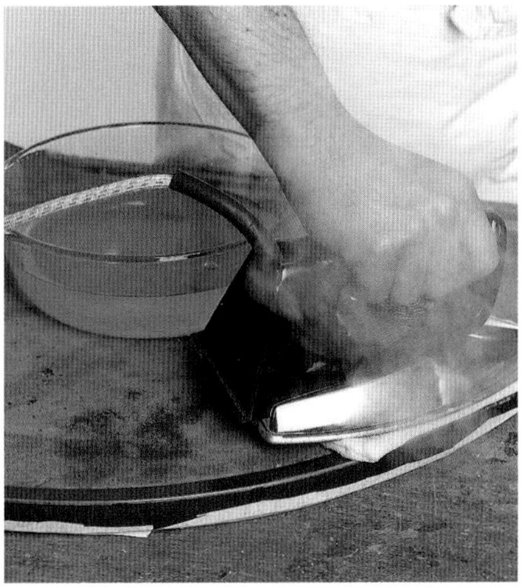

4 Immerse a cloth (cotton rag) in a bowl of water, then lay it over part of the banding. Place a hot iron on the damp cloth and press down for a few seconds, then remove the iron and cloth. The steam will soften the glue holding the banding on to the core. Take care not to scorch the banding.

5 Slide a flat-bladed knife under the banding while the glue is still malleable, and lift a section of it from the flap. The stringing should be removed at the same time. Continue steaming and lifting sections of the banding and stringing until all of it has been removed.

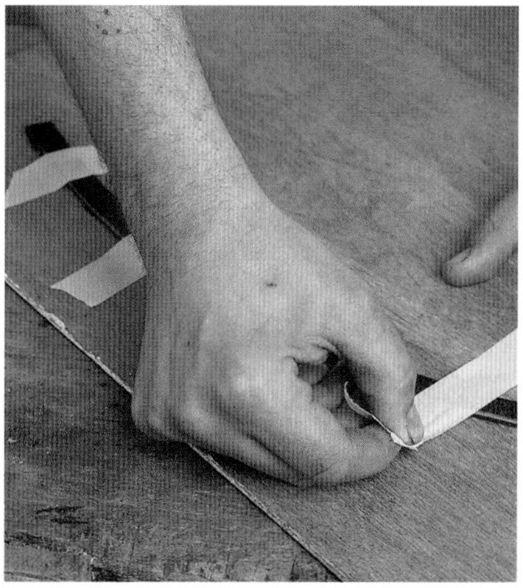

6 Tape the pieces of the banding and stringing together on to a board in the same positions that they occupied on the table. This will ensure that they can be replaced in the correct order.

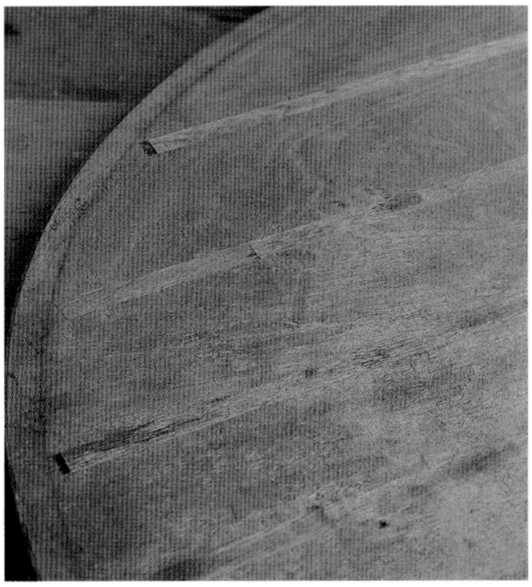

◁ 7 Scrape any remaining baize from the flap with a scraper. In this case, evidence of a previous, and unsuccessful, restoration can now be seen. This method involved removing strips of wood from the warped upper layer, flattening the table, then replacing them with new wood.

▷ 8 Scribe a line around the edge of the flap, just inside the banding's position, with a marking gauge. Turn the flap over, remove the padded packaging, then turn it back again. Removing the packaging will allow the flap to lie completely flat.

Tip

To hold a table flap securely while working on it, you will need to make several holding blocks, which can be screwed down over the table flap on to a chipboard (particle board) base. Make each block 5–7.5cm/2–3in long from softwood that is at least 12mm/½ in thicker than the flap. Cut a rebate (rabbet) along the length of each block to the depth of the flap, producing an L-shaped end profile. Drill two screw holes in each block. Place the flap on the chipboard base and clamp the edges down by screwing the blocks to the base, using chipboard screws (see right).

9 Place the flap on a piece of chipboard (particle board) and press it flat with both hands. Place holding blocks (see Tip) at regular intervals around the edge. ▷

Correcting a warped card table...continued

10 Select a suitable thickness of MDF (medium-density fiberboard) for the core. Remove sections of the flap to this depth, leaving borders to support the router.

11 Cut away the supporting border with a gouge. Take great care not to cut too deeply because you risk damaging the veneer from the underside.

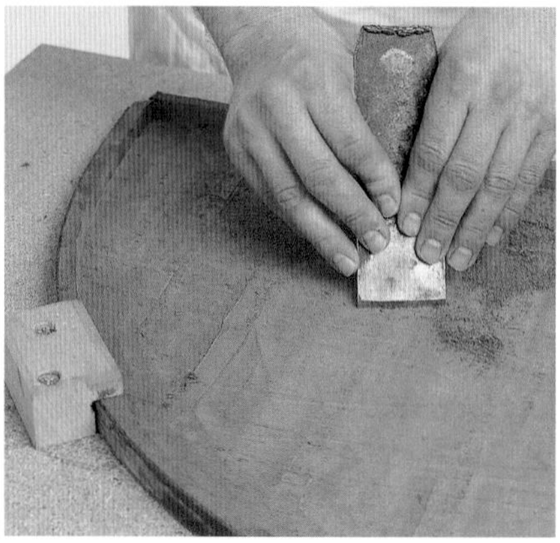

12 Level the surface with the iron from a smoothing plane, continuing until it is completely smooth.

13 Place the flap on the MDF and draw around the outline. Remove the flap and cut along this line with a jigsaw (saber saw).

14 Mark another line on the MDF that approximately matches the width of the banding, and cut along this line. Check that the MDF core fits the cut-out area of the flap, sanding it to fit if necessary.

15 Spread PVA (white) glue over the cut-out area of the flap, then insert the MDF. Place the flap between two pieces of wood and use G-clamps to apply even pressure. Leave to dry.

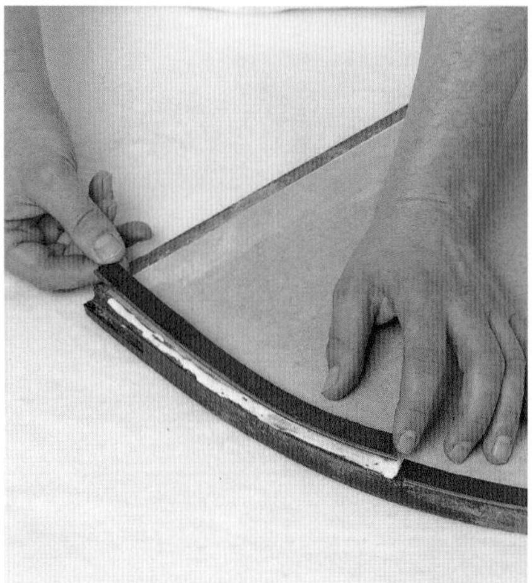

◁ **16** Remove the clamps and wood, turn the flap over, and remove the masking tape from the veneered side. Place the flap, veneered side down, on a protected workbench. Apply PVA glue to the edge of the flap and replace the pieces of banding and stringing.

▷ **17** Reattach the flap to the table and lightly polish the banding with shellac polish. This will remove any traces of watermarks that may have occurred when it was being steamed off.

18 Scrape any remaining baize from the rest of the table with a scraper and then use the scraper to fill any damage with wood filler. Protect the banding and stringing by covering them with masking tape.

19 Cut a piece of baize about 7.5cm/3in larger all around than the table and flap. Apply glue to the surface and lay the baize on top. Working from the centre, push the baize outward to remove any creases.

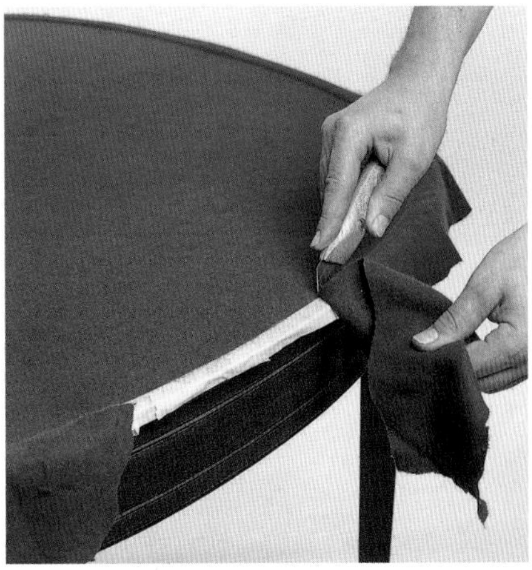

20 Cut the baize with a utility knife so that it lies flush with the inner edge of the banding. Take care to cut in an even line and not to cut the banding. Leave to dry. Remove the protective masking tape.

◁ **21** Seal the baize by heating a tooling wheel on a hotplate and then running it around the edge of the baize. Apply a firm, even pressure from start to finish.

Tip

If a surface is warped only slightly, it may be best to leave it as it is. To assess the extent of a warped surface, hold a long ruler alongside it. As a guide, if you can fit your little finger between the ruler and the surface, restoration is required.

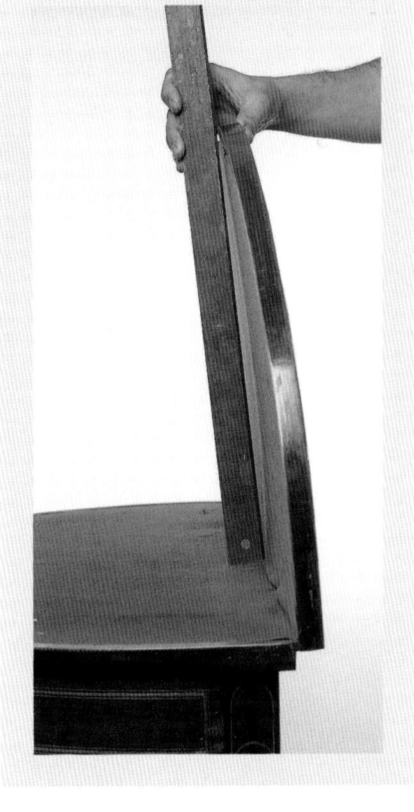

Below: *MDF (medium-density fiberboard) does not warp easily so there should be little or no risk of this card table warping again.*

Repairing a split pedestal table

Splits to table tops occur either along the grain of the wood or, if the top is made from glued boards, along the joints. Splits along the grain should be secured with butterfly keys (see p.230), but splits along the joints can simply be reglued and clamped.

The top of this mahogany pedestal table is made from two pieces of wood. The original glue that held them together has perished, allowing the pieces to separate and a gap to appear. The task of regluing is a relatively simple procedure – most of the work involved in this instance lies in dismantling and reassembling the table.

MATERIALS AND EQUIPMENT

- screwdriver
- chalk
- flat-bladed knife
- drill
- flat-bottomed grain plug drill bit
- chisel
- plane
- PVA (white) glue
- sash clamps
- clamping blocks
- hammer
- hardwood block
- mahogany
- grain plug cutter
- fine brush
- stain
- rubber
- polish
- cloth (rag)
- wax

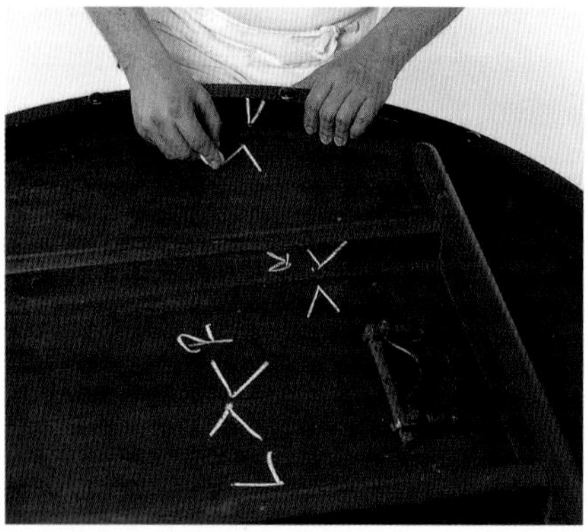

1 Place the table upside down on a protected workbench, and unscrew the column and legs from the bearers. Mark the position of each separate section of the table top with chalk.

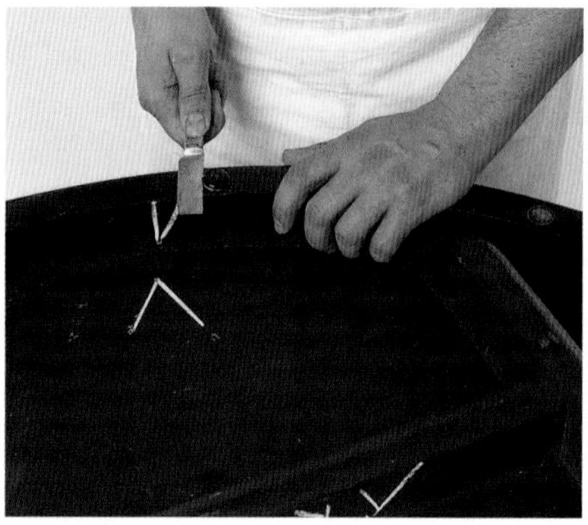

2 Remove the decorative mahogany plugs that cover the steel screw heads on the rim, lifting them out with a flat-bladed knife. Place these in a labelled container for safe keeping (see Tip).

3 Unscrew each of the screws on the rim, remove them and place them in the container. Lift the rim from the underside of the table top and place it to one side.

Tip

Small fittings and fixtures are easy to lose, and if you are working on more than one piece of furniture, you may waste time trying to attach the fitting from one piece of furniture to another piece. To prevent this from happening, always store small parts from a single item of furniture – such as plugs, screws, hinges and knobs – together in a labelled container, such as a glass jar, a can or a box with a lid. Keep them on your workbench for easy access.

4 Drill out the wooden plugs that cover the screws in the bearers with a flat-bottomed grain plug drill bit, but stop short of the heads of the screws. Remove any remaining wood above the screw heads with a chisel.

5 Loosen the screws on the bearers with a screwdriver, remove them, and put them in the container. Lift the bearers from the top and place them to one side.

6 Set a plane to the shallowest cut possible and go over the mating edges of the top once or twice. Apply PVA (white) glue and clamp the pieces together. Tap down raised edges with a hammer and a hardwood block.

7 Cut new plugs from a piece of mahogany using a grain plug cutter. Taper one end of each plug with a chisel, making small grooves down the length at the same time.

◁ **8** Screw the bearers back on to the table top with the original screws. Apply some PVA glue to the holes, then tap the plugs into the holes to cover the screws.

▷ **9** Pare the plugs down with a chisel until they are flush with the bearers. Avoid scratching the bearers as far as possible.

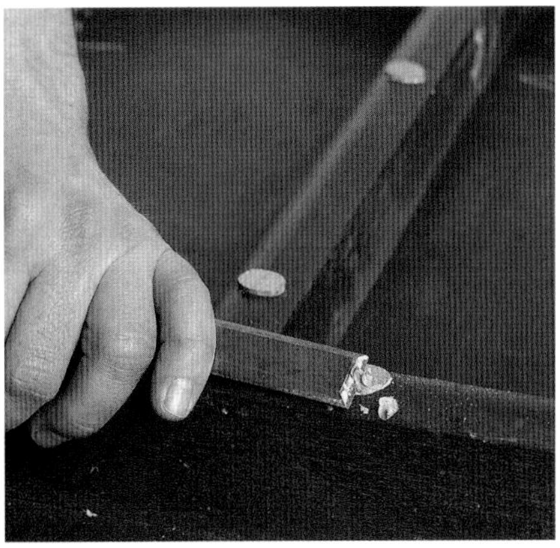

10 Mix a water- or spirit-based (alcohol-based) stain to match the bearers (see p.41) and apply with a brush. When the stain is dry, attach the column and legs. Charge a rubber with polish and apply a light layer to the table top (see pp.66–67), then add a wax finish (see p.68).

Left: *The gap between the sections of the top has gone. This technique is quick and simple, and produces a very satisfying result.*

PROJECT: DROP-LEAF TABLE

During the early 18th century, the drop-leaf table became a favoured type of dining table. This design allowed the table to be stored with its flaps down when not in use, thus saving space. Nowadays, such tables are still extremely popular, and are particularly practical in modern homes where space may be at a premium. Unfortunately, like so many other items of antique furniture, drop-leaf tables may have led hard lives and may now suffer from all manner of ills, ranging from stained and discoloured tops to severe damage to the structure.

ASSESSING THE PROJECT

This George II table, constructed in c.1745, is made from dense red walnut, and its distinctive moulded pad-foot design suggests that it is Irish in origin. It has sustained a sprung glue line in a panel on the flap, which reveals a previous dowel-joint repair. There is also veneer and bracket damage to the carcass, several pieces of one of the feet are missing, and one of the swing legs has broken off and been lost, so needs to be replaced.

The top

- split top, previously repaired with dowels
- watermarks and scratches

The legs

- foot broken
- one swing leg missing

The carcass

- veneer missing
- damaged shoulder
- broken brackets

Repairing the top

Damp caused the glue joining two sections of the table top to perish, producing a split. This revealed an earlier dowel-joint repair. As the dowels were in good condition, they can be incorporated into the new repair. The table top is also marred with various marks and scratches, so the surface needs to be revived thoroughly.

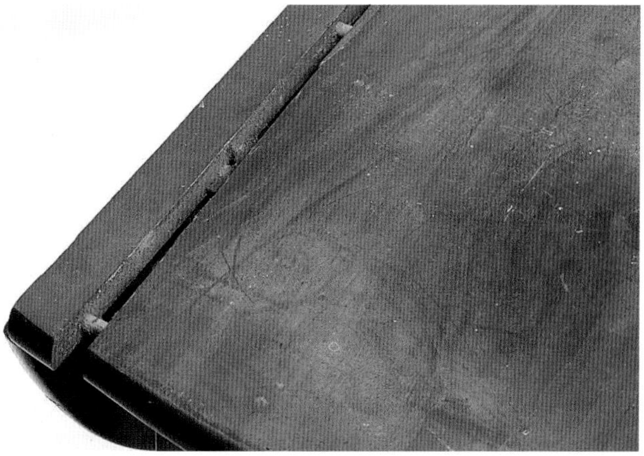

MATERIALS AND EQUIPMENT

- screwdriver
- chalk
- pliers
- plane
- PVA (white) glue
- sash clamps
- long clamping blocks

1 Place the table upside down on a protected workbench. Remove the fixing screws and put the frame and legs aside. Now the frame is off, the pivoted gates and the remaining swing leg can be lifted clear.

2 Unscrew the flap hinges from the main section of the table top. Mark the underside of the top with chalk so that you can tell which flap belongs on which side. Remove the dowels with pliers.

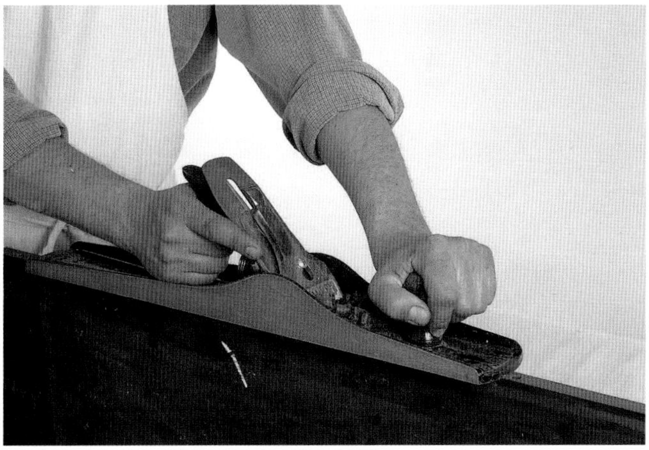

3 Place the main section of the top in a vice and plane the split side of the wood until smooth. Do not take off too much wood, as this will reduce the width of the table. Repeat for the other split side.

4 Apply PVA (white) glue along both split edges, replace the dowels and secure with sash clamps and long clamping blocks. Leave to dry, then remove the clamps.

▷

Repairing the carcass

The carcass, or framework, of the table is in good order and does not need to be knocked apart and reglued. There are, however, missing areas of veneer and two brackets that have fallen off and need refitting. One of the shoulders is also damaged. Due to the untouched patination of the piece, only old surface breaker veneer is used for repairs.

Refixing the brackets

One of the brackets had broken cleanly off and needed gluing back in place. A second bracket had also fallen off, due to damage at the point where it joined the table leg. This meant that the shoulder needed to be repaired before the bracket could be refixed in place.

MATERIALS AND EQUIPMENT

- **toothbrush**
- **PVA (white) glue**
- **spring clips**
- **tenon saw**
- **red walnut**
- **plane**
- **G-clamp**
- **clamping blocks**
- **gouges**
- **fine-grade sandpaper**

◁ **1** Remove the old glue from both the brackets that have fallen off using a toothbrush and hot water. Refit the bracket that sits under the missing veneer patch using PVA (white) glue. Use spring clips (see p.215) to hold the bracket in place while the glue dries.

◁ **2** Turning now to the leg with the damaged shoulder, use a fine tenon saw to cut away a small section to allow for an inset patch to be applied. Cut a new section from a piece of red walnut.

▷ **3** Glue and clamp the new piece of wood in place. When it is dry, plane it flush with the shoulder. There is now a level surface to which the bracket can be reattached.

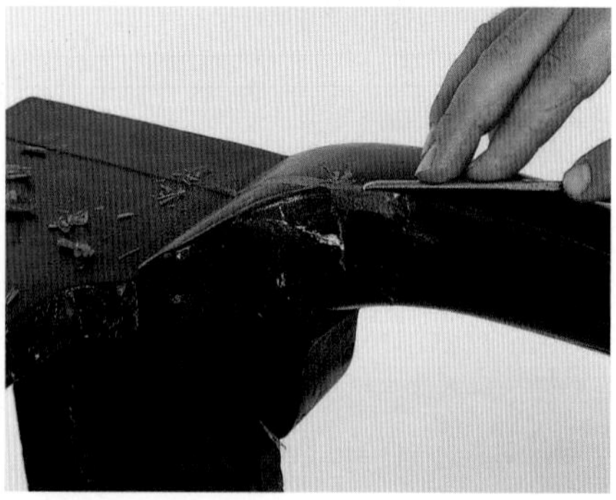

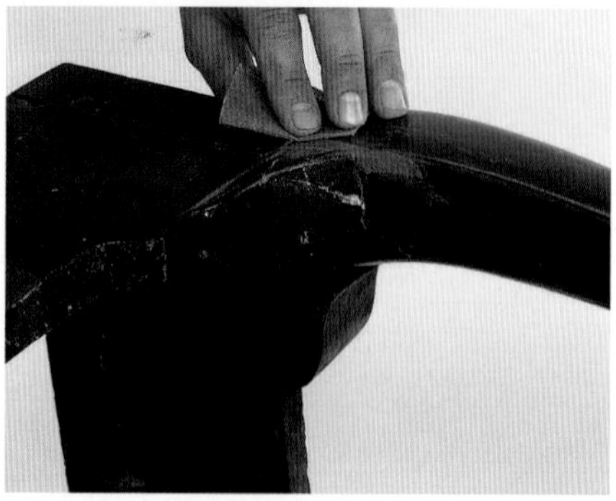

4 Glue the original bracket back into place, sandwiching the new wood between the leg and the bracket. Clamp until dry. Using a shaped gouge, pare away the excess wood to give a smooth, flowing repair.

5 With a smaller, rounded gouge, carve the moulded edge to the bracket, so that the repair is unnoticeable.

6 Finally, finish the repair by using fine-grade sandpaper to remove any rough edges. Take care not to mark the polished areas.

REPLACING THE VENEER

Parts of the decorative veneer on the base have become detached and been lost after the animal glue has perished. The veneer must be replaced with matching old surface veneer.

MATERIALS AND EQUIPMENT

- **old veneers**
- **toothing plane**
- **utility knife**
- **PVA (white) glue**
- **clamping blocks**
- **G-clamps**
- **fine-grade sandpaper**

◁ **1** Select a few possible replacement veneers for the missing patch on the frame, and hold them by the table to see which provides the best match to the original, paying attention to grain and colour.

◁ **2** Before laying the new piece of veneer, remove all traces of the old animal glue with the iron from a toothing plane. Scrape away only the residue of old glue without altering the actual groundwork.

◁ **3** Trim the veneer to roughly the correct size and glue it into position. Make sure that the veneer is laid with the grain pattern running in the correct direction, otherwise the repair will be all too obvious.

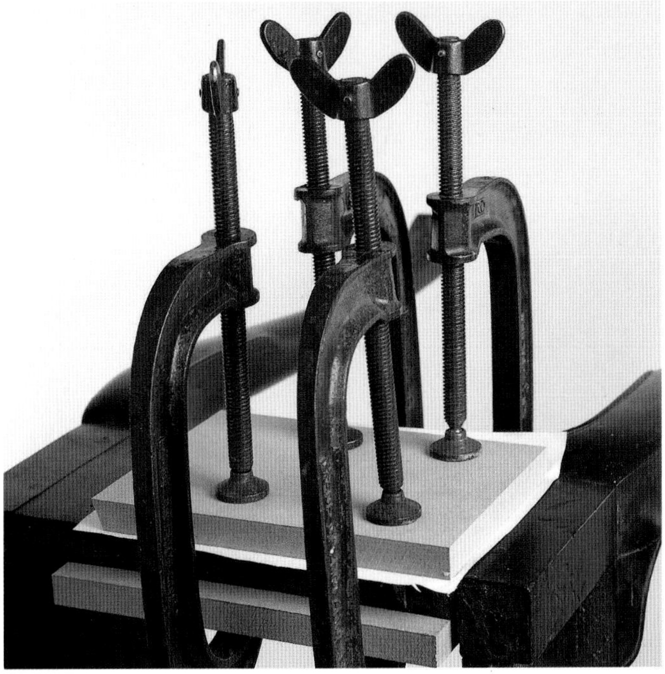

◁ **4** Place some paper on top of the veneer and then put clamping blocks on either side of the damaged frame. Clamp securely with G-clamps and leave to dry. Remove the clamps and blocks.

5 Hold one of the clamping blocks at an angle against the front of the frame to form a cutting base. Use a utility knife to trim the veneer, following the outline of the carcass, then sand the edge.

▷

Repairing the legs

This table is unusual because it has two different styles of leg. The four fixed corner legs are cabriole with shaped lozenge feet. One of these feet has been damaged and needs to be rebuilt. The other two legs, which are swing legs, are turned club legs with small pad feet. They are attached to the frame by swing gates, which support the table flap when it is lifted. One of these swing legs in now missing and a replacement must be made to match the remaining leg.

MATERIALS AND EQUIPMENT

- **red walnut**
- **steel straightedge**
- **tenon saw**
- **drill**
- **wood drill bit**
- **lathe**
- **callipers**
- **turning tools**
- **dividers**
- **fine-grade sandpaper**

TURNING A NEW LEG

Legs on tables seldom break into pieces, but if they do sustain substantial structural damage, they must be replaced, as it is important that they are extremely robust and strong. One of the swing legs on this red walnut drop-leaf table had been removed, then misplaced, so a new leg needs to be turned and fitted.

1 Cut a piece of red walnut slightly larger than the final size of the leg. Mark the centre of each end of the block by drawing two diagonal lines with a steel straightedge. Cut a shallow groove along one of the lines at one end with a tenon saw.

2 Drill a hole in the centre of each end, about 1cm/⅜in deep. The tail stock of the lathe will be housed in the end with just the hole, and the head stock will sit in the end with the groove and hole.

▷ **3** Secure the block of walnut in the lathe and make a shallow cut with a tenon saw where the turned area will finish and the square section will begin.

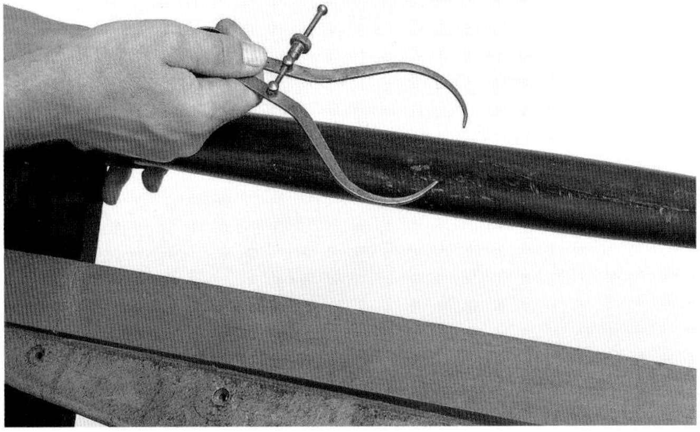

4 Use callipers to measure the widest part of the other swing leg so that you can turn the new leg to the correct size.

5 Turn the wood until you achieve the required diameter. Check the size of the new leg frequently with the callipers so that you do not inadvertantly remove too much wood.

◁ **6** Use dividers to transcribe the various dimensions of the decorative foot area from the other swing leg.

7 Turn the decorative parts of the leg with a very small gouge. Always remove less wood than you think you should, at first, and take measurements regularly from the existing leg.

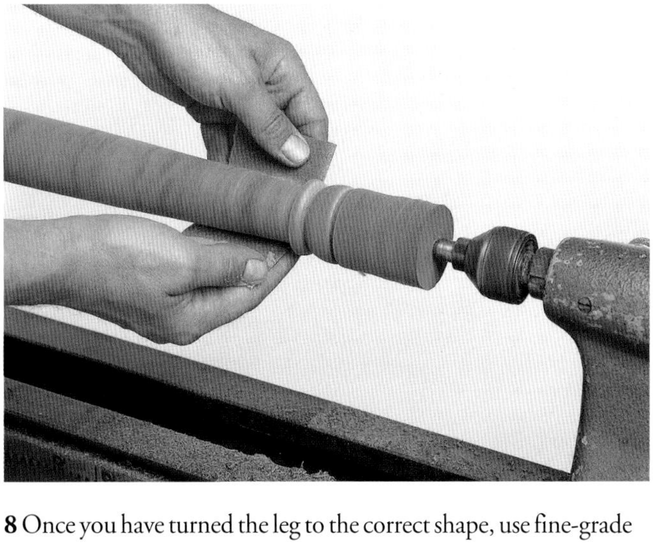

8 Once you have turned the leg to the correct shape, use fine-grade sandpaper to finish off and smooth it. Remove the leg from the lathe and cut it to shape.

▷

Cutting the mortise

The newly turned leg now needs to have a mortise cut into the square section that was left at the top. The leg can then be attached to the tenon on the gate.

MATERIALS AND EQUIPMENT

- set (carpenter's) square
- utility knife
- mortise gauge
- G-clamp
- clamping blocks
- mortise chisel
- cardboard
- tenon saw
- PVA (white) glue
- sash clamp
- fine-grade sandpaper
- bichromate of potash
- fine brushes
- water-based stain
- rubber
- shellac polish
- screwdriver

1 Detach the other swing leg from its gate and place the new leg side by side with it. Using a set (carpenter's) square and a utility knife, mark across the shoulder lines.

2 Set a mortise gauge to match the width of the tenon on the swing gate that belonged to the missing leg.

◁ **3** Mark the correct position of the mortise between the scribed shoulder lines on the new leg.

▷ **4** Clamp the leg securely to the workbench, using a clamping block to stop any possible bruising to the leg, and cut out the mortise with a mortise chisel of a suitable size.

5 Take a cardboard template (pattern) of the top of the other swing leg, then mark out this shape on the top of the new leg. Cut away the unwanted wood with a tenon saw.

6 Apply PVA (white) glue to the end of the original tenon and insert it into the newly cut mortise. Clamp the joint under pressure using a sash clamp and clamping blocks. Leave the joint to dry then remove the clamp and blocks.

7 Sand the top of the leg with fine-grade sandpaper, wetting the wood in between sandings to raise the grain. The benefit of this is that the grain will not be raised when a water-based stain is applied.

8 Apply a thin layer of bichromate of potash to the entire new leg. This will change the reddish tone of the walnut to a more suitable brown.

9 After selecting and mixing a suitable water-based stain, apply this to the leg to match the other swing leg.

10 Charge a rubber with shellac polish and apply it to the leg. Distress the leg to match the other swing leg.

Repairing a foot

One of the pad feet has various broken and missing parts, which, due to their damaged edges, cannot simply be reglued, and so must be replaced. A template (pattern) must be taken of an undamaged foot, so that the extent of the repairs can be determined and the new pieces of wood cut to size.

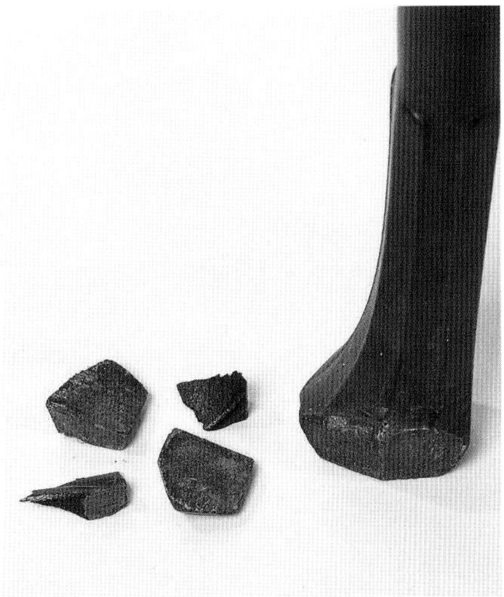

MATERIALS AND EQUIPMENT

- **profile gauge**
- **mount card (stock)**
- **red walnut**
- **tenon saw**
- **PVA (white) glue**
- **spring clips**
- **utility knife**
- **block plane**
- **coping saw**
- **rasp**
- **carving tools**
- **bichromate of potash**
- **fine brushes**
- **polish**
- **cloth (cotton rag)**
- **fine pumice powder**

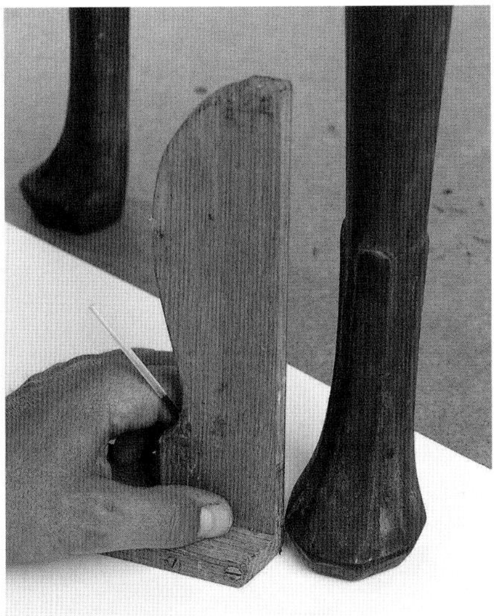

◁ **1** Draw the outline of an undamaged foot using a profile marker (see p.110) on a piece of stiff mount card (stock). This will be used as a template (pattern) to repair the damaged foot.

▷ **2** Place the damaged foot on the template and mark along the broken edges. This will indicate what shape and size the new pieces of red walnut need to be. Cut the pieces of walnut to a suitable size to fill the gaps. Glue them into place one piece at a time so that you build up the profile. This gives extra strength.

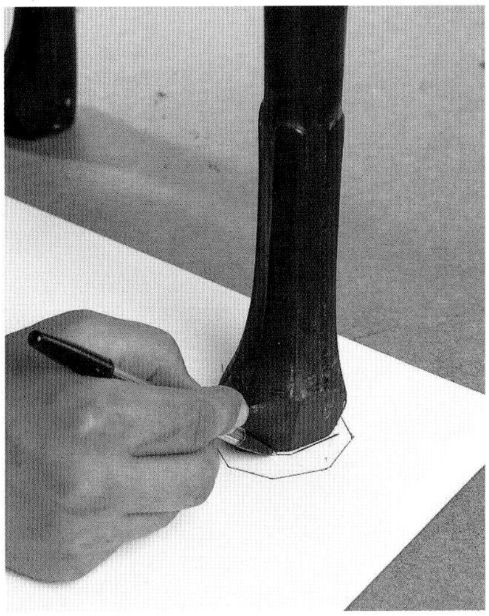

▷

Repairing a foot...continued

3 Using a tenon saw, trim the excess wood away, but remember that the foot has yet to be shaped, so allow enough extra thickness for the shaping to be done.

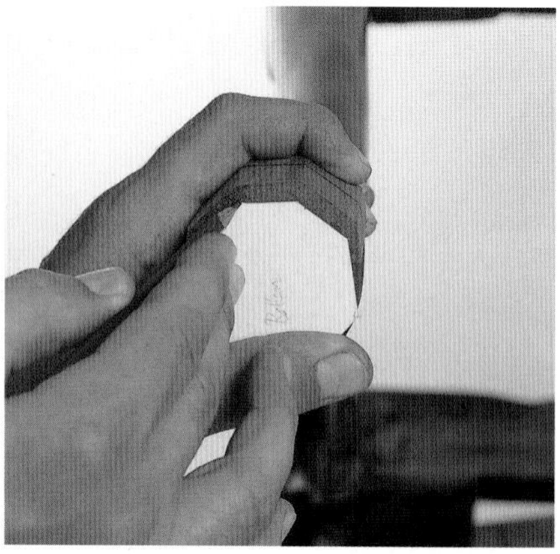

4 To get the profile of the undamaged foot's chamfer, make a second template, this time of the bottom of the complete foot. Cut it out and place it on the bottom of the foot being restored and mark the outline.

5 Using a small block plane, follow the mark on the bottom of the foot to obtain the correct chamfer. Remember to work with the grain and not across it, as this would result in the wood tearing.

◁ **6** Use a coping saw to create the shape of the actual pad foot. The coping saw allows an angled cut to be made, which helps to shape the foot.

▷ **7** Use a rasp to shape the desired profile. Do not to go too far, because there is still a raised lozenge foot to be carved.

8 By cross-referencing to an undamaged foot and by following the line of the raised decoration on the original leg, sculpt the moulding on the restored foot.

9 Give the new wood a thin coat of bichromate of potash – a chemical stain that will react with the tannin of the wood and change the walnut's natural red tone to a more suitable brown.

10 Brush on a thin layer of polish to fill the grain of the walnut. Put some polish on a cloth (cotton rag) and sprinkle some fine pumice powder on it. Use this to work the polish into the grain, blending the old and new surfaces.

Reassembling and polishing

With all the structural work now complete, the restored table can be reassembled. The old screws will be used again and as all parts were labelled prior to disassembling, and the correct position of the top marked, this should be a fairly straightforward process.

MATERIALS AND EQUIPMENT

- screwdriver
- methylated spirits (methyl alcohol)
- cloths (cotton rags)
- fine brush
- stain
- rubber
- polish
- wax

1 Turn the table top upside down and place it on a protected workbench to avoid any unnecessary scratches or marks. Screw the frame and legs back in place, as well as the gates for the two swing legs, using the original screws.

2 Put some methylated spirits (methyl alcohol) on a cloth (cotton rag) and cut back the surface, taking care to remove as little of the original surface as possible. Attend to any surface scratches or marks (see pp.54–59).

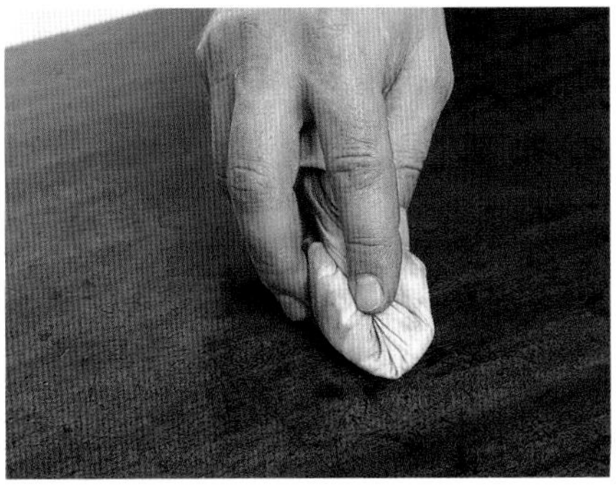

3 Stain the repairs (see p.69). Polish the table (see pp.66–67) and when it has hardened, wax and burnish it (p.68).

Above: *The restored table, with its brackets refitted, missing veneer replaced, foot repaired, a new swing leg attached and the surface revived and polished, can be fully enjoyed and appreciated once again.*

Project: Sofa table

The term "restoration" can cover a multitude of necessary techniques, ranging from simply removing a scratch or two, to having to undertake what may seem, at first glance, a lost cause. This George III sofa table, c.1810, is veneered in rosewood and is of good quality and colour. Originally designed to stand behind a sofa, it had stood under a bedroom window and been used as a dressing table. Unfortunately, a pair of reading glasses left on the table during a very hot day had magnified the sun's rays on to the curtains (drapes), which caused them to ignite. This led to the back edge of the sofa table catching fire, which completely destroyed some areas and damaged others.

Assessing the project

The cross-banding along the front and top edge has been completely destroyed, and the damage has gone through to some of the groundwork beneath. The drawer front of one false drawer has been lost, along with the turned rosewood knobs. On one of the flaps, the heat of the fire has caused the glue line in the mahogany core to spring apart. Fortunately, the veneer has separated cleanly with no tearing occurring. A few pieces of cross-banding are missing from the edge. General wear and tear had caused some of the legs to become loose, so these needed to be detached, cleaned off, and reassembled, and some veneer and stringing were missing from the base pedestal.

The top
- flap split along glue line
- veneer, cross-banding and stringing damaged on the edge of the top

The frame
- veneer and groundwork destroyed
- knobs destroyed

The base
- veneer and stringing missing on base
- legs loose

Repairing the top

The heat of the fire has caused the glue line in one of the flaps to perish, causing a split. The fire has also caused extensive damage to the edge of the table – the veneer, banding and stringing. The first task is to repair the split, after which the damaged edge can be restored.

SECURING THE FLAP

The damage to the flap appears worse than it is. It has split along the glue line, so can simply be reglued and clamped.

MATERIALS AND EQUIPMENT

- **screwdriver**
- **toothing plane**
- **PVA (white) glue**
- **sash clamps**
- **clamping blocks**
- **G-clamps**

◁ **1** Turn the table upside down on top of a protected workbench. Remove the base, then unscrew and remove the frame. Separate the twin flaps from the top. Store all the screws carefully for reuse (see p.182).

2 Separate the two parts of the split flap carefully. Remove the residue of glue from the glue line with the iron from a toothing plane, which will also provide a key for the new joint line.

3 Glue the two parts of the flap back together. Apply sash clamps and clamping blocks to keep the join under pressure, and use G-clamps to keep the join flat, using paper to prevent any sticking.

▷

Rebuilding the Edge

The edge of the table top has suffered some serious damage. The groundwork, veneer, stringing and cross-banding have all been destroyed and must be replaced. Luckily, the damage has not gone any further than the stringing inlay, so a line exists at which the new veneer can join the undamaged parts, with the stringing hiding the joint.

MATERIALS AND EQUIPMENT

- router
- guide fence
- softwood
- tenon saw
- PVA (white) glue
- masking tape
- plane
- chisel
- toothing plane
- old veneer
- boxwood stringing
- clamping block
- utility knife
- fine-grade sandpaper

1 Using a router fitted with a guide fence, remove some of the damaged area of veneer and groundwork, but leave a rebate (rabbet) into which sections of new groundwork can be glued.

2 Cut pieces of softwood to replace the routed-out section of groundwork. Apply PVA (white) glue and fit these in place, securing them with masking tape while the glue dries.

3 Plane the new groundwork flush with the front edge. Remove the remainder of the veneer up to the stringing line with a chisel. Scrape the planed groundwork with the iron from a toothing plane.

4 Select a piece of old surface veneer that best matches the original veneer, and glue it over the old and new groundwork. This will ensure that the edge retains its original strength. Lay the replacement stringing at the same time (see p.83) to ensure a tight-fitting joint.

5 Trim the replacement banding flush with the edge (see step 5 on p.187) then sand with fine-grade sandpaper. Use more of the old surface veneer to repair the damaged areas of the cross-banded edge, following the same method.

Repairing the frame

Half of the front of the frame has been reduced to charcoal. Although it appears to be beyond repair, the careful application of new groundwork, the selection of a good match for the new veneer and the construction of some new drawer knobs will make a complete repair possible.

REPLACING THE GROUNDWORK AND VENEER

The charred wood must be removed before a replacement piece can be added and the new veneer applied.

MATERIALS AND EQUIPMENT

- router
- guide fence
- smoothing plane
- tenon saw
- pine
- PVA (white) glue
- G-clamps
- clamping blocks
- plane
- rosewood
- utility knife
- chisel
- scratch gauge
- boxwood strip
- hammer
- sash clamp

◁ **1** The damaged areas of the drawer front must be repaired before the drawer can be re-veneered. Set a router to a suitable depth to cut away the charred veneer and groundwork. To maintain an even depth of cut, clamp a guide fence to the frame for the router to run on.

2 Go over the routed area with the blade from a smoothing plane. This will level the surface and key it so that the glue can achieve a good grip. Measure the area and and cut a piece of pine slightly larger than this.

3 Spread glue over the routed area, then place the new piece of pine in position. Clamp it with G-clamps and clamping blocks and leave it to dry. When it is dry, remove the clamps and blocks, then plane the pine flush with the top and bottom edges of the frame. ▷

Replacing the groundwork and veneer...continued

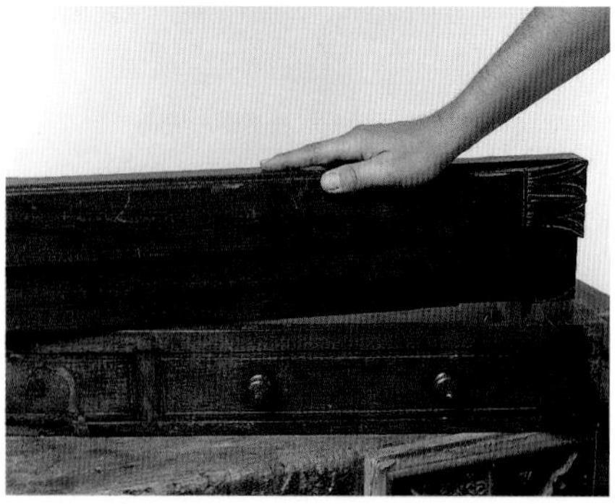

4 Select a piece of old surface rosewood that matches the colour and grain of the original veneer as closely as possible, and then steam or cut the veneer off (see p.77).

5 Place the frame in a vice. Starting with the top drawer rail. Make matching angled cuts on the original and new veneers with a utility knife. Glue the new piece in place.

6 Remove the remaining areas of damaged veneer by lifting them gently away with a large chisel.

7 Glue a piece of the previously selected veneer on to the damaged false drawer front. Place a clamping block on top to ensure that no blistering occurs, then apply a G-clamp.

8 Remove the frame from the vice. Replace the piece of veneer that is laid at right angles over the joint between the two false drawer fronts. This is set proud to imply that the drawer fronts are real.

9 In preparation for adding the inlaid boxwood strip, cut a groove using a scratch gauge set at the correct width. Keeping the cutting blade sharp ensures a clean trench.

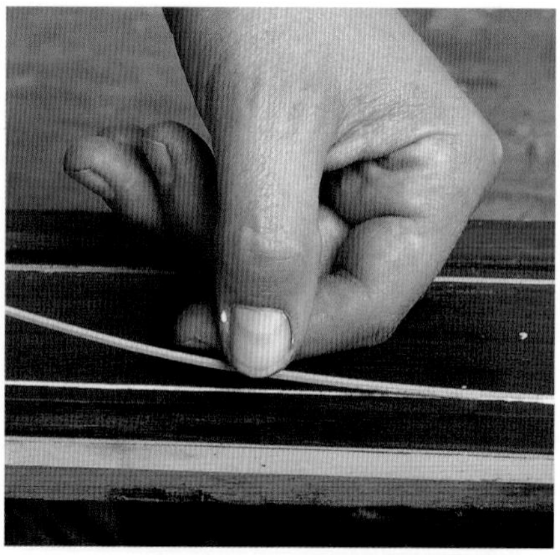

10 Choose and prepare a boxwood strip (see p.83). Lay the strip into the groove, then push it firmly into position using the back of a hammer.

11 Glue more pieces of the selected veneer over the damaged end panel. Clamp these into place using a sash clamp and a clamping block.

Replacing the knobs

Two new knobs must be turned to match the old ones. It is important to take several measurements from the existing knobs to ensure that the new ones are exactly the same shape.

MATERIALS AND EQUIPMENT

- **callipers**
- **rosewood or walnut**
- **lathe**
- **turning tools**
- **dividers**
- **fine-grade sandpaper**
- **drill**
- **wood drill bit**
- **screws**

◁ **1** Measure the diameter of an original knob with some callipers. Solid rosewood can be difficult to source, so if you cannot find any rosewood, choose well-figured walnut, which makes a suitable alternative.

2 Turn the new piece of wood to a diameter marginally larger than the dimension set on the callipers. Make frequent checks because if you remove too much material, you will have to start again.

3 Using some dividers, and referring back to the original knob for guidance, mark the approximate positions and sizes of the various parts of the knob, such as the handle, neck and back.

4 Having scored the various marks, trim the knob to the correct length. Remove the tailstock from the lathe, release the turned wood from the headstock and place it in the chuck.

5 Using the original knob as a pattern, turn the new knob to the same size and shape.

▷

Replacing the knobs...continued

6 Finish off the turned knob by giving it a light sanding with fine-grade sandpaper. Repeat steps 2 to 6 to make the other knob.

7 Find the location for the knobs by using dividers to transfer the dimensions from the undamaged drawer to the repaired one.

8 Drill the drawer front and fit the knobs dry. Do not glue; it is better to stain and polish them first.

Repairing the base

The legs have become loose due to general wear and tear. They need to be removed, cleaned off, then reattached. There are also some patches of veneer and stringing missing on the pedestal.

MATERIALS AND EQUIPMENT

- screwdriver
- chalk
- hammer
- hardwood block
- toothbrush
- PVA (white) glue
- sash clamp
- clamping blocks
- rosewood veneer
- utility knife
- chisel
- masking tape
- steel straightedge
- boxwood strip
- fine brush
- stain
- methylated spirits (methyl alcohol)
- rubber
- polish
- cloth (cotton rag)
- wax

1 The legs were joined to the table by dovetail tenons, which had been reinforced by metal brackets. Remove these brackets, making identifying marks with chalk.

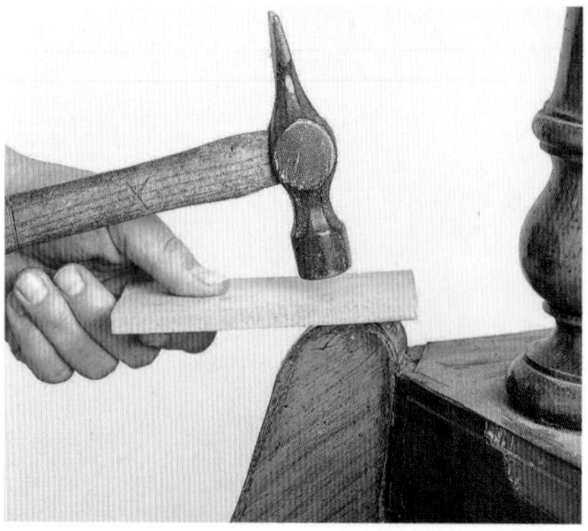

2 Knock the legs apart using a hammer and a hardwood block to ensure that no damage is caused to the legs.

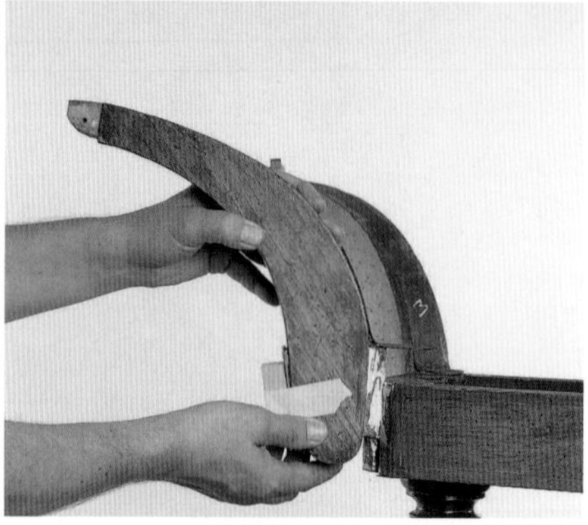

3 Clean off all the old adhesive with a toothbrush and hot water. Reglue the legs, securing them with sash clamps, and replace the metal brackets.

4 After selecting a piece of rosewood veneer that is a close match for the original veneer, hold it over the damaged area and mark around it with a sharp utility knife. Remove the old veneer from within the marks with a sharp chisel.

5 Glue the veneer into place, securing it with masking tape. Use a steel straightedge and a utility knife to cut a rebate (rabbet) in the new veneer for a boxwood strip. Choose and prepare a boxwood strip (see p.83).

6 Glue the boxwood strip into the rebate, pushing it into place with the back of a hammer. When the glue has dried, trim the inlay flush using a sharp chisel, taking care not to damage any polished areas. Reassemble the table.

7 To finish, apply a matching stain to all the replacement areas of stringing. Stain other new repairs, including the knobs, and refit them.

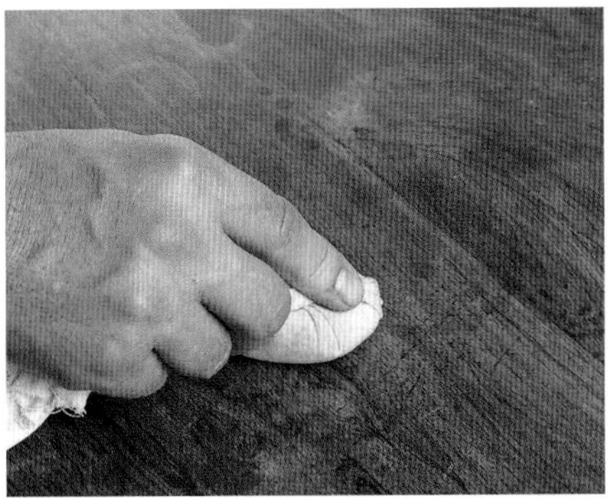

8 Finally, wash the surface with methylated spirits (methyl alcohol). Polish the table (see pp.66–67) and when it has hardened, wax and burnish the surface (see p.68).

Above: *With the fire-damaged areas removed and replaced with old surface veneer, and the entire table's surface revived, polished and waxed, there is no indication of the sorry state it was in before restoration began.*

Chests and cabinets

Cabinets and especially chests of drawers, by the very nature of their design, will have a number of restoration requirements that are unique to them alone. Working parts such as drawers may need their runners or stops replaced. Drawer linings will shrink, causing splits. Doors may need reglazing or refitting and, on rare occasions, the entire carcass may need to be dismantled and reglued.

HISTORY OF CHESTS AND CABINETS

Unlike chairs or tables, cabinets and chest of drawers have changed radically throughout their history. While their function has always been primarily for storage, in certain periods, particularly during the 18th century, they also became a symbol of the owner's wealth and position in society. As such, the chest of drawers was displayed in a prominent position in the main room of the house, the drawing room, and was known as a commode.

The modern chest of drawers evolved from the chest or coffer (the terms were interchangeable in medieval times). During the 15th century, when coffers first appeared in a form that would be recognizable today, furniture was a rare commodity. Even the largest hall's furniture would consist of little more than a large chair for the master of the house, stools for the rest of the household, a large table at which the household would dine, a cupboard and a coffer to store valuables, clothes and food.

The earliest coffers, dating from the late 13th century, were simply hollowed-out logs with the outsides squared off and the lids attached by raised peg hinges. The next advance was a coffer constructed from roughly hewn boards that were fixed together with wooden dowel pegs; shaping the taller ends formed simple feet. They were made secure by crude iron strap hinges and locks. The obvious problem with this form of construction – especially as most of the wood used was unseasoned – was that the planks often split. Most decoration was fairly crude, although the earliest forms of carving are found as well as some paintwork. Some coffers, mainly those designed for travel, were bound in iron and covered with

Above: *The earliest coffers were little more than planks of oak nailed and held together with iron straps.*

Left: *By the 15th century, panel construction allowed more elaborate decoration.*

studded leather. These coffers, with their distinctive shape and rope handles at the ends, were known as trussing coffers, or standards.

The next major development, during the late 15th and early 16th centuries, was the framed or panel coffer. This, as the name suggests, was a coffer made up of an oak framework joined by mortise and tenons. The panels were simply fitted loose into grooves in the styles, rails and muntins, which allowed for shrinkage without the wood splitting. The more stable coffer gave the craftsman greater scope for decoration, and from this period onward many of the chests were highly carved. By the late 16th century, decorative inlays of bone and of wood such as holly or box are also found. Some of the earliest decorated coffers were carved with the linenfold pattern, which perhaps mimics the natural ripple in the wood. Carvings became more and more complex, and by the late 17th century not only were carved figures incorporated into the panels and uprights but also regional differences had begun to develop, each with their own distinctive style of manufacture and decoration.

During this period, with more people owning books (themselves a valuable commodity at the time), bookcases began to appear. At first they had solid panel doors, but by the late 17th century the finest examples had mirror plate or hand blown glass doors.

The first chest of any description, more commonly known as the mule chest, was in fact a coffer with a large drawer set at the bottom. It appeared during the late 16th century, but it was not until the 17th century that the chest of drawers in the form we recognize today actually developed.

The chest, still made in the majority in oak, rapidly changed its form. At first the drawers were made by simply nailing the softwood linings together and housing them on inset runners. Then finer linings were cut from quarter-sawn oak and joined with dovetails to aid strength and rigidity. The second half of the 17th century saw an increased use of walnut and the introduction of veneers. The latter brought about a change in construction in cabinets and chests of drawers: where before they were made from solid oak or walnut, the carcass was now constructed from a softwood such as pine on to which was applied the decorative veneer. This was taken to an even greater extreme in France, where tortoiseshell and intricate brass inlays were being used by the royal cabinet-maker André-Charles Boulle (1642–1732). This was also used, but perhaps not to the same level, in England by the royal cabinet-maker Gerreit Jensen (fl.1680–1715), who is more commonly associated with the use of intricate seaweed marquetry.

With the use of veneer becoming more fashionable in the better houses, long-grain moulding was replaced with bolder cross-grain moulding, which gave a more decorative finish. It is interesting to note that it was due to economic rather than technical restrictions that the use of marquetry ceased in English furniture toward the end of the 17th century, although it continued to feature in French and Italian furniture. In England, the use of decorative veneers once again came to the fore, supplemented with decorative herringbone bandings and inlay.

Above: *A late 17th-century English chest of drawers showing the influence of the imported fashion of inlaid marquetry.*

The late 17th century saw a number of structural changes to the chest and cabinet. A new method of allowing the drawers to slide in and out of the carcass was introduced: the previously side-hung drawer runners were replaced with runners applied to the drawer bottoms. The practice also emerged of raising the chest off its feet with the use of a low stand, itself often fitted with a drawer. While commonly found in either oak or walnut veneer, these pieces were sometimes, when made for the wealthiest of patrons, constructed in Europe and then transported to China to be lacquered. On their return they were placed on elaborate carved stands that would be silver gilded. The chest on stand, while continuing occasionally to be ▷

commissioned during the 18th century, was largely replaced by the tallboy, or chest on chest. As the name suggests, these were two chests, one on top of the other, which offered double the storage. The better examples would have canted corners, a secretaire interior or perhaps an inset sunburst to the base drawer.

The form of the chest of drawers and cabinet changed very little until around 1720, when mahogany imported from Cuba and Honduras began to be used in the manufacture of the finest pieces of furniture. With its dense grain and ease of working, mahogany ideally suited the needs of an emerging wealthy clientele who were demanding a wider diversity of furniture to house their ever-growing collections of valuable objects and expanding libraries. While the chest's primary function was still the storage of clothing, a new piece of furniture emerged from France – the commode.

The commode was grander and far more intricate than the simple chest, its place being in the drawing room under an imposing work of art and surrounded by fine objects collected from around the world. The leading makers and designers of the 18th century, such as Thomas Chippendale, published design and pattern books for commodes and cabinets, which were subscribed to by all the leading members of the European aristocracy. Commodes and cabinets were constructed from the finest mahogany and decorated with elaborate carving. With the importation of exotic woods during the mid-18th century, combined with the desire for a lighter and more elegant look, marquetry decoration re-emerged. Its revival was short-lived, as by the end of the century the chest was once again largely being consigned to the role of clothes storage, while bookcases and cabinets developed both in scale and variety to include secretaire drawers, opening cupboard bases and elaborate cornices and pediments.

During the early to mid-19th century, chests of drawers gradually became larger. In previous centuries, most people owned a very limited number of clothes, but now the emerging merchant classes had more changes of dress than before. Therefore larger, more utilitarian chests were required. To help keep the costs of manufacture down, making the chests more accessible to the new market, mahogany veneer was often used instead of solid wood. The ability to knife-cut rather than saw-cut the expensive imported mahogany facilitated the manufacture of a more affordable yet still desirable product.

The overall style and design of the chest and cabinet was to remain largely unaltered from the early 20th century onward, although they did undergo stylistic changes during the early part of the century with a cleaner, less elaborate style being favoured by the emerging designers of the Art Deco period.

Above: *By the 18th century, the finest French commodes were often lacquered and embellished with fire-gilded mounts.*

Left: *This Georgian mahogany breakfront bookcase with drawers, possibly Chippendale, dates from around 1760.*

Chest construction

The chest, be it 17th-, 18th- or 19th-century, consists of a series of drawers enclosed in a carcass. The drawers, depending on their date, will have to run on drawer runners. Chests vary in size from small bachelors' chests, often no larger than 75cm/30in wide, to chests so tall that the top drawers cannot be seen into. Their location was usually in the bedroom, but the finest commodes were prominantly displayed in the drawing room.

On mid-17th-century chests, drawer runners were often attached to the carcass sides and slotted into the side linings of the drawers. By the late 17th century, the runners were attached to the underside of the drawer. This meant that the weight was better dispersed and the runners could easily be replaced when worn.

To ensure that the drawers stopped neatly in the right place when pushed in, drawer stops were used. Like the runner, however, they were susceptible to wear and needed replacing from time to time. By the 18th century, dust boards were incorporated between the drawers. These helped to strengthen the carcass and enabled locks to be fitted on each drawer, if required.

The earlier chests of drawers, dating from the 16th to the mid-17th centuries, were generally made of solid wood and had long-grain mouldings. Some were decorated with carving or limited inlays.

With the arrival of veneers in the latter part of the 17th century, the carcass was usually made of softwood on to which walnut veneers or even marquetry were applied. The veneer was laid with quarter patterns embellished with herringbone inlay bandings. The use of long-grain mouldings was replaced with cross-grain mouldings, which, like the veneer, gave a far more decorative look. In France this went even further with elaborate brass boulle (buhl) inlays inset to tortoiseshell or ebony backgrounds.

By the early 18th century mahogany was once again being used in its solid form, with the use of veneer not returning until the importation of exotic timbers such as satinwood some 40 years later. The chest was further enhanced with decorative features such as canted corners, detailed carving, applied blind fret decoration or a brushing slide.

The feet would reflect the style of the time. Bun feet were the choice of the 17th century, giving way to the shaped bracket foot of the 18th century, and by the 19th century plinths were often used on bedroom chests. The changing fashions are often reflected in the hardware, and it is not unusual to find a chest that has had its handles changed a number of times.

Right: *The basic construction of the chest of drawers varied little during the 18th and 19th centuries.*

DISMANTLING AND REBUILDING CHESTS

It is unusual to have to dismantle a chest of drawers, but you may have to do this when a chest has become very loose or when a side or top has been badly damaged and must be removed from the chest in order to be repaired.

The techniques required and steps taken are equally applicable for the majority of carcass furniture, such as bureaus, bookcases or tallboys. The main consideration is to examine the construction of the piece closely prior to commencement to make sure that no unnecessary damage is caused to either the constituent parts or joints during the dismantling process. All polished areas should be laid on a protective surface and any hammer blows or pressure to dismantle joints should be applied next to joints to ensure that no unnecessary splintering occurs.

Dismantling the chest

This George III chest, c.1760, has become loose and a split has appeared in the top. It is a typical example of 18th-century carcass construction, and closer examination shows that there are no through dovetails that have been veneered over, and no nails or screws have been added to give strength at a later date. Before any work can be done, the chest must be dismantled.

MATERIALS AND EQUIPMENT
- chalk
- hardwood lengths and blocks
- nails
- hammers
- mallet
- wide chisel
- flat-bladed knife

1 The back of the chest consists of a number of boards. Their location should be marked before removal; a suitable method is to mark them with chalk lines, as shown here.

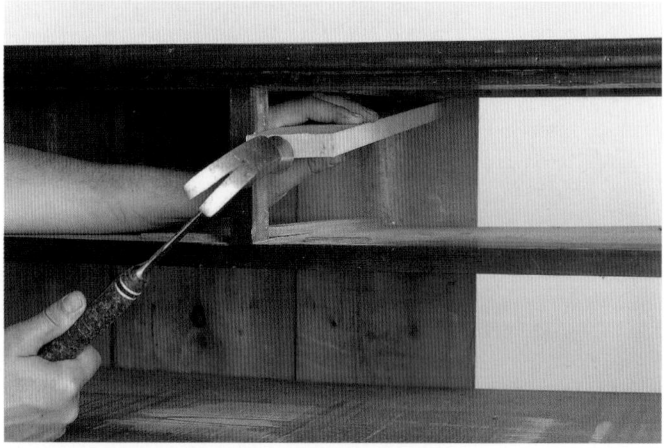

2 Remove the backboards by placing a length of hardwood against the location of the holding nails and tapping it with a hammer. Make sure that only the areas nailed are struck, to avoid unnecessary splintering of the boards.

3 Remove the kickers, which help to make the drawers run level, as well as the wedges, which hold the dust boards in place, by using a mallet to tap a wide chisel between each board and kicker.

◁ **4** Remove both facing strips, which cover the rebates (rabbets) for the dust boards along the front edges, by sliding a flat-bladed knife along the glue line. Use a hammer to help the knife move down each facing edge.

5 Remove the dust boards from the long drawers by knocking them out either backward or forward (depending on the construction of the chest). Place a hardwood block between the board and hammer to avoid any unnecessary damage to the wood.

6 As well as being nailed together, the top and side joints are given extra strength by glue blocks. Remove these by placing a chisel behind each block in turn and giving it a sharp blow with a mallet. The glue line holding the blocks should come away easily.

7 Having removed the dust boards from the long drawers, there still remains the frame from the two short drawers, which is jointed with the twin drawer centre stile. In this case the joint is a through tenon, and therefore the stile and frame must be knocked apart.

◁ **8** Remove the top from the sides using a hammer and hardwood block as for the backboards. Slide out the remaining dust board. Now lift the remainder of the carcass clear of the workbench with the aid of a helper and place it the right way up.

▷

Dismantling the chest...continued

◁ **9** Now dismantle the sides, which are dovetailed into the base, using a hammer and hardwood block, as before. Tap the base while lifting one side clear, then repeat for the other side.

▽ **10** The chest is now dismantled. The feet have not been removed to prevent further damage to the chest of drawers.

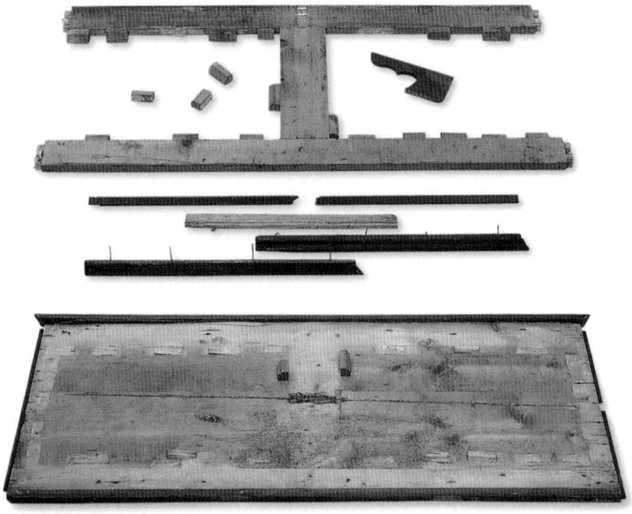

Reassembling the chest

When the necessary repairs have been made (in this case, the table had developed a split top, which needed gluing together), the chest of drawers can be rebuilt.

MATERIALS AND EQUIPMENT

- toothbrush
- PVA (white) glue
- cloths (rags)
- sash clamps
- clamping blocks
- snap clamps
- gauge sticks
- hammer
- length of hardwood
- masking tape
- nails
- animal glue
- rubber
- polish
- wax

1 Remove traces of the old animal glue using an old toothbrush and hot water. The water will soften the glue and enable it to be removed without any damage to the actual joints.

◁ **2** Apply only a small amount of PVA (white) glue to the joints between the sides and bottom, then refit the sides and the drawer frame. Wipe away any excess glue with a cloth (cotton rag) immediately. Apply sash clamps and a snap clamp.

3 Before the glue sets, fit a drawer to check that the drawer frame is square, and check the carcass for squareness using gauge sticks.

4 Slide the long dust boards back into position, then gently tap the kickers and wedges back into place using a length of hardwood to guard against unnecessary bruising.

◁ **5** Glue the top back on and clamp it securely into place with snap clamps and sash clamps. Refit the old glue blocks using animal glue. Leave to dry. Also reglue the facing strips, holding them in position with masking tape while they dry.

◁ **6** Finally, nail the backboards back into place, remembering to match up the chalk lines to ensure the correct positioning.

Right: *With the chest reassembled, any surfaces that need it can be revived, polished and waxed, and any missing handles replaced.*

REPAIRING CARCASSES AND TOPS

Traditionally, carcasses are very strong and rarely suffer serious structural damage in normal use. Exceptions occur when changes in humidity cause carcasses and tops to crack, heavy doors put undue strain on hinges, and plinths and feet become scuffed and damaged. None of these problems is insurmountable, provided the correct repair and restoration techniques are employed, and the results can be very pleasing.

Repairing a split top

Changes in humidity can cause chest tops to split in exactly the same way that table tops split. If a split occurs along the line where two pieces of wood are joined, they can simply be reglued and clamped to secure. If a split occurs away from a natural join, the top must be repaired with butterfly keys.

This c.1845 pine chest of drawers, veneered in Cuban mahogany, has a split top, due to the pine core shrinking away from the mahogany until the resulting tension caused the core to split apart. The mouldings must be removed, the split must be separated and reglued and then re-secured with butterfly keys, glued into cut-outs routed into the underside of the top.

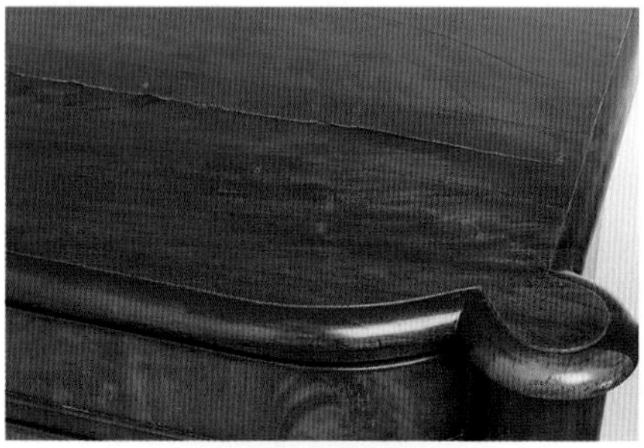

MATERIALS AND EQUIPMENT

- hammer
- hardwood block
- flat-bladed knife
- tenon saw
- PVA (white) glue
- sash clamps
- clamping blocks
- softwood
- deep-throated clamps
- cardboard
- utility knife
- router
- chisel
- jack plane
- water-based stain
- fine brushes
- cabinet scraper
- fine-grade sandpaper
- rubber
- polish
- stopping wax
- spirit-based (alcohol-based) stain
- cloth (cotton rag)
- wax

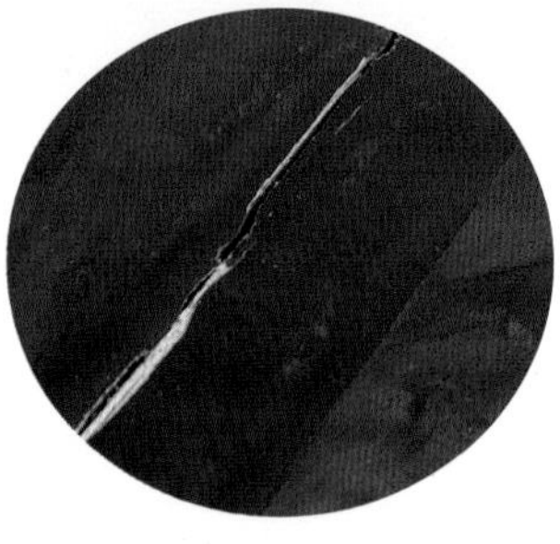

Above: *The split in the top.*

1 Remove the top from the carcass using a hammer and hardwood block and place it upside down on a protected workbench. Blocks of wood had been glued to the underside in a previous attempt to repair the split. Remove these now with a flat-bladed knife, then turn the top over.

2 Carefully cut the mahogany long-grain mouldings that pass the end of the split from the pine core with a tenon saw. The mouldings have not split, and so they can be removed intact and reglued later (see step 5). Apply PVA (white) glue along the split in the top.

3 Clamp the width of the top together using sash clamps and clamping blocks. Place a piece of paper, then a piece of softwood, along the length of the split, then secure both with deep-throated clamps to make sure the two parts of the top remain level. Leave to dry.

4 Cut butterfly keys from pine and rout matching holes along the underside of the split (see p.230). Glue in the keys and plane them down until flush with the underside. Stain the keys to match the top.

5 Turn the top over and work along the split with a cabinet scraper to remove any loose veneer. Take great care to scrape only along the split, to avoid damaging the rest of the veneer. Reglue any un-split mouldings.

6 Smooth the area along the split by rubbing with fine-grade sandpaper. Avoid sanding too wide an area around the split.

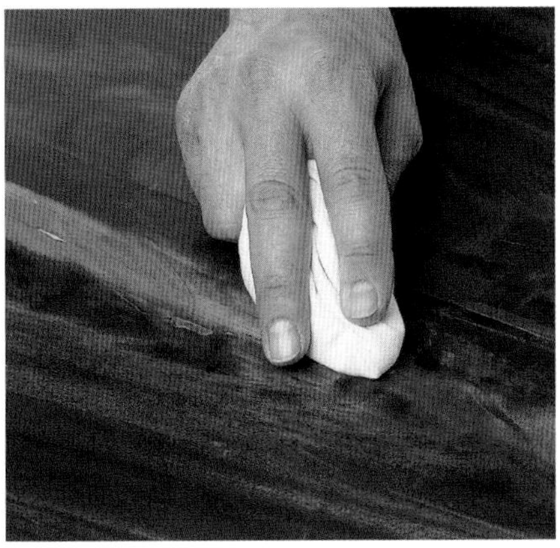

7 Charge a rubber with polish and apply a layer to the split area to conceal any tiny missing areas of veneer (see pp.66–67). The split will now be almost invisible.

8 Select a stopping wax to match the colour and tone of the veneer. Fill the small areas of missing veneer with the wax, using a flat-bladed knife.

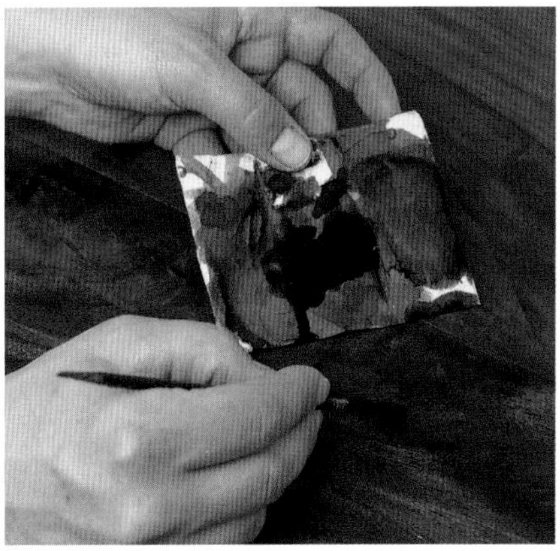

9 Mix a spirit-based (alcohol-based) stain to match the colour and tone of the veneer (see p.41), and apply it to the sanded and polished area. This will blend the two pieces together and help to mask the joint.

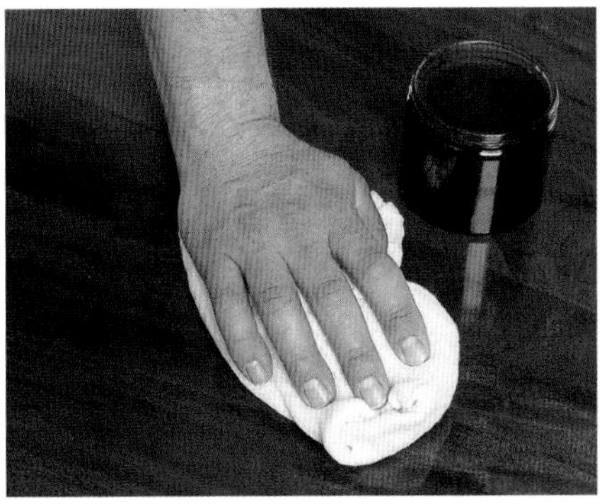

10 Put the top back on. Treat the entire top with a wax chosen to match the colour and tone of the veneer. Take care not to rub too hard on the split area, because you risk removing the applied colour and wax.

Left: *Now stained and waxed, the split is almost invisible. With the inset butterfly keys on the underside securing the joint, no further restoration should be necessary.*

Replacing a bracket foot

The bracket foot was introduced during the early 18th century and remained basically unchanged in its construction through the rest of the century. When replacing a single missing foot, you can copy one of the remaining feet, but if all the feet are missing you will need to seek advice from an expert in this field to determine the correct shape and style required. This chest of drawers is missing one of its mahogany feet, although some of the glue blocks remain.

MATERIALS AND EQUIPMENT

- cardboard
- utility knife
- mahogany
- coping saw or band saw
- jack plane
- mitre box
- scotch glue
- spring clips
- softwood
- rasp
- chisel
- screwdriver
- rubber
- polish
- fine brush
- stain

1 Make a cardboard template (pattern) of one of the remaining feet and mark this outline twice on the selected old surface mahogany, once for each side of the foot.

2 Cut out both pieces of the foot by hand with a coping saw or by machine with a band saw. Plane the joining mitres with a jack plane, ideally using a mitre box.

3 Attach both parts of the foot to the carcass and each other with scotch glue. Rub each part back and forth a few times to create suction between the foot and carcass, then apply pressure with spring clips.

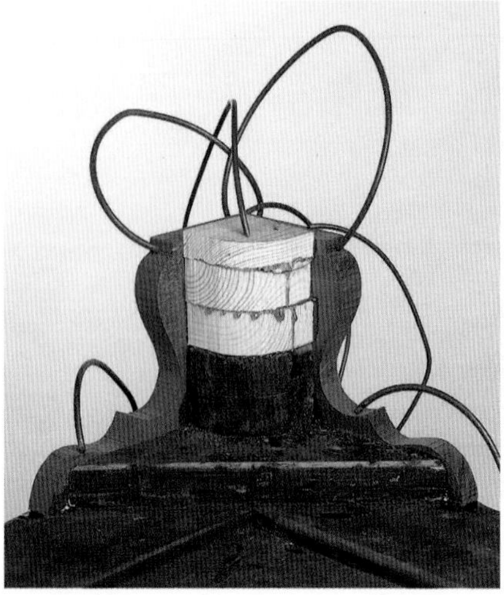

◁ **4** Cut new glue blocks from softwood. With the clips still in place, glue these blocks, into position and secure them with more spring clips. Leave them slightly proud of the foot so that they can be trimmed flush later. This will help to distribute the weight of the chest.

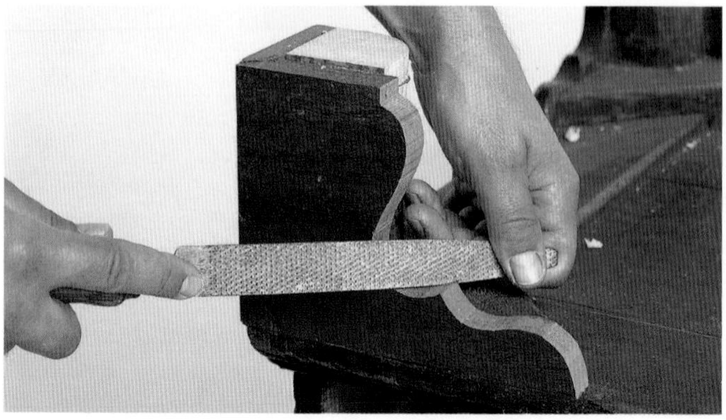

5 If the foot parts were cut with a band saw, use a rasp to remove the blade marks that will have been left. Note the wear patterns on the opposite original foot and try to mirror them.

6 Trim the glue blocks flush with a chisel or plane. Round over all the sharp edges with the shank of a screwdriver. This mimics the natural process of years of waxing and handling. Also, if a clean piece of mahogany has been used to make the foot, add a few knocks to match the existing feet.

Left: *Polish the exterior of the foot, and stain the interior and the glue blocks. The new foot now matches the carcass in grain, colour and finish. The wear and patination also match the other feet on the chest, and no casual observer should be able to spot the replacement.*

Spring clips

There are numerous types of clamp designed to help in the restoration of antique furniture. One of the most versatile, used for difficult and awkward clamping, is the spring clip. This is home-made from old upholstery springs, and is ideal for applying pressure or simply holding small pieces of wood or furniture in place.

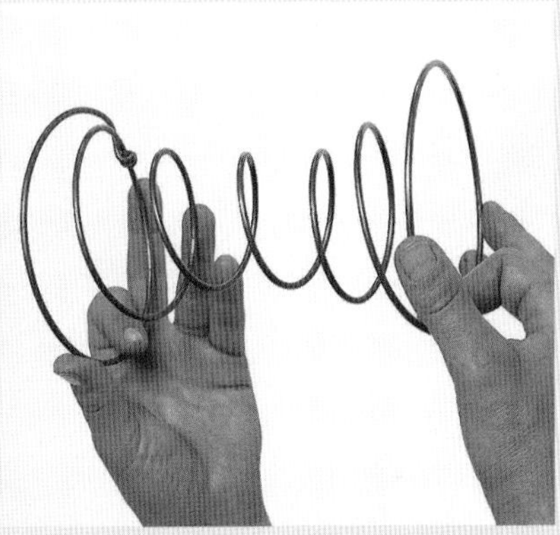

◁ **1** *Choose a large old upholstery spring; this will allow you to make several clips of different sizes. The spring steel will keep its shape and will apply considerable pressure when pulled apart.*

2 *Using a bench grinder, cut through the tensile-steel spring at two points to form a circular clip, the two ends of which should meet. When pulled apart, the natural curve of the spring should give the necessary pressure to hold any parts together.*

3 *Grind a point on each end of the clip. These points will make sure that the clip remains in place when it is being used.*

4 *When completed, the clip can be used for a variety of awkward clamping tasks. To keep the tension, push the two end points until they overlap, then pull them apart and place them in the required holding position.*

REPAIRING DRAWERS

Prior to the late 17th century, the majority of drawers would have run on rebated (rabbeted) side drawer runners. After this time, the runners were fitted on the bottom of the drawer. Due to their constant action, drawer stops and drawer runners are sometimes worn away. A sure sign that they need to be replaced is when a drawer begins to stick. Failure to attend to this can, in extreme cases, make the chest unusable.

Replacing cock beading

Cock beading is the name given to the moulding that runs around the edge of inset drawers. This decorative feature, which was introduced during the early 18th century, also protects the edge of applied veneers from flaking and splitting. Sometimes the beading can become loose or broken due to being snagged. On this drawer, part of the beading had become detached and lost and another part was damaged.

MATERIALS AND EQUIPMENT
- paring chisel
- mahogany
- utility knife
- PVA (white) glue
- spring clips
- block plane
- fine-grade sandpaper
- fine brush
- stain
- rubber
- polish

1 Using a paring chisel, remove the damaged area of cock beading. Select a piece of mahogany for the new beading.

2 Cut 45-degree mitres with a sharp utility knife at either end of the new cock beading. Glue it in place with PVA (white) glue and hold it with spring clips (see p.215).

3 Cut a piece of cock beading to replace the missing beading. Cut 45-degree mitres at both ends, then secure the piece as in step 2.

4 When the glue is dry, use a block plane to remove any excess wood so that the beading is flush with the side of the drawer.

5 As the cock beading will almost certainly have a rounded edge this can be first shaped using a small paring chisel and followed by papering with fine-grade sandpaper.

Above: *The new cock beading should be stained and polished to match the existing beading, with efforts made to match any light distressing on the original.*

Replacing drawer runners

The drawer runners on this drawer have been completely worn away in places. Further damage has been done by the carcass drawer stops, which have grooved trenches into the drawer bottom (see p.218). The damaged runners must be removed and replaced with new ones.

MATERIALS AND EQUIPMENT

- flat-bladed knife
- hammer
- smoothing plane
- beech or mahogany
- tenon saw
- PVA (white) glue
- snap clamps
- toothbrush
- plane
- chisel

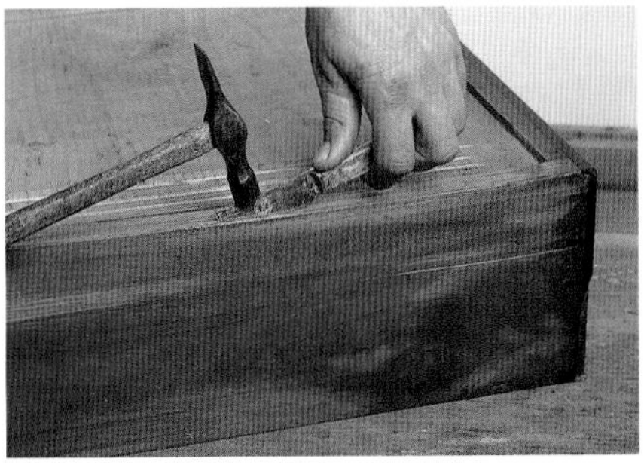

1 If the runners are glued to the sides and bottom, tap a flat-bladed knife slid between the runner and the side to break the joint.

2 Remove the damaged runners from the bottom by sliding the knife underneath and gently tapping it with the hammer.

3 Use the iron from a smoothing plane to remove any traces of old and perished glue.

4 Choose a similar wood to the old runners (usually beech or mahogany) and cut some runners to the same width and length as the old ones, but deeper to allow for planing at a later stage. Glue them into place.

5 Hold the new runners firmly in place with snap clamps and leave to dry. Remove any excess glue using a toothbrush and water.

6 This drawer also had runners attached to the exterior of the drawer sides, and these too had become worn. Remove and replace these with new ones, as before, gluing them to the replacement bottom runners.

◁ **7** When dry, plane the runners to the correct depth to enable the drawer to sit evenly in the carcass. This is very much a case of trial and error, but take care not to plane the runners too thin, or the drawer will sit unevenly.

▷ **8** The final touch is to cut an angled mitre at the back of each runner. This will help the drawer to run smoothly as well as preventing snagging.

▷

Replacing drawer runners...continued

◁ **9** Use a sharp chisel to cut a bevel at the back of each mitred runner. This will make removing the drawer and inserting it back into the carcass much easier.

Right: *With its new runners in place, the drawer will slide smoothly and freely.*

Replacing drawer stops

Drawer stops are designed to prevent a drawer from sliding in too far, and ensure that all the drawers line up correctly when closed. Stops are normally fitted so that they come into contact with the back of the drawer front, although they may be placed at the back of the drawer. If the runners wear, the stops may also become worn. In this case, the stops had worn away to expose their fixing nails, which had gouged the drawer bottoms.

MATERIALS AND EQUIPMENT

- flat-bladed knife
- hammer
- pincers
- tenon saw
- wood blocks
- PVA (white) glue
- pins (tacks)

1 Using a flat-bladed knife and a hammer, gently tap the knife between the worn stops and the carcass, and lift the stops away.

2 When the stops have been removed, they may leave behind the fixing nails. Remove these with a pair of pincers.

3 Insert one of the drawers into the carcass. Pulling the drawer forward slightly, measure the gap between the drawer bottom and the carcass. Cut a block of wood to a thickness that will be less than this measurement, to ensure that it does not interfere with the smooth running of the drawer, then cut it into two squares of suitable size. Repeat for the other drawers.

4 Glue the new drawer stops to the carcass, setting them slightly forward of the original positions. Before the glue has dried, insert both drawers, carefully aligning them with the front of the chest. This will push the blocks into their correct positions. Leave the glue to dry completely before removing the drawers. If extra strength is required, drive a few pins (tacks) through the stops.

Cutting a dovetail joint

The dovetail joint was one of the most common types of joint used in the construction of furniture in the 18th and 19th centuries. In the main, it was used when two flat sections overlapped each other and a strong, secure joint was required, such as in carcass, plinth, drawer and cornice construction. Small dovetails can be difficult to cut, and the skill of the cabinet-maker is demonstrated by the quality of his dovetails.

This drawer, which dates from 1780, has lost one of its sides, but fortunately the interior parts used to house the ink bottles have survived. Before work starts, the drawer must be dismantled by gently tapping it apart using a cabinet hammer and a block of protective hardwood. The drawer dovetails are finer than normal so care must be taken not to damage them during the dismantling process. The drawer was made from Cuban mahogany, and a piece of matching wood must be found for the new side. Once the new dovetail joints have been cut, the drawer can be reassembled.

MATERIALS AND EQUIPMENT

- Cuban mahogany
- tenon saw
- marking gauge
- utility knife
- fine dovetail saw
- G-clamp
- clamping blocks
- chisel
- mallet
- hammer
- hardwood blocks
- mortise gauge
- narrow chisel or router
- PVA (white) glue

1 Dismantle the drawer. Find a matching piece of mahogany for the new side. If the colour is slightly different, it can be stained to match at a later stage, but it is important that the grain is the same. Cut it to the same size as the existing drawer side.

2 Measure the length of the dovetail pins on the existing drawer side, then mark them out on both ends of the new side using a marking gauge.

3 Hold the front of the drawer against the corresponding end of the new side, and transfer the pin lines with a utility knife. Repeat with the back, holding it against the other end of the new side.

4 Place the side in a vice with the marked lines held vertical. Using a fine dovetail saw, cut along the waste side of the marked lines. This will help to achieve good tight joints.

▷

Cutting a dovetail joint...continued

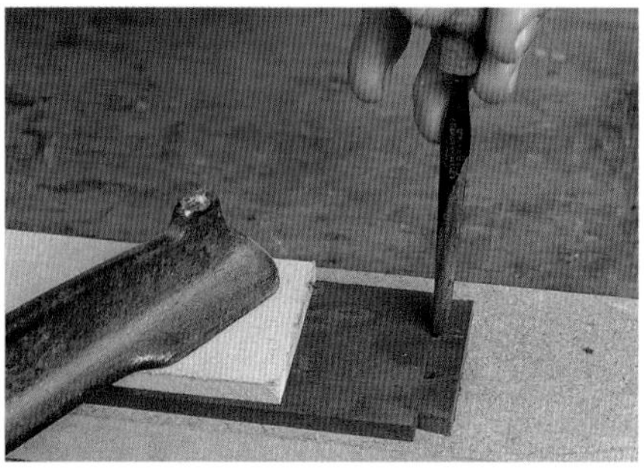

5 Clamp the side to a flat piece of wood and use a sharp chisel and a mallet to cut halfway through the top of the waste wood. Turn the side over and cut through from the other side. This will ensure a clean cut.

6 Some drawer bottoms are nailed in place, but this one is housed in a groove. Mark this groove on the new side with a mortise gauge set to the thickness of the bottom.

7 Cut the new groove for the drawer bottom with a narrow chisel or a router.

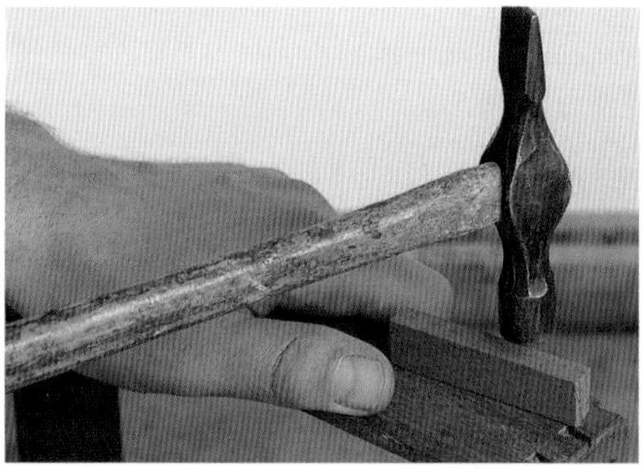

8 Tap the dovetail joint gently together with a small hammer and a hardwood block. The joint should be tight with no gaps. If necessary, make small adjustments by paring the wood with a utility knife.

Left: *The drawer can now be reassembled and the internal parts glued back into place.*

Cutting a dovetail housing

__1__ Lay the newly cut dovetail pins against the end grain of the corresponding piece of wood. Mark the outline of the pins clearly with a utility knife.

__2__ Measure the depth of the pins with a marking gauge, then score a line across the wood. Use a dovetail saw to cut on the waste side of the marked lines for a good fit, using the scored line as a depth guide.

__3__ Bring the two parts of the joint together. It should be tight with no gaps. Apply a small amount of glue, then remake the joint. Before it sets, check that the drawer is square by using gauge sticks (see p. 142).

Repairing a split drawer bottom

During the 18th and 19th centuries, drawer bottoms were made up from a number of pieces. They were then either slotted into grooved drawer sides or nailed flush. Due to the fact that wood will shrink across its grain, it is not uncommon to find that the original glue line has come away with the shrinkage of the various sections of a drawer bottom, leaving gaps. This drawer has an unsightly gap, so the bottom must be removed and the gap reglued before the drawer can be reassembled.

MATERIALS AND EQUIPMENT
- chalk
- stiff-bladed knife
- hammer
- smoothing plane
- PVA (white) glue
- sash clamps
- clamping blocks
- nails
- cloth (cotton rag)

1 Mark the underside of the various pieces of the drawer bottom with chalk before removing them. This shows which way around the boards should be and also how the parts join together.

2 The bottom slides into grooves on the drawer sides but is nailed to the drawer back, and the nails have been punched below the surface. To remove them, insert a stiff-bladed knife between the wood and the back, then tap it with a hammer to cut through the nails.

3 Remove the bottom pieces and clean off the old glue with the iron from a smoothing plane. Replace the bottom pieces in the correct order, applying a small amount of PVA (white) glue along the glue lines.

4 Clamp the bottom pieces together with a sash clamp and clamping blocks, and nail the back piece to the drawer back at the same time. Finally, wipe off any excess glue and chalk marks with a cloth (cotton rag).

Right: *Once restored, the drawer bottom will be gap-free, giving an aesthetically more pleasing appearance.*

REPAIRING DOORS

The doors in pieces of furniture can suffer from a number of problems, some of which are easier to put right than others. Broken glass is common in glazed doors, while doors of all types can stick in their openings or become distorted. As with other types of furniture, any carved detail or mouldings may be damaged over the years, while the hardware (hinges, catches and locks) can also give trouble.

Repairing a glazed door

From the late 17th century onward, glass was introduced into furniture construction. It was hand blown and rolled into very thin sheets. During the 18th and 19th centuries, the style of the glazing bars, or astragals, found in bookcase and cabinet doors varied greatly, but the actual method of securing the glass remained fairly constant.

This door is from a mid-18th-century bookcase. One of the smaller panes has been cracked and so needs to be replaced. Once the glass has been removed, a new pane must be inserted. This will be held in place with plaster rather than putty. Once dry, the plaster can be stained to match the original putty. There are various sources for suitable glass (see Selecting glass, p.224).

MATERIALS AND EQUIPMENT

- iron
- chisel
- glass
- methylated spirits (methyl alcohol)
- fine wire (steel) wool
- felt-tipped pen
- diamond-tipped glass cutter
- steel straightedge
- plaster
- ochre
- flat-bladed knife
- fine brush
- water-based stain

1 First, remove the original mid-18th century putty. Do this by heating the putty with an iron to soften it.

2 When the putty is soft, begin to pare it away with a sharp chisel.

3 Remove all the old putty from the back of the astragal with the chisel, making sure not to cut into the wood supports, since this would weaken the construction of the door.

◁ **4** When the putty has been removed, carefully lift out the broken pieces of glass (you may wish to wear protective gloves for this job). If the glass is antique and hand blown, do not discard any pieces of a reasonable size, but store them carefully for a possible later use.

▷ **5** Period hand-blown glass was often not flat but uneven in texture, so it was bedded on to a putty base to counter any movement. This was the case in this door, so pare away the bedding putty as well.

6 Clean your selected piece of glass using methylated spirits (methyl alcohol) and fine wire (steel) wool, and check that it matches the existing glass in both colour and type.

7 Place the glass over the astragal and mark out the shape with a felt-tipped pen.

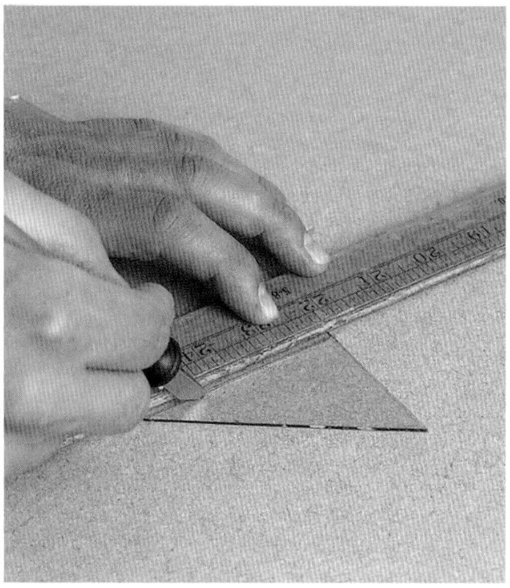

8 Using a diamond-tipped glass cutter, scribe along the marked line and cut the glass to size and shape.

◁ **9** Putty was used to hold the original glass in this door, and you could use putty to fix the new pane, but it takes several days to harden fully. A better choice is plaster, which hardens in minutes and can be pre-coloured. Mix the plaster with a small quantity of ochre before stirring in the water.

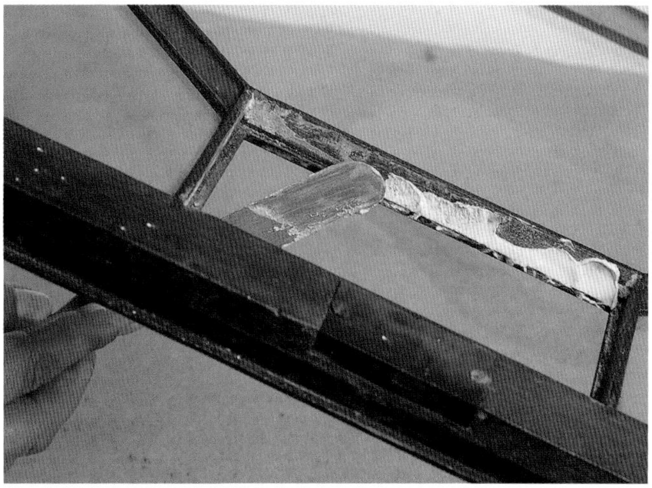

10 The glass will not be completely flat, so apply a small layer of plaster with a flat-bladed knife to act as a levelling base. ▷

Repairing a glazed door...continued

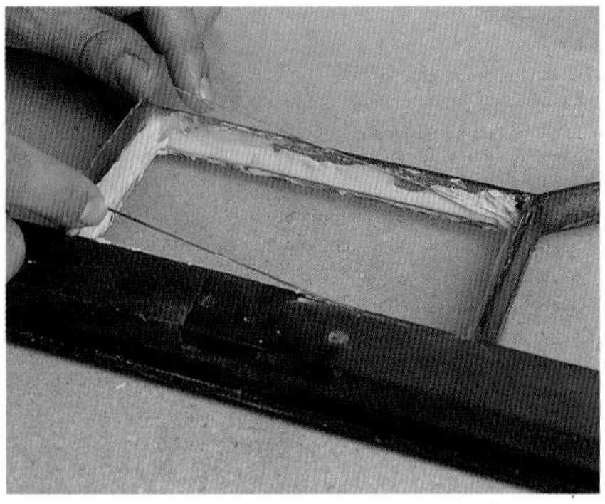

11 Press the glass gently into position on the wet plaster.

12 Apply more plaster with a flat-bladed knife and shape it into a bevel.

13 While the plaster is still malleable, trim away the excess with a sharp chisel.

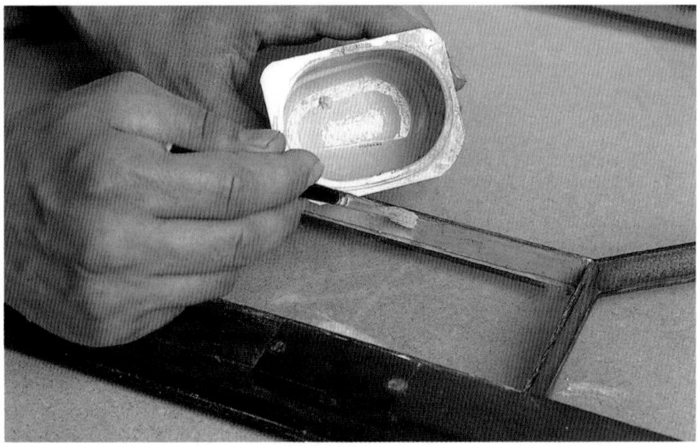

14 When the plaster is dry, stain it with a water-based stain mixed to match the colour of the original putty.

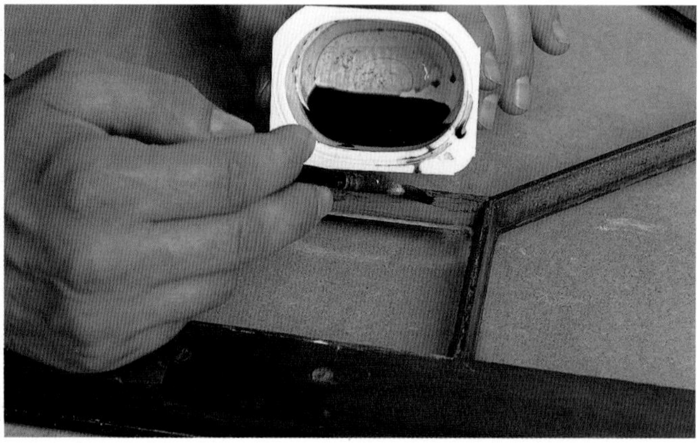

15 Finally, apply a darker stain on top of the coloured plaster to try to mimic the patina of the original putty. This should blend the repaired glazed panel to match the others.

Right: *As the restored pane is of a matching glass and was fitted properly, it is u ndetectable from the original when viewed from the exterior.*

Selecting glass

It is always preferable to use an old piece of glass to replace glass lost from antique furniture, as new glass will stand out. While certain specialist glass manufacturers still supply old-style glass, the best sources are old picture frames and stocks collected from previous repairs, which can be cut down to the required size.

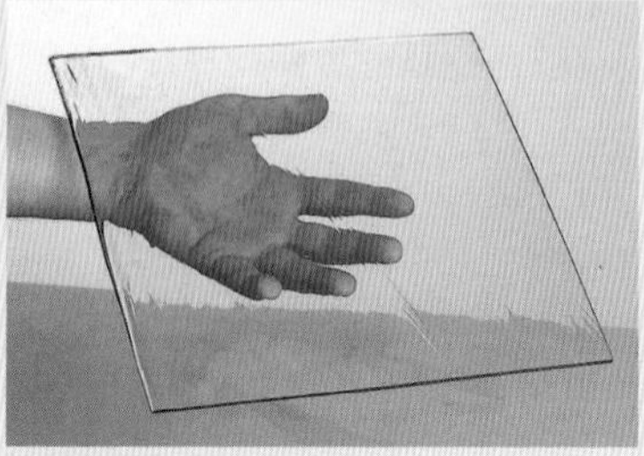

Repairing a sliding tambour

Sliding tambours were introduced in the 18th century. Their construction method is simple: lengths of wood are bonded to a cloth backing, which can be slid back and forth around a curve.

Several lengths of wood have become loose on this 18th-century Dutch cabinet, and closer inspection revealed that a previous repair was causing the problem. The tambour must be detached from the cabinet, the pieces of wood removed from the old backing and reglued to a new linen cloth.

MATERIALS AND EQUIPMENT
- masking tape
- flat-bladed knife
- long-shanked screwdriver
- smoothing plane
- Irish linen
- PVA (white) glue

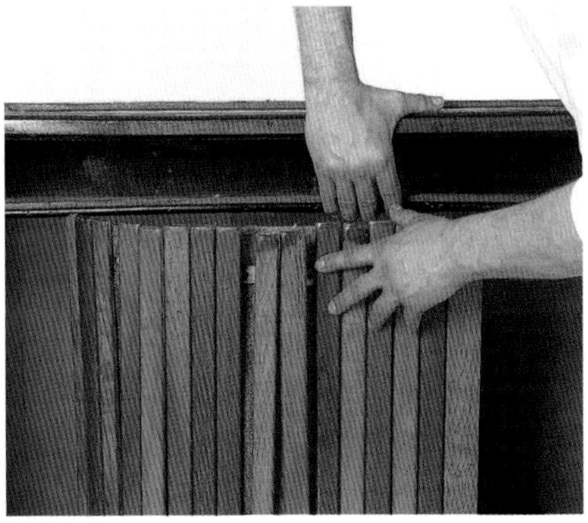

1 The tambour is held in place only through tension, so, once the frieze at the top has been removed, pulling the top of the frieze should release it. Alternatively, the back of the cabinet may have to be removed.

2 Lay the tambour face up on a flat surface. Secure the lengths of wood with 5cm/2in strips of masking tape, laid at right angles to the strips, at 10cm/4in intervals.

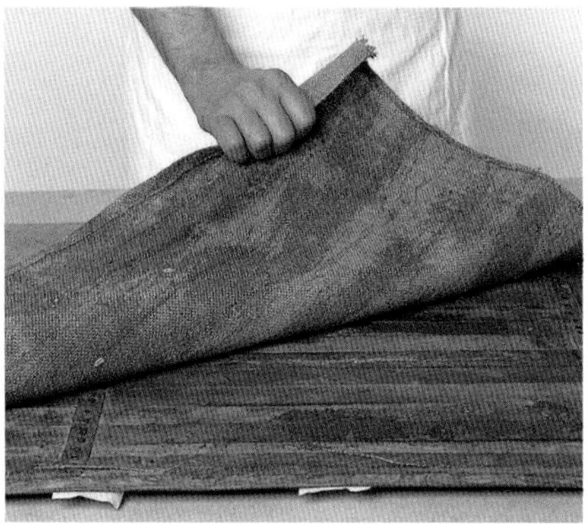

3 Turn the tambour over. Lift up a corner of the backing material with a flat-bladed knife, then pull it away and discard it.

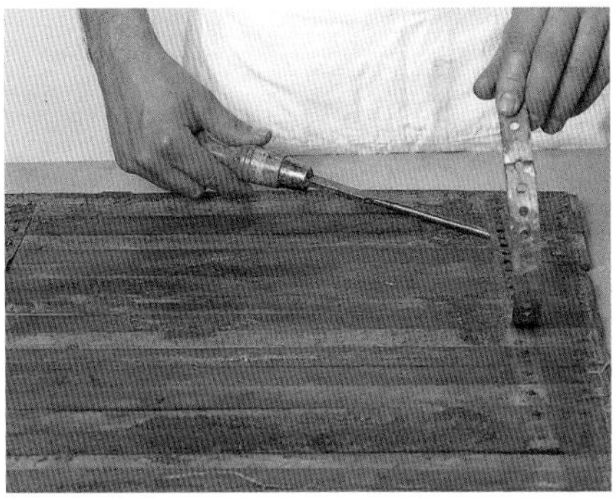

4 Some metal strips from an earlier repair were revealed. These would have held the tambour together, but would have been too stiff to allow it to run freely. Use a long-shanked screwdriver to remove these strips. Scrape away any remains of glue with the iron from a smoothing plane.

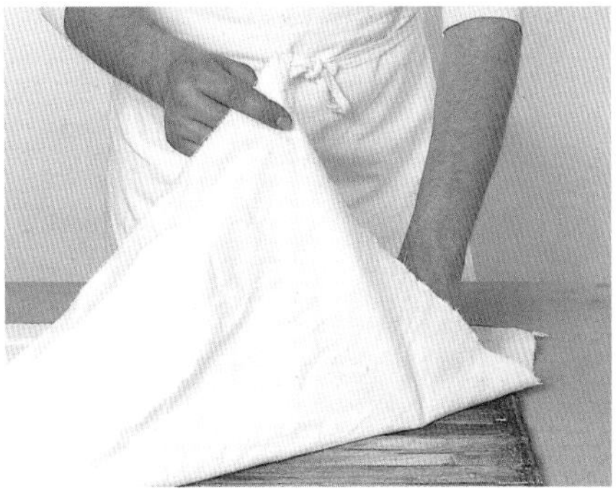

5 Cut a piece of Irish linen to match the height and width of the tambour. Coat the back of the tambour with glue, then smooth the linen over the surface, making sure that there are no air bubbles or wrinkles. Leave to dry. Remove the masking tape and test the flexibility of the tambour by manipulating it into a curved shape, then refit it.

Above: *The restored sliding tambour, with its decorative parquetry frieze replaced, now operates smoothly in the cabinet.*

Refitting a door

The door on this 18th-century wall cupboard has dropped due to wear on the pin hinge. This has resulted in the door no longer sitting square in the frame, and a gap can be seen at the top. The two alternatives are to have the hinge remade or to pack up the bottom of the door, which is an easier and quicker method.

MATERIALS AND EQUIPMENT
- **flat-bladed knife**
- **hammer**
- **tenon saw**
- **wood**
- **hand drill**
- **fine brush**
- **stain**

1 Due to the construction of the cabinet, the hinges have been attached with hand-made clout nails rather than screws. Ease the nails out gently by tapping a flat-bladed knife in behind the hinge.

2 Fold the detached part of the hinge forward to reveal the housing. Cut a thin packing piece of wood to size and trim to fit in the recess of the housing. This will counteract the dropping of the hinge.

3 Drill pilot holes into the packing piece (see p.235). These will make sure that the original clout nails, which will be weakened by their age, will not shear off when they are refitted. Stain the packing piece to match the surrounding wood.

Left: *With the packing piece in place and the hinge replaced, the door once again sits squarely in its frame.*

Correcting a minor twist

Doors come in many styles and designs, but one theme that is common to all doors is that they can warp, twist or bind due to climatic change. In extreme cases, the door may need to be completely remade, with the core wood being replaced. In most cases, however, there are a number of steps that can be taken to help alleviate the problem. The door on this mid-18th-century bookcase has twisted slightly and no longer closes flush against the opposite door. Since the problem is fairly minimal, a technique known as half and half (half packing/half paring) will be employed to correct the twist.

MATERIALS AND EQUIPMENT

- screwdriver
- tenon saw
- wood
- hand drill
- wood drill bit
- chisel

1 Unscrew both hinges from the carcass and remove the bookcase door. Keep the original screws safely.

2 Cut a small packing piece of wood to fit in the bottom hinge recess. This will push the bottom of the door out slightly. Drill pilot holes for the screws and refit the hinge.

◁ **3** Pare down the top hinge recess slightly then refit the hinge. This will pull the top part of the door nearer to being flush with the opposite side. Both the packing and paring have an element of trial and error about them, so make small changes at a time and refit the door regularly to make sure that a correct balance is obtained. Note that the packed and pared areas do not need staining because they are completely covered by the refitted hinges.

Right: *With the corrective work undertaken, the door is once again able to close flush against the opposite side.*

Project: 19th-century desk

When this desk was originally purchased, its age was unknown. It was not immediately apparent, therefore, whether or not it was worth carrying out restoration. After some investigation and upon close examination, however, it was discovered to be a 19th-century English oak-veneered writing desk, and, despite the generally distressed condition of the piece, it was indeed worth restoring to its former glory.

Assessing the project

The desk is damaged in several areas, particularly the top, the drawers and the carcass, with areas of veneer missing in some places. An initial assessment was made of each problem in order to decide in which order to proceed. The final decision was to split the restoration work into three sections – first the top, then the drawers and finally the carcass – after which the whole desk would be polished and cleaned.

The top

- split wood
- torn and worn leather

The carcass

- damage to frame supports
- splits to pedestal
- missing veneer on plinth corners

The drawers

- damaged runners
- missing knobs

Repairing the desk top

The wood of the desk top needs extensive restoration, but the leather is too badly damaged to be saved and so must be replaced. The first stage is to secure the splits in the wood from underneath using butterfly keys. Then the splits in the top surface should be filled, planed and polished, and finally some new leather applied.

SECURING THE SPLITS

Although the splits in the desk top appear dramatic, they require one of the more straightforward repairs, using softwood butterfly keys that are inset and glued underneath the top at right angles to the split. These keys secure the split and so prevent any further movement.

MATERIALS AND EQUIPMENT

- screwdriver
- long pole
- G-clamp
- clamping block
- toothing plane
- cardboard
- softwood
- tenon saw
- utility knife
- router
- chisel
- PVA glue
- jack plane
- fine brush
- water-based stain or ochre

1 Remove the top drawers and lift the desk top and frame off the pedestals. Prise a corner of the leather free and wrap it around a long pole. Pull the leather gently away while rolling the pole toward you.

2 Remove the second piece of leather in the same way. As the leather is removed, you can assess the extent of the damage to the top. In this case, the splits in the top go right through the wood.

3 Secure the top to the workbench with a G-clamp and clamping block, then run a toothing plane over the wood to remove any old glue or pieces of leather.

4 To clean the edges, remove the iron from the toothing plane and scrape it along the surface, parallel to the polished edge, until no traces of old glue or leather remain.

5 Remove the clamp and turn the top over. In this instance, a previous owner had tried, unsuccessfully, to restore the desk top by screwing a wooden panel over the split. This has to be removed.

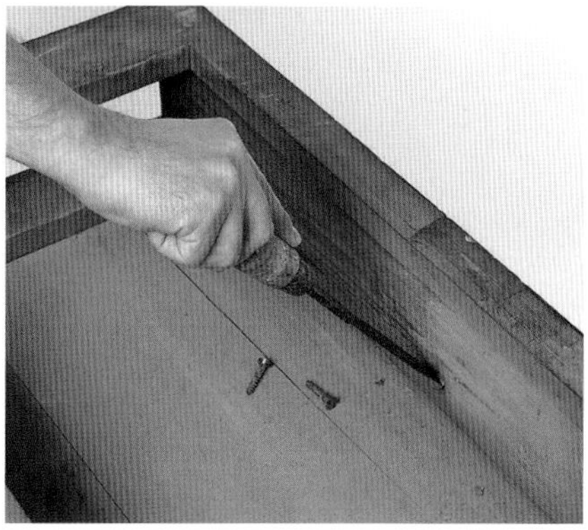

6 Detach the frame from the top by removing the recessed screws, known as pocket screws, with a screwdriver. This will provide complete access to the desk top. Set the frame aside for later repairs.

▷

Securing the splits ...continued

7 Make a cardboard template for the butterfly keys (see right). Mark out as many keys as you need on a piece of softwood and cut them out with a tenon saw.

Butterfly keys

Butterfly keys are dovetail-shaped blocks of wood that are inset at right-angles to a split, thus preventing the split from opening up further. They should be made from a softwood, such as pine, and their size and number depend upon the size of the split and the depth of the wood. In the case of a split that cannot be closed up, the keys will secure the surface in its current position. If the split can be glued and clamped (such as the Windsor chair, p.147), the keys will secure the glued join.

8 Place a butterfly key over one end of the first split, about 13cm/5in from the edge of the desk top, with the waist of the key directly over the split. Mark out the position of the key with a utility knife.

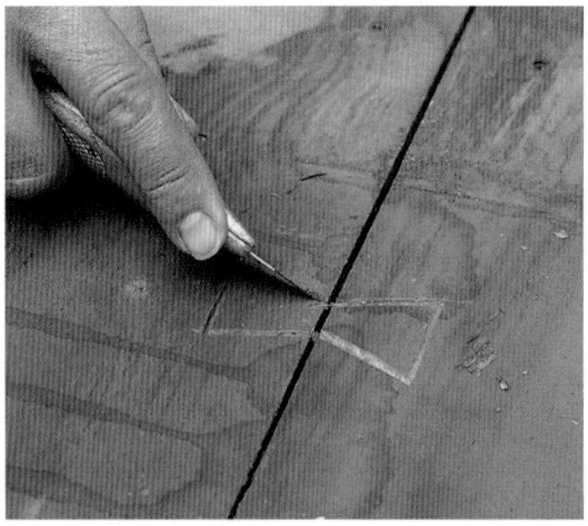

9 Cut an angled back chamfer around the key outline with the utility knife. This will prevent the edge from splintering when it is routed.

10 Set the depth stop on a router to slightly less than the thickness of the key, then cut out the marked key shape.

11 Use a sharp chisel to straighten the edges of the cuts. It is important to match the recess exactly to the shape of the key to ensure a snug fit. Continue cutting shapes at 23cm/9in intervals along all the splits.

12 Apply a thin coat of glue to each recess and press in a key. When they are dry, plane the keys level with the surface of the desk top using a jack plane.

13 Use a water-based stain or ochre that matches the colour of the wood to tint the keys. Although the underside of the desk top will not be seen, this is a finishing touch that should always be made.

Preparing the Top

Any cracks or dents in the upper surface of the desk top will show through the leather, as the construction of the desk top made it simply impossible to glue the top together. Therefore, they must be filled and the top smoothed down. A two-part wood filler can be applied to smaller cracks, but larger splits also require filling with thin strips of wood. The veneer around the edge of the upper surface requires some patching, and must be cleaned and polished before the leather is applied.

MATERIALS AND EQUIPMENT

- **softwood**
- **tenon saw**
- **PVA (white) glue**
- **hammer**
- **chisel**
- **two-part wood filler**
- **putty knife**
- **smoothing plane**
- **veneer patch**
- **fine wire (steel) wool**
- **methylated spirits (methyl alcohol)**
- **rubber**
- **polish**

1 Cut strips of softwood to the correct width and length to fit the larger splits snugly. Apply a generous amount of PVA (white) glue to the splits.

2 Put each sliver of wood over its split and set it in place by lightly tapping it down with a hammer. Wipe away the excess. Leave to dry.

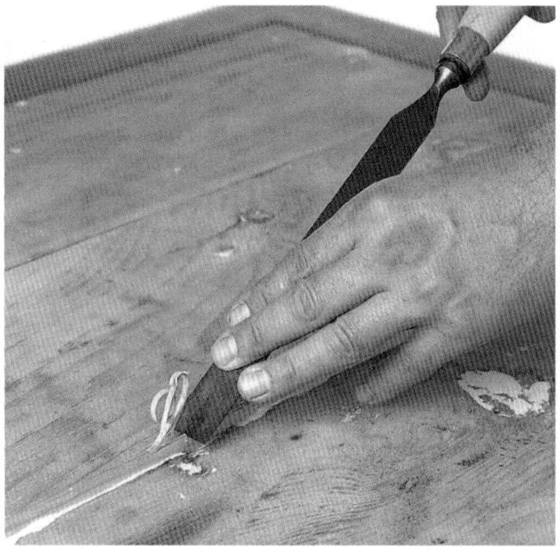

3 Use a sharp chisel to pare away any excess wood. Continue until each insert is flush with the desk top.

4 Apply a two-part wood filler to all cracks and knot holes with a putty knife, packing the filler in well. Leave to dry.

5 Plane the surface with a smoothing plane to smooth off the filler and to produce a surface to which the leather can adhere.

6 Patch the damaged areas of veneer banding on the edge of the top, making sure the grain and figure match (see p.239). ▷

Preparing the top...continued

7 Lightly rub the veneered edge with fine wire (steel) wool to remove any top wax and loose dirt. Always work in the direction of the grain, otherwise you will leave scratches.

8 Moisten the wire wool with methylated spirits (methyl alcohol) and lightly rub the veneered edge again. This will give a surface to which the new polish can adhere.

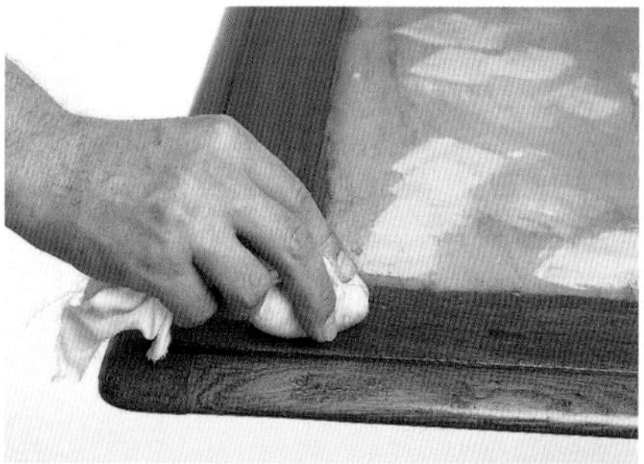

9 Charge a rubber with polish and apply a layer to the veneered edge to enhance the grain and colour of the veneer. A final polish will be applied when the desk is reassembled.

LEATHERING THE TOP

The value of the desk demands that a best-quality piece of hide should be selected and purchased from a tannery. Prior to cutting it, examine it for scars, scratches and stretch marks, all of which will be emphasized when coloured and polished (see p.43). Time taken at this stage will ensure that the finished result complements the rest of the restoration work undertaken.

MATERIALS AND EQUIPMENT

- large brush
- PVA (white) glue
- leather
- "bone"
- utility knife
- cloths (cotton rags)
- leather sealant
- water-based stain
- tooling wheel
- pressurized spray gun
- cellulose lacquer
- dividers
- roll of gold leaf
- steel rule
- decorative pattern wheel
- stamp
- wax (optional)

1 Spread PVA (white) glue evenly over the wood, making sure it covers the whole area, especially up to the edges. Lay the new piece of leather down on the desk top, making sure it covers the whole area.

2 With the aid of a tool known as a "bone", flatten out any blisters and uneven areas, working from the centre outward. Use the edge of the "bone" to make sure the leather is pushed into the corners (see p.43).

3 Use a sharp utility knife to cut away the excess leather, taking care that the cut is accurate and no gaps are left. Use the edge of the veneer banding as a cutting guide.

4 When the leather is dry, wipe the surface with a leather sealant, applied with a cloth (cotton rag). This will make sure that the leather dyes will give an even covering and not become blotchy.

5 Apply a water-based stain with a cloth in a circular motion and gradually build the colour to the desired intensity. Avoid the veneer banding around the edge.

6 Heat a tooling wheel to create a decorative border. Apply even pressure and, once the wheel is rolling, do not stop until you reach the end of the leather.

7 With the leather fitted, coloured and sealed, the next stage is to lacquer it. To make sure the lacquer will not mark the veneer, mask it off (wrap it) with paper.

8 Using a pressurized spray gun, apply an even coat of cellulose lacquer. If necessary, apply a second coat once the first has dried. Lacquering gives a protective layer to the leather as well as locking in the colour and stopping it bleeding out.

9 When the lacquer has dried, and the paper has been removed, decide on a decorative border. There are many styles and patterns to choose from, but it is a good idea to seek advice on what would be suitable. Use dividers to decide the best proportions.

10 Lay a roll of gold leaf in place and put a steel rule on top, then run the tooling wheel along the leaf. Keep the pressure even and ensure the wheel is at spitting heat: if too hot, it will burn through the gilt, and if too cold, the gilt will not stick to the leather.

11 Apply a more decorative pattern wheel inset inside the original single line, working freehand. Carefully peel the gold leaf away.

12 Join the corners using a stamp, which again has been heated to spitting heat. This gives a neat appearance and completes the process. The top can now be sealed with a coat of wax or another thin layer of lacquer.

13 Finally, using a utility knife, carefully lift off any excess areas of gilt and tidy up the finish. Obtaining a perfectly straight and even line, like many restoration techniques, takes many years of practice.

▷

Repairing the drawers

All the drawers are suffering from worn runners, which cause the drawers to sit unevenly and to stick. Two of the drawers are also missing knobs, which need replacing, and there are several patches of chipped and missing veneer to be restored.

Replacing the runners

Drawer runners are often attached to the drawer bottoms, and are designed to allow the drawer to run smoothly and evenly in the carcass. In this case they are attached to the drawer sides, so the drawer will have to be dismantled before work can begin. Remove the plinths first; these will be repaired at a later stage.

MATERIALS AND EQUIPMENT

- **masking tape**
- **marker pen**
- **stiff-bladed knife**
- **hammer**
- **hardwood block**
- **circular saw**
- **mahogany**
- **PVA (white) glue**
- **snap clamps**
- **flat piece of wood**
- **plane**
- **gauge sticks**
- **small pins (tacks)**
- **G-clamps**

1 Remove the drawers from the pedestals and place them on the workbench. Label each part of each drawer in a way that identifies not only which drawer it belongs to but also its position within that drawer.

2 Starting with the first drawer, slide the bottom out of the frame. You may need to remove small pins in order to be able to do this (see p.221, step 2). Put the drawer bottom to one side.

3 Stand the drawer up and place a hardwood block on the inside of one of the sides. Gently knock the block with a hammer until the dovetail joints loosen and the pieces come apart.

4 Using a circular saw with the fence set, cut a small amount from the drawer runner. This is to provide a parallel edge for the new wood to attach to. Note that the guard has been removed for the photograph.

5 Cut a straight strip of matching mahogany to the same length as, but marginally deeper than, the drawer side and glue it to the freshly cut edge of the runner. Apply snap clamps and leave to dry.

6 Place a flat length of wood between the drawer side and the workbench, then clamp them both securely to the bench. Plane the edge of the runner flush with the drawer side. Repeat steps 2–6 for all the other worn drawer runners.

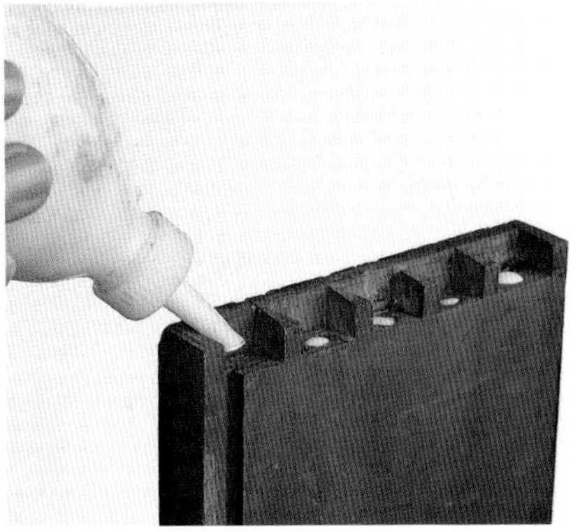

7 Now all the drawers can be reassembled. Apply only a small amount of PVA (white) glue to the inside of the dovetails on the drawer backs and fronts, as the tightness of the joints will hold them together.

8 Immediately after applying the glue, tap the dovetail joints together using a hammer and a block of wood. Apply only light pressure to avoid unnecessary damage to the delicate dovetail pins.

9 Use gauge sticks to check that each drawer is square (see p.142). Do this straight after gluing, so any minor adjustments can be made.

10 When the glue has set, slide each of the drawer bottoms back in place, and secure them with three or four small pins (tacks).

Pre-drilling a nail hole

When hammering a small pin (tack) or clout nail into a hardwood, you may find that it can bend or shear off. An easy remedy is to pre-drill the hole at a slightly smaller diameter than the nail (a pilot hole).

◁ **11** Clamp a hardwood block at the back of the workbench to keep each drawer securely in place, then plane the runners so that they fit into the desk and run smoothly.

▷

REPLACING THE KNOBS

The desk retains its original oak wooden knobs, although a number have become detached and are now missing. Using an original as a template (pattern), copies must be turned to match.

MATERIALS AND EQUIPMENT

- callipers
- oak
- lathe
- turning tools
- paring tool
- dividers
- skew chisel
- very fine-grade sandpaper
- spirit-based (alcohol-based) stain
- fine brush
- rubber
- polish

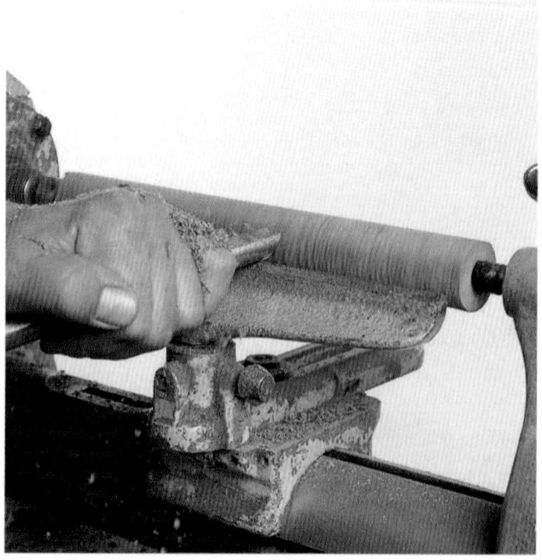

1 Take a measurement from an original knob using a pair of callipers, and use this to determine the diameter of the new knob. Prepare a piece of oak for the lathe (see p.153), then turn it to the correct diameter.

2 Mark out the depth of the knob using a paring tool, then remove it from the lathe and pare it away from the rest of the wood. Replace the knob into a lathe chuck.

3 Turn the shape of the wooden knob, constantly comparing its shape and size to the original using dividers.

4 With the proportions determined, turn the final shape, using a skew chisel to create the domed shape of the knob.

5 Finish off the knob by lightly sanding it while it is still rotating in the lathe. Take care during this process that you do not alter the shape of the knob.

◁ **6** The completed replacement knob should be identical to the original. Repeat this procedure to make as many knobs as are needed. Stain and polish them to match the other knobs, before fitting them in place.

Repairing the carcass

The drawer runners have worn deep grooves in the frame; one of the pedestals has a large split in the back due to shrinkage; and both plinths are missing sections of veneer and have sustained damage to the core wood. The frame supports for the drawer runners will be repaired with new pieces of wood, while the split will be glued and clamped. Damaged core wood on the plinths will be replaced and the veneer patched.

MATERIALS AND EQUIPMENT

- screwdriver or pincers
- hardwood block
- hammer
- circular saw
- softwood
- PVA (white) gluc
- jack plane
- sash clamps
- clamping blocks
- nails

Repairing the drawer supports

The action of opening and shutting the top drawers over many years has resulted in deep grooves being worn into the frame supports. This damage must be repaired, as otherwise the frame will continue to be worn away until it breaks in two.

1 Place the frame on the workbench and remove the screw or nail that secures each end of a support to the frame. Place a piece of hardwood over the support and gently knock the support out using blows from a hammer.

2 Make two parallel cuts down the centre with a circular saw. Reset the saw and turn the support on to its side. Making sure the depth is set correctly, run the support over the saw to remove the worn parts. Note that the guard should always be in place.

3 Using the circular saw, cut two fillets of softwood to replace the worn parts of wood that have been removed, and glue them into position.

4 Plane the new wood flush with the original. The inserts will allow the replaced drawer runners to run on a level surface. Repeat for the other damaged support.

◁ **5** Glue the restored frame supports back into position and clamp until dry. Hammer nails into each end while the supports are still firmly clamped.

▷

Repairing the pedestal

Shrinkage has caused a crack to develop from the top to the bottom of the back panel of one of the pedestals. The panel is attached to the sides by dovetail joints, which have been veneered over. To leave the dovetails and veneer intact, the back is scribed down each side and only the broken sections removed. Once the crack is repaired, the split is glued and clamped in place and a fillet is added to fill the gap.

MATERIALS AND EQUIPMENT
- marking gauge
- circular saw
- stiff-bladed knife
- hammer
- iron
- oak
- PVA (white) glue
- sash clamps
- G-clamps
- clamping blocks
- plane
- nails
- veneer

1 Place the pedestal on the workbench and scribe along both edges of the back with a marking gauge. Cut along the lines with a circular saw to free the broken sections.

2 Cut through the fastening rails with a stiff-bladed knife and hammer, then prise the broken sections off the pedestal. Turn the pedestal on to its front.

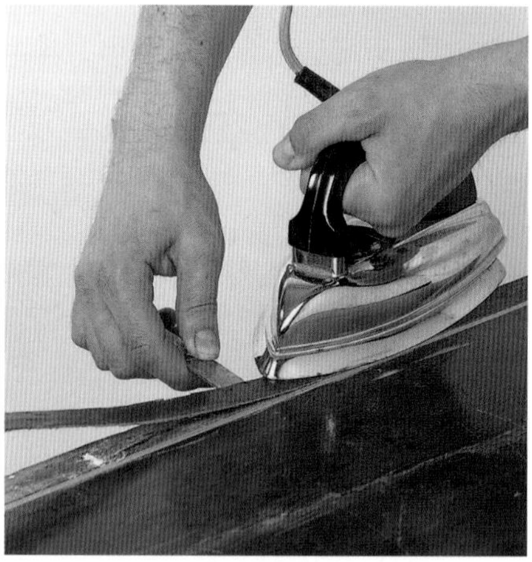

3 Remove the thin strip of veneer left between the right-hand edge and the scribing line by placing a hot iron on it to soften the glue and prising it away.

◁ **4** Before mending the split, cut a fillet of oak to compensate for the back being narrower now than it was. Apply glue to both sides of the split and also to the fillet, and glue this to the right-hand edge of the back. Clamp the pieces together, using sash and G-clamps and clamping blocks. Leave to dry.

5 Trim the fillet and plane it to the correct width. Glue the new back into place and nail it at top and bottom. Apply a strip of veneer to cover the fillet and bare edge.

Restoring damaged wood and veneer

Sections of veneer are missing from the corners of the plinths, after years of being kicked and knocked, and the core wood on to which the veneer was laid is also damaged. The core wood needs to be rebuilt, and the veneer patched and polished to restore the piece. This is a relatively straightforward task but it is important that the new core wood is cut and fitted correctly before the more cosmetic veneer can be applied.

MATERIALS AND EQUIPMENT

- **snap clamp**
- **set (carpenter's) square**
- **utility knife**
- **router**
- **wood**
- **tenon saw**
- **bench hook**
- **PVA (white) glue**
- **masking tape**
- **small block plane**
- **veneer**
- **scotch glue**
- **cabinet scraper**
- **fine-grade sandpaper**
- **sanding block**

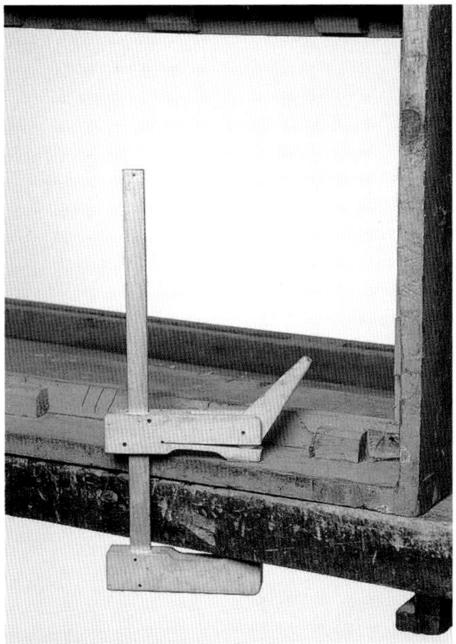

◁ **1** Place one of the plinths on the workbench. Clamp it firmly to the bench using a snap clamp, or fix it into the vice.

▷ **2** Score a line close to one of the damaged sections of veneer and core wood, using a set (carpenter's) square and a utility knife.

3 Cut away the damaged area of core wood with a router. Repeat this procedure on each of the damaged corners, removing the wood and veneer if necessary, or just the veneer if the core wood is undamaged.

4 Cut replacement pieces of core wood from a suitable wood using a tenon saw and bench hook.

▷

Restoring damaged wood and veneer...continued

5 Glue the replacement patches into place using PVA (white) glue.

6 Apply strips of masking tape, pulled tight, to secure each patch as it sets. Make sure that all the edges are square, to achieve a firm joint.

7 Plane each new section of wood with a small block plane. Continue until there is enough depth to allow for a replacement piece of veneer.

8 Select a piece of oak veneer that matches the original. Cut it to size. Apply scotch glue to the new wood and tape the veneer firmly into place. Leave to dry.

9 Using a cabinet scraper, level the veneer patch to match the original veneer. Trim off any excess using a sharp utility knife.

10 Sand the veneer with fine-grade sandpaper and a sanding block. Repeat steps 1–10 for the other plinth.

11 Note the importance of choosing new wood that matches the original grain of the existing veneer.

Reassembling and polishing

With all the carcass repairs completed and the surface cleaned and revived, the desk can now be reassembled. This will involve replacing the knobs after they have been coloured and stained to match the originals, and may include servicing the locks.

MATERIALS AND EQUIPMENT
- screwdriver
- brush
- stain
- ground pumice
- soft cloth (rag)
- polish

1 Reattach the plinths to the pedestals using the original screws. If you have carefully labelled the fittings when the carcass was dismantled you can ensure that they are put back on the right pedestal.

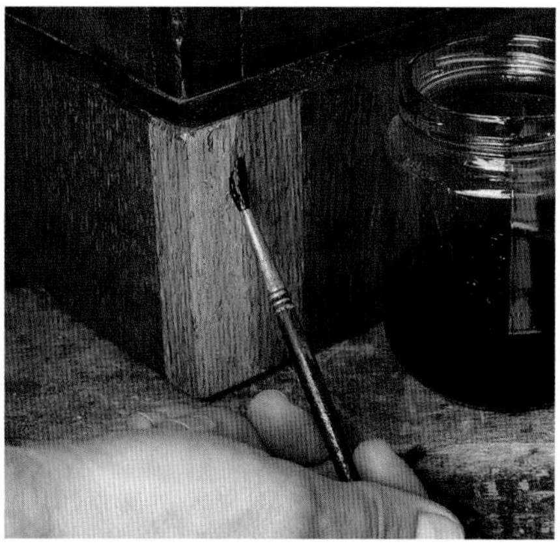

2 Stain any replacement veneer or moulding to match the original finish before polishing.

3 After filling the grain with ground pumice and polish, polish the new patches of wood until they match the rest of the desk (see pp.66–67).

Left: *The restored and reassembled desk is ready once again to be used. Treated with care, it should not need further attention for several generations.*

PROJECT: GRANDFATHER CLOCK

The longcase, or, as it is more commonly known, the grandfather clock, was a familiar part of home furnishings during the mid-18th and 19th centuries. Although they were commissioned during the late 17th and early 18th centuries, their use became more widespread after 1800. They came in various shapes, styles and sizes, and by the mid-19th century the cases were often made of the finest veneers by master cabinet-makers. Like all furniture, however, they can suffer the ravages of time, as is the case with this example.

ASSESSING THE PROJECT

This longcase contains an illustrated mahogany clock. The clock is in good working order, but the case is damaged in several areas and requires new mouldings to be made, loose ones replacing, as well as general repairs to the carcass. The veneer, which has good colour and patination, needs patching and blisters putting down. Finally, a missing roundel on the hood will need to be replaced and the surface revived, polished and waxed.

The hood

- loose and missing veneer
- missing pediment roundel and core wood
- missing inner slip

Tip

The clock workings are in good order. Prior to work on the case, the workings should be carefully removed and stored in a dry, dust free environment until the clock is ready for reassembly.

The trunk and plinth

- missing and blistered veneer
- loose and missing mouldings

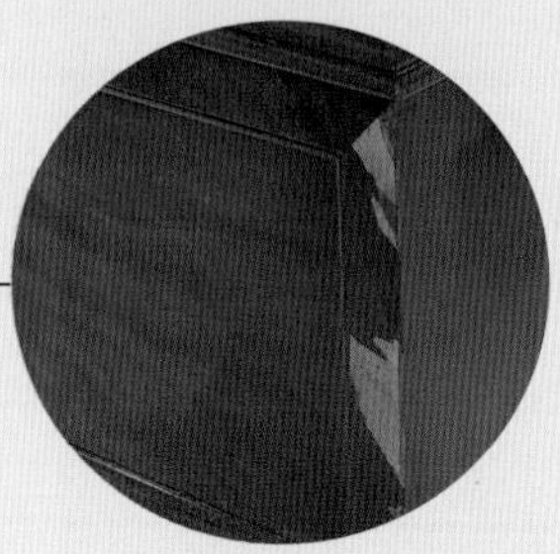

Repairing the hood

The decorative scrolls on the pediment of a longcase are easily damaged when the clock is moved. In this instance, veneer has been damaged, some of the long-grain moulding is loose or has been lost, some groundwork is missing and a roundel has been lost. Finally, an inner slip by the hood door is missing and needs to be replaced.

Securing veneer and restoring the core

Much of the loose veneer can simply be removed, reglued and clamped. It is best to remove large areas, rather than cut through the veneer with a knife, but if the veneer is in danger of breaking, score a line with a sharp utility knife to make sure of a straight edge. Before starting work, the hood must be removed and placed on a workbench and the works should be removed and carefully stored.

MATERIALS AND EQUIPMENT

- **flat-bladed knife**
- **smoothing plane**
- **softwood**
- **tenon saw**
- **PVA (white) glue**
- **paper**
- **G-clamps**
- **jigsaw (saber saw)**
- **snap clamps**
- **lengths of wood**
- **spokeshave**
- **utility knife**
- **Cuban mahogany**
- **veneer**

◁ **1** Gently prise away both pieces of loose moulding, and then the veneer (which came away in two pieces), with a flat-bladed knife. Put the pieces of moulding and veneer to one side.

▷ **2** Scrape the core wood with the iron from a smoothing plane to remove any traces of old glue. Cut a softwood clamping block to fit the shape of the area that is to be re-veneered.

3 Apply PVA (white) glue to the hood and put the pieces of old veneer back in place, matching the edges as exactly as possible.

4 Place a piece of paper and the clamping block on top of the relaid veneer. Apply G-clamps and leave to dry. Repeat steps 1–4 for all the remaining loose veneer.

5 Place a piece of softwood behind the swan-neck moulding that is missing its core, and trace around the moulding. Cut out this shape with a jigsaw (saber saw). ▷

Securing veneer and restoring the core...continued

6 Glue the softwood shape to the back of the pediment, then clamp it in place using snap clamps braced against lengths of wood. When the glue has dried, remove the clamps and shape the core with a spokeshave.

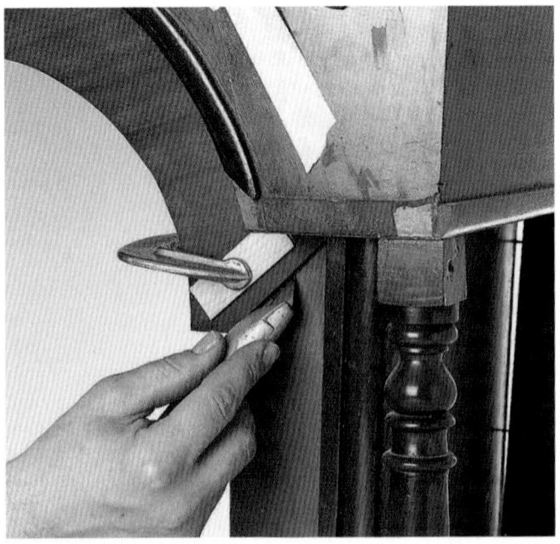

7 One of the inner slips is missing on the door of the hood. Cut a piece of Cuban mahogany to size, secure it in place with a small G-clamp, then mark the mitre with a utility knife.

8 Secure the new piece of wood in place by gluing veneer patches on to the back. This is a good way of joining two pieces of wood together when there is only a small area of joint between them.

TURNING AND ATTACHING A ROUNDEL

One of the roundels on the pediment is missing and needs to be replaced. This is done by using a faceplate on a lathe, which allows a flat surface to be turned to the required size and profile. The original remaining roundel can be removed to act as a template (pattern).

MATERIALS AND EQUIPMENT

- faceplate
- tenon saw
- wood
- steel rule
- jigsaw (saber saw)
- screws
- screwdriver
- flat-bladed knife
- mahogany
- PVA (white) glue
- paper
- G-clamp
- lathe
- dividers
- parting gauge
- skew chisel
- hammer
- spring clips

1 Choose a faceplate of a suitable size for the new roundel. Cut a square piece of wood and mark its centre point. Lay the faceplate on the wood and mark out its circumference.

2 Cut the circumference out with a jigsaw (saber saw), then screw the faceplate to the wood. Use a flat-bladed knife to remove the original roundel from the hood, so that it can be used as a template (pattern).

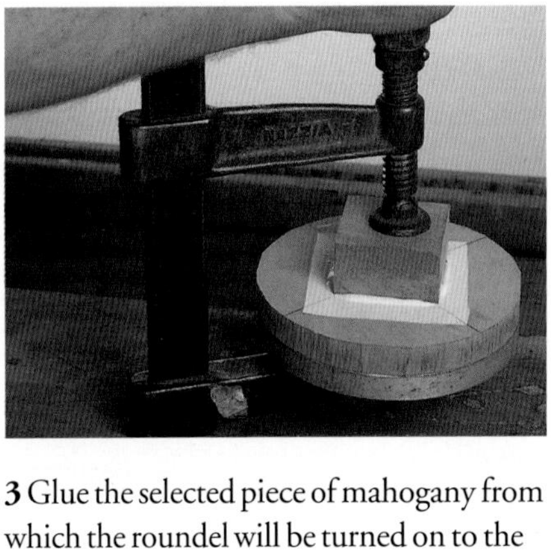

3 Glue the selected piece of mahogany from which the roundel will be turned on to the wooden side of the faceplate. Placing paper with glue on either side between the wood blocks will aid removal at the end of turning.

4 Screw the faceplate on to the end of the lathe and put the lathe rest in place.

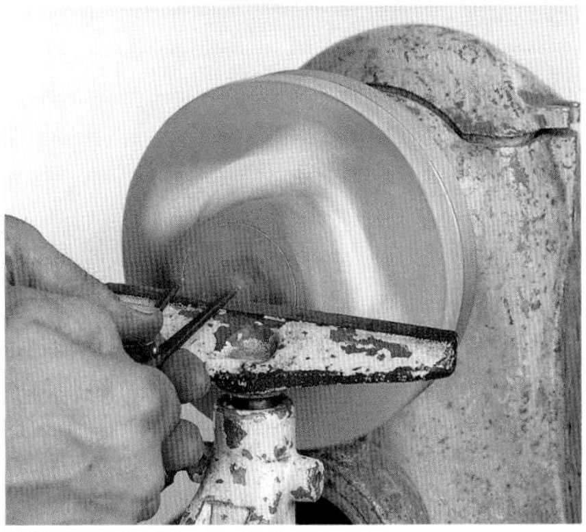

5 Measure the circumference of the original roundel with dividers, then, with the lathe turning, transfer this to the new wood.

6 Use a parting gauge to turn the roundel to the correct diameter. Make sure that the sides are at right angles to the front.

7 When the correct size has been obtained, turn the shape of the face with a skew chisel. Keep checking the shape against the original roundel.

8 When the correct size and shape have been achieved, hold a handful of shavings, removed earlier, lightly against the turning while it is spinning to give a smooth finish.

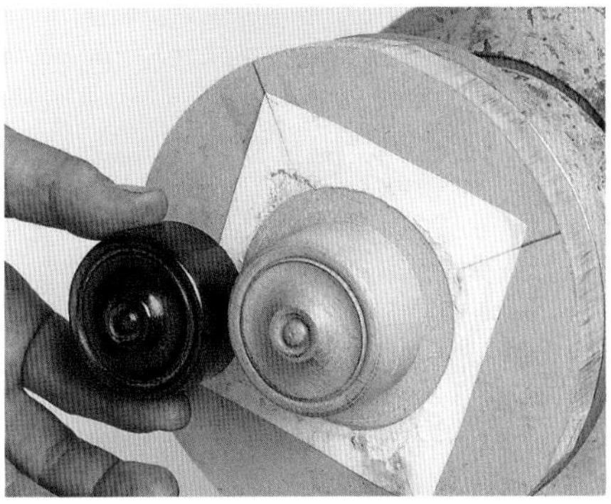

9 When finished, the roundel should be exactly like the original. Remove it from the faceplate by tapping a flat-bladed knife between the paper–glue joint.

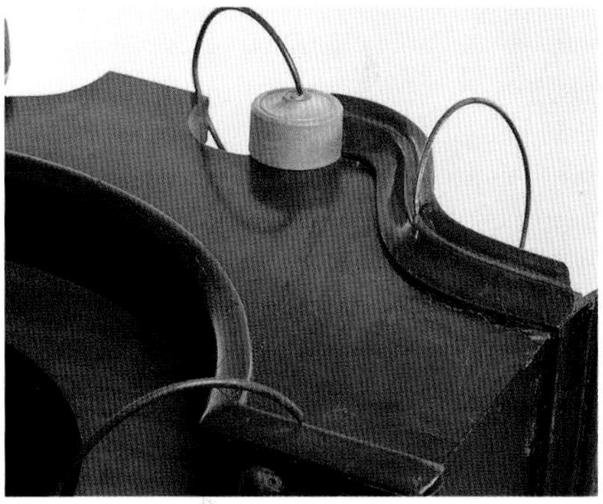

10 Both roundels can now be glued into place on the restored hood, along with the two areas of missing moulding, and held with spring clips while the glue sets.

Restoring the trunk and plinth

While the trunk is in fairly good order, there are some mouldings that need to be replaced, some blisters to put down and some damaged areas of veneer to be patched. These are all typical of the types of damage that you would expect to find on any period carcass or trunk furniture.

MATERIALS AND EQUIPMENT

- block of MDF (medium density fiberboard)
- iron
- paper
- clamping blocks
- G-clamps
- cloth (cotton rag)
- flat-bladed knife
- veneer
- circular saw
- utility knife
- PVA (white) glue

Repairing and replacing veneer

Some pieces of veneer can be reglued, but others are missing, so some old pieces of veneer must be sourced. Whenever possible, reuse all veneer that is removed from the clock elsewhere on the longcase. For example, one of the cross-banded lengths was missing several pieces, so the remaining pieces were used as patches for other areas, while a new strip was fitted to replace the whole length.

▷

Repairing and replacing veneer...continued

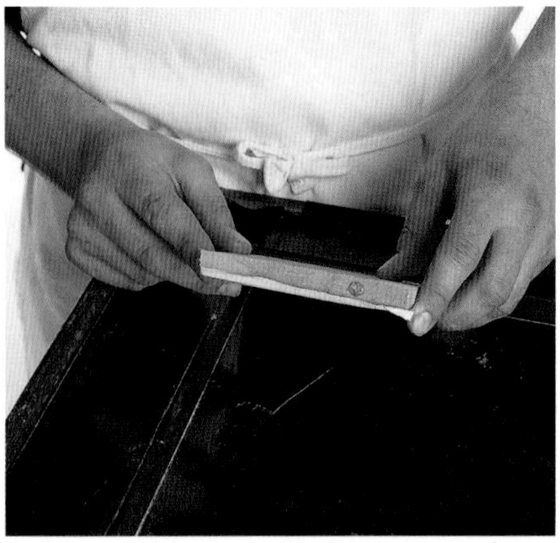

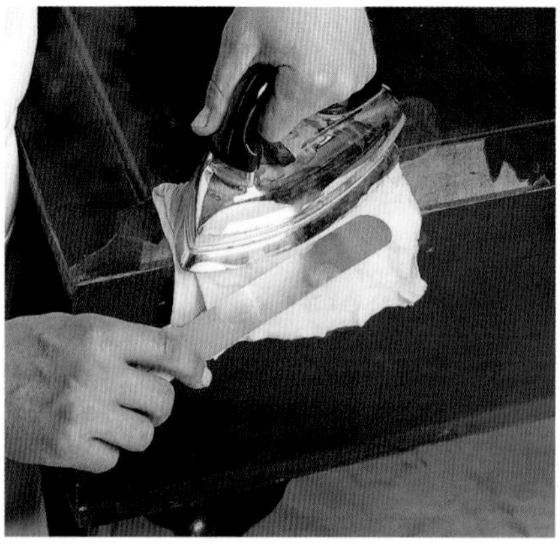

1 Put any blisters down with a hot block (see p.78). The heat generated from the previously heated block will soften the glue underneath the veneer. Clamping the veneer will rebind it to the core as it cools.

2 Place a damp cloth on the remaining veneer of the most damaged cross-banded length. Place a hot iron on the cloth to loosen the glue. Remove the veneer by lifting it with a flat-bladed knife.

3 Select a closely matching section of veneer. It is vital to match colour, figure and patination as closely as possible, and it is here that the importance of a well-stocked breaker store (see p.28) can be seen.

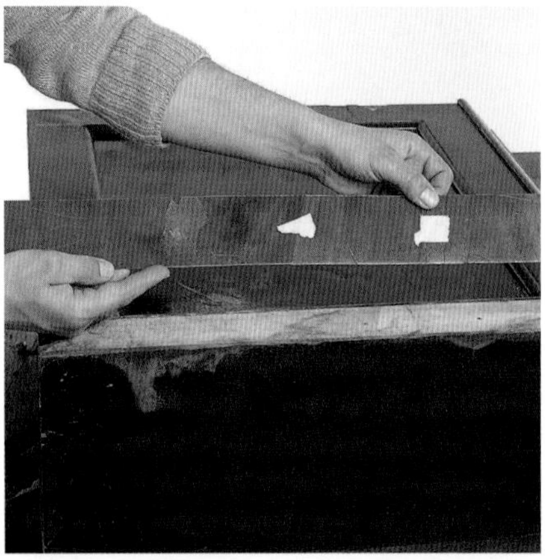

◁ **4** In this instance, cut the veneer away from its backing with a circular saw rather than steaming it off. This is to make sure that the surface is not marked and retains its original surface. Make sure that this replacement veneer is cut to match the thickness of the existing veneer.

▷ **5** Cut mitres at the ends of the veneer length to match the existing veneer corners, and then, after trimming it to fit with a utility knife, glue the veneer into position with PVA (white) glue. Clamp until dry.

6 Use the veneer previously removed to patch the less-damaged length, trimming the damaged areas first to ensure good joints.

7 When completed, and if the grain is carefully matched, the joints should be barely visible.

Replacing and Restoring Mouldings

Loose mouldings need to be refixed, missing cock beading replaced and damaged areas patched.

MATERIALS AND EQUIPMENT

- toothbrush
- wood
- tenon saw
- PVA (white) glue
- chisels
- fine-grade sandpaper
- G-clamps
- clamping blocks
- jack plane
- flat-bladed knife
- smoothing plane

◁ **1** There are a number of missing pieces of moulding on the trunk. Clean away all traces of the old glue with a toothbrush, then cut a new piece of matching wood to size and glue it into position with PVA (white) glue.

2 Using a sharp paring chisel, round off the square edges to give the cock beading its standard rounded profile.

3 Smooth the moulding with fine-grade sandpaper, making sure not to mark the polished surfaces.

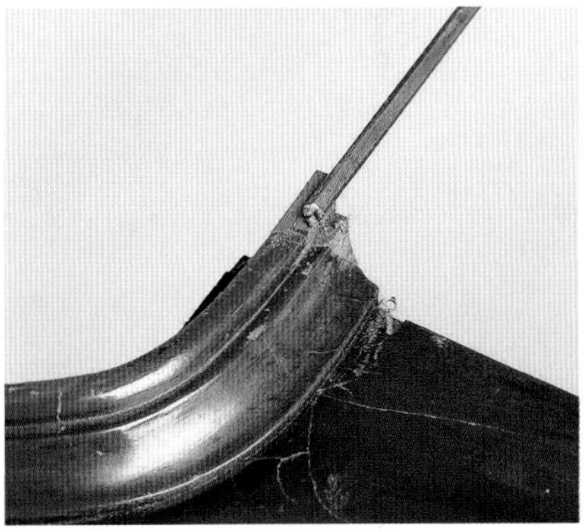

4 Patch any other areas of missing moulding and, with the aid of chisels or carving tools, flow in the new areas to follow the profile of the original (see p.169).

◁ **5** Part of the plinth moulding is missing. Find a suitable piece of matching wood, plane it to match the original, then glue it to the base. Apply G-clamps and clamping blocks.

▷ **6** Remove very loose mouldings on the trunk of the clock with a flat-bladed knife.

▷

Replacing and restoring mouldings...continued

◁ **7** Remove any loose glue from the carcass and mouldings with the iron from a smoothing plane.

▷ **8** Reglue the mouldings. Due to their unusual shape, it is often necessary to cut clamping blocks to match the mouldings, so that an even pressure can be applied.

Polishing

Due to the excellent untouched colour of the mahogany veneer, the polishing was confined to colouring the repairs and lightly reviving the surface.

MATERIALS AND EQUIPMENT

- fine wire (steel) wool
- fine brush
- stain
- rubber
- polish
- cloth (cotton rag)
- wax
- mutton cloth

◁ **1** After all the restorations have been completed, give the polished surface a light dusting with fine wire (steel) wool. The aim is to remove any loose dirt and wax but not to damage the patinated surface.

2 Stain all the repairs, then charge a rubber with polish and apply a thin layer to revive the surface of the clock (see pp.66–67). As the majority of repairs to the surface were carried out using old surface veneers, this is more a case of reviving than repolishing the surface.

3 When the polish has hardened, cut it back with fine wire wool, wax it, then finally buff it with a soft mutton cloth.

Setting up the clock

A clock, with its precision movement, must be perfectly level to work properly. When you have chosen a suitable position, level the case, using a spirit level to check, and then screw it to the wall to give it stability. Add the pendulum and weights, and, if balanced correctly, the clock should begin to work once you start off the pendulum. If the clock does not keep good time or keeps stopping, seek the advice of a qualified clock-restorer unless you know what you are doing. Remember that all grandfather clocks should be cleaned and oiled by a qualified clock-restorer every ten years.

MATERIALS AND EQUIPMENT
- spirit level
- screws
- screwdriver
- coins

1 After levelling and screwing the clock case in place, sit the works on top of the trunk. The seat board, to which the works are attached, must be perfectly level; use coins to help to achieve this.

2 With the clock screwed into position, and the works in place, replace the hood and fit the door if necessary (the majority of clocks have a door already fixed to the hood).

Right: *The clock, now restored and in place, will need no further attention for several years, other than being wound up once a week.*

Glossary

animal glue Also known as scotch glue and traditionally used from the 17th century onwards.
astragals Glazing bars on cabinet furniture, forming a geometric pattern.
bain-marie A pot containing hot water in which another container, holding animal glue, gesso or bole, for example, can be gently heated.
banding Decorative inlays of veneer that are used for aesthetic effect. They can be either long-grained or cross-grained and on earlier pieces can be joined to give a chevron effect, known as herringbone.
blister A bubble that forms on a surface when part of the veneer has become detached from its core.
blooming The name given to the white marks left on a polished surface that has been water-damaged or chilled.
bole A clay-like substance that is used in the gilding process.
boulle Also known as buhl, this is the use of fine brass inlay inset into tortoiseshell or ebony backgrounds.
bracket foot A square foot which might have a shaped profile on the inside. The foot most commonly used during the 18th century.
breaker A piece or a collection of pieces of furniture used in the restoration of another item of furniture.

bun feet A ball type of foot favoured during the 17th century and replaced by the bracket foot in the 18th century.
butterfly key A butterfly-shaped piece of wood used to secure and hold splits. It is inset into a piece so that the grain runs at right angles to the main wood. Also known as a dovetail key.
carcass The actual framework of a piece of furniture. Depending on the period, this would be either in the solid or veneered.
cascamite A glue used when forming laminates or shape work. It is very strong but also brittle.
cock beading Thin strips of decorative beading often found around drawer fronts.
colour The tone or shade that wood develops over time.
conservation To maintain a piece by undertaking as little work as possible so as not to alter its present or original form (*see* restoration).
core The moulded shape on to which veneer or mouldings are applied.
cornice The top of a carcass piece of furniture often decorated with dental mouldings, cross bandings or a pediment.
cross-grain mouldings Wood applied to a softwood backing and planed to a moulded profile, applied to a carcass for aesthetic reasons. Introduced during the 17th century, they are more decorative than long-grain mouldings.
Cuban mahogany Mahogany imported from Cuba during the 18th and 19th centuries and the preferred wood for quality furniture. It is densely grained and red in tone when first polished.
cutting gauge A tool fitted with a small blade that is used across the grain to cut a groove. Often used prior to fitting boxwood lines.
de-nibbing The removal of dust that has combined with polish to form small raised nibs on a surface after polishing. This is done by lightly using fine wire wool in the direction of the grain. The surface is then waxed.

dental mouldings Small rectangular pieces applied to a cornice and resembling square teeth. Popular during the mid-18th century.
dovetail saw A fine-bladed saw used for cutting accurate and delicate dovetails.
escutcheon The brassware used in conjunction with locks for both aesthetic and protective reasons.
fading/fad Filling the grain in wood with a mixture of polish and pumice powder. The cloth with which it is applied is known as a fad.
fire gilding A mixture of gold and mercury applied to a metal base and heated until the mercury evaporates and binds the gold to the metal. Favoured during the 18th century; used on the mounts and handles of the finest pieces.
French curve A kidney-shaped scraper used on concave curves.
French polishing Using shellac polish, which is usually applied with a linen and wadding (batting) rubber.
fret A lattice-like decoration, in which open fret is pierced and blind fret is applied to a solid background.
gauge sticks Two lengths of stick which are held together and used to check the equal diagonal measure of a frame to ensure it is square.
gesso A plaster-like substance that is used in the gilding process.
graining Using surface stains and colours to mimic the grain of a solid piece of wood. Favoured during the early 19th century.
Honduras mahogany Mahogany imported from Honduras during the 18th and 19th centuries and favoured for carcass construction.
kickers Strips of wood applied to the inside carcass of a chest, running along the top of the drawer linings, to stop the drawers tipping forward when extended.
linings The name given to the sides and often the bottom of a drawer.
long-grain mouldings Mouldings planed from one length of wood along the grain and applied to a carcass for aesthetic or structural reasons.

marquetry Inlays of decorative scenes.
marriage Two parts of a piece of furniture that started life separately but have now been brought together. Such an example would be a bureau bookcase in which both halves would have started life with another part.
mortise The hollow housing part of a mortise and tenon joint, which is the most widely used joint in furniture construction.
mortise gauge A marking tool that has a small steel point and is used along the grain to mark the shoulders of a mortise.
overloe A shaped block used in conjunction with sandpaper.
parquetry Inlays of geometric patterns.
patera A round or oval, raised decoration often found on cornices or the tops of legs. Can also be used in veneer form.
patination This refers to the build up of waxes, natural greases and dust that over numerous years combines to form a desirable finish on a surface.
pediment Found on top of a carcass and, depending on the period, can be arched, broken-arched or swan-necked in shape.
piecrust The name used to describe the shape of a top usually applying to a tripod table. The top, as the name suggests, looks like the top of a pinched pastry pie top.
plinth The platform base on which a carcass will sit.
PVA glue Polyvinylacetate glue, also known as white glue. Ideal for day to day use.
reeded decoration A raised decoration of parallel, tapering lines, usually found on chair and table legs.
reeds Raised dome-shaped decoration applied along the length of a surface.
restoration To undertaken any necessary work to return a piece as near as possible to its original form but retaining its integrity (*see* conservation).
revive a surface The action of attending to any minor damage or surface oxidation of a polished surface while not repolishing the whole top.
rubber Wadding (batting) wrapped in linen, which is used to apply shellac polish.
runners The strips of wood attached to the bottom or sides of a drawer on which the drawer will run. Sometimes also found as part of the carcass.
scratch box A workshop-made tool that allows parallel reeds to be scratched on a leg (*see* reeded decoration).
shellac Polish that is obtained from the shellac beetle.
skiver Leather taken from sheep. Not as good quality as cow hide.
splay feet A shaped bracket foot that is splayed in profile. Favoured during the late 18th century.

spring clip A workshop-made cramping device made from upholstery springs. Ideal for securing awkward shapes.
stains Usually bought in powder form and mixed with water, spirit or oil depending on the intended use.
stringing Thin lines of inlay, usually of ebony or box, which were used for both aesthetic reasons and as protective edges.
tenon The protruding part of a mortise and tenon joint, which is the most widely used joint in furniture construction.
twist When wood bows in two directions.
warp When a piece of wood has bowed along its length or width.

FURTHER INFORMATION

British Antique Furniture Restorers' Association (BAFRA)
18 Merry Lane, Sansaw Heath
Shrewsbury, SY4 3JS
UK
Tel: 01939 210826
Email: headoffice@bafra.org.uk
Web: www.bafra.org.uk

British Antique Dealers' Association (BADA)
21 John Street
Holborn
London WC1N 2BF
UK
Tel: 020 7589 4128
Email: info@bada.org
Web: www.bada.org

Association of Art and Antique Dealers' (LAPADA)
535 Kings Road
Chelsea
London SW10 0SZ
UK
Tel: 020 7823 3511
Email: lapada@lapada.org
Web: www.lapada.co.uk

The Antiques Council
3867 Medina Road, 254
Akron
OH 44333
USA
Tel: (413) 436 7064
email: antiquescouncil@gmail.com
www.antiquescouncil.com

Art and Antique Dealers' League of America, Inc. (AADLA)
PO Box 2066, Lenox Hill Station
New York
NY 10021
USA
Tel: (212) 879–7558
Email:secretary@artantiquedealersleague.com
www.aadla.com

Australian Antique Dealers' Association
PO Box 294
Apollo Bay
Victoria 3233
Australia
Tel: (03) 9576 2275
Fax: (03) 9576 2106
Web: www.aada.org.au
Email: info@aaada, USA.com.au

PICTURE CREDITS

INDEX

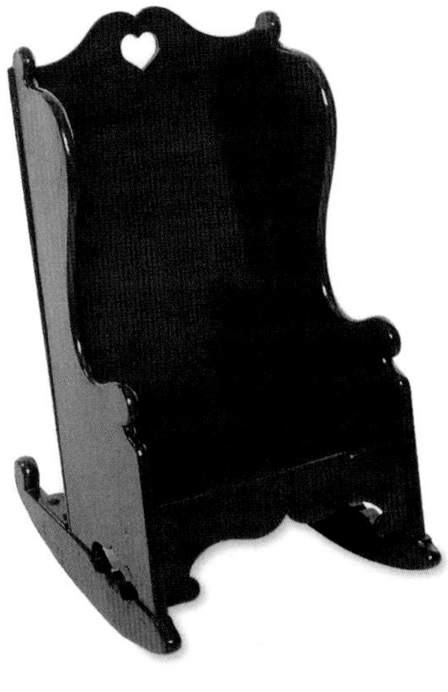

WILLIAM COOK · W.J. COOK & SONS

Above: *clockwise from left, Bill, Stephen, Richard, Billy and Catherine Cook.*

About the Author

Ever since childhood Billy Cook has been in and around the family workshop learning about furniture restoration. After studying at the London College of Furniture, he spent four years working for one of the country's leading furniture dealers before joining Christie's Auctioneeers in London.

He left to join his family's restoration business, W.J. Cook & Sons, where he developed the independent retail side of the business, specializing in late 17th- to 19th-century furniture, both buying and selling around the world. As well as exhibiting at antique shows in the UK and America, the company has a permanent retail presence in both the picturesque market town of Hungerford and the City of Charleston, USA.

Billy has researched and written various specialist catalogues and gives lectures on the subject of restoration and furniture history. Based in Marlborough, Wiltshire, he is a member of The London and Provincial Antique Dealers' Association and a board member of The Antiques Council of America. W.J. Cook & Sons is a senior member of The British Antique Furniture Restorers' Association.

About the Company

W.J.Cook & Sons was established by Bill Cook in 1962. His reputation for outstanding work quickly spread and since those early days clients have included the British Royal Household and Government, museums, collectors, dealers and private individuals.

While still retaining a London workshop, the business is based in Marlborough, Wiltshire. With the cabinet-making, machine and polishing shops it is a business that is recognized as one of the leaders in its field. After training at the London College of Furniture, three of Bill's sons joined the business and have helped develop and further expand its range and facilities. Now their own children are being encouraged to pick up the tools with a view to taking the family tradition to a third generation.

The services carried out are many and include cabinet-making, gilding, carving, polishing, lock repairs, leathering and upholstery. Being a true family business it means that every restoration commission is undertaken with great care. With almost 60 years of experience at the very highest level, together with an extensive in-house library and access to furniture archives, any restoration carried out is authentic in every detail.

Virtually all the restoration work is still carried out using 18th- and 19th-century tools: their band saw was used in the construction of the panelling for the *Queen Mary*.

A final note: antique furniture if badly restored can rarely be returned to its original glory. Therefore, it is important that a suitably qualified restorer should be consulted when necessary.

Contact Details:

High Trees House
Savernake Forest
Marlborough, Wiltshire
SN8 4NE
01672 513017
info@wjcookandsons.co.uk
www.wjcookandsons.co.uk
instagram: williamjcookandsons

167 Battersea High Street
London, SW11 3JS

William Cook
15 Bridge Street,
Hungerford, Berkshire
RG17 0EG
01488 681254
07885 031301
billy@williamcookantiques.com
www.williamcookantiques.com
instagram: williamcookantiques

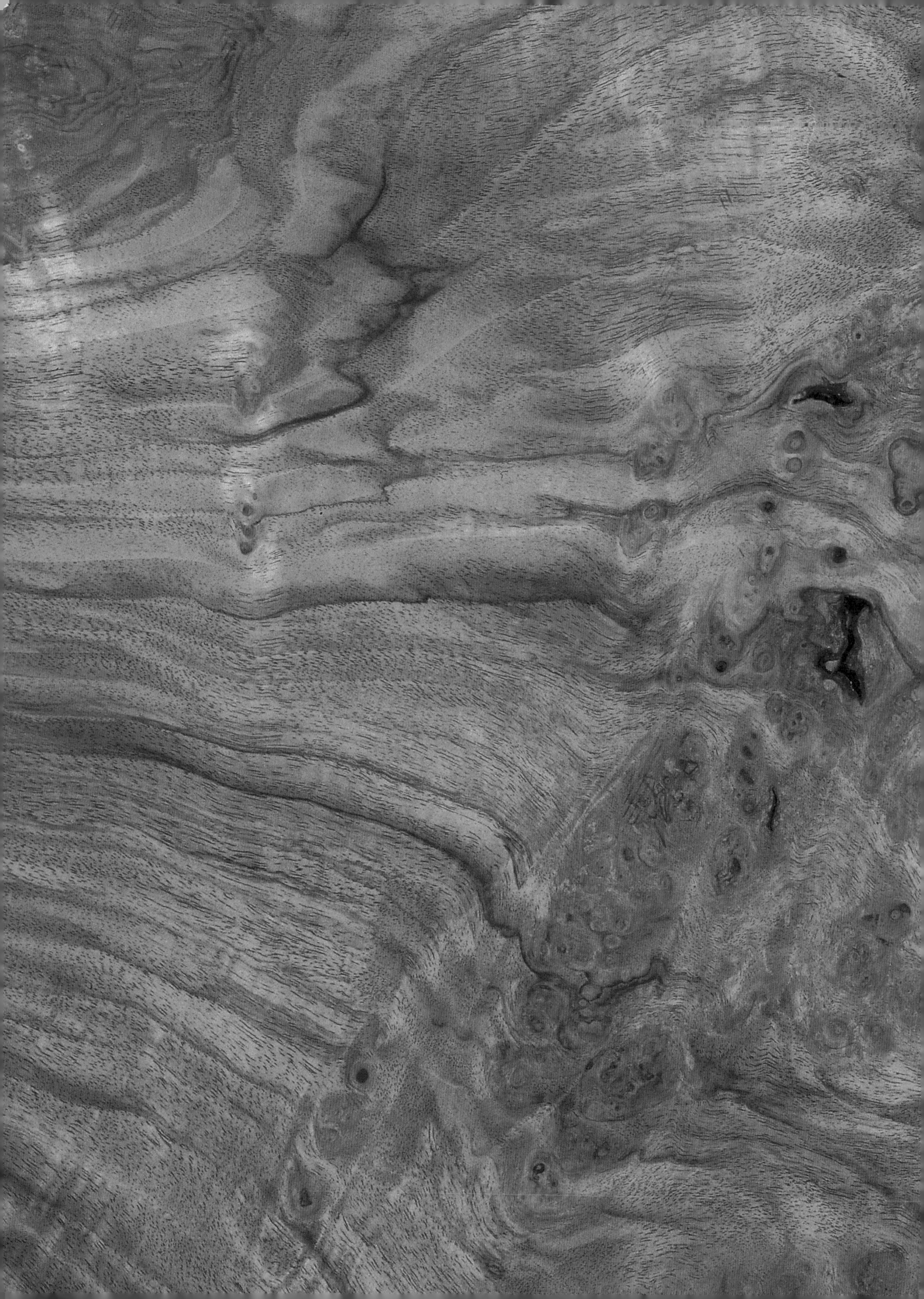